First World War
and Army of Occupation
War Diary
France, Belgium and Germany

57 DIVISION
Headquarters, Branches and Services
Royal Army Medical Corps
Assistant Director Medical Services
12 February 1917 - 23 March 1919

WO95/2969/2

The Naval & Military Press Ltd
www.nmarchive.com
Published in association with The National Archives

Published by

The Naval & Military Press Ltd

Unit 10 Ridgewood Industrial Park,
Uckfield, East Sussex,
TN22 5QE England
Tel: +44 (0) 1825 749494

www.naval-military-press.com

www.nmarchive.com

This diary has been reprinted in facsimile from the original. Any imperfections are inevitably reproduced and the quality may fall short of modern type and cartographic standards.

© Crown Copyright
Images reproduced by permission of The National Archives, London, England, 2015.

Contents

Document type	Place/Title	Date From	Date To
Heading	WO95/2969/2 Assistant Director Medical Services		
Heading	War Diary Of Assistant Director Of Medical Services 57th Division From 12th February 1917 To 27th February 1917 Volume 1		
War Diary	Havre	12/02/1917	15/02/1917
War Diary	Merris	16/02/1917	24/02/1917
War Diary	Sailly	25/02/1917	26/02/1917
Heading	War Diary Of A.D.M.S. 57th Division		
War Diary	Sailly	27/02/1917	30/03/1917
Miscellaneous	Medical Arrangements 57th (West Lancs) Division	04/03/1917	04/03/1917
Miscellaneous	Medical Arrangements 57th (West Lancs) Division	21/03/1917	21/03/1917
Heading	War Diary Of R.A.M.C. 57th Division From 31st March 1917 To 30th April 1917 Volume 1		
War Diary	Sailly	31/03/1917	30/04/1917
Operation(al) Order(s)	57th Division R.A.M.C. Operation Order No. 1	15/04/1917	15/04/1917
Operation(al) Order(s)	57th Division R.A.M.C. Operation Order No. 2	25/04/1917	25/04/1917
Operation(al) Order(s)	57th Division R.A.M.C. Operation Order No. 3	28/04/1917	28/04/1917
Heading	War Diary Of R.A.M.C. 57th Division From May 1st 1917 To May 31st 1917 Volume 1		
War Diary	Sailly	01/05/1917	01/05/1917
War Diary	Croix Du Bac	02/05/1917	31/05/1917
Miscellaneous	Summary Of Medical War Diaries For 57th Divn. 11th Corps 1st Army		
Miscellaneous	57th Divn. 11th Corps 1st Army A.D.M.S.Col. T.F. Dewar	17/05/1917	17/05/1917
Heading	War Diary Of A.D.M.S. 57th Division From June 1st 1917 To June 30th 1917 Volume I		
War Diary	Croix Du Bac	01/06/1917	30/06/1917
Operation(al) Order(s)	57th Division R.A.M.C. Operation Order No. 4	01/06/1917	01/06/1917
Operation(al) Order(s)	57th Division R.A.M.C. Operation Order No 5	08/06/1917	08/06/1917
Operation(al) Order(s)	57th Division R.A.M.C. Operation Order No 6	09/06/1917	09/06/1917
Operation(al) Order(s)	57th Division R.A.M.C. Operation Order No 7	12/06/1917	12/06/1917
Operation(al) Order(s)	57th Division R.A.M.C. Operation Order No 8	15/06/1917	15/06/1917
Map	Map		
Operation(al) Order(s)	57th Division R.A.M.C. Operation Order No 9	24/06/1917	24/06/1917
Heading	War Diary Of A.D.M.S. 57th Division From July 1st 1917 To July 31st 1917 Volume		
War Diary	Croix Du Bac	01/07/1917	31/07/1917
Operation(al) Order(s)	57th Division R.A.M.C. Operation Order No. 10	04/07/1917	04/07/1917
Operation(al) Order(s)	57th Division R.A.M.C. Operation Order No. 11	08/07/1917	08/07/1917
Miscellaneous	Matters Receiving Attention By The A.D.M.S. 57th Divn	09/07/1917	09/07/1917
Operation(al) Order(s)	57th Division R.A.M.C. Operation Order No 12	16/07/1917	16/07/1917
Heading	War Diary Of A.D.M.S 57th Division From 1st August 1917 To 31st August 1917		
War Diary	Croix Du Bac	01/08/1917	31/08/1917
Heading	War Diary Of A.D.M.S. 57th Division From September 1st 1917 To September 30th 1917		
War Diary	Croix Du Bac	01/09/1917	17/09/1917
War Diary	Norrent Fontes	17/09/1917	30/09/1917

Type	Description	Date From	Date To
Operation(al) Order(s)	57th Division R.A.M.C. Operation Order No. 13	10/09/1917	10/09/1917
Map	Map		
Heading	A.D.M.S. 57th Division		
War Diary	Norrent Fontes	01/10/1917	17/10/1917
War Diary	Renescure	18/10/1917	18/10/1917
War Diary	Proven	19/10/1917	24/10/1917
War Diary	Welsh Farm	25/10/1917	31/10/1917
Heading	Summary Of Medical War Diaries For 57th Divn. 14th Corps 5th Army		
Miscellaneous	57th Divn. 14th Corps 5th Army A.D.M.S. Col. J.F. Dewar		
Miscellaneous	57th Divn. 19th Corps 5th Army A.D.M.S. Col. J.F. Dewar		
Miscellaneous	57th Divn. 14th Corps 5th Army A.D.M.S. Col. J.F. Dewar		
Miscellaneous	57th Divn. 14th Corps 5th Army A.D.M.S. Col. J.F. Dewar	29/10/1917	29/10/1917
Miscellaneous	57th Divn. 14th Corps 5th Army A.D.M.S. Col. J.F. Dewar		
Miscellaneous	Appendix A		
Operation(al) Order(s)	57th Division R.A.M.C. Operation Order No. 14	23/10/1917	23/10/1917
Miscellaneous	Memorandum Regarding Evacuation	30/10/1917	30/10/1917
Heading	A.D.M.S. 57th Division		
War Diary	Welsh Farm	01/11/1917	08/11/1917
War Diary	Zutkerque	09/11/1917	30/11/1917
Miscellaneous	Summary Of Medical War Diaries For 57th Divn. 14th Corps 5th Army		
Miscellaneous	Casualties R.A.M.C.		
Miscellaneous	57th Divn. 19th Corps 5th Army A.D.M.S. Col, J.F. Dewar	14/11/1917	14/11/1917
Miscellaneous	57th Division Medical Arrangements for Evacuation Of Wounded During Quiet Period	02/11/1917	02/11/1917
Miscellaneous	57th Division R.A.M.C. Operation Order No 15	05/11/1917	05/11/1917
Miscellaneous	Medical Officer. Appendix 6	14/11/1917	14/11/1917
Heading	A.D.M.S. 57th Division		
War Diary	Zutkerque	01/12/1917	07/12/1917
War Diary	Rousbrugge	08/12/1917	17/12/1917
War Diary	Elverdinghe	18/12/1917	31/12/1917
Operation(al) Order(s)	Addenda To R.A.M.C. Operation Order No 16	05/12/1917	05/12/1917
Operation(al) Order(s)	57th Division R.A.M.C. Operation Order No 16	05/12/1917	05/12/1917
Operation(al) Order(s)	57th Division R.A.M.C. Operation Order No 17	14/12/1917	14/12/1917
Miscellaneous	Medical Arrangements	14/12/1917	14/12/1917
Diagram etc	Diagram of Evacuation Arrangements		
Miscellaneous	Detailed Instructions Regarding French Preventive Treatment Of Trench foot	25/12/1917	25/12/1917
Operation(al) Order(s)	57th Division R.A.M.C. Operation Order No 18	26/12/1917	26/12/1917
Operation(al) Order(s)	57th Division R.A.M.C. Operation Order No 19	30/12/1917	30/12/1917
Heading	War Diary Of A.D.M.S. 57th Division From 1st January 1918 To 31st January 1918 Volume 1		
War Diary	Elverdinghe	01/01/1918	02/01/1918
War Diary	Steenwerck	03/01/1918	31/01/1918
Miscellaneous	57th Division Medical Arrangements	06/01/1918	06/01/1918
Diagram etc	Diagram Of Evacuation Of Wounded. Armentieres Sector		
Miscellaneous	List Of Returns Rendered By A.D.M.S 57th Division Appendices C		

Miscellaneous	Note Of Admissions To And Evacuations From Field Ambulance Of 57th Division	31/01/1918	31/01/1918
Heading	War Diary Of A.D.M.S 57th Division From 1st February 1918 To 28th February 1918 Volume 1		
War Diary	Steenwerck	01/02/1918	15/02/1918
War Diary	Merville	16/02/1918	28/02/1918
Operation(al) Order(s)	57th Division R.A.M.C. Operation Order No. 20	10/02/1918	10/02/1918
Heading	War Diary Of A.D.M.S. 57th Division From 1st March 1918 To 31st March 1918		
War Diary	Merville	01/03/1918	20/03/1918
War Diary	Croix Du Bac	21/03/1918	31/03/1918
Operation(al) Order(s)	57th Division R.A.M.C. Operation Order No 21	18/03/1918	18/03/1918
Operation(al) Order(s)	57th Division R.A.M.C. Operation Order No. 22	30/03/1918	30/03/1918
Operation(al) Order(s)	57th Division R.A.M.C. Operation Order No. 23	31/03/1918	31/03/1918
Heading	War Diary Of A.D.M.S, 57th Division From 1st April To 30th April 1918		
War Diary	Croix Du Bac	01/04/1918	01/04/1918
War Diary	Lucheux	02/04/1918	04/04/1918
War Diary	Coullemont	05/04/1918	08/04/1918
War Diary	Beauquesne	09/04/1918	11/04/1918
War Diary	Lucheux	12/04/1918	13/04/1918
War Diary	Pas-En-Artois	14/04/1918	30/04/1918
Miscellaneous	57th Division A.D.M.S. 57th Div. No, MS 219/3. Medical Arrangements	17/04/1918	17/04/1918
Miscellaneous	57th Division A.D.M.S. 57th Div. No, MS 219/3. Medical Arrangements	19/04/1918	19/04/1918
Heading	War Diary Of A.D.M.S. 57th Division From 1st May To 31st May 1918		
War Diary	Pas-En-Artois	01/05/1918	05/05/1918
War Diary	Couin	06/05/1918	31/05/1918
Operation(al) Order(s)	57th Division R.A.M.C. Operation Order No 24	03/05/1918	03/05/1918
Heading	War Diary Of A.D.M.S. 57th Divn. From 1.6.18 To 30.6.18		
War Diary	Couin	01/06/1918	30/06/1918
Miscellaneous	Medical Arrangements 57th Division	01/06/1918	01/06/1918
Operation(al) Order(s)	57th Division R.A.M.C. Operation Order No. 25	05/06/1918	05/06/1918
Operation(al) Order(s)	57th Division R.A.M.C. Operation Order No. 26	28/06/1918	28/06/1918
Heading	War Diary Of A.D.M.S.57th Division From 1/7/18 To 31/7/18		
War Diary	Couin	01/07/1918	01/07/1918
War Diary	Authie	02/07/1918	14/07/1918
War Diary	Pas-en-Artois	15/07/1918	29/07/1918
War Diary	Bouquemaison	30/07/1918	30/07/1918
War Diary	Hermaville	31/07/1918	31/07/1918
Miscellaneous	Medical Arrangements 57th Division	01/07/1918	01/07/1918
Operation(al) Order(s)	57th Division R.A.M.C. Operation Order No. 27	28/07/1918	28/07/1918
Operation(al) Order(s)	57th Division R.A.M.C. Operation Order No. 28	30/08/1918	30/08/1918
Heading	War Diary Of A.D.M.S. 57th Division From August 1st To August 31st 1918		
War Diary	Hermaville	01/08/1918	02/08/1918
War Diary	Etrun	03/08/1918	31/08/1918
Miscellaneous	Medical Arrangements 57th Division	02/08/1918	02/08/1918
Miscellaneous	Medical Arrangements 57th Division	08/08/1918	08/08/1918
Miscellaneous	Addendum To Medical Arrangements 57th Division Issued Under M. S 288/25	08/08/1918	08/08/1918
Operation(al) Order(s)	57th Division R.A.M.C. Operation Order No 29	15/08/1918	15/08/1918

Type	Description	Date From	Date To
Operation(al) Order(s)	R.A.M.C. 57th Division Operation Order No. 30	27/08/1918	27/08/1918
Miscellaneous	Provisional Medical Arrangements 57th Division	31/08/1918	31/08/1918
Heading	War Diary Of A.D.M.S. 57th Division From 1st Sept To 30th Sept 1918 Vol. 19		
War Diary	In The Field	01/09/1918	01/09/1918
War Diary	Blairville	01/09/1918	07/09/1918
War Diary	Near Queant	08/09/1918	16/09/1918
War Diary	Bavincourt	17/09/1918	30/09/1918
Operation(al) Order(s)	57th Division R.A.M.C. Operation Order No 31	06/09/1918	06/09/1918
Miscellaneous	Amendment To 57th Division R.A.M.C. Operation Order No 31	07/09/1918	07/09/1918
Miscellaneous	Medical Arrangements	07/09/1918	07/09/1918
Miscellaneous	Amendment No.1 To Medical Arrangements, 57th Division, Issued Under M.S. 306/5	09/09/1918	09/09/1918
Operation(al) Order(s)	57th Division R.A.M.C. Operation Order No. 32	15/09/1918	15/09/1918
Miscellaneous	Outline Of Medical Arrangements For The Evacuation Of Wounded During Active Operation	24/09/1918	24/09/1918
Miscellaneous	Medical Arrangements	24/09/1918	24/09/1918
Heading	War Diary Of A.D.M.S. 57th Division From 1st October To 31st October 1918		
War Diary	Near Canal Du Nord	01/10/1918	11/10/1918
War Diary	Barlin	12/10/1918	13/10/1918
War Diary	L' Epinette	14/10/1918	18/10/1918
War Diary	Englos	19/10/1918	19/10/1918
War Diary	Petit Ronchin	20/10/1918	20/10/1918
War Diary	Willems	21/10/1918	31/10/1918
Operation(al) Order(s)	57th Division R.A.M.C. Operation Order No. 34	07/10/1918	07/10/1918
Operation(al) Order(s)	57th Division R.A.M.C. Operation Order No 35	13/10/1918	13/10/1918
Operation(al) Order(s)	Medical Arrangements 57th Division R.A.M.C. (Published With 57th Division/ Operation Order No 35	13/10/1918	13/10/1918
Operation(al) Order(s)	R.A.M.C. Operation Order No 36. 57th Division	29/10/1918	29/10/1918
Heading	War Diary Of A.D.M.S. 57th Division From 1st November 1918 To 30th November 1918		
War Diary	Lille	01/11/1918	06/11/1918
War Diary	Mon En Baroeul	07/11/1918	30/11/1918
Operation(al) Order(s)	R.A.M.C. Operation Order No 37 57th Division	29/11/1918	29/11/1918
Operation(al) Order(s)	R.A.M.C. 57th Division Operation Order No 37	29/11/1918	29/11/1918
Heading	War Diary Of A.D.M.S. 57th Division From 1/12/18 To 31/12/18		
War Diary	Mons En Baroeul	01/12/1918	02/12/1918
War Diary	Duisans	03/12/1918	31/12/1918
Heading	War Diary Of A.D.M.S. 57th Division From 1st January 1919 To 31st January 1919		
War Diary	Duisans	01/01/1919	31/01/1919
Heading	War Diary Of A.D.M.S. 57th Division From 1st February 1919 To 28th February 1919		
War Diary	Duisans	01/02/1919	28/02/1919
Heading	War Diary Of A.D.M.S. 57th Division From 1st March 1919 To 31st March 1919		
War Diary	Duisans	01/03/1919	23/03/1919
Heading	57th Division C.R.E 1915 Sep-1916 Feb-1917 Feb-1919 Mar		

WO95/29691
Assistant Director Medical Services

Confidential

War Diary

of

Assistant Director of Medical Services.

57th DIVISION.

from 12th February 1917 to 27th February 1917

(Volume 1.)

COMMITTEE FOR THE
MEDICAL HISTORY OF THE WAR
Date 4 - APR. 1917

WAR DIARY or INTELLIGENCE SUMMARY

Army Form C. 2118.

Place	Date	Hour	Summary of Events and Information	Remarks and references to Appendices
HAVRE	1917 Feb. 12	—	After some two years of residence and about 8 months training in the Aldershot area, the 57th (West Lancs) Division, a 'Second line' Territorial Division chiefly recruited from the cities and large towns of south-west Lancashire, but including two Field Companies R.E. and two Field Ambulances from the Wessex Territorial Area, commenced a few days ago to move overseas and the Headquarters of that Division arrived in Havre today; one Field Ambulance (the 3/2nd West Lancs Field Ambulance) preceded it by one day; another the 2/2nd Wessex and the 2/1st (that is, Second line) West Lancs Cas. Clearing Station accompanied it; while the third, the 2/3rd Wessex Fd Amber. follows one day later. The crossing was smooth and uneventful.	
	Feb. 15		Leaving HAVRE at 9 p.m. on the 13th the Divisional Headquarters with the 2/2nd Wessex Fd Amb. and other troops in the same long train proceeded slowly and deviously by DIEPPE, BOULOGNE and HAZEBROUCK to the back area behind BAILLEUL where the Division is to assemble before going into the line. The journey lasted 41 hours and two nights spent in the train were excessively cold. HQ of Division proceeded to MERRIS, 2/2nd Wessex	

Army Form C. 2118.

WAR DIARY
or
INTELLIGENCE SUMMARY.
(Erase heading not required.)

Instructions regarding War Diaries and Intelligence Summaries are contained in F.S. Regs., Part II. and the Staff Manual respectively. Title pages will be prepared in manuscript.

Place	Date	Hour	Summary of Events and Information	Remarks and references to Appendices
	1917			
			Field Ambulance to STRAZEELE, the 3/2nd WEST LANCS. F. AMB. being already at OUTTERSTEENE.	Page 2.
MERRIS	Feb. 16		The 2/3rd WESSEX F. AMB. and the 57th Divisional Sanitary Section arrived today, proceeding to BORRE and MERRIS respectively. All three Field Ambulances visited today, and found satisfactorily settled.	
do.	Feb. 17		The 3/2nd Westlancs. F. Ambce. took over Main Dressing Station and work of evacuation from 1st New Zealand Field Ambulance. Visited Advanced Dressing Stations with A.D.M.S. New Zealand Division.	
do.	Feb. 18		Visit to Field Ambulances at BORRE and STRAZEELE.	
do.	" 20.		Owing to continuance of damp, foggy weather, much with illness of catarrhal nature about. Visited Main Dressing Station and Divisional Rest Station. SAILLY Sector. Met the 57th Division is taking over.	
do.	" 22		Conference of Divisional A.D.'s M.S. in Office of D.D.M.S. II ANZAC Corps, BAILLEUL. The 67th (Westlancs) Division is in the II ANZAC Corps with the 3rd AUSTRALIAN DIVISION. The II Anzac Corps has Headquarters in BAILLEUL and is in the II Army, Headquarters at CASSEL. We are	

Army Form C. 2118.

WAR DIARY
or
INTELLIGENCE SUMMARY.
(Erase heading not required.)

Place	Date	Hour	Summary of Events and Information	Remarks and references to Appendices
	1917.		in process of taking over line from N.Z. Division which has held it for 3-4 months.	Page 3.
MERRIS	Feb 24		Considerable number of cases of Rubella have already occurred in 57th Div. since its arrival in France.	
SAILLY	Feb 25		Proceeded from MERRIS to SAILLY and took over from A.D.M.S. New Zealand Division. Office documents to. Left Capt. Edmiston D.A.D.M.S. at Australian Casualty Clearing Station with Septic Sore throat, possibly of diphtheric nature. Capt. Godsell Asst 3/2 WEST LANCS Fd A.M.B. came as substitute. Sunshine today, first since Feb 10th.	
do.	Feb 26		Office routine now beginning to run smoothly.	

J.F.Dixon
Colonel, A. Med. S.
A.D.M.S. 57th (W.L.) Division,

Confidential

War Diary
of
A.D.M.S., 57th Division

from 27/2/17 to 30/3/17.

(Volume 1)

140/2057
Vol 172

COMMITTEE FOR THE
MEDICAL HISTORY OF THE WAR
Date 11 MAY 1917

WAR DIARY
or
INTELLIGENCE SUMMARY
(Erase heading not required.)

Army Form C. 2118.

Place	Date	Hour	Summary of Events and Information	Remarks and references to Appendices
SAILLY	1917 Feb. 27		Visited Advanced Dressing Station and Regimental Aid Posts of Rhineland Sector now held by 57th Division. Line runs from 2⅔ miles S.S.E. of Armentières (Sheet 36 I 20 d) to 3 miles E. by S. of LAVENTIE (Sheet 36. N.8.a) Heavy artillery fire on rest sector to left during last night and some enemy counter-fire. Two casualties in 57th Division.	
	Feb 28		Medical arrangements of Division now on established routine.	
	Mar 1		Visited Advanced Dressing Station and Aid Posts in right sector – see Appendix I. "Medical arrangements 57th Division".	Vide APP I.
		2.	Visited similarly left sector. See Appendix I	do
		3.	Visited Officers' Rest House at LA MOTTE. Chateau in part devoted to the purpose of Corps Officers' Convalescent Hospital. Administered by T.H. & N.Z. Army Corps; accommodation for 25 Officers in pleasant woodland country. Received information of appointment of O.C. 57 Div. Sanitary Section as Specialist Sanitary Officer, and order for the establishment of Divisional School of Sanitation for training of Sanitary Personnel. A suspected case of Cerebro Spinal Meningitis admitted to C.C.S. Diagnosis proved correct.	

Army Form C. 2118.

WAR DIARY
or
INTELLIGENCE SUMMARY.
(Erase heading not required.)

Place	Date	Hour	Summary of Events and Information	Remarks and references to Appendices
SAILLY	1917 Mar 5		D.A.D.M.S. returned to duty from HAZEBROUCK after 9 days sick (bronchitis) in hospital. Medical Officers ordered to Army School of Sanitation, HAZEBROUCK and Medical Officers training course (Corps School) at ESTAIRES. Those who have attended these schools especially the latter speak most highly of their value. Divisional Sanitary School for Sanitary personnel about to be established. Attended first meeting of Divisional men with D.D.M.S. (D.A.Q.M.G., C.R.E, & A.D.M.S.)	
	6.		Routine work; nothing of importance to report.	
	7.		Receipt of Operation Order No 4. Copy No 12 from Divisional H.Q. reference possible taking over of more line from 3rd Australian Division. April 3rd Australian Division called here for consultation	
	8		Orders received from Divisional H.Q. that 10th Brigade 3rd Australian Division to be relieved by 170th Brigade. Main Dressing Station and Advanced Dressing Station No 10th Brigade to be relieved by the 3/2 Wessex Fd Amba. 3/2 Wessex Fd Amba. to take over Advanced Dressing Station at La Corree relieves from 3/2 Wessex Fd Amba at 6 pm 9/3/17	

WAR DIARY or INTELLIGENCE SUMMARY

Army Form C. 2118.

Place	Date	Hour	Summary of Events and Information	Remarks and references to Appendices
SAILLY	1917. Mar. 9		Relief of Field Ambulance attached to 10th Brigade, 3rd Australian Division by 3/2nd 10th Brigade 4th Aust. Div. by 6.30 p.m. Taking over Advanced Dressing Station at Chapelle d'Armentieres on same. Left sector relief of 3/2nd Westpana. Field Ambulance at Advanced Dressing Station carried out by 6.30 p.m. Hq 2/3rd Wessex ft Aubers.	
	10.		Relief of 10th Brigade 3rd Australian Division carried out by noon. Everything quiet. During night of 10/11 bombardment of lactrine right sector. Some gas shells. Everything quiet. Some hostile aeroplanes came over lines during forenoon. Regimental Aid Post and portion of new sector visited by D.A.D.M.S. A.D.M.S. visited new Regimental Aid Post at lactrine right sector.	
	11.		Clear morning hostile aeroplanes over our lines fired at our own balloon. Pt Course of Divisional Sanitary School began at builders situated G.D.A.S.S. (sheet 36). 35 N.C.O's and men present from sanitary personnel of units. Telephone intercommunication (portable) broken down from 9 am to 2 pm. Inconvenience to this Office slight as Field Medical Units are not on telephone. Divisional Headquarters informed.	
	12.			

Army Form C. 2118.

WAR DIARY
or
INTELLIGENCE SUMMARY.
(Erase heading not required.)

Instructions regarding War Diaries and Intelligence Summaries are contained in F.S. Regs., Part II. and the Staff Manual respectively. Title pages will be prepared in manuscript.

Place	Date	Hour	Summary of Events and Information	Remarks and references to Appendices
SAILLY	1917 Nov/13		Quiet again on right sector. ADMS held conference of Officers Commanding Medical Units and Regimental Medical Officers. 14 Officers present.	
	14		Signs of enemy activity at 7.15 p.m. N.E. of D.H.Q. Request from D.H.Q. to report on cases gassed on night of 11th. ADMS visited Regimental Aid Posts right sector of line.	
	15	9.30 p.m.	ADMS attended Conference at D.D.M.S. Office I ANZAC. Message received 9.30 p.m. G O C II Anzac Army Corps to visit Medical Units on 16th. Units notified.	
	16	10 a.m.	G.O.C. II A. & N.Z. Army Corps visited Divisional Rest Station at 10 a.m. Accompanied by ADMS, met by RAMC Officers & Mdcl Officers of Unit. Seemed very pleased with inspection. Proceeded 2/2 Wn Yn at SAILLY. From here to 3/2 Wfans for Amb. at FORT ROMPU Afterwards visited Advanced Dressing Station at LA CROIX ESCURNEZ. Suggested that at least one hut should be made shell proof. This to be attended to. Notice from ADM II Anzac that next course of instruction at Medical Officers Training School for Officers Commanding Sections	

Army Form C. 2118.

WAR DIARY
or
INTELLIGENCE SUMMARY.
(Erase heading not required.)

Instructions regarding War Diaries and Intelligence Summaries are contained in F.S. Regs., Part II. and the Staff Manual respectively. Title pages will be prepared in manuscript.

Place	Date	Hour	Summary of Events and Information	Remarks and references to Appendices
SAILLY	1917. Mar 7		Weather quite changed, temperature much higher. Pond froze. Reynolds died. Bots and Advanced Dressing Station at Grandfire Kensha in BUSNES + BOIS GRENIER Sector.	
	18		Continuance of better weather. Several hours sunshine. N.O. 2/6 King's Liverpool Regt. admitted to Hospital – 3/2 W/ance. St. Aubin. Corpl water Donoual lookitchin. Telegram received stating 73 Amb School of Sanitation class until further notice.	
	19		Second course at Div School of Sanitation commenced. Col'd Andrews visited SDS and 3/2 W/ance to Amb. Main Dressing Station. Weather quite changed – dull cloudy & rain. Some showers.	
	20.		Weather becoming more wintry – little sunshine, there are twenty five north of Wy seen. One Officer supposed the suffering from effects of gas sent down sick. Bowl met Col. W. barrow being of 3/2 W/ance to A. Her. T.A.N.L.O. Routine Order 1090 received. 25th Division totals to Second Army & Anyac Corps – made NERRIS to be completed by March 22nd Visit by A. D.m.s. y D.A Dm.s. to Advanced Dressing Station, 3/2 W/ance. to Amb.	

WAR DIARY
or
INTELLIGENCE SUMMARY.
(Erase heading not required.)

Army Form C. 2118.

Place	Date	Hour	Summary of Events and Information	Remarks and references to Appendices
SAILLY	1917 Mar 21 (cont)		Coy at Chapelle d'Armentières, close to Regimental Aid Post at T.15.b.2.4 and T.14.d.5.4. Cold, with showers of sleet, clear at times. Several observation towards evening; wind dropped, clear at 4pm. Several observation balloons ascended. H.O. d/o KL kept accurate to have horses mov[ed] arrangements issued for Divisor (Appendix I)	Appendix I
	22.		April 5 at conference with 2 and 11 Anzac. Weather conditions much altered - covering of snow on ground at 7am. Snow warm during morning. Snow by 11am. Overcast afternoon with very heavy snowfalls. Relatively heavy blizzard 11.30 am & 3 pm. Wind fell on now cleared late	
	23.		While frost during night 22/23. 23/4/17 Secret Memo from 2nd and 11 Anzac Corps "Offensive Scheme" 2nd wire Divisional training School Divisional Institution and 2HQ in morning, and Bois Grenier. Slides in afternoon.	
	24.		B.M.S.9. 170th Infantry Brigade received acknowledged. To proceed to casualties Hostile artillery over line - heavily shelled by aircraft. Summertime from 11 pm.	

Army Form C. 2118.

WAR DIARY
or
INTELLIGENCE SUMMARY.
(Erase heading not required.)

Instructions regarding War Diaries and Intelligence Summaries are contained in F.S. Regs., Part II. and the Staff Manual respectively. Title pages will be prepared in manuscript.

Place	Date	Hour	Summary of Events and Information	Remarks and references to Appendices
SAILLY	1917 May 25		No increase in number of wounded. Desultory bombardment in early hours lasting only 10 minutes followed by heavy hostile bombardment for 30 minutes.	
	26		All sectors quiet. Artillery activity moderate. Weather bad – snow showers. Forty four remounted with two Thresh Disinfectors arrived. Third convoy at Divisional Sanitary School commenced.	
	27		Everything remains quiet. Some activity on part of enemy. Cascailles recall in minutes. Small raiding parties of the enemy noticed. Dull & cloudy with low in morning – intermittent sunshine in afternoon. Conference of Medical Officers at A.D.M.S. Office 2.45 pm	
	28		Enemy Artillery had own. G.S.O. 2 wounded at LA VESEE 12 noon. Died in Casualty Clearing Station during afternoon. Lieutenant Stelling H.2.L.d. 2.2 (Sheet 36) between 12 noon and 1 pm. – 18 soldier casualties, one died in Field Ambulance. 5 civilians wounded, one died on way to Field Ambulance, shrapnel wound abdomen. Shelling ceased 12 pm, 1 pm. Weather clear, visibility good. Course of instruction for Officers Commanding Section of Field Ambulance finished.	
	29		A.D.M.S. attended Conference with D.D.M.S. Corps. 2nd Lt Angus 3/7/?	

Army Form C. 2118.

WAR DIARY
or
INTELLIGENCE SUMMARY.
(Erase heading not required.)

Instructions regarding War Diaries and Intelligence Summaries are contained in F.S. Regs., Part II. and the Staff Manual respectively. Title pages will be prepared in manuscript.

Place	Date	Hour	Summary of Events and Information	Remarks and references to Appendices
SAILLY	1917 Mar 29	30	Secret Scheme amended from March 21st. Weather changeable - travel of GSO2. Weather again squally with shovers of rain & sleet. Some eucochine Aired visits hade at BOURGHAM. Enemy great allway, not at much movement opposite left Sector. 1st course of instruction at T'Arque Medical Officer Training School at ESTAIRES commenced at 9.30 am. 4 Regimental Medical Officers and 2 Field Ambulance Medical Officers detailed to attend.	

J. F. Edmeston
Captain, R.A.M.C.T.
D.A.D.M.S
for A.D.M.S., 57th (W.L.) Division.

SECRET.   Appendix I

MEDICAL ARRANGEMENTS
57th (West Lancs) Division.

Reference Map 36.

1. **EVACUATION FROM RIGHT SECTOR.**

REGIMENTAL AID POSTS and BEARER RELAY POSTS.	RIFLE VILLA.	N.2.d.6.9.
	EATON HALL.	N.3.b.4.3.
CAR COLLECTING POINTS.	TWO TREE FARM.	N.2.c.3.6.
	CROIX BLANCHE.	H.33.a.4.3.
	RUE DE BASSIERES.	N.3.b.7.8.
ADVANCED DRESSING STATION.	LA CROIX LESCORNEX.	H.26.d.1.2.
MAIN DRESSING STATION.	FORT ROMPU.	H.7.d.6.3.

   ROUTES OF EVACUATION. From Regimental Aid Post at RIFLE VILLA (RUE DU BOIS) by wheeled stretcher by RUE DE BOIS and RUE DES BASSIERES to Advanced Dressing Station at LA CROIX LESCORNEX. Thence by car to Main Dressing Station. Should the RUE DU BOIS be unavailable owing to shell fire, wounded may be evacuated by V.C.AVENUE to Car Collecting Post at TWO TREE FARM and thence by car direct to Main Dressing Station.

   From Regimental Aid Post at EATON HALL (whither wounded are brought from front line trenches by CELLAR AVENUE) by wheeled stretcher along RUE PETILLON and RUE DES BASSIERES to Advanced Dressing Station at LA CROIX LESCORNEX (where one car is continuously kept). Thence by RUE DE BIACHE to Main Dressing Station.

   DISTRIBUTION OF PERSONNEL.

Regimental Aid Posts.	4 men at each as relief bearers.
Advanced Dressing Station.	1 Medical Officer and 15 N.C.Os. and men.

   In case of necessity, extra bearers can be supplied from Advanced Dressing Station to either Regimental Aid Post or both: these in turn will be replaced or augmented from Main Dressing Station. In action or on notification of raid, the bearer personnel at Advanced Dressing Station will be increased according to requirements.

2. **EVACUATION FROM CENTRE SECTOR.**

REGIMENTAL AID POSTS and BEARER RELAY POSTS.	CONVENT AVENUE.	N.5.a.4.2.
	ENGINEER DUMP near WYE FARM.	H.35.b.8.2.
CAR COLLECTING POINTS.	LA CROIX MARECHAL. (from CONVENT AVENUE).	H.34.a.8.7.
	ELBOW FARM. (from WYE FARM).	H.29.c.1.3.
ADVANCED DRESSING STATION.	PORT A CLOUS FARM.	H.21.a.2.8.
MAIN DRESSING STATION.	N.E. of SAILLY.	G.17.a.8.3.

   ROUTES OF EVACUATION. From Regimental Aid Post at CONVENT AVENUE by hand to RUE DAVID. Thence by wheeled stretcher to LA CROIX MARECHAL. Thence by car to Advanced and Main Dressing Stations.

   From Regimental Aid Post near WYE FARM to ELBOW FARM by wheeled stretcher by day and by car at night.

From ELBOW FARM to Main Dressing Station by car. To the Aid Post neare WYE FARM cases are brought by tramway by day, by hand stretcher via GUNNERS' WALK by night, the tramway being unsafe owing to machine gun fire.

DISTRIBUTION OF PERSONNEL.

Regimental Aid Posts   4 men at each, as relief bearers.
Advanced Dressing Station.   1 Medical Officer 1 N.C.O. and 6 men, also two motor ambulances.

These can be rapidly reinforced at need from Main Dressing Station.

3. EVACUATION FROM LEFT SECTOR.

REGIMENTAL AID POSTS and BEARER RELAY POSTS.	WHITE CITY. TRAMWAY AVENUE.	I.31.a.4.6. I.20.c.0.0.
ADVANCED DRESSING STATION.	BOIS GRENIER.	H.24.d.5.0.
MAIN DRESSING STATION. (as for Right Sector).	FORT ROMPU.	R.7.d.6.3.

ROUTE OF EVACUATION. From Regimental Aid Posts on trolleys by tramway to main road (RUE d' ANCARDERIE). Thence by wheeled stretcher to BOIS GRENIER (Advanced Dressing Station) and thereafter by car.

DISTRIBUTION OF PERSONNEL.

Regimental Aid Posts.   4 men at each as relief bearers.
Advanced Dressing Station.   1 Medical Officer and 15 other ranks.

4. During action communication is kept up between Advanced Dressing Stations and Main Dressing Stations by motor cycle.

5. Sick in the front area are evacuated in the same manner as wounded.

6. There is a Medical Officer and orderly at each Regimental Aid Post: all sick and wounded in the sub sector are to receive medical attention at the Aid Post irrespective of unit.

7. Two Medical Officers are medically responsible for the gun positions: two others for artillery details behind the line, and the wagon lines respectively.

8. The Divisional Rest Station is situated at LE NOUVEAU MONDE - G.27.c.6.3.

9. Cases requiring evacuation are conveyed by NO.14 MOTOR AMBULANCE CONVOY to NO.1. AUSTRALIAN CASUALTY CLEARING STATION, ESTAIRES - L.29.d.9.8. via Main Road South of the River Lys.

4th March, 1917,

Colonel. A.Med.S.
A.D.M.S., 57th Division.

SECRET.

Appendix II

MEDICAL ARRANGEMENTS

57th (West Lancs) Division.

Reference Map 36.

1. **EVACUATION FROM RIGHT SECTOR - RIGHT SUBSECTION.**

REGIMENTAL AID POSTS.	EATON HALL.	N.3.b.4.2.
BEARER RELAY POSTS at EATON HALL and on RUE PETILLON opposite the end of	IMPERTINENCE SAP.	N.3.c.8.5.
CAR COLLECTING POINTS.	RUE DESBASSIERES.	N.3.b.7.8.
ADVANCED DRESSING STATION.	LA CROIX LESCORNEX.	H.26.c.8.4.
MAIN DRESSING STATION.	N.E. of SAILLY.	G.17.a.8.3.

    ROUTES OF EVACUATION. From Regimental Aid Post at EATON HALL (whither wounded are brought from front line trenches by CELLAR AVENUE) by wheeled stretcher along RUE PETILLON and RUE DESBASSIERES to Advanced Dressing Station at LA CROIX LESCORNEX (where one car is continuously kept). Thence to Main Dressing Station.

    DISTRIBUTION OF PERSONNEL.

Regimental Aid Posts.	4 men at each as relief bearers.
Advanced Dressing Station.	1 Medical officer and 15 N.C.Os. and men.

    In case of necessity, extra bearers can be supplied from Advanced Dressing Station to either Regimental Aid Post or both: these in turn will be replaced or augmented from Main Dressing Station. In action or on notification of raid, the bearer personnel at Advanced Dressing Station will be increased according to requirements.

2. **EVACUATION FROM RIGHT SECTOR - LEFT SUBSECTION.**

REGIMENTAL AID POSTS.	R.E.DUMP near WYE FARM	H.35.b.8.2.
BEARER RELAY POSTS.	R.E.DUMP near WYE FARM, and near CONVENT AVENUE.	H.35.b.8.2. N.5.a.4.2.
CAR COLLECTING POINTS.	LA CROIX MARECHAL (from CONVENT AVENUE). ELBOW FARM (from WYE FARM).	H.34.a.8.7. H.29.c.1.3.
ADVANCED DRESSING STATION.	PORT A CLOUS FARM.	H.21.a.2.8.
MAIN DRESSING STATION.	N.E. of SAILLY.	G.17.a.8.3.

    ROUTES OF EVACUATION. From Bearer Relay Post at CONVENT AVENUE by hand to RUE DAVID. Thence by wheeled stretcher to LA CROIX MARECHAL, and so by car to Advanced and Main Dressing Stations.
    From Regimental Aid Post near WYE FARM to ELBOW FARM by wheeled stretcher by day and by car at night.

From ELBOW FARM to Main Dressing Station by car. To the Aid Post near WYE FARM cases are brought by tramway by day, and by hand stretcher via GUNNERSV WALK by night.

DISTRIBUTION OF PERSONNEL.

Regimental Aid Posts.   4 men at each as relief bearers.
Advanced Dressing Station.   1 Medical Officer 1 N.C.O. and 6 men, also two motor ambulances.

These can be rapidly reinforced at need from Main Dressing Station.

3. EVACUATION FROM LEFT SECTOR - RIGHT SUBSECTION.

REGIMENTAL AID POSTS.   at   TRAAMWAY AVENUE.   I.25.b.9.1.
BEARER RELAY POSTS.   at   I.31.a.5.5.
   and   I.19.c.8.5.
ADVANCED DRESSING STATION.   BOIS GRENIER.   H.24.d.5.0.
MAIN DRESSING STATION.   FORT ROMPU.   H.7.d.6.3.

ROUTE OF EVACUATION.   From Regimental Aid Posts and Bearer Relay Posts on trolleys by tramway to main road (RUE d'ANCARDERIE). Thence by wheeled stretcher to BOIS GRENIER (Advanced Dressing Station) and thereafter by car.

DISTRIBUTION OF PERSONNEL.

Regimental Aid Posts.   4 men at each as relief bearers.
Advanced Dressing Station.   1 Medical Officer and 15 other ranks.

4. EVACUATION FROM LEFT SECTOR - LEFT SUBSECTION.

REGIMENTAL AID POSTS. and)   WELLINGTON AVENUE.
BEARER RELAY POSTS.   ) (near FME   I.14.d.5.8.
      DESPLANQUE.)
   and   COWGATE AVENUE.   I.15.b.2.9.

ADVANCED DRESSING STATION.   LA CHAPELLE d'ARMENTIERES.   I.8.a.5.4.

CAR COLLECTING STATION.   at   I.9.c.4.5.

ROUTES OF EVACUATION.   From COWGATE AVENUE by hand to SALVAGE DUMP where a wheeled stretcher carriage is kept. Thence to Car Collecting Post by carrier.
From WELLINGTON AVENUE by trolleys on old railway or by wheeled stretcher carrier to Car Collecting Station. By night cars may go almost to Aid Post.

DISTRIBUTION OF PERSONNEL.

Regimental Aid Posts.	4 men at each as relief bearers.
Advanced Dressing Station.	1 Medical Officer, 2 N.C.Os. and 25 men (R.A.M.C.) and 2 men (A.S.C.M.T.).

5. During action communication is kept up between Advanced Dressing Stations and Main Dressing Stations by motor cycle.

6. Sick in the front area are evacuated in the same manner as wounded.

7. There is a Medical Officer and orderly at each Regimental Aid Post: all sick and wounded in the sub sector are to receive medical attention at the Aid Post irrespective of unit.

8. Two Medical Officers are medically responsible for the gun positions: two others for Artillery Details behind the line, and the wagon lines respectively.

9. The Divisional Rest Station is situated at LE NOUVEAU MONDE - G.27.c.6.3.

10. Cases requiring evacuation are conveyed by NO.14 MOTOR AMBULANCE CONVOY to NO.1.AUSTRALIAN CASUALTY CLEARING STATION, ESTAIRES - L.29.d.9.8. via Main Road South of the RIVER LYS.

21st March, 1917.   Colonel. A.Med.S.
                                     A.D.M.S, 57th Division.

Confidential.

War Diary
of
A.D.M.S. 57th Division.

from 31st March 1917 to 30th April, 1917.

(Volume I.)

Army Form C. 2118.

WAR DIARY
or
INTELLIGENCE SUMMARY.
(Erase heading not required.)

Instructions regarding War Diaries and Intelligence Summaries are contained in F.S. Regs., Part II. and the Staff Manual respectively. Title pages will be prepared in manuscript.

Place	Date	Hour	Summary of Events and Information	Remarks and references to Appendices
SAILLY	31/3/17		A.D.M.S. visited D.M.S. 2nd Army at HAZEBROUCK in accordance with instructions received from D.M.S. Left here 11am arrived back about 3 p.m. Scots very quiet, one client hit in cook-house. Average admissions daily sick to Field Ambulance 37.9, average daily evacuations wounded & sick 24.	
	1/4/17		Case of Scarlet Fever reported from 2/5 K. Royal Regt. 17th S. Bn in the line. No case of infectious disease notified during 24 hours now 31st inst now 1st. Weather fair at first, but cold showers during afternoon with periods of sunshine. Advanced Dressing Station at CHAPELLE D'ARMENTIÈRES apparently shot at. I.1.d.5.8 that car collecting post at La Ardenneca Dressing Station.	
	2/4/17		Very cold and windy which facilitates apparently general use of Western Europe. A/C L.P. in now in Divisional Area. Followed by burst of ADMS Officer sustaining and todays very high wind and drifting snow. Officer doubles great. Wounded of the enemy in March was the 186 sick ———— to rate moderate. Scabies fairly abundant. No special incidence of infectious disease.	
	3/4/17		Capt. Look R.A.M.C. T.F. posted for duty with 2/5 Wessex Fd Ambulance.	

Army Form C. 2118.

WAR DIARY
or
INTELLIGENCE SUMMARY.
(Erase heading not required.)

Place	Date	Hour	Summary of Events and Information	Remarks and references to Appendices
SAILLY	4/4/17		Visited new Advanced Dressing Station on outskirts of ARMENTIÈRES - about 400-600 yards behind front line which was hit by shells on 31st March. New Advanced Dressing Station in spacious cellar of large self contained house. Also being shepherded. O.C. Divisional Coy. Shown new car collecting post. Visited subsidiary line in front of mobile gun pits.	
	5/4/17		Conference of Assistant Directors of Medical Services of II Anzac Corps at BAILLEUL. Shell Shock, Mumps, and Adams Office Report discussed. NZADMS inspected V.C. manner and enquired into case of Scarlet Fever at 2/2 Rifle Bgde. Envid, Leeson Camp and D.D.M.S. I Anzac Corps visited Medical Unit thorough inspection. D.M.S. expressed warm approval of all conditions he has found.	
	7.4.17		Five cases of Scarlet fever having occurred lately (in 2/2, 2/8, & 2/10 Rutland) visited 2/10 K. Lpool hosp. yesterday and today. Visited 2/2 Wiltshire Anbur and 2/2 Worcesters the Anbur regarding measures accommodation available in case of great pressure. Visited Divisional Reinforcement	

T2134. Wt. W708–776. 50C000. 4/15. Sir J. C. & S.

Army Form C. 2118.

WAR DIARY
or
INTELLIGENCE SUMMARY.
(Erase heading not required.)

Instructions regarding War Diaries and Intelligence Summaries are contained in F. S. Regs., Part II. and the Staff Manual respectively. Title pages will be prepared in manuscript.

Place	Date	Hour	Summary of Events and Information	Remarks and references to Appendices
SAILLY	7/4/17		Camp to which cases thrown from lictherham Crumpy Alearing Station are now being returned. Divisional School of Sanitation has closed its four course (and Monday to Saturday) all the Sanitary men of the Division have received oral and practical instruction. D.A.D.M.S. - O.C. School. Capt. McKenzie - Adjutant.	
	8/4/17		Office routine. Weather bright sunshine warm Advance Dressing Station visited the Regimental Aid Post bearer Relay Posts. Advanced Dressing Station in the right Brigade Sub-sector at present occupied by 146th Brigade. The evacuation from this area is carried out by 2/2 A. Wessex fd Ambce. The Officer Commanding accompanied C.O.S.M. through inspection of front line was carried out at same time. time occupied 4 hours. Marked aerial activity.	
	9/4/17		Weather completely changed. Snow sleet and hail showers. Some sunshine at intervals. Wind cold and dangerous. Advance with Divisional Reinforcement Camp. Reinforcement party 3 O.R. arrives to Westhoa. Ye Aubes. 5] Div. Operation Order No 6 received - Relief of 17th by 172nd Inf Bde.	

T/134. Wt. W708-776. 50000. 4/15. Sir J. C. & S.

Army Form C. 2118.

WAR DIARY
or
INTELLIGENCE SUMMARY.
(Erase heading not required.)

Instructions regarding War Diaries and Intelligence Summaries are contained in F. S. Regs., Part II. and the Staff Manual respectively. Title pages will be prepared in manuscript.

Place	Date	Hour	Summary of Events and Information	Remarks and references to Appendices
SAILLY.	10/4/17		Notification received of relief by 12th Infantry Brigade. Zero hour 10.15 p.m. Very quiet day. Weather capricious. Snow, sleet and rain, very cold indeed. Moving from Wet. At 10.30 p bombardment commenced. Very heavy bombardment followed by bombardment by enemy. Raiding party of 30 left our trenches. Casualties numbered 1 Officer 29 other ranks. Nine 2 killed out & known to us officially. Only 4 serious cases evacuated at once. The remainder were brought in from rifle billets. Moto Ambulance Convoy unable to deal with cases - evacuated to Casualty Clearing Station by Field Ambulance Motor Ambulances. The took place in BOIS GRENIER Sector. All the Casualties were passed through Advance Dressing Station at BOIS GRENIER to Main Dressing Station 3/2 Wdane. H Ambulance at FORT ROMPU. Absence time bombardment and apparently en masse from sector immediately on our right LAVENTIE Sector.	
	11/4/17		It was on this day snow began to fall heavily and continued for about 30 hours, very soon melted. About 7 pm. turned to rain and was fair for an interval of 8.30 pm	

Army Form C. 2118.

WAR DIARY
or
INTELLIGENCE SUMMARY.
(Erase heading not required.)

Place	Date	Hour	Summary of Events and Information	Remarks and references to Appendices
SAILLY	12/4/17		ADMS attended long conference of ADIs NS of II Anzac Corps at office of DDMS BAILLEUL chiefly regarding evacuation of wounded on new front. Lt. Col. Cook OC 2/3rd Wessex F. Amb unofficially announced to have been appointed ADMS 55th Division. A DMS visited NEUVE EGLISE area to which this Division may move later.	
	13/4/17		ADMS visited ESTAIRES No 1 Australian Casualty Clearing Station and Bayer at LA GORGUE and saw men wounded on night of 10-11th about to be evacuated; also 2 Medical Officers - Major Williams MO 2/5 W. Ryd Regt and Capt Kennedy MO 2/5 Lan. Regt. - injured by shell in theatre wall and Capt Kennedy MO 2/5 Lan. Regt. - injured by shell in theatre wall and Capt Kennedy severely shelled with H.E. from 3-5. No casualties but building much battered, one motor ambulance car injured. All night trail of the injured to convey the above by Motor Guild from PORT L CROIX to all Medical Units and ADMS.	
	14/4/17		Weather at last at work at spring-like. Visited 3rd Australian Divisional Rest Station at L'ESTRADE and road being repaired by 2/2 W. Wessex F. Amb.	

Army Form C. 2118.

WAR DIARY
or
INTELLIGENCE SUMMARY.
(Erase heading not required.)

Place	Date	Hour	Summary of Events and Information	Remarks and references to Appendices
SAILLY	14/4/17		G.19/k/2012 to improve line of evacuation. A.D.M.S. and Divisional Gen. Officers visited all Main and Advanced Dressing Stations and gave orders to the being more gas proof. Formal intimation received that Lt Col H.D. Brock OC 2/3rd Wessex Field Amb. is appointed A.D.M.S. 55th (W.Lanc.) Division, to take up duty at once.	
	15/4/17		Sanitary Section ceases to be Divisional unit from today. Conference in afternoon of Field Ambulance Commanders regarding Evacuation. In order that all may have an opportunity of acquiring experience in evacuation, 2/3rd Wessex Field Ambulance to take over evacuation from 4 pm. (La Croix Reserve) Sector — see Operation Order No. 1. Raid by enemy last night carried about 30 evacuation to men of this Division.	Appendix I
	16/4/17		Redistribution of Evacuation duty among Field Ambulances from today. 2/3rd Wessex to Ancre Mains (Courcelly now left) and left, 2/2 Wessex No. 3 to Hypre. No. 4 to taken over by 2/3rd Wessex to Ancre from R.A.P. Wessex to Ancre. Increased demands from Medical Units of the Division by I Anzac Corps from today. 3 Sergeants & 40 other	

WAR DIARY or INTELLIGENCE SUMMARY

Army Form C. 2118.

Place	Date	Hour	Summary of Events and Information	Remarks and references to Appendices
SMILY	16/4/17		Inspected and from tomorrow 8 G.S. wagons, horse and drivers visited Field Ambulance regarding preparations of speedy evacuation in the event of a raid. Col. Brooks departure to 55th Division postponed. Medical rendezvous practise. 8 G.S. wagons to attend to 11th August. Yth Aust. Cond. supt at 8 p.m.	
	17/4/17		At 3.30 a.m. a raiding party from the 171st Brigade entered the enemy trenches. Our casualties 2 O.R. killed and 2 Officers and 7 O.R. wounded. D.M.S. visited Main Dressing Station in the early morning at FORT RONPU. The work of evacuation was carried out with all possible speed. A barrage was put down at 3.30 a.m. the raid actually commencing a little later. The casualties began to arrive at their Dressing Station after being collected and passed through Regimental Aid Posts and moved to Cambligneul Station at 6.15 p.m. and were attended to and passed to ARMENTIÈRES at following times — Le Jully 1/3 Heyland and 10 men 10/4th ARMENTIÈRES at following times — LE NOUVEAU MONDE 1 Sergt + 20 men at 6 p.m., from 2/2 West's M. Cent. SALLY 6.30 a.m. One Sergt. and 10 men, FORT RONPU 1 Sergt + 10 men at 7 a.m. Message received from D.D.S. Second Army, that Capt. Smith withdrawn from School of Musketry	

WAR DIARY or INTELLIGENCE SUMMARY

Army Form C. 2118.

Place	Date	Hour	Summary of Events and Information	Remarks and references to Appendices
SAILLY	17/4/17		To report to O.C. 1/5th Wore't Regt Aubers, 8th Division. Weather very blustery all morning. Afternoon cold wind with snow.	
	18/4/17		Confirmation received of postponement of Col Brook's departure. 11.30 am B.15th Telegram through Division HQ from Second Army asking explanation of telegram from Cpl Sibitaris General memo No. 6 of 15000 premises captured by 2nd Army, the question put was that C. & M.M. had Received message Salient at Bois Grenier, which has not received any hostile shells for 4 days. The reports to the Observation Post which observe the fire on this area not to be complete. Observation Post probably abandoned.	
	19/4/17		Col Wild attended conference at D.H.Q and T/ Auryas. Telegram received from 8th that if Col Brook should not proceed to 58th Division would further at once received. Very quiet day. Ethold but rainy. DAZ will send Line & 2/21st Medical Field Ambulance for evening state.	
	20/4/17		Telephone communication cut off all by letter or telegram. Telegram in code Message received 57th Division Order No. 7 re move of 171st & 170th Infantry Brigade cancelled. 171st Brigade Order No. 8 received referred to move that is cancelled.	

WAR DIARY or INTELLIGENCE SUMMARY

Army Form C. 2118.

Place	Date	Hour	Summary of Events and Information	Remarks and references to Appendices
SAILLY	2/4/17		By Div. H.Q. telegram preliminary warning received to take over portion of line from 3rd Australian Division, namely that occupied by the 2nd Australian Brigade, to include 2 Regimental Aid Posts and 2 Advanced Dressing Stations. The Advanced Dressing Stations will be taken over by 3/2 & 1/Qn.ers. Field Ambulance. Move to be completed on 26th April about visited R.A. Units, H.Q. and 5th Australian Division, and also 3rd F/Ambulance. 5th Australian, to make preliminary arrangements.	Appendix I
	3/4/17		Operation Order No. 9 – 5th Division enclosing new boundary received. New line taken over extends from I.16.6.2.8 Rue De La BLANCHE to RIVER LYS all on Sheet 36 NW FRANCE. The boundary is a very irregular one. The area was seen by a guide with O.C. 3/2 F/Amce. 5th Amb. and found to include 2 Advanced Dressing Stations and 3 Regimental Aid Posts, one of which was looked after by a Field Ambulance Medical Officer. It caused the due to High Explosive falling in midst of a relieving party. Very few due to being carried out about 2.30 am. Operation Order No. 8 revised 17th Infantry Brigade to go into new trenches and one Brigade received.	

Army Form C. 2118.

WAR DIARY
or
INTELLIGENCE SUMMARY.
(Erase heading not required.)

Instructions regarding War Diaries and Intelligence Summaries are contained in F.S. Regs., Part II. and the Staff Manual respectively. Title pages will be prepared in manuscript.

Place	Date	Hour	Summary of Events and Information	Remarks and references to Appendices
SAILLY	21/4/17		From 25th Division to be in billets behind ERQUINGHEM as reserve. The move not to take place same day. 171st Brigade Order No 9 received giving order of Battalions to march into new area. 2/5 K.L.Regt. Regt first to take over as has left when 2/5 K.L.Regt. Regt. within sight — move to commence with 23rd. Orders received about new duties of Sanitary Sections — not responsible for scavenging etc.	
	22/4/17		Capt. E. Jephcott reported from Base Hospital, BOULOGNE. Very quiet day. Visited Casualty 3rd Australian Division and made a complete tour of the new Main Dressing Stations and Advanced Dressing Stations in ARMENTIÈRES and HOUPLINES before taking them over. Officer commanding 3/2nd W. Lanc. 1/5 Amb. accompanied him. The day proved quickly. Weather becoming stronger.	
	23/4/17		Capt. Newton, R.A.M.C.T.F. relieved by Capt. Gibbs, 2/5 N.O.F Lancs Regt. Was suffering from nervous breakdown — sent to Hospital. Colonel started 3/2 W. Lanc. Fd Ambce. to see some cases of N.Y.D. & Shell Shock — one serious case. Letter received from R.A.M.D advising arrival of a new Medical Officer who to complete establishment. Not 1 arrived and remains substance. Very chilly sharp eastern in the air, still cold wind from the east. 3 layers.G	

Army Form C. 2118.

WAR DIARY
or
INTELLIGENCE SUMMARY.
(Erase heading not required.)

Place	Date	Hour	Summary of Events and Information	Remarks and references to Appendices
SAILLY	23/4/17		Cars no now sent to 1st Australian Field Ambulance. Worked to one line Field Ambulances.	
	24/4/17		Clear spring day, very little wind. Marked aircraft activity. Aeroplanes and balloons. "B.A.B." trench code corrections received. Wind visited Advanced Dressing Station at LA CROIX-L'ESCORNEZ. Enquiries of proposed Medical offices at 2.45 pm. Ambulance fair.	
	25/4/17		Advanced parties from 17th Brigade in new Sector. Arranged with 9 Squad 3rd Australian Division Sectors in ARMENTIÈRES, in company with D.A.D.M.S. 3rd Australian Division. Medical supply from town water supply station. See and enquired into. Medical supply from town ample. Supply Coys high standards found in different quarters of the town for the purpose of filling carts. Supply to shut off and spared at extra hours. Plans to prevent waste. Now and Advanced Dressing Station visited. Horse lines taken far away from reserves. Stables at L'EPINETTE, 2 miles from town, but very good. Wagon lust in ARMENTIÈRES. A.D.M.S. moved from line Contemine Section.	
	26/4/17		Increase large scale - march proper scale today. Ration Officer	

WAR DIARY
or
INTELLIGENCE SUMMARY

Army Form C. 2118.

Place	Date	Hour	Summary of Events and Information	Remarks and references to Appendices
SAILLY	2/4/17		Adjt. left instructions to move 16th Oct to Oct. to hosp Mary's received to file.	
	2/4/17		A.D.M.S. visited O.R.S. O.H.M.S. visited stables 2/3 West Lanc. Arrange details of move of 3/3 W. Lanc Field Ambulances at 12 noon to Main Dressing Station at FORT ROMPU to Main Dressing Station at Ecole des Filles ARMENTIERES. 3rd West Lanc. to move up to FORT ROMPU and also take over Advanced Dressing Station at BOIS GRENIER, the move to take place on Monday 30th April. A.D.M.S. visited Advanced Dressing Station at CHAPELLE D'ARMENTIERES to confer with Regimental Medical Officers 2/4 and 2/5 S. La. Regt. with reference to an extra Regimental Aid Post for leave left of the RUE DU BOIS Sector, which is to take over of Regimental Aid Post. D.A.D.M.S. attended conference at Divisional H.Q. for special purpose. Cancelled Medical Orders to Special Corps. Re. stretcher bearers etc. Refused and asked permission to send cases from his own companies to Main Dressing Station. A.D.M.S. visited No 3/5 K.O.R. Lanc Regt. to see inspection carried out.	

Army Form C. 2118.

WAR DIARY
or
INTELLIGENCE SUMMARY.
(Erase heading not required.)

Instructions regarding War Diaries and Intelligence Summaries are contained in F. S. Regs., Part II. and the Staff Manual respectively. Title pages will be prepared in manuscript.

Place	Date	Hour	Summary of Events and Information	Remarks and references to Appendices
SAILLY	28/4/17		57th Div. R.A.M.C. Operation Order No 3 issued; move of 3/2nd Wessex and 2/3rd Wessex Field Ambulances thereon. O/C.s visited the backs to be proceeded over. C.O. visited the Tramway, Ostella Sidings and the 2/3rd Wessex to Ankles. Carrier parties carried empty panniers. Divisors also arranged emergency loads.	Appendix III
	29/4/17		Carrying out of new SAILLY-ARMENTIÈRES road. About seven Reinforcement Camps near the Regimental Aid Post. up to 1/2am, before then the V.C. Stamens on the outskirts of the advance line. before then V.C. Stamens taken all over. The ADMS visited the 2/3rd Wessex at Ankles. He arranged visits to the 3/2nd Wessex Fd. Amb. and to the 3/2nd Wessex Fd. Amb. Very quickly shell fell in GARGUÉ area. Strong defensively arrived	
	30/4/17		Move of 3/2nd Wessex Fd. Amb. for Mainwaring Station at FORT ROMPU completed at noon. 2/2nd Wessex to Ankles. also took over BOIS GRENIER Advanced Dressing Station. Sgt. Argus and D.A.D.M.S. visited Anvil OC 57th Div. Train inspected transport of 2/3 Wessex Fd. Amb. at 2.30 hrs. Train entire stable. Officers accompanied him. O.C. Train very satisfied with inspection. Strong a little disturbance. Army visited 2/2	

Army Form C. 2118.

WAR DIARY
or
INTELLIGENCE SUMMARY.
(Erase heading not required.)

Instructions regarding War Diaries and Intelligence Summaries are contained in F. S. Regs., Part II. and the Staff Manual respectively. Title pages will be prepared in manuscript.

Place	Date	Hour	Summary of Events and Information	Remarks and references to Appendices
SAILLY	30/11		Went to Amba. Officer in cmd at New Brewery Salien at FORT ROMPU STRAND visited 3/L W Lancs. F Amba at ARMENTIERES and at the Stables on LERMITTE Rd. No ams to Amba at ARMENTIERES. Received "camp of gassing" testid not to be due to enemy gas. Actual cause very suspicious. 1st case from 2/3 W Welsh to Camp. Orders to move 1 Sgt. J.C. 12 men to reinforce from Camp Commandant.	

J.C. Edmiston
Captain, R.A.M.C.T.
D.A.D.M.S.
for A.D.M.S., 57th (W.L.) Division.

SECRET.　　　　　　57th DIVISION.　　　　　　　　　　Copy No. 8.

APPENDIX I

Headquarters,
15-4-1917.

R.A.M.C. Operation Order No.1.

Reference sheet 36 - 1/40,000.

1. The Officer Commanding 2/3rd Wessex Field Ambulance will detail a party to relieve the 2/2nd Wessex Field Ambulance at the Advanced Dressing Station, H.26.c.2.8., and the two Bearer Relay Posts attached. Move to be completed by 10-30am 18-4-1917.

2. The Officer Commanding 2/3rd Wessex Field Ambulance will detail an advance party of 1 officer and 4 other ranks to report on morning of 16/4/1917 to Officer in Charge of Advanced Dressing Station H.26.c.2.8. Arrangements will be made by Officers Commanding units concerned.

3. Completion of move to be notified to this office by WIRE.

4. ACKNOWLEDGE.

Issued at 7.30 pm. to

DISTRIBUTION:-
　　　　　　　　　　　　　　　　　　Colonel.A.Med.S.
　　　　　　　　　　　　　A.D.M.S., 57th Division.

Copy No. 1.　　to Headquarters, 57th Division.
　　　　2.　　　-ditto-　　　-ditto-
　　　　3. to Officer Commanding, 2/2nd Wessex Fd Amblce.
　　　　4. to Officer Commanding, 2/3rd Wessex Fd Amblce.
　　　　5. to Officer Commanding, 3/2nd WEST Lan. Fd Amblce.
　　　　6. to D.D.M.S., 11 Anzac.
　　　　7. to　-ditto- -ditto-
　　　　8. to War Diary.
　　　　9. to File

SECRET. 57TH DIVISION. Copy No. 16.

APPENDIX II

Headquarters,
23rd April 1917.

R.A.M.C. OPERATION ORDER NO. 2.

Reference Sheet 36 - 1/40,000.

1. The Officer Commanding, 3/2nd West Lancs. Field Ambulance will detail one section to relieve the 11th Australian Field Ambulance of the 3rd Australian Division and take over the two Main Dressing Stations at B.30.c.6.4., (MATERNITE HOSPITAL), and C.19.c.1.1.(ECOLE, RUE MESSINES): the two Advanced Dressing Stations at I.8.b.3.7. (BRICKFIELDS), and C.26.d.5.9.(HOUPLINES): also the Regimental Aid Post I.4.b.2.7.(WILLOW WALK). Move to be completed by noon on 26th instant.

2. The Officer Commanding 3/2nd West Lancs. Field Ambulance will detail an advance party to report to the Officer Commanding 11th Australian Field Ambulance at B.30.c.5.4. at noon on Tuesday 24th instant. Details to be arranged between Officers Commanding Units concerned.

3. Evacuation will be by Divisional Motor Ambulance Cars to No. 2 Australian Casualty Clearing Station at TROIS ARBRES.

4. Completion of move to be notified to this Office by wire.

5. ACKNOWLEDGE.

J.F. Dwan

ISSUED AT ...1.0... p.m. to

Colonel, A.Med.S.,
A.D.M.S., 57th Division.

DISTRIBUTION :

Copy No. 1 to   H.Q., 57th Division.
       2.   do.
       3.   O.C., 2/2nd Wessex Field Ambce.
       4.   O.C., 2/3rd Wessex Field Ambce.
       5.   O.C., 3/2nd West Lancs. Field Ambce.
       6.   D.D.M.S., II ANZAC.
       7.   do.   do.
       8.   H.Q., 170th Infantry Brigade.
       9.   H.Q., 171st   do.
      10.   H.Q., 172nd   do.
      11.   C.R.A., 57th Division.
      12.   C.R.E.,   do.
      13.   O.C., Signals.
      14.   O.C., 57th Division Train.
      15.   A.D.M.S., 3rd Australian Division.
      16.   War Diary.
      17.   do.
      18.   File.
      19.   Spare.
      20.   do.
      21.   do.

Appendix III

SECRET.   57th DIVISION.   Copy No. 15

M 1046/54.
                                                Headquarters,
                                                28th April, 1917.

R.A.M.C. OPERATION ORDER NO. 3.

                                        Reference Sheet 36 - 1/40,000.

1. The 2/2nd Wessex Field Ambulance will take over from the 3/2nd West Lancs. Field Ambulance the Advanced Dressing Station at the BREWERY, BOIS GRENIER H 24 d 5.0. and the Main Dressing Station at FORT ROMPU H 7 d 6.3. on Monday next 30th instant. Move to be completed by 12.0 noon. Details to be arranged between Officers Commanding Units concerned.

2. Advance Parties will proceed on Sunday 29th instant.

3. The Officer Commanding 2/2nd Wessex Field Ambulance will leave a small rear party at present Main Dressing Station G 17 a 8.3. until further orders are received.

4. The 3/2 West Lancs. Field Ambulance will march out of FORT ROMPU and establish their Headquarters at the Main Dressing Station at G 19 c 1.1. (ECOLE DES FILLES).

5. Evacuation from FORT ROMPU will be by Divisional Motor Ambulance Cars to No. 1 Australian Casualty Clearing Station, ESTAIRES.

6. Completion of moves to be notified to this office by wire.

7. ACKNOWLEDGE.

                                                    J.J. Dlwar

                                                Colonel, A.Med.S.,
ISSUED AT 7.45 a.m. to   A.D.M.S., 57th Division.

        DISTRIBUTION.

Copy No. 1   to   H.Q., 57th Division.
        2   do.
        3   O.C., 2/2nd Wessex Field Ambulance.
        4   O.C., 2/3rd Wessex Field Ambulance.
        5   O.C., 3/2 West Lancs. Field Ambulance.
        6   D.D.M.S., II ANZAC
        7   do.
        8   H.Q., 170th Infantry Brigade.
        9   H.Q., 171st   do.
       10   H.Q., 172nd   do.
       11   C.R.A., 57th Division.
       12   C.R.E., 57th Division.
       13   O.C., Signals.
       14   O.C., 57th Divisional Train.
       15   War Diary.
       16   do.
       17   File.
       18   Spare.
       19   do.
       20   do.

Confidential

War Diary.

of

ADMS

R.A.M.C. 57th Division

From May 1st 1917   to May 31st 1917.

Volume I.

Army Form C. 2118.

WAR DIARY
or
INTELLIGENCE SUMMARY.
(Erase heading not required.)

Instructions regarding War Diaries and Intelligence Summaries are contained in F. S. Regs., Part II. and the Staff Manual respectively. Title pages will be prepared in manuscript.

Place	Date	Hour	Summary of Events and Information	Remarks and references to Appendices
	MAY			
SAILLY	1/5/17		War Diary sent to Base. 31 case of nephritis reported from 2/3rd Wessex Field Ambulance. Enquiries made by D.A.D.M.S. do not point to this being a case of nephritis due to exposure on service. D.A.D.M.S. visited 2/3rd Wessex Field Ambulance with reference to the case. Medical Boards on "P.B." men held at SAILLY, VIEUX BERQUIN, ESTAIRES, and ARMENTIERES.	
CROIX DU BAC	2/5/17		Divisional Headquarters moved from SAILLY to CROIX DU BAC. Sheet 36., G.6.c.6.2. about 2½ miles N.E. of SAILLY. Enemy bombarded a gun position S.E. of ARMENTIERES causing casualties to 7 Officers and 17 other ranks. The new officer was opened and working fully by noon, move having been at 9-30 am. In the afternoon the A.D.M.S. visited the ARMENTIERES Huts and the RUE DU BOIS and BOUTILLERIE Sectors. Instructions received from D.D.M.S. 11 A. with N.Z. Stony Cafs and Divisional Headquarters for Lieutenant Colonel 76 O Bush 2/1 Wessex Field Ambulance to assume a course of instruction in the duties of an A.D.M.S. A.D.M.S. 57th Division wrote Lieutenant Colonel 76 O Bush to report to his office on Saturday May 5th, 1917.	
	3/5/17		A.D.M.S. attended conference at BAILLEUL office of D.D.M.S. II A. and N.Z. Stony Cafs and	

Army Form C. 2118.

WAR DIARY
or
INTELLIGENCE SUMMARY.
(Erase heading not required.)

Instructions regarding War Diaries and Intelligence Summaries are contained in F. S. Regs., Part II. and the Staff Manual respectively. Title pages will be prepared in manuscript.

Place	Date	Hour	Summary of Events and Information	Remarks and references to Appendices
CROIX DU BAC	3/5/17		Received instructions with reference to the evacuation of sick and wounded. The Main Dressing Station at ARMENTIERES to evacuate by convoys of its own cars to No 2. Stationary Casualty Clearing Station at TROIS ARBRES. 2/2nd and 2/3rd Wessex Field Ambulances, Main Dressing Station at FORT ROMPU and LE NOUVEAU MONDE respectively to be evacuated by No 22 M.A.C. B Section to No 1. Australian Casualty Clearing Station	
ESTAIRES			D.A.D.M.S. visited the Main Dressing Station at Fort Rompu, with reference to two cases of Pneumonia.	
	4/5/17		The weather was fine and visibility good, great aeroplane activity and shelling of back areas by heavy guns. A.D.M.S. visited the CORDONNERIE and BOUTILLERIE Sectors, M.O. 2/10th Kings Liverpool Regt. and M.O. 2/5 Royal West Lancs Regt. with reference to the situation of Regimental Aid Posts and Bearer Relay Posts.	
	5/5/17		Lieutenant-Col. H. O. Brasher reported for instructional routine with Light A.D.M.S. visited Baths at SAILLY and Divisional Reinforcement Camp. Enemy bombardment made necessary continued special attention being given to the main roads from FORT ROMPU through ERQUINGHAM to ARMENTIERES, also Shelling Battery wagon lines, north of the river LYS, behind ERQUINGHAM.	

Army Form C. 2118.

WAR DIARY
or
INTELLIGENCE SUMMARY.
(Erase heading not required.)

Instructions regarding War Diaries and Intelligence Summaries are contained in F. S. Regs., Part II. and the Staff Manual respectively. Title pages will be prepared in manuscript.

Place	Date	Hour	Summary of Events and Information	Remarks and references to Appendices
Croix Du Bac	6/5/17		Lieutenant Colonel 16. O. Booth again in the office. Quiet day in office work. A.D.M.S. visited Divisional Headquarters to make contact at A.D.M.S. then back to his Headquarters. Hunting areas as usual so far as possible. A.D.M.S. visited baths again to arrange for inspection of stables to be confirmed if possible.	
	7/5/17		Great activity in the air and by enemy heavy guns many rounds reach SAILLY to ARMENTIERS and on the roads LYS. Obliered factor in BAC ST MAUR, shells causing casualties to civilians and soldiers. Great numbers of civilian H.F. B.E.G. ST MAUR and SAILLY flying temporary refugees shells falling just short of CROIX DU BAC. A.D.M.S. and Lieutenant-Colonel H. D. Booth visited the ARMENTIERE Section Regiment Station Posts and the RUE du BOIS and BOIS GRENIER Cases of Typhoid Enteric civilians Fibrilans LA ROLANDERIE removed to Hospital Enemy launched gas attack about 8.p.m. Good bathing nearby at several places. Our artillery opened a heavy bombardment from 8/6. am lasting until about 10:30 p.m. Gas heavy artillery shoot was First part of bombardment was engaged by the enemy Strange cooler shoot along whole Army Front was anticipated day one ships of Pale artillery an addition it to hushh up a battle raid. This alarm of gas was given by H.Howls 16 Corps at 8-10 p.m. attack was only an own ridge of the front clouds gas, we had no casualties from it 2 civilians	

WAR DIARY or INTELLIGENCE SUMMARY

Army Form C. 2118.

Place	Date	Hour	Summary of Events and Information	Remarks and references to Appendices
Croix Du Bac	7/5/17		Casualties BAC ST MAUR.	
	8.5.17		Message received at 12.45 am from 3/2nd West Lancs Field Ambulance, that they required two additional motor ambulances which were despatched from 2/3rd Wessex Field Ambulance.	
			Also to cope with evacuation of casualties from previous evening, carried out by Divisional Motor Ambulance cars, to No. 2 Stationary Casualty Clearing Station at TROIS ARBRES.	
			Total casualties evacuated during night from health-shelling which was ends wid 1 officer 33 others ranks and 4 civilians, 2 civilians killed by BAC ST MAUR. ADMS visited 2/10 Kings Liverpool Regt. during the afternoon. Information received that Major W.R.E. WILLIAMS and Captain G.D. NEWTON R.A.M.C.T.F. 3/2nd West Lancs Field Ambulance returned from No 2 Stationary Casualty Clearing Station, to duty with his unit. Enemy again bombarded BAC ST MAUR apparently for this purpose using a mortal gun of large calibre. Numerous during night rounds through Field Ambulance, 39.	
			Weather very fair.	
	9.5.17		Enemy again shelling back area Cpl. R.E. dumps by Divisional Reinforcement Camp received 19 little shells. The Reinforcement Camp received a large number. The back area from SAILLY to BAC ST MAUR was also	

Army Form C. 2118.

WAR DIARY
or
INTELLIGENCE SUMMARY.
(Erase heading not required.)

Place	Date	Hour	Summary of Events and Information	Remarks and references to Appendices
CROIX DU BAC	9-5-17		Shelled. The enemy made a raid during night of 8th and 9th but were repulsed. Fires killing and said our casualties numbered 82, treated in our own Field Ambulances all on the EPINETTE and RUE DU BOIS Sectors. During the early hours of the morning continued with evacuating BFG ST MAUR. ADMS visited Baths. DADMS visited Horse Lines of the 2/3rd Wessex Field Ambulances at	
			LE NOUVEAU MONDE	
	10-5-17		Much quieter night only 9 wounded. Our aeroplanes out in floors up all day, not much enemy aeroplane activity. Shelling back areas still continues. Though not light than previous days. ADMS attended conference at DDMS II Army NZ Engh. Still evacuation from Divn from today to be to No 2 Stationary Casualty Clearing Station, TROIS ARBRES. Only little holt however into Ambulance Convoy sent on still to be done by Divisional Motor Ambulances Cars. ADMS took Lieut-Col HG D Book on tour of inspection of right half of Divn Thus making complete tour of Regimental Aid Posts, Brass Relay Posts and Advanced Dressing Stations. Some doubt as to the ability of BOIS GRENIER Advanced Dressing Station to two uses. The track will having been considerably damaged by enemy	

WAR DIARY or INTELLIGENCE SUMMARY.

Army Form C. 2118.

(Erase heading not required.)

Place	Date	Hour	Summary of Events and Information	Remarks and references to Appendices
CROIX DU BAC	10.5.17		Shell fire. Slow evacuation report to be called for.	
	11.5.17		Morning very quiet. In the afternoon ADMS visited M.O. 2/5th Kings Own Royal Lancs Regt on visit to see M.O. carrying out inspections of men for scabies. The incidence of scabies is now low, but has been very high. Lieut-Colonel BROOK HD. attended sick on at REMY SIDING on "Scabies". ADMS visited stables of 2/3rd West Lancs Field Ambulances at EPINETTE with reference to question of manure. A great quantity left behind by previous units to be dealt lightly and removed with earth. Region to be grouped. Regt declining to carry it away and leaving cart to be guarded. Only 8 wounded in the 24 hours ending noon.	
	12.5.17		Enemy shewed most of his forces & H.E shelling back areas. Great army aeroplane activity. Great army aeroplane activity. Notification of arrivals from 2/3rd Wessex Field Ambulance of a casualty suspected Cerebro-Spinal-Meningitis, evacuated to British Isolation Hospital at BAILLEUL. ADMS visited M.O's of units in back areas. DADMS visited stables of 2/3rd Wessex Field Ambulances. Unit has left behind a large quantity of manure. This to be treated by hashing lighting.	
	13.5.17		Very quiet day. ADMS with DADMS visited the XI. Corps DDMS headquarters.	

WAR DIARY
or
INTELLIGENCE SUMMARY.

(Erase heading not required.)

Army Form C. 2118.

Place	Date	Hour	Summary of Events and Information	Remarks and references to Appendices
CROIX DU BAC	13.5.17		at HINGES. Great aerial activity. The line is very much quieter, the shelling of back areas not so persistent. The Bosche guns which were shelling our front in this front now seem to devote to ***(?)*** out of action not confirmed. DADMS visited two H.S.C. Companies with regard to Sanitation Everything satisfactory.	
	14.5.17		A.D.M.S. went to BAILLEUL to see DDMS II A and NZ Corps, saw DADMS. In the afternoon DDMS took Lieut Colonel H.D. Brook, who is undergoing a course of instruction in ADMS. (57th Division) office, to see I A and NZ Can Main Dressing Station at PORT D'ACHELLES, which is just nearing completion. also the No 2 Australian Casualty Clearing Station at TROIS ARBRES. ADMS visited BOIS GRENIER on the afternoon, his received information that the Commander of this area including 57th Division will hear from II ANZAC, 2nd Army, to II Corps first thing at noon on May 20th 1917. Lieut Col H.D. Brook completed his course of instruction II ANZAC and 57th Division HQ preparatory notified.	
	15.5.17		ADMS visited Divisional Reinforcement Camp, during the morning, to see the H.O., with reference to a scheme for making Divisional Rest Camp, into a	

Army Form C. 2118.

WAR DIARY
or
INTELLIGENCE SUMMARY.
(Erase heading not required.)

Instructions regarding War Diaries and Intelligence Summaries are contained in F. S. Regs., Part II. and the Staff Manual respectively. Title pages will be prepared in manuscript.

Place	Date	Hour	Summary of Events and Information	Remarks and references to Appendices
CROIX DU BAC	15.5.14		Reserve Camp for light duty, as well as its real duty. In the afternoon he visited the Main Dressing Station of 2/3rd West Lancs Field Ambulance and the Advanced Dressing Station at FOURLINES. Was shown a case of mental disease which is to be evacuated. This was shown to ADMS in his report to forwards requesting a Medical Board at Base. DADMS worked upon lines 2/9th Hamps Loresphel Regt transport.	
	16.5.14		2md Army forwarded instructions through DAAG 57th Division that Lieut Col. H.O. Birth should report to DDMS IX Corps for a ten days course of instructions under ADMS 16th Division. Lieut Colonel H.O. Birth notified ADMS visited BOIS GRENIER. Very quiet day on whole line. Nothing to report on Divisional Front	
	17.5.14		Cars of S.S.S. Service notified to O.C. 2/3rd Wessex Field Ambulances, inspected ADMS attended conference of AD'sMS at DDMS Office BAILLEUL. ADMS inspected Main Dressing Station of 3/2 West Lancs Field Ambulance at RUE DE MESSINES, ARMENTIERE, Advanced Dressing Station, CHAPELLE ARMENTIERE, BRICKFIELD Car Collecting Post from Regimental Aid Post, SQUARE FARM on	

A6915 Wt. W14122/M160 35,000 12/16 D,D,&L. Forms/C/2118/14.

WAR DIARY or INTELLIGENCE SUMMARY

Army Form C. 2118.

Place	Date	Hour	Summary of Events and Information	Remarks and references to Appendices
CROIX DU BAC	17-5-17		Bearer Relay Post at LEITH WALK. Very quiet day on whole, short day dull with poor visibility, no aircraft movement.	
	18-5-17		Warm sunny day, considerable aircraft activity, enemy commenced shelling our Observation Balloons being sent up in the air at no time. During morning HDMS visited Divisional Baths at ERQUINGHEM. Enemy commenced shelling Baths making several direct hits on the Baths and Laundry completely wrecking the machinery in use at the laundry. Also some direct hits on barges on the canal moored behind the laundry. Total casualties - Officers and Other Ranks - Inland Water Transport, killed, 5 Other ranks wounded. The baths were being used at the time of shelling, no casualties among Everhams employed at Laundry. Baths and Laundry both closed refuse to machinery until late 14 days at least. About 5:30 p.m. enemy aircraft suddenly swept down on observation balloons at ERQUINETTE and opened machine gun fire. Men in balloon descended by Parachute notwithstanding subjected to m.g. heavy gun fire and fumes to return causing no casualties and leaving balloon on fire. Enemy attempted to reach	
	19-5-17		Very quiet day although visibility good. Enemy attempted to reach	

WAR DIARY
INTELLIGENCE SUMMARY.
(Erase heading not required.)

Army Form C. 2118.

Place	Date	Hour	Summary of Events and Information	Remarks and references to Appendices
CROIX DU BAC	19.5.17		Draft of Officers & men left without nurses 377th and 378th Batteries of 169th Brigade B.F.A from England required assistance with regards to Medical treatment. DADMS visited Main Dressing Station, FORT ROMPU and RUE DE MESSINES to show them to DADMS First Stamp, and Officer Commanding No. 2 Motor Ambulance Convoy who will carry out evacuation from the Division. SM case to be evacuated to MERVILLE, only serious cases to ESTAIRES. Private Osborn 29 Kings Liverpool Regt. diagnosed Cerebro-Spinal-Meningitis necessary precautions taken.	
	20.5.17		Divisional Stores and Division came into 2nd Stamp at noon. During the hours of early morning a combined action with 49 Division took place with success. Officer Commanding No. 2 Motor Ambulance Convoy reported with Motor cars one to be stationed at each Main Dressing Station, to evacuate seriously wounded cases to Casualty Clearing Station. ADMS with DA.Q.M.G. and Officer Commanding Sanitary Section visited the various mans water supplies, the Divisional Shear. Officer Commanding 54th Casualty Clearing Station and Captain M.C. Nec Officer in Charge No. 3 Mobile Laboratory both belonging to the 1st Army, called at our ADMS. 54th Casualty Clearing Station, MERVILLE opening small Hospital at	

Army Form C. 2118.

WAR DIARY
or
INTELLIGENCE SUMMARY.
(Erase heading not required.)

Instructions regarding War Diaries and Intelligence Summaries are contained in F. S. Regs., Part II. and the Staff Manual respectively. Title pages will be prepared in manuscript.

Place	Date	Hour	Summary of Events and Information	Remarks and references to Appendices
CROIX DE BAC	20.5.17		ESTAIRES two more serious cases. Probably ready to receive cases by Friday 25th inst. Quarter Master Sergeant Howell from A.D.M.S Staff left in the morning to go to England to take up a commission.	
	21.5.17		Many changes in office. Bowles, Perkins etc. owing to change of Divisions from II ANZAC Corps. Records slowing to XI Corps. First Stamp DADMS went on leave to England until 1st June. Captain McKenzie to be M.O. i/c Headquarters in his stead. ADMS visited town Dressing Stations and Divisional Rest Stations. 2/3rd Wessex Field Ambulance in detail, remarkably after a considerable number of H.E. shells fell just towards and to the west of it. Causing no casualties and no damage beyond breaking glass. G.O.C. Division inspected hours of 3/2nd West Lancs Field Ambulance 2/2nd Wessex Field Ambulance and 2/3 Wessex Field Ambulances. ADMS met him at that place. IDMS, XI Corps. Colonel Wright inspected all town Dressing Stations. (ADMS did not see him.) DMS. – Brig. General Pike with DADMS and Officer Commanding 54th Casualty Clearing Station, MERVILLE visited town Dressing Stations at LE NOUVEAU MONDE, FORT ROMPU and ECOLE des FILLES.	

WAR DIARY or INTELLIGENCE SUMMARY

Army Form C. 2118.

Place	Date	Hour	Summary of Events and Information	Remarks and references to Appendices
CROIX DU BAC	21.5.17		ARMENTIERES. The ADMS accompanied him and inspected factory at G.18.6.9.4. as BHQ St MAUR Bridge, as to its fitness to be a site for Casualty Clearing Station (It formerly was so.) Later meeting of Divisional Motor Boards. New Caps and IMS First Stamp have sufficed pointed instructions as received. Latter which are very helpful.	
	22.5.17		Captain W.E.L.K. Kennedy 2/3rd Wessex Fields Ambulances on Office as I.O. in charge Divisional Headquarters and acting IADMS. Often routine very hard owing to practically entire change in detail of Routine Memoranda on matters medical as between Second Army First Army. It is not certain that toward the end of the third year of the war the Government is not arriving at so definitely adverse that consider a very forcible part of the you the change from onetime to another should make an almost intolerable fuss stress for several days. Main Club worked about 15 hours today and after not much less. Difference conference at No III Stationary Evacuation Road evacuation Medical Officer of ERQUINGHEM closures/season.	

Army Form C. 2118.

WAR DIARY
or
INTELLIGENCE SUMMARY.
(Erase heading not required.)

Instructions regarding War Diaries and Intelligence Summaries are contained in F. S. Regs., Part II. and the Staff Manual respectively. Title pages will be prepared in manuscript.

Place	Date	Hour	Summary of Events and Information	Remarks and references to Appendices
CROIX DU BAC	23.5.19		Office still much congested owing to radical changes and adjustments arising from recent advance and early to bank. H.M.S. XI Corps critical Sarn and Steenwerck Amusing Stations of 519th Field Section on roads near FRMENTIERES and 2 pairs 2 generally working in this connection Numbers various coming and going but the Offices the permanent no H.D.&M.S. of I Corps area hold on H.T.M.S. offices Corps H.Q. of H.D.&M.S. XI Corps and H.D. of S., 49th, 57th and 66th Divisions.	
			HINGES – Present H.M.S. H.D.M.S. XI Corps and H.D.S. of Medical Services. The position of Medical Arrangements in respect of the wounded to us on present front was subject of consideration. Armies 20 miles Areas held by 2 Divisions and attack would be made without march-ing to my of transport and in abstraction of this Division onto the forces the Indians so only possible. The H.D.M.S. visited 57th Corps Clearing Station at	
			ST VENANT (on loading of Forward Stations) afford by him has to assist this month.	
	24.5.19		Began after 6.30 am. and 10.30 pm of nearly 14 thousand lumber etc etc Marcs) about 10' acres from them to new Equipment Wing.	

Army Form C. 2118.

WAR DIARY
or
INTELLIGENCE SUMMARY.
(Erase heading not required.)

Instructions regarding War Diaries and Intelligence Summaries are contained in F. S. Regs., Part II. and the Staff Manual respectively. Title pages will be prepared in manuscript.

Place	Date	Hour	Summary of Events and Information	Remarks and references to Appendices
CROIX DU BAC	24.5.17		Officer Commanding 3rd Divisional Train inspected horse lines & harness of 3/3rd West Lancs Field Ambulance and 2/3rd Wessex Field Ambulance. He made some favourable comment on the state of both Field Ambulances at the last inspection.	
	25.5.17		D.D.M.S. XI Corps made extensive and minute inspections of Main and Advanced Dressing Stations of 2/2nd Wessex Field Ambulance at FORT ROMPU and BOIS GRENIER, respectively. No inspection could be more searching or instructive. On the other hand the peculiar characteristics of Territorial Force units should be borne in mind. The Medical Officers of 2nd line Territorial Force units are mostly men there would be at great loss to themselves, and from the highest motives. To expect them to have memorised the items in the "Unit" Mobilization Store Table does not seem to me to be reasonable. This opinion is fairly generally expressed that the 76 of chloroform & syringe issued to Medical Units and Medical Officers are of a type unsuitable for such emergency work that provided for use of surgeons in the Navy.	
			I.M.S. Fort Sheng (Bessies [illegible] there) came to the Advanced Dressing Station with [illegible] at 10 a.m. there after felt 4 h.m.s. visited all Advanced Dressing Stations	
	26.5.17			

WAR DIARY OR INTELLIGENCE SUMMARY

Army Form C. 2118.

Place	Date	Hour	Summary of Events and Information	Remarks and references to Appendices
CROIX DU BAC	26/5/17		Regimental Aid Posts at TRAMWAY AVENUE and new Regimental Aid Post at H30.b.10.8. also New Dressing Station at 4/9m Avenue 2/8m Avenue and 3/9 of West Lanes. Field Ambulances and Advanced Baths are still established particularly as regards officers' wards and sheets. Sufficient sections of the manure in which the 3/6m West Lanes and 4m Avenue Field Ambulances have no provision. New Dressing Stations and practice amongst the.	
	27/5/17		Owing to alteration of Divisional areas - the two lines of the 3/9 of West Lanes Field Ambulances have to be moved from their present stations. Infantry like over this New Division Station in ARMENTIERES chosen. Considerable correspondence regarding establishment of units and list of available dry accommodation for troops cote no 100/10 and 1.C.C. to be circulated. Reports the states organisation and arrangement movement expansion of the new Cars and Stores as attend to the troops movement.	
	28/5/17		Two Battalions of 170th Brigade are to be detached from 57th Division temporarily and included in II ANZAC Corps as working relations while two Battalions two 49th Division are to replace them. Special arrangement is undertaken	

WAR DIARY
or
INTELLIGENCE SUMMARY.
(Erase heading not required.)

Army Form C. 2118.

Place	Date	Hour	Summary of Events and Information	Remarks and references to Appendices
CROIX DU BAC	28.5.17		Inspection of equipment of men of Field Ambulances and other Horse Drivers	
			Men in motor convoy inspected.	
	29.5.17		Work of ADMS gradually resuming smooth routine after the dislocation caused by change from Cap. and from Strong to Strong. Procedure regarding evacuation from Advn Dressing Stations, Infectious Diseases, Water Supplies, Shell Shock cases, Self-inflicted Wounds, etc, is radically different, also there were 50 or 51 returns rendered by this officer when in 2nd Strong area. Now there are approximately as many but almost all are different. The fact that in IInd Instructions Corps standing Orders and Corps Note "M" there are all explicitly laid down, goes far to simplify the work. As officers of ADMS, conference of Field Ambulance Commanders of the Division (as representatives) regarding painting of vehicles, units distinguishing marks, marking of Field Ambulance Medical Officers, to Regimental Duty, messages regarding ambulances cars etc.	
	30.5.17		Boulens. Very quiet on Army Front. ADMS visited (forenoon) Hd. Qrs. of 4 days ago has quite ceased for the present. ADMS visited (forenoon) Hd. Qrs. of Field Ambulances and 2/10 Kings Liverpool Regt. 51st Division Artillery actively shelling	

Army Form C. 2118.

WAR DIARY
or
INTELLIGENCE SUMMARY.
(Erase heading not required.)

Instructions regarding War Diaries and Intelligence Summaries are contained in F. S. Regs., Part II. and the Staff Manual respectively. Title pages will be prepared in manuscript.

Place	Date	Hour	Summary of Events and Information	Remarks and references to Appendices
CROIX DU BAC.	31.5.17		Two Battalions of 170th Brigade of this Division - 2/4th and 2/5th Loyal North Lancs Regt - have been attached to II Anzac Corps. 3rd Australian Division for Instructional operations and have moved to north-west of LYS near ARMENTIERES. Their Medical Officers and Regimental Medical arrangements have of course gone with them. Two Battalions of 49th Division have taken their place in CARDONNERIE Sector. Orders has been received for a Relieves of Units of the 2/4 and 2/5 Loyal North Lancs Regt. on the LE TONQUET-BERTHE Sector. II M S. II Corps inspected Main Dressing Station of 2/3rd Wessex Field Ambulance at LE NOUVEAU MONDE and Advanced Dressing Station at LA CROIX LESGORNEZ.	

J.J. Dunn
Colonel, A. Med. S.
A.D.M.S. 57th (W.L.) Division.

B.E.F.

SUMMARY OF MEDICAL WAR DIARIES FOR 57th Divn. 11th Corps 1st Army.

WESTERN FRONT May. 1917.

A.D.M.S. Col. T.F. Dewar.
D.A.D.M.S. Capt. J.F. Edmiston.

SUMMARISED UNDER THE FOLLOWING HEADINGS.

Phase "B" Battle of Arras April- May. 1917.

2nd Period Capture of Siegfried Line May.

B.E.F.

SUMMARY OF MEDICAL WAR DIARIES FOR 57th Divn. 11th Corps 1st Army.

WESTERN FRONT May. 1917.

A.D.M.S. Col. T.F. Dewar.
D.A.D.M.S. Capt. J.F. Edmiston.

SUMMARISED UNDER THE FOLLOWING HEADINGS.

Phase "B" Battle of Arras April- May. 1917.

2nd Period Capture of Siegfried Line May.

B.E.F.

<u>57th Divn. 11th Corps 1st Army.</u>   <u>WESTERN FRONT.</u>
A.D.M.S. Col. T.F. Dewar.   <u>May. '17.</u>

<u>Phase "B" Battle of Arras- April- May. 1917.</u>
2nd Period Capture of Siegfired Line May.

1917.	<u>Headquarters.</u> at Croix Du Bac.
May. 20th.	<u>Administration. Transfer.</u> Command of area including 57th Divn. passed from 2nd Anzac Corps 2nd Army to 11th Corps 1st Army.
31st.	<u>Operations R.A.M.C.</u> "Section held by Divn., very quiet". Routine.

<u>Location of Field Ambulances</u>:-

2/2nd Wessex F.A. at Fort Rompu.
2/3rd   "   "   " Nouveau Monde.
3/2nd West Lancs. " Armentieres.

<u>Appendices.</u> Nil.

B.E.F.

57th Divn. 11th Corps 1st Army.　　WESTERN FRONT.
A.D.M.S. Col. T.F. Dewar.　　May. '17.

Phase "B" Battle of Arras- April- May. 1917.
2nd Period Capture of Siegfired Line May.

1917.
May. 20th.　Headquarters. at Croix Du Bac.
Administration. Transfer. Command of area including 57th Divn. passed from 2nd Anzac Corps 2nd Army to 11th Corps 1st Army.

31st.　Operations R.A.M.C. "Section held by Divn., very quiet". Routine.
Location of Field Ambulances:-
2/2nd Wessex F.A. at Fort Rompu.
2/3rd　　"　　"　　"　Nouveau Monde.
3/2nd West Lancs.　" Armentieres.

Appendices. Nil.

Confidential

War Diary.

of

A.D.M.S. 57th Division

from. June 1st 1917   to June 30th 1917.

(Volume I)

WAR DIARY or INTELLIGENCE SUMMARY

Army Form C. 2118.

Place	Date	Hour	Summary of Events and Information	Remarks and references to Appendices
CROIX DU BAC	1-5-17		Arrangis for "B" Section, 2/2nd Wessex Fd Ambulance (Major ADAMS commanding) to proceed tomorrow to Advanced Dressing Station at BREWERY (G.14.d.1.5.) to perform evacuation for 2 Battalions incorporated from 57th Division to II ANZAC Corps front holding LE TOUQUET – BERTHE sector between River LYS at G.10.6.0.0. and U.14.6.0.0. Sheet 28.	
			Visited ADMS 3rd Australians Division at T.10.a.7.6 re arranging Operation Orders A. This means that including the two Battalions attached to 57th Division from 49th Division (now holding CORDONNERIE Sector), and the two attached to II ANZAC Corps from 57th Division front, a new about 11000 + 6000 + 5000 = 22,100 yards or 12.55 miles from the new Sector evacuation is to be to Advanced Dressing Stations at 3rd/2nd West Sears Fd Ambulances at RUE DES MESSINES ARMENTIÈRES. Last evening (11th and 31st) about 9 hrs on 9.30. 6 ambulance cars to N.E. was supplied by ourselves and carry clears via Sailly. Medical Boards holds today to examine "P.B." men at ARMENTIÈRES, SAILLY and ESTAIRES presided over by O.C. 2/2nd West Lancs F/A. Names and 2/3 Wessex Fd Ambulances as Members.	Appendix "A"
	2-5-17		Captain EDMISTON D.A.D.M.S. returned today from leave, after eleven days absence. No news to hand that changes are to great that practically all ranks muscular returns.	

Army Form C. 2118.

WAR DIARY
or
INTELLIGENCE SUMMARY.
(Erase heading not required.)

Place	Date	Hour	Summary of Events and Information	Remarks and references to Appendices
CROIX DU BAC	2.6.17		hours of return forms of scabies are different, even the subject's death with are on the mend radically suffered. This is available to the different methods recorded, and interest of test and Second Stories but still more to the question to Lieut. H. ANZ H.Q and XI Corps. Newcastle admitted to Field Strength as of 31st October. May are 314 as against 166 on March and 228 on April. Say there are nearly weekly with Casts. Bilharzia admissions keep very low, a little above 2/3 daily as should be. N.Y.D. that is accepted as normal. There is no prevailing disease. P.U.O. and I.C.T being suspected at scarce of very heavy special and local symptoms. N.Y.D. There is very little infectious disease and only one case of Enteric "Group" so reported from the Devision of approximately 17000 in our 100 days. ADMS today visited Steenwerck Dressing Station at LES CROIX LESCORNEY and Reserve T.S. Pat at ERTON HALL and ROUGE DE BOUT. At the former he met Captain SCOTT R.A.M.C. Medical Officer 11th West Riding Regt. and at the latter Captain CAIRNEY, and Captain Medical Officer (pro Captain GREEN) of 1/5 West Riding Regt. The former made useful suggestions about special clothes for convalescence of scabies from the CORDONNERIE Field Post one para company served for R.E.M.C. As marched and left in front seat	

WAR DIARY or INTELLIGENCE SUMMARY.

Army Form C. 2118.

Place	Date	Hour	Summary of Events and Information	Remarks and references to Appendices
CROIX DU BAC	2.6.17		at Tramway Corner. EATON HALL Regimental Aid Post was an excellent order. It would accommodate 6-8 lying cases for a time. It is situated on what it was told was a tram line as three night ago and proved very satisfactory.	
	3.6.17		Visited new Advanced Dressing Station at BREWERY two miles N.E. of ARMENTIERES which is lighted by B section ½/2nd West Lancs twelve stretchers, bed neighbourhood being under heavy shellfire and our own guns any actors Advanced Dressing Station at O1.d.4.5. (Sheet 28.S.W.) Walked with Capt ADAMS to fields and communication trenches to Regimental Sub Post at DESPIERRE FARM. C.3.c.8.4. on night of June 1st/2nd by 2/5th Loyal North Lancs Regt. Captain W.G. McKENZIE I/C Returned by New Dressing Station at 0/2 2nd West Lancs twelve Stretchers ARMENTIERES, to which wounded and dying evacuated. Later went to Advanced Dressing Station at BOIS GRENIER and Regimental Aid Post at TRAMWAY AVENUE, now front as Advanced Dressing Station of this section. Quick shrapnel also from enemy.	
	4.6.17		Members Medical Board, ADMS President, Major E.L. ANDERSON and Capt. EDMISTON examined men – about 150 on all employed at Divisional Headquarters. cavon	

A6945 Wt.W14427/M1160 35,000 12/16 D.D. & L. Forms/C./2118/14.

WAR DIARY or INTELLIGENCE SUMMARY

Army Form C. 2118.

Place	Date	Hour	Summary of Events and Information	Remarks and references to Appendices
CROIX DU BAC	4.6.17		Divisional duties along establishment. About two fifths stands in category B. ADMS. visited Main Dressing Stations of 3/2nd West Lancs Field Ambulance. Captain ASPINALL temporary Medical Officer in charge 2/5th Loyal North Lancs Regt. stated evacuated with measles. Case of suspected Cerebro-spinal Meningitis removed from 2/3rd Main Field Ambulance Main Dressing Station to Casualty Clearing Station, MALASSISE.	
	5.6.17		Long spell of colder, hot weather continues, roads very dusty and roadside verges to breaks. ADMS, XI Corps carried no enemy aircraft and gunfire. administration of 3/2nd West Lancs Field Ambulance with which he was still greatly dissatisfied. He was also concerned regarding repair of evacuation roads. Also training of Field Ambulances and arranging for a scheme for reviewing condition of men in cases. Medical Boards continued categorisation of men retained by Divisional Headquarters.	
	6.6.17		Routine Detail to the next list. Visit of Medical Officers to area admin. of Harvets stations in table and means of establishing gasstores of efficiency of water carts of repairs of evacuation roads of re-education of water supplies. DADMS	

Army Form C. 2118.

WAR DIARY
or
INTELLIGENCE SUMMARY.
(Erase heading not required.)

Instructions regarding War Diaries and Intelligence Summaries are contained in F. S. Regs., Part II. and the Staff Manual respectively. Title pages will be prepared in manuscript.

Place	Date	Hour	Summary of Events and Information	Remarks and references to Appendices
CROIX DU BAC	6.6.17		Visited Headquarters of 2/2nd West Lancs. Field Ambulance, which has been fairly busy with evacuation of wounded chiefly from LE TOUQUET - BERTHE Sector.	
	7.6.17		II ANZAC Corps heavy barrage MESSINES RIDGE in early morning and tps. advanced. Walked towards Dressing Station at BREWERY Cor. of PLOEGSTEERT. About 70 cars kept on night relieving many guns and no tks. to the tks. Stretcher Works there and evacuation has been very good so far. Walked through considerable enemy gun fire to Corps Dressing Station at ARMENTIERES and went over it carefully. ARMENTIERES under considerable shell fire at present.	
	8.6.17		Three Battalions of PORTUGUESE Expeditionary Forces are coming into the 57th Divisional Lines. Warned Dressing Stations stationed there to stand by 2/2 W. Lancs. Field Ambulance to evacuate to Main Dressing Station 2/2 W. Lancs. Field Ambulance. Long visit of D.D.M.S. to Divns. mons. 9th inst. (see Operation Order.) Still very hot weather. After regarding many matters of administrative detail (II ANZAC Corps and Second Army general Hy.) am Great Bombardment by our artillery Heavy Hot. Magunid Opn. of Messines Strong is being carried out very carrying. satisfactorily	APPENDIX "B"

Army Form C. 2118.

WAR DIARY
or
INTELLIGENCE SUMMARY.
(Erase heading not required.)

Place	Date	Hour	Summary of Events and Information	Remarks and references to Appendices
CROIX DU BAC	9-6-17		Met and saw Divisional Headquarters regarding Tramway Trolley for Medical use. Note: supplies disinfections of clothing. D.A.D.M.S. in morning, awaiting teams. Dressing Station of 3/2nd West Lancs Field Ambulance ARMENTIERES, which has been under shell fire, and Stationed Dressing Station at the BREWERY. In the afternoon A.D.M.S. visited A.D.M.S. 2nd Sheltarian Division regarding handing over of Stationed Dressing Station at BREWERY, tomorrow. Thereafter visited Sheltarian Orders No 6 — I.C. Heavy artillery fire last two days in ARMENTIERES, APPENDIX "G" on gun positions in ARMENTIERES Section and on Headquarters 142/151 Field Engr R.E.	
	10-6-17		Visited 3/2nd West Lancs Field Ambulance Cars Dressing Station at ARMENTIERES and went over with Officer Commanding and Sjt. Major inspecting quarters on ground floor of ECOLE in detail. Conditions generally satisfactory though the building is not one that can be made to look well. ARMENTIERES experience is never finely continuous H.E. shell fire, one shell fell in three dines of 3/2nd West Lancs Field Ambulance advanced billing no loss, entirely destroying a G.S. wagon and considerably damaging 2 horse ambulance wagon. Duck'd barge moved on canal at LYS near JESUS FARM, where water (from river) is obtained and filtered	

Forms/C./2118/14.

Army Form C. 2118.

WAR DIARY
or
INTELLIGENCE SUMMARY.
(Erase heading not required.)

Instructions regarding War Diaries and Intelligence Summaries are contained in F. S. Regs., Part II. and the Staff Manual respectively. Title pages will be prepared in manuscript.

Place	Date	Hour	Summary of Events and Information	Remarks and references to Appendices
CROIX DU BAC	10-6-17		Owing to large drafts, about 180,000 gallons and 65 cars for lorries daily, but there is owing to the difficulty of water and transport. The ADMS co-ordinated reports on that matter supplied by all Field Ambulances, Commanders and Regimental Medical Officers and sent them to "Q" Branch, Divisional Headquarters	
	11-6-17		Bat at SAILLY. Medical Board (ADMS President, DADMS and Captain PARKINSON, members) Infantrymen to examine and categorize men attached to Divisional Headquarters and to establishment. ADMS with Divisional Baths at SAILLY and saw FODEN Disinfector at work. ADMS visited 2/3rd Wessex Field Ambulance, Main Dressing Station at LE NOUVEAU MONDE and saw Lieutenant Foran ROUGE en ROUT walked with Captain SCOTT RAMC, Medical Officer in charge 1/4th WEST RIDING Regt. to inspect Temporary Steam-disinfector. Response to S.M.O. Z of S/H averages 9 to dealing with up to 50 casualties on night of June 15-16th, arrivals on doubtful. Last entry "B" Section 2/2nd Wessex Field St Ambulance returned from Divisional Dressing Station BREWERY near LE BIZET to Headquarters of unit.	
	12-6-17		Considerable enemy artillery activity about this Divisional front from 1 to 3 a.m. 56 wounded admitted in 24 hours ending 9 a.m. today. Strength for	

WAR DIARY
or
INTELLIGENCE SUMMARY.
(Erase heading not required.)

Army Form C. 2118.

Instructions regarding War Diaries and Intelligence Summaries are contained in F. S. Regs., Part II. and the Staff Manual respectively. Title pages will be prepared in manuscript.

Place	Date	Hour	Summary of Events and Information	Remarks and references to Appendices
CROIX DU BAC	12.6.17		successive mars of Field Ambulances of Division, so that each will in turn have more days clear at LE NOUVEAU MONDE for thorough overhaul of equipment etc.	
			New distinguishing marks now being affixed to all Field Ambulance vehicles of 57th Division namely	
			2/2nd Wessex Field Ambulance ⊡⊡	
			2/3rd Wessex Field Ambulance ⊡⊡	
			3/2nd West Lancs Field Ambulance ⊡⊡	
			Operation order No.7. issued regarding Advanced Dressing Stations at LACROIX, LESGORNEZ during taking over by 2/2nd Wessex Field Ambulances from 2/3rd Wessex Field Ambulances which will then close for training. Issued general notes on training suggested.	APPENDIX "D"
			It appears that the artillery activity mentioned on yesterday entry was no later	
	13.6.17		at 49th Division as might, not in the Divisional Area) ARMENTIERES has been heavily shelled last 3 days fortunately last three and most of all yesterdays and last night many shells having fallen over Main Dressing Station at 3/2 W. Lans. training Ambulance, ROE de MESSINES, and one at least on the building. Officer Commanding came today regarding possibility of moving elsewhere, and DADMS went with him and	

Army Form C. 2118.

WAR DIARY
or
INTELLIGENCE SUMMARY.
(Erase heading not required.)

Instructions regarding War Diaries and Intelligence Summaries are contained in F. S. Regs., Part II. and the Staff Manual respectively. Title pages will be prepared in manuscript.

Place	Date	Hour	Summary of Events and Information	Remarks and references to Appendices
CROIX DU BAC	13/6/17		Inspected returning that a man of Messrs Drying Station to ERQUINGHAM seemed inadequate. Information received from T.M.S. through DDMS that Lieut Colonel BROOK, Officer Commanding 2/3rd Wessex Field Ambulance attributes to be ADMS. ADMS is asked to give his views as to the succession to the command. Report by Major ADAMS regarding an much of his section (B 2/3 Wessex Field Ambulances) which attaches two 8 days to 3rd Lancashire Division further arrangements in connection with intended to be undertaken on CARDONNERIE sector by 1/4th and 1/6th Battalions West Riding Regt. operative attached to 57th Division as one night towards the end of this month.	
	14/6/17		ADMS visited DDMS VI Corps HINGES regarding command of 2/3rd Wessex field ADMS and DADMS visited 49th Divisional Baths and VI Corps Laundry, both at LAGORGUE, and at both. Medical inspected mental men attached to 57th Division of Headquarters. Proceeded with ADMS to ERQUINGHAM to meet Officer Commanding 3/2nd West Lancs Field Ambulances, regarding change of the Main Drying Station from ECOLE des FILLES, RUE de MESSINES, ARMENTIERES, to ECOLE at ERQUINGHAM. Conference in ADMS	

Army Form C. 2118.

WAR DIARY
OR
INTELLIGENCE SUMMARY.
(Erase heading not required.)

Instructions regarding War Diaries and Intelligence Summaries are contained in F.S. Regs., Part II. and the Staff Manual respectively. Title pages will be prepared in manuscript.

Place	Date	Hour	Summary of Events and Information	Remarks and references to Appendices
GROS DE B.HG	14.6.17		offices of AA and QMG, DAAG, ADMS, and DADMS. regarding procedure in cases of shell-shock. Further arrangements for entertains to be undertaken in CORDONNERIE Salient area by 59th Division. (14th and 15th West Riding Regts. at present are of 3rd Division) The work by 19th Division and instructions and right of our early date. The long tract of still hot anti-cyclone weather still continues. There have been no wet days since this day 4 weeks May 17th. The trees are in full leaf making .... a dense natural camouflage in front area.	
	15.6.17		Lieut Colonel H.D. BROOK. Officer Commanding 2/3rd Wessex Field Ambulance, to be ADMS, 55th Division with temporary rank of Colonel. To take up duty at once. Instructions received today. Training of 2/3rd Wessex Field Ambulance when Shenanments continued for dawn of MDS is new shed commenced today. Main Dressing Station at RUE de MESSINES ARMENTIERES on account of heavy shelling and shipping of Main Dressing Station at ERQUINGHEM undertaken. ADMS. IIDMS, XI Corps created on the places today and was already exchange. Lieut Colonel BROOK (2/3rd Wessex Field Ambulance) Major O. WILLIAMS (2/1st West Lanes Field Ambulance) and Captain SCHOLEFIELD (2/2nd Wessex Field Ambulance)	APPENDIX "E"

Army Form C. 2118.

WAR DIARY
or
INTELLIGENCE SUMMARY.
(Erase heading not required.)

Instructions regarding War Diaries and Intelligence Summaries are contained in F. S. Regs., Part II. and the Staff Manual respectively. Title pages will be prepared in manuscript.

Place	Date	Hour	Summary of Events and Information	Remarks and references to Appendices
CROIX DU BAC	15.6.17		Proceeded to LILLERS, Headquarters 1st Army, and were shewn amounts of sanitary and ambulance matériel and full size affiliated by DMS and DADMS (Army) 1st Army. Ambulance training party visited 57th Casualty Clearing Station and were shewn over by Officer Commanding of that unit.	
	16.6.17		DADMS visited Headquarters 2/2nd Wessex Field Ambulance at FORT ROMPU and also ERQUINGHEM regarding move that is to take place tomorrow. Interview with Divisional Commander regarding closing of Divisional Rest Station. Loan of Main Dressing Station from ARMENTIERES to ERQUINGHEM general conditions and affiliation of Field Ambulances and formation of units succession to (are command of 2/3rd Wessex Field Ambulance) Lieut. Colonel BROOK. Diagrams of evacuation from Sector at present held by 57th Division.	APPENDIX F.
	17.6.17		Vide the F. "B" Section 2/2nd Wessex Field Ambulance with officers Major H.G. ADAMS, action commander Captain J.P. RACE and Captain W.G. McKENZIE (also Captain S.R. GIBBS on leave) and also Captain ROGERS, ASPINALL (acted Captain CAMERON (Australian) never from Sick were evacuated sick with measles and Captain CAMERON Divisional Dressing Station, THE BREWERY, LOMME from 2nd to June 10th at Attached Dressing Station, LOMME.	

WAR DIARY
or
INTELLIGENCE SUMMARY.
(Erase heading not required.)

Army Form C. 2118.

Place	Date	Hour	Summary of Events and Information	Remarks and references to Appendices
CROIX DU BAC	17-6-17		South of PLOEGSTEERT and on 3rd Australian Division. II ANZAC Corps Record Shoot south so far as the operators which resulted in the taking of the MESSINES RIDGE. The Officer Commanding "B" Section specially mentions Staff Sergt. ROACH as invaluable and indefatigable worker by night and day. Lance Corporal FRENCH as rendering valuable and Private MERRICK A.S.C. M.T. who drove Motor Ambulance Car absolutely under shell fire, also Private FARRANT and others. ADMS visited 2/3rd Wessex Field Ambulance Main Dressing Station Headquarters 170th Labour Company whose ordes and sanitation is very excellent. Advanced Dressing Station LA CROIX LESCORNEY. Headquarters 2/6th Battalion King's Liverpool Regt. at CANTEEN FARM Rest Room Dressing Station Bde. ERQUINGHEM and Headquarters Sussex Yeomanry FORT ROMPU. 2/27 Wessex Field Ambulance marched today from FORT ROMPU to ERQUINGHEM 1/2 West Lancs Field Ambulance from HR FLEURBAIX to FORT ROMPU. Horse Lines of both to be at H.q.a. 6.6.	
	18.6.17		T.H.D.M.S. visited Main Dressing Station at ERQUINGHEM and	

Army Form C. 2118.

WAR DIARY
or
INTELLIGENCE SUMMARY.
(Erase heading not required.)

Instructions regarding War Diaries and Intelligence Summaries are contained in F. S. Regs., Part II. and the Staff Manual respectively. Title pages will be prepared in manuscript.

Place	Date	Hour	Summary of Events and Information	Remarks and references to Appendices
CROIX DU BAC	18.6.17		FORT ROMPU. Medical Officer to remain in charge of Dressing Station at	
			RUE DE MESSINES, ARMENTIERES; visits arrangt. made for Turn of Erquinghem 171st	
			Infantry Brigade. Motor ambulances to be at Brigade Headquarters at night	
			t.M. of Manuir Contval	
	19.6.17		D.F.D.M.S. spent nearly whole day on inspection of equipment of 2/3rd Wessex	
			Field Ambulances which he found very satisfactory. A.D.M.S. discussed with HA + GNIG	
			question of RAMC personnel at Divisional Baths, braziers & shots etc.	
	20.6.17		Appointment of Major (Temp. Lieut. Colonel) NIGHTINGALE R.A.M.C. to	
			Command 2/3rd Wessex Field Ambulances in succession to Lt.Colonel PENN-NALTON,	
			2/3rd Wessex Field Ambulances, o/c Divisional Baths notified. February 18th, so as to	
			be replaced by Colonel WALES, and will return to his unit tomorrow. D.H.D.M.S.	
			visited Advanced Dressing Stations at ARMENTIERES, LILLE ROAD and HOOPLINES	
			and Regimental Stick Post at TISSAGE DUMP, AUCKLAND ROAD and SQUARE FARM.	
	21.6.17		A.D.M.S. visited house-lines of 3/2nd West Lancs Field Ambulance (at H.2.a.6.3)	
			and those of 2/6th Wessex Field Ambulance, which have been moved to the flat lands	
			by the road LYS at H.2.a.8.7. also Main Dressing Station 3/2nd West Lancs Field	

WAR DIARY
INTELLIGENCE SUMMARY

Army Form C. 2118.

Place	Date	Hour	Summary of Events and Information	Remarks and references to Appendices
GROMBUBER	21.6.17		Ambulances with regard to two cases of men up ASC attacked (Ammo transport) returned as Shell Shock Wounds. On Saturday January 4th the Keen Lanes of the 3/2nd West Lancs Field Ambulance were shelled repeatedly. Three men were slightly wounded and three horses also received severe wounds. Two men received an adjacent billet where two shells struck it and were severely shaken. The S.S.L. (DOUGLES) is reputed to have shown great coolness and presence of mind and hereby standy promoted a large incidents of casualties. Short 11-15 today Lt. Donald Commanding 286th Brigade R.F.A. and Lieut R.G. BROADWOOD Lieut Colonel SHORT, Officer Commanding 286th Brigade R.F.A. and Lieuts MORGAN and HASLAM R.F.A. were wounded when crossing railway bridge and was LYS at ESTAIRES. The other two officers were not dangerously wounded ADMS on late afternoon visited Main Dressing Station at ERQUINGHEM Advanced Dressing Stations at HOUPLINES and RUE do MESSINES in regard to evacuation of the sick and wounded and the event of a	

WAR DIARY or INTELLIGENCE SUMMARY

Army Form C. 2118.

Place	Date	Hour	Summary of Events and Information	Remarks and references to Appendices
CROIX DU BAC	21/6/17		No operations to take place tonight.	
	22/6/17		Our Officers and 6 others ranks wounded in air raid.	
			HOUPLINES Sector last night.	
			Funeral of Lieut Colonel R.G. BROADWOOD at 6 p.m.	
	23/6/17		A.D.M.S. visited 2/5th Wessex Field Ambulance new HQrs at LE NOUVEAU MONDE.	
			Training in proper evacuation of equipment to Division Sutures and Medical Work during active operations. Corespondance regarding provision of wounded from town of ARMENTIERES has been taking place. Gas stations at various places on outskirts and telephones now installed at ERQUINGHEM to effectively overcome situation and aerial activity on neighbourhood today. Three of our divisions Infantry Batterys which are, and one enemy aeroplane brought down.	
	24/6/17		Issued Operation Orders No 9. regarding complementary parties of 2/5 & 2/7 W.Ls & Field Ambulances and 2/6 & 2/7 West Lancs Field Ambulances. Coys of Bns.	APPENDIX G.
			D.A.D.M.S. visited Advanced Dressing Stations at BOIS GRENIER and LA CROIX LESCORNEZ and Regimental Aid Post at WYE FARM, regarding gas-mask arrangements in the places. Instructions for evacuation etc., also of Aid Posts of BOIS GRENIER	

WAR DIARY or INTELLIGENCE SUMMARY

Army Form C. 2118.

Place	Date	Hour	Summary of Events and Information	Remarks and references to Appendices
Croix Du Bac	24.6.17		Sub-section at present held by 2ⁿᵈ PORTUGUESE Regt. with special reference to their sanitary arrangements, which it is found are some respects defective. Captain JEPHCOTT, Medical Officer in charge 4/5 Royal Fus: Loyals	
	25.6.17		Regt. left today to be commandant at No 7 Stationary Station, now relieved at BRAQUEMONT, now NOEUX-LES-MINES. Lieut Colonel J. NIGHTINGALE arrived from 6th Division where he had commanded a Regimental Field Stretcher-bearers to command and this 2/5th Manc. Field Stretchers, vice Lieut. Colonel (now Temporary Colonel) H.D. BROOK. A/ARMED A.D.M.S. 55th Division. Hears that the PORTUGUESE, who have been in line on front of BOIS GRENIER Section, are likely to be withdrawn and given a "B" Section. C.R.A. (Brigadier General WRAY) who is commanding Division in absence of General BROADWOODS thinks their defects F.D.M.S. to visit 286th Brigade R.F.A. especially "B" by tomorrow, especially as regards their fitness to man a further so long gas alarm. D.A.D.M.S. and Captain LEIGHTON (representing 2" Brigade) visited the various billets by PORTUGUESE and made inspection of Sanitary arrangements. A.D.M.S. visited Divisional Baths which have recently been altered and are now empowered to supply baths with subsequent plunge. Inspected also experience arrangements to these	

Army Form C. 2118.

WAR DIARY
or
INTELLIGENCE SUMMARY.
(Erase heading not required.)

Instructions regarding War Diaries and Intelligence Summaries are contained in F. S. Regs., Part II. and the Staff Manual respectively. Title pages will be prepared in manuscript.

Place	Date	Hour	Summary of Events and Information	Remarks and references to Appendices
CROIX DU BAC	25.6.17		A.D.M.S. visited Hq. 49th Divisional Sanitary Section, workshops at LA GORGUE. Congratulated the two joining units and troubled to make sanitary arrangements on white. Decisions from times were this inflicted. It is advisable that by Officers Commanding 49th Sanitary Sections.	
	26.6.17		A.D.M.S. visited ARMENTIERES, generally saw various gun positions of A. B and D Batteries 286th Brigade R.F.A. with Battery Commanders and Medical Officers. Saw Officer Commanding 286th Brigade R.F.A. Visited Detachments Dressing Stations at RUE des MESSINES, HOUPLINES and MATERNITY HOSPITAL. Visited Headquarters of 171st and 173rd Machine Gun Corps regarding medical attendance. Visited also New Dressing Station at 2/2nd Wessex Field Ambulance at ERQUINGHAM and Headquarters of 2/9th and 2/10 Kings Liverpool Regiments, seeing Medical Officers on each case regarding water-supply, slaughter houses training, water duties men, sanitary squads etc. A.D.M.S. interviewed O.C. 2/3rd Wessex Field Ambulance at 2/3rd Wessex Field Ambulance about the attached Officer Commanding Colonel NIGHTINGALE about the attached Officer Commanding.	
	27.6.17		2/3rd Wessex Field Ambulance moved today from LE NOUVEAU MONDE where it has been stationed for four months to FORT ROMPU, 1 the 3/2nd West Lancs	

Army Form C. 2118.

WAR DIARY
or
INTELLIGENCE SUMMARY.
(Erase heading not required.)

Instructions regarding War Diaries and Intelligence Summaries are contained in F. S. Regs., Part II. and the Staff Manual respectively. Title pages will be prepared in manuscript.

Place	Date	Hour	Summary of Events and Information	Remarks and references to Appendices
CROIX DU BAC	27.6.17		Field Ambulances moving from FORT ROMPU to LE NOUVEAU MONDE to close the tramway.	
			DADMS. Officer Commanding 2/5th Sanitary Section and party of N.C.O's and men, went to LILLERS. First Army H.Q. in conference, to see practical Sanitary Appliances.	
	28.6.17		ADMS. paid visits of inspection to HOUPLINES, L'EPINETTE and RUE DE BOIS Sub-sections, especially with regard to Brown's Relay Post, Gas-proofing arrangements and use of Kettles and Tramways. With Captain GIBBS visited HOUPLINES Advanced Dressing Station which he is handing over to Captain PENN-MILTON today. Tissage Dump Regimental Aid Post, AUCKLAND ROAD Post, Square Farm Regimental Aid Post, LEITH WALK Post, and WELLINGTON AVENUE Post, Gas-affecting Post at BRICKFIELD and Advanced Dressing Station at LILLE ROAD, ARMENTIERES. ADMS. also visited Headquarters "D" Battery 286th Brigade RFA. at ARMENTIERES, which had been occasionally shelled one course of morning. ADMS. interviewed Medical Officers of 2/17 and 2/19 Kings Liverpool Regts and 2/5th South Lancs Regt. on their Regimental Aid Posts.	
	29.6.17		ADMS. discussed revised arrangements for dealing with (1) gassed and	

A6915 Wt. W1422/M1160 35,000 12/16 D.D. & L. Forms/C./2118/14.

Army Form C. 2118.

WAR DIARY
or
INTELLIGENCE SUMMARY.
(Erase heading not required.)

Instructions regarding War Diaries and Intelligence Summaries are contained in F. S. Regs., Part II. and the Staff Manual respectively. Title pages will be prepared in manuscript.

Place	Date	Hour	Summary of Events and Information	Remarks and references to Appendices
CROIX DU BAC	29/6/17		(2) so called "shell shock" cases - though that term is no longer to be used - will AA's & MG and DAAG, and drafted demiort on the subject for general (ASMS Medical Officers). ADMS, visited Main Dressing Station Sailly and also Dressing Station (BOIS GRENIER) of 2/6.3rd Manor Field Ambulance and also Regimental Sub Post TRAMWAY AVENUE regarding arrangements for evacuation of casualties that may occur in a raid projected for the afternoon. ADMS visited Main Dressing Station of 2/3rd Masson Field Ambulance at FORT ROMPU at 6.45 and 8.40 pm. Thirty wounded of 2/10th King's Liverpool Regt. where admitted between 6 and 7 pm. There at least twenty unconscious cases.	
	30/6/17		Finds that a total of 55 cases in 2/10th King's Liverpool Regt. were admitted wounded to Main Dressing Station of 2/3rd Manor Field Ambulance of which 2 died. Evacuation to Casualty Clearing Stations went smoothly. SM arrangements satisfactory. (This section that has not hitherto dose any evacuation of wounded.) ADMS interviews Officers Commanding Sanitary Sections regarding water supplies, and general low incidence of sickness.	

J. J. Lewis ....Colonel, A. Med. S.

A.D.M.S. 57th (W.L.) Division.

57TH DIVISION.   Copy No. 9

SECRET.

M.1730/54.

R.A.M.C. OPERATION ORDER - No. 4.

Reference Sheet 36 - 1/40,000.
and Sheet 28 SW - 1/20,000.

1. The Officer Commanding 2/2nd Wessex Field Ambulance will detail one Section to relieve personnel of 9th Australian Field Ambulance at the "BREWERY" C.1.d.4.5., and posts associated therewith. Section transport, with the exception of two motor ambulance cars, to be left at the Headquarters of the unit.

2. The Section in question will report at the "BREWERY" at 12-0 noon, 2/6/1917. The taking over will be completed by 10-0pm, 2/6/1917.

3. Details of arrangements for taking over will be made direct between the Commanding Officers concerned.

4. Completion of move to be reported to this office by wire.

5. ACKNOWLEDGE.

Headquarters,
1/6/1917.

Colonel. A.Med.S.
A.D.M.S., 57th Division.

Issued at ......9-15..... pm to

Distribution -

Copy No. 1. to H.Q. 57th Division.
      2.   -do-
      3.   O.C. 2/2nd Wessex Field Ambulance.
      4.   O.C. 3/2nd West Lancs. Field Ambulance.
      5.   A.D.M.S., 3rd Australian Division.
      6.   D.D.M.S., XI Corps.
      7.   -do-
      8.   War Diary.
      9.   -do-
    10.   H.Q., 170th Infantry Brigade.
    11.   File.
    12.   Spare.
    13.   -do-
    14.   -do-
    15.   -do-

SECRET.　　　　　　　57th DIVISION.
　　　　　　　　　　　　　　　　　　　　　　　　Copy No. 7

　　　　　　R.A.M.C. OPERATION ORDER - No. 5.　　M. 1883/54.

　　　　　　　　　　　　　　　　　Reference Sheet 36 - 1/40,000.

1.　　　Evacuations of Sick and Wounded from the Advanced Dressing
　　　Station at LA CROIX LESCORNEZ (H.26.c.8.4.) will be to the Main
　　　Dressing Station at FORT ROMPU (H.7.d.9.3) from noon on Saturday,
　　　9th instant.

2.　　　Personnel of 2/3rd Wessex Field Ambulance will still remain at
　　　LA CROIX LESCORNEZ.

3.　　　All cases so evacuated will be passed through Admission and Dis-
　　　charge Books of 2/2nd Wessex Field Ambulance.

4.　　　ACKNOWLEDGE.

Headquarters,
　　8/6/1917.
　　　　　　　　　　　　　　　　　　　　　　　Colonel, A.Med.S.,
　　　　　　　　　　　　　　　　　　　　A.D.M.S., 57th Division.

Issued at ....8.0........p.m. to

　　　Distribution -

Copy No. 1. to H.Q., 57th Division.
　　　　2.　　　　-do-
　　　　3.　　O.C., 2/2nd Wessex Field Ambulance.
　　　　4.　　O.C., 2/3rd Wessex Field Ambulance.
　　　　5.　　D.D.M.S., XI Corps.
　　　　6.　　　　-do-
　　　　7.　　War Diary.
　　　　8.　　　　-do-
　　　　9.　　File.
　　　10.　　Spare.
　　　11.　　　　-do-

SECRET   Copy No....10....

57th DIVISION

R.A.M.C. Operation Order No. 6.

M 1908/54.
Ref. Sheet 36 - 1/40,000
and sheet 28S.W. 1/20,000

1. "B" Section, 2/2nd Wessex Field Ambulance will be relieved by 4th N.Zealand Field Ambulance at the "Brewery" C.1.d.4.5. and posts associated therewith.

2. Advance party of 4th N.Zealand Field Ambulance will report at the "Brewery" at 12.0 noon, 10/6/17.

3. Details of arrangements for taking over will be made direct between the Commanding Officers concerned.

4. Move to be completed by 6.0 p.m.

5. Completion of move to be reported to this office by wire.

6. ACKNOWLEDGE.

Headquarters,
9/6/17.

Colonel, A. Med.S.,
A.D.M.S., 57th Division.

Distribution -   Issued at .....9.30.....p.m.

Copy No. 1 to H.Q., 57th Division
      2   do.
      3   O.C. 2/2nd Wessex Field Amblce.
      4   O.C., "B" Section, 2/2nd Wessex Field Amblce.
      5   O.C. 3/2nd West Lancs. Field Ambulance.
      6   A.D.M.S., 3rd Australian Division.
      7   O.C., Detached Force (57th Division.)
      8   D.D.M.S., XI Corps.
      9   do.
     10   War Diary
     11   do.
     12   File
     13   Spare
     14   do.

"D"

SECRET. **57TH DIVISION.** COPY No...7.....

R. A. M. C. OPERATION ORDER No.7.   M. 1968/54.

Reference sheet 36 - 1/40,000.

1. 2/2nd Wessex Field Ambulance will take over Advanced Dressing Station, LA CROIX LESCORNEZ, (H.26.c.8.4.) from 2/3rd Wessex Field Ambulance on 14th June, 1917.

2. Evacuation will be carried out in accordance with R.A.M.C. Operation Order No.6.

3. Details to be arranged direct between Commanding Officers concerned.

4. Move to be completed by 6-0pm.

5. Personnel of 2/3rd Wessex Field Ambulance will return to unit at LE NOUVEAU MONDE.

6. Main Dressing Station of 2/3rd Wessex Field Ambulance, LE NOUVEAU MONDE (G.27.c.3.2.) will close 14th June, 1917.

7. 2/3rd Wessex Field Ambulance to commence training on 15th June, 1917.

8. Completion of move to be notified to this office by wire.

9. Acknowledge.

J F Dwan
Colonel. A.Med.S.
A.D.M.S., 57th Division.

Headquarters,
12th June, 1917.

Issued at 4.30 pm.

Distribution -

Copy No. 1 to H.Q., 57th Division.
     2   do.   do.
     3   O.C., 2/2nd Wessex Field Ambulance.
     4   O.C., 2/3rd Wessex Field Ambulance.
     5   O.C., 3/2nd West Lancs. Field Ambulance.
     6   D.D.M.S., XI Corps.
     7   War Diary.
     8   do.
     9   File.
   10   Spare.
   11   do.

SECRET

Copy No......7....

57th DIVISION.

R.A.M.C. Operation Order No. 8.

Headquarters,
   15th June, 1917.

M. 2052/54.
****

Reference sheet 36 - 1/40,000.

1. The 2/2nd Wessex Field Ambulance will establish a Main Dressing Station at Billet 145, Rue de la Lys, ERQUINGHEM, on Sunday 17th June, 1917.

2. The 2/2nd Wessex Field Ambulance will detail a holding party to take over from the 3/2nd West Lancs. Field Ambulance at the RUE DE MESSINES (C.19.c.1.1.) and the MATERNITE HOSPITAL (B.30.c.6.3.), 17th June, 1917.

3. The 2/2nd Wessex Field Ambulance will take over the Advanced Dressing Stations from the 3/2nd West. Lancs Field Ambulance at HOUPLINES (C.26.d.5.9.), and Rue de Lille, ARMENTIERES (I.1.d.5.8.), 17th June, 1917.

4. The 2/2nd Wessex Field Ambulance will take over the stables of the 3/2nd West Lancs. Field Ambulance at H.5.a.2.7., 17th June, 1917.

5. The 3/2nd West Lancs. Field Ambulance will take over the Main Dressing Station at FORT ROMPU, (H.7.d.6.3.), and the Advanced Dressing Stations at BOIS GRENIER (H.24.d.5.0.), and LA CROIX LESCORNEZ (H.26.c.8.4.), and the Car Collecting Post at PORT A CLOUS, (H.21.a.3.8.), on 17th June, 1917.

6. The 3/2nd West Lancs. Field Ambulance will take over the stables at present occupied by the 2/2nd Wessex Field Ambulance at H.9.a.6.8., 17th June, 1917.

7. Advance parties will proceed on Saturday, 16th June, 1917.

8. Details will be arranged direct between the Commanding Officers concerned.

9. Moves to be completed by 6-0pm.

10. Completion of moves to be notified to this office by wire.

11. ACKNOWLEDGE.

J.S. Edmiston.

Captain. R.A.M.C., TF.,
Issued at 11.30 pm.   D.A.D.M.S. for A.D.M.S., 57th Division.

Distribution -

Copy No. 1 to H.Q.57th Division.
     2   do.
     3   O.C., 2/2nd Wessex Field Ambulance.
     4   O.C., 3/2nd W.L. Field Ambulance.
     5   D.D.M.S., XI Corps.
     6   War Diary.
     7   do
     8   File.
     9   Spare.

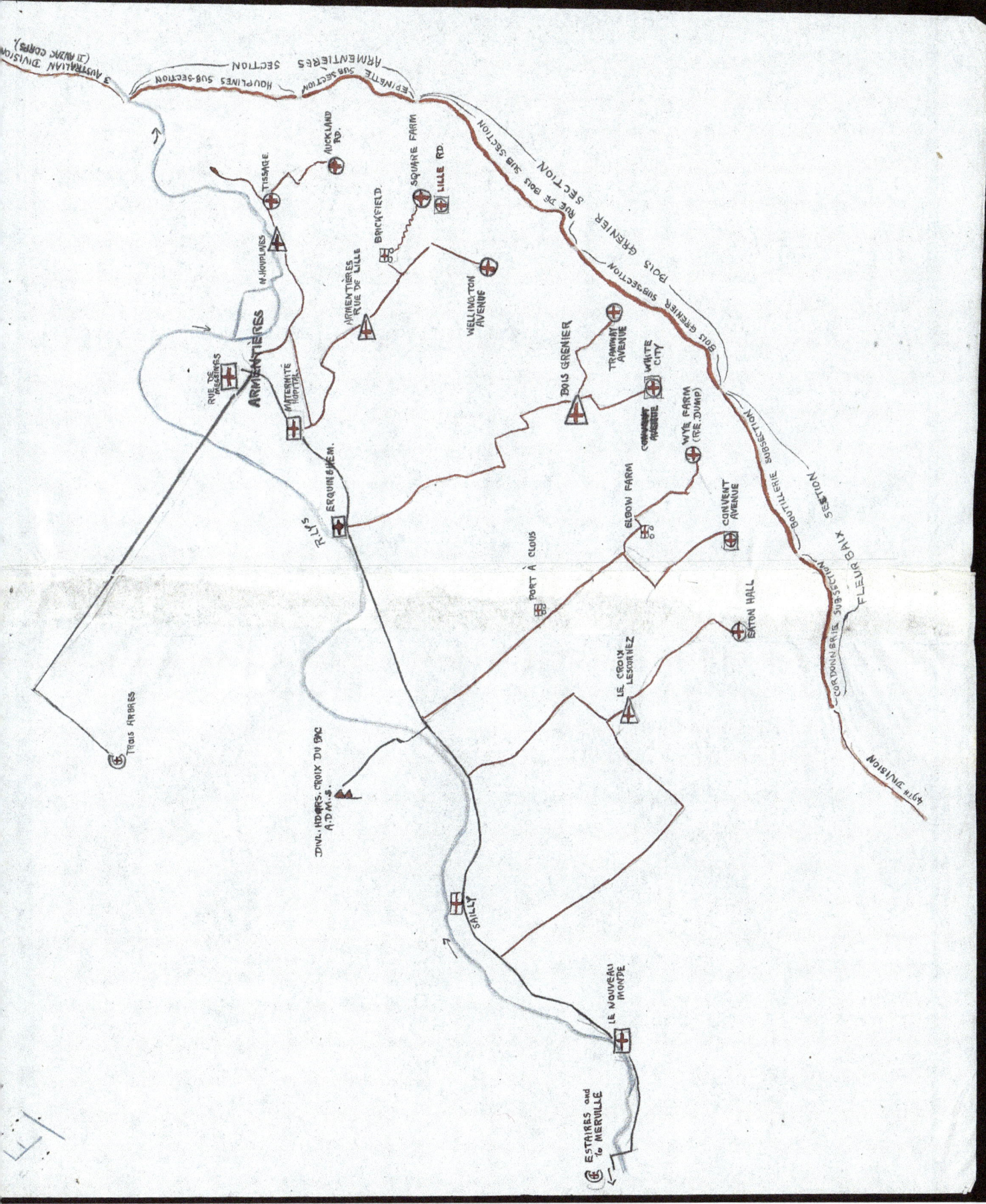

SECRET. 57th DIVISION. Copy No. 14.

R.A.M.C. Operation Order No. 9. M.2052/54.

Reference Map Sheet 36 - 1/40,000.

1. The 2/3rd Wessex Field Ambulance will take over the Main Dressing Station at FORT ROMPU, (H.7.d.6.3.), Advanced Dressing Stations at BOIS GRENIER, (H.24.d.5.0.), and LA CROIX LESCORNEZ, (H.26.c.8.4.), and Car Collecting Post at PORT A CLOUS, (H.21.a.3.8.) from 3/2nd West Lancs. Field Ambulance on Wednesday, 27th June, 1917.

2. The 2/3rd Wessex Field Ambulance to be accompanied by its full complement of motor ambulance cars.

3. The 3/2nd West Lancs. Field Ambulance will take over quarters at present occupied by 2/3rd Wessex Field Ambulance at LE NOUVEAU MONDE (G.27 c 3.2.) on 27th June, 1917.

4. The 3/2 West Lancs. Field Ambulance will commence training on 28th June, 1917.

5. Advance parties will proceed on Tuesday, the 26th June 17.

6. Details to be arranged direct between Commanding Officers concerned.

7. Moves to be completed by 6.0 p.m.

8. Completion of move to be notified to this Office by wire.

9. ACKNOWLEDGE.

Headquarters,
24th June, 1917.

Issued at 7.30 pm.

Colonel, A. Med. S.
A.D.M.S. 57th Division.

Distribution -

Copy No. 1	to H.Q. 57th Division.	Copy No.	
2	- do -	14.	War Diary.
3	O.C. 2/2nd Wessex Fd.Amb.	15.	War Diary.
4	O.C. 2/3rd Wessex Fd.Amb.	16.	File.
5	O.C. 3/2nd W.Lan. Fd.Amb.	17.	Spare.
6	D.D.M.S. XI Corps.	18.	Spare.
7	H.Q. 170th Infantry Bde.		
8	H.Q. 171st Infantry Bde.		
9	H.Q. 172nd Infantry Bde.		
10	C.R.E. 57th Division.		
11	C.R.A. 57th Division.		
12	O.C. 57th Divl Signal Co.		
13	O.C. 57th Divl Train.		

Confidential

War Diary.

of

A.D.M.S. 57th Division.

From July 1st 1917.   to July 31st 1917.

(Volume   )

Army Form C. 2118.

WAR DIARY
or
INTELLIGENCE SUMMARY.
(Erase heading not required.)

Instructions regarding War Diaries and Intelligence Summaries are contained in F. S. Regs., Part II. and the Staff Manual respectively. Title pages will be prepared in manuscript.

Place	Date	Hour	Summary of Events and Information	Remarks and references to Appendices
CROIX DU BAC	1/7/16		A.D.M.S. visited Main Dressing Station of 2/3rd Wessex Field Ambulance at FORT ROMPU. Stationary Dressing Station at LA CROIX LESCORNEX; also Headquarters of 2/2nd West Lancs Field Ambulance — now closed for training and overhaul at LE NOUVEAU MONDE. D.A.D.M.S. visited front line at CORDONNERIE section. EATON HALL Regimental Aid Post.	
	2/7/16		A.D.M.S. had an interview with new Divisional Commander, Major General R.W.R. BARNES (11th Hussars) regarding sickness, Field Ambulances, Regimental Medical Officers, etc. Lectured to 3/2nd West Lancs Field Ambulance at LE NOUVEAU MONDE, after formal inspection on parade, on "Medical Service in Operations on a large scale". A.D.M.S. visited Divisional Baths where there is now sufficient underclothing for adequate issue.	
	3/7/16		Medical Officer arrived as reinforcement. Captain H. ROBERTSON, R.A.M.C.T.C.. He serves in South Africa and on present war (H.ms) August 1914 to 1915. Wounded admitted to Field Ambulances of 57th Divisions and belonging to the Division, as from 622, as against 166, 228 and 314 in March, April and May respectively. Sickness rate consistently low. Admission rate runs from 0.1 to 0.2%. No flannel specially provided. Evacuated to Casualty Clearing Station. 42% of those admitted sick to Field Ambulances. One case of Enteric Fever reported yesterday, investigation being made.	

Army Form C. 2118.

WAR DIARY
or
INTELLIGENCE SUMMARY.
(Erase heading not required.)

Instructions regarding War Diaries and Intelligence Summaries are contained in F. S. Regs., Part II. and the Staff Manual respectively. Title pages will be prepared in manuscript.

Place	Date	Hour	Summary of Events and Information	Remarks and references to Appendices
CROIX DU BAC	4/7/17		Operation Orders No. 10. (RAMC 57th Division) for exchange of Headquarters. Mains Dressing Stations and Advanced Dressing Stations - but not location of horse lines - of 2/2nd Wessex and 2/3rd Wessex Field Ambulances. DADMS with DAQMG and accompanied by Medical Officers in charge 2/4 N.LAN.R. made exhaustive inspection of water supply arrangements in front area of CORDONNERIE Sub-section. DDMS VI Corps and DADMS visited 57th Divisional Headquarters.	APPENDIX A
	5/7/17		ADMS interviews with Officer Commanding 57th Sanitary Section regarding water supplies, sanitary workshop and general co-operation on sanitary affairs, with G.S.O.I regarding inspected quarters; with D.A.Q.M.G. regarding water supplies; Medical attended at Divisional School. DADMS visited 2/3rd Wessex Field Ambulance, horse-lines, and Senior Supply Officer regarding issue of Chlorinating Powder in bulk. 2/3rd Wessex Field Ambulance moved from FORT ROMPU to ERQUINGHEM	
	6/7/17		exchanging quarters and evacuation duties with 2/2nd Wessex Field Ambulance. Considerable number of civilians evacuated in ARMENTIERES. DADMS with DAQMG made exhaustive investigation of water supplies in	
	7/7/17		BOUTILLERIE Sub-section. Much artillery and aerial activity by enemy last night.	

WAR DIARY
or
INTELLIGENCE SUMMARY.
(Erase heading not required.)

Army Form C. 2118.

Place	Date	Hour	Summary of Events and Information	Remarks and references to Appendices
CROIX DU BAC	7-7-17		Bomb from aeroplane burst in hut occupied by B Section Divisional Ammunition Column near HALLOBEAU killing four and wounding four others. Enemy's trench mortar on BOIS GRENIER Instruction in night 10 p.m. til midnight, killed a considerable number and wounded 12. Also considerable bombardment of communication trenches on L'EPINETTE. Subsections during relief. A.D.M.S. visited 2/3rd Wessex Field Ambulance at ERZUINGHEM - foot and escaped quarters. Advanced Dressing Stations at RUE des MESSINES, and swimming bath. ARMENTIERES. Headquarters 172nd Machine Gun Coy, RUE du MARLE. several bad roads in evacuation south. Advanced Dressing Station at LA CROIX LESCORNEZ. Headquarters of 3/3rd West Lancs Field Ambulance at LE NOUVEAU MONDE etc. Captains S.R.GIBBS 2/3rd Wessex Field Ambulance came to office to-day for fortnight training in duties of D.A.D.M.S.	
	8-7-17		Orders received for one section of Field Ambulance of 61st Division to take over Field Ambulance of 49th Division at ZELOBES on departure of 49th Division, and to take and dispose of British sick and wounded from centre section of XI Corps front, which is about to be taken over by Portuguese. D.A.D.M.S., and Captains S.R.GIBBS went to arrange. Section to be provided from 3/3rd West Lancs Field Ambulance. Date not yet	

Army Form C. 2118.

WAR DIARY
or
INTELLIGENCE SUMMARY.
(Erase heading not required.)

Instructions regarding War Diaries and Intelligence Summaries are contained in F. S. Regs., Part II. and the Staff Manual respectively. Title pages will be prepared in manuscript.

Place	Date	Hour	Summary of Events and Information	Remarks and references to Appendices
CROIX DU BAC	8.7.17		announced. A.D.M.S. visited Main Dressing Station of 2/3rd Wessex Field Ambulance at ERQUINGHEM, and went over with Officer Commanding 2/300 duty examined proposed for sectional occupation as a Main Dressing Station. Operation Orders No. 11. issued regarding moves of 2/2nd Wessex Field Ambulance and 3/2nd West Lancs Field Ambulance to the 119 (?)	APPENDIX. B.
	9.7.17		A.D.M.S. visited Divisional B.H.s at SAILLY, and watched process of inspection of men for scabies etc and also carefully examined skin about to be inoculated. Found many dead flies adherent, but no sign of any on life. Total dones spent by A.D.M.S. on officers, 62. For list of duties, diseases, etc, appendix G. Note this is not an exceptional day. This date was selected for the record a weeks ago.	APPENDIX. G.
	10.7.17		Boards held at LE NOUVEAU MONDE and ERQUINGHEM, for examining "P.B." mens. S/t Lt+u A.D.M.S. Major STOKES and Captain GIBBS. A.D.M.S visited 2/10th Loyal Regt H.Q's., and saw Medical Officer regarding new Regimental Aid Post, his former Post having been slightly shelled and no longer tenable. A.D.M.S discussed with Officer Commanding 2/3rd Wessex Field Ambulance many details of sanitary administration, etc. A.D.M.S, in afternoon, with A.A. & Q.M.G visited Divisional Baths, SAILLY.	

Army Form C. 2118.

WAR DIARY
or
INTELLIGENCE SUMMARY.
(Erase heading not required.)

Instructions regarding War Diaries and Intelligence Summaries are contained in F. S. Regs., Part II. and the Staff Manual respectively. Title pages will be prepared in manuscript.

Place	Date	Hour	Summary of Events and Information	Remarks and references to Appendices
CROIX DU BAC	10-7-17		where 22 men of Field Ambulances are still employed; 2/2nd Wessex Field Ambulance Main Dressing Station, regarding its general immediately employing it fully; and a section at ERQUINGHEM on which the Field Ambulances could open their next advantages. Orderlies to limb and car to Officers Commanding 49th Sanitary Section and 20 RAMC men temporarily to 54th Casualty Clearing Station.	
	11-7-17		2/2nd Wessex Field Ambulance proceeded today from FORT ROMPU to LE NOUVEAU MONDE, and closed for overhaul and training, exchanging with 3/2nd West Lancs Field Ambulance which opened Main Dressing Station at FORT ROMPU and Advanced Dressing Stations at BOIS GRENIER and LA CROIX LESCORNEZ. B Section 3/2nd West Lancs Field Ambulance proceeded to ZELOBES and opened Main Dressing Station for British troops in Portuguese Divisional area. Two nursing orderlies and two general duty men went from 2/2nd Wessex Field Ambulance to 54th Casualty Clearing Station for temporary duty. ADMS saw DDMS XI Corps at Corps Headquarters regarding moving 2/2nd Wessex Field Ambulance Headquarters and Main Dressing Stations from ERQUINGHEM to SAILLY; also with unflicted wounds; wearing of trousers only; carriage of rifles for A.S.C. men attached to Field Ambulances; motor ambulances for	

T.131. Wt. W708—776. 50t000. 4/15. Sir J. C. & S.

Army Form C. 2118.

WAR DIARY
or
INTELLIGENCE SUMMARY.
(Erase heading not required.)

Instructions regarding War Diaries and Intelligence Summaries are contained in F.S. Regs., Part II. and the Staff Manual respectively. Title pages will be prepared in manuscript.

Place	Date	Hour	Summary of Events and Information	Remarks and references to Appendices
CROIX DU BAC	11-7-17		Officer Commanding Sanitary Sections, etc. ADMS visited "B" Section 3/2nd West Lancs Field Ambulance at ZELOBES and 2/2nd Wessex Field Ambulance at LE NOUVEAU MONDE. ADMS visited Divisional Baths regarding 22 RAMC. N.C.Os and men still employed there. DADMS with DAQMG made exhaustive audit of inspection of Water Supplies in BOIS GRENIER subsections.	
	12-7-17		ADMS visited wagons lines R.F.A. (286th Brigade) and Reinforcement Camp. ADMS saw G.O.C. 57th Division, regarding re-occupation of former Main Dressing Station at SAILLY. He agrees H.S.O. Company can be accommodated elsewhere.	
	13-7-17		ADMS met DDMS XI Corps and with him went over old Main Dressing Station at SAILLY, about to be re-opened as Main Dressing Station, and met in forenoon of H.S.C. Company 57th Division. ADMS wrote DDMS XI Corps, regarding the considerable and ever increasing work of conveying wounded – and sometimes also sick-civilians to HAZEBROUCK (if french) or POPERINGHE (if Belgian) Average figures for 57th Division 15-2-17 to 11-7-17. (See next page)	

WAR DIARY
or
INTELLIGENCE SUMMARY.

(Erase heading not required.)

Army Form C. 2118.

Place	Date	Hour	Summary of Events and Information	Remarks and references to Appendices
CROIX DU BAC	13.7.17		Admitted Field Ambulances 4,466	
			Evacuated to Casualty Clearing Stns. Sick 1,284	
			Wounded 1,764 3,048	
			Killed 374	
			Sent home to receive Commissions 120	
			3,542	
			Received as Reinforcements 2,242	
			Net wastage 1,300	
	14.7.17		A.D.M.S. visited Main Dressing Stations of 2/2nd Wessex Field Ambulances and 3/2nd West Lancs: Field Ambulances regarding various points; also Advanced Dressing Stations at BOIS GRENIER. A.D.M.S. with Medical Officer in charge, 2/10th King's Liverpool Regt., visited SHAFTESBURY AVENUE, regarding site of new Regimental Aid Post. A.D.M.S. in afternoon attended conference at BETHUNE, Institute St. VAAST (No.35. Clearing Station) of D.D.M.S., A.D.M.S., D.A.D's.M.S., Sanitary Officers and Sanitary Officers	

WAR DIARY
or
INTELLIGENCE SUMMARY.
(Erase heading not required.)

Army Form C. 2118.

Place	Date	Hour	Summary of Events and Information	Remarks and references to Appendices
CROIX DU BAC.	14-7-17		Communion at first Army. Colonel WESTCOTT. A/DMS presiding. Chiefly discussed the subject of Sanitary administration, construction of appliances, sanitation of newly occupied areas, training of sanitary personnel etc. ADMS visited Dressing Station staffed by "B" Section, 3/2nd West Lancs Field Ambulance at ZELOBES.	
	15-7-17		A.D.M.S. visited Reinforcement Camp regarding water supply and sheds etc, about to be reoccupied as Main Dressing Station at SAILLY. Received from Divisions and issued orders for move of Field Ambulances. thus — 2/3rd Wessex Field Ambulance from ERQUINGHEM to FORT ROMPU on 17th instant, 3/2nd West Lancs Field Ambulance from FORT ROMPU to SAILLY same day. DADMS forwarded chart of present Medical arrangements in Divisional area. DADMS with DAQMG visited Water Supplies in RUE de BOIS	APPENDIX II
	16-7-17		Bluecheno in early morning. Issued 57th Divisional RAMC Order No 12, regarding move of 2/3rd Wessex Field Ambulance and 3/2nd West Lancs Field Ambulance tomorrow. ADMS with A/DMS 1st Army (Colonel WESTCOTT), and DDMS XI Corps and DADMS 1st Army (Lieut Colonel DAVIDSON) visited Headquarters 2/2nd Wessex Field Ambulance, 3/2nd West Lancs Field Ambulance at LE NOUVEAU MONDE; Main Dressing Station, 3/2nd West Lancs Field Ambulance at	

Army Form C. 2118.

WAR DIARY
or
INTELLIGENCE SUMMARY.
(Erase heading not required.)

Instructions regarding War Diaries and Intelligence Summaries are contained in F. S. Regs., Part II. and the Staff Manual respectively. Title pages will be prepared in manuscript.

Place	Date	Hour	Summary of Events and Information	Remarks and references to Appendices
CROIX DU BAC	16-7-17		FORT ROMPU and Lains Dressing Station, 2/2nd Wessex Field Ambulance at ERQUINGHEM, and Advanced Dressing Station at HOUPLINES.	
	17-7-17.		ADMS 57th Division went to 3/2nd West Lancs Field Ambulance at SAILLY to meet DDMS II Corps and planned an extensive alteration to existing site. Plans to be made and submitted as soon as possible. At this site are many wooden buildings which could be utilised as accommodation for stretcher cases while awaiting evacuation, could not be used to retain patients for several days. DADMS visited here several of several units and infected water cart. Lieut Col PARSONS, Officer Commanding, 2/2nd Wessex Field Ambulance, reported to Divisional Headquarters to act as ADMS during absence of Colonel DEWAR.	
	18-7-17.		ADMS went away on leave at 2 p.m. Lieut Col PARSONS, Officer Commanding, 2/2nd Wessex Field Ambulance, reported to Divisional Headquarters to act as ADMS during absence of Colonel DEWAR. Gunner FILLINGHAM evacuated suffering from enteritis on 17-7-17, was notified to ADMS as now diagnosed dysentery, first case in this Division in this area since 57th Division took over. 2/1/17 No. 11 — 2/3rd Wessex Field Ambulance and 3/2nd West Lancs Field Ambulance moved their Headquarters and Lains Dressing Stations. The 2/3rd Wessex Field Ambulance to FORT ROMPU, but continuing the evacuation from the ARMENTIÈRES sectors. The 3/2nd West Lancs Field	

Army Form C. 2118.

WAR DIARY
or
INTELLIGENCE SUMMARY.
(Erase heading not required.)

Instructions regarding War Diaries and Intelligence Summaries are contained in F. S. Regs., Part II. and the Staff Manual respectively. Title pages will be prepared in manuscript.

Place	Date	Hour	Summary of Events and Information	Remarks and references to Appendices
GROS DU BAC	18.7.17		Ambulances moved to the Laundry at AILLY which was occupied in the early part of the year by the 92nd Russ. Field Ambulance as a Headquarters and Main Dressing Station. Work completed at btwn. This Headquarters Company 57th Divisional Train moved out and occupied stables evacuated by 57th Divisional R.E. Company marched our Trenches at some times as was ascertained thus in rear - Ache - BOUTILLERIE.	
	19.7.17		Recommendation to Headquarters 57th Division for a reinforced concrete building to be erected on the communication trench running between Halfest and subsidiary lines as a Regimental Aid Post from the Battalion in Line on the BOIS GRENIER Instruction. Plans to be drawn up and material supplied by C.R.E. Labours by R.A.M.C. Captains R.S. ASPINALL, R.A.M.C., S.R. reported to impact emergency roads to be used by Field Ambulance vehicles in case main roads were being shelled. There were not found to be sufficient repair to this work. Repair are being made on this subject to this Officer an Krity. Lethe from Medical Officer in charge 2/8th King's Liverpool Regt., references medical arrangements for a raid to be carried out by battalion on Line via EPINETTE instructions. Probable date not available.	

T2134. Wt. W708 - 770. 500,000. 4/15. Sir J. C. & S.

Army Form C. 2118.

WAR DIARY
or
INTELLIGENCE SUMMARY.
(Erase heading not required.)

Instructions regarding War Diaries and Intelligence Summaries are contained in F. S. Regs., Part II. and the Staff Manual respectively. Title pages will be prepared in manuscript.

Place	Date	Hour	Summary of Events and Information	Remarks and references to Appendices
CROIX DU BAC	19/7/17.		Captain FAULKNER, Medical Officer, in charge 2/8th Kings Liverpool Regt. asked to call on A.D.M.S. on Saturday 21st.	
	20/7/17.		Enemy shelled town of ARMENTIERES very considerably with aerial observation, as available was very good. He also shelled our hut balloons with shrapnel. D.A.D.M.S. visited 10 Field Medical Units at their Main Dressing Stations.	
	21/7/17.		Enemy shelled ARMENTIERES in the early morning with gas-shells. He is reported to have put 3,000 large calibre gas shells into the town. Partly containing a new form of gas, supposed to be mustard oil vapour. These did not appear to be much shrapnel. There were 79 casualties reported, of these 59 were gas cases, only 5 very serious of these. Still the remainder appeared to have been in contact with the gas. The eyes, in these cases were very inflamed and both upper and lower lids were very oedematous and painful. Two cases were blistered by the gas on the conjunctiva. Men engaged in removal of samples for analysis gives district, in the cases where the body did not come into actual contact with the shell. One man carried a shell on his back keeping his tunic and clothes on, he had a large blister.	

Army Form C. 2118.

WAR DIARY
or
INTELLIGENCE SUMMARY.
(Erase heading not required.)

Instructions regarding War Diaries and Intelligence Summaries are contained in F. S. Regs., Part II. and the Staff Manual respectively. Title pages will be prepared in manuscript.

Place	Date	Hour	Summary of Events and Information	Remarks and references to Appendices
Crom Du Bag.	21/7/17	—	Thin attack took place on the back areas of both L'EPINETTE and HOUPLINES subsection. Cases of delayed actions were reported, but these were for the most part gassed late on in the day which out as working parties. 8 Special men working at a cable took advantage of a shell hole to bury cable, and were gassed though performing the lifting of the hole for the cable. The Medical Officer in charge 2/8th Mang Lancport Regt. called with reference to Medical arrangements for a special scheme, enabling the assistance of two Medical Officers in addition to his establishment for this special scheme. The could not be arranged, as Division is now 6 Medical Officers below Establishment, and 2 Medical Officers on leave. IIADMS and Capline Ellis RAMC[?] visited the CORDONNERIE Subsection to investigate tramways, with special reference to their positions as routes of evacuation. This reelos is well supplied by a system of tramways which branches off in three main routes to support and front lines. H/ADMS visited the Casualty Clearing Station, at the request of the I.G.O.C. to investigate cases of gas poisoning evacuated there.	
	22-7-17		A second batch of cases through the gas bombardment of previous day. Enemy minutely Headquarters of battalions were sent from RUE du BOIS section, for a	

Army Form C. 2118.

WAR DIARY
or
INTELLIGENCE SUMMARY.
(Erase heading not required.)

Instructions regarding War Diaries and Intelligence Summaries are contained in F.S. Regs., Part II. and the Staff Manual respectively. Title pages will be prepared in manuscript.

Place	Date	Hour	Summary of Events and Information	Remarks and references to Appendices
CROIX DU BAC	22/7/17		Brigade Headquarters and bombarded it heavily during the evening. Several officers were wounded and had to be evacuated. Captain R.B. Stspand R.A.M.G.S.R. was admitted to Field Ambulance, suffering from N.Y.D.N. and was evacuated to Hospital. Just before midnight enemy aeroplanes came over the back area but dispersed. Officer Commanding 2/3rd Wessex Field Ambulance wrote to A.D.M.S. that his Advanced Dressing Station in ARMENTIERES was being very badly shelled. The Advanced Dressing Station at RUE de MESSINES having had several direct hits. This had to be given up and the party moved to the Cellars at the Institut St JUDE.	
	23/7/17		Directly after midnight enemy aeroplanes returned and dropped 7 bombs just behind the village of BAC St MAUR, very close to river banks, one burst on river trawler less than 10 feet from the BAC St MAUR Bridge, another fell just on Divisional Ordnance Store, penetrating the officers quarters, a third fell on a barge in river causing damage to the barge and two casualties, one died almost immediately, the second was brought to Hospital and remained to special hospital for wounded soldiers, other bombs fell in the open and did no damage. A/A.D.M.S went to LE NOUVEAU MONDE to preside of a Medical Board on two men. Letter received from D.M.S. enclosing D.M.S. instruction to nominate	

Army Form C. 2118.

WAR DIARY
or
INTELLIGENCE SUMMARY.
(Erase heading not required.)

Instructions regarding War Diaries and Intelligence Summaries are contained in F. S. Regs., Part II. and the Staff Manual respectively. Title pages will be prepared in manuscript.

Place	Date	Hour	Summary of Events and Information	Remarks and references to Appendices
CROIX DU BAC HQ	23-7-17		3 Medical Officers to be ready at 24 hours notice to go wherever required. Captains Penn-Molton, Pindar, and Robinson nominated. IADMS and Captain Gibbs RAMCF visited Advanced Dressing Station at HOUPLINES, to see Medical Officer who complained of heavy bombardment and that his area was being tracked by heavy gunners, to make a shot cut with ammunition. The town of ARMENTIERES was badly shelled all day with heavy material. Gas still hanging about. This Medical Officer of CHAPELLE d'ARMENTIERE had to evacuate this building and go to the BRICKFIELD. Very large fire was noted at STEENWERCK at night and one in ARMENTIERES.	
	24-7-17		Very quiet day. Hot and sunny. Kaye all rounds making airship trial. No aircraft at work. Captain S.R. GIBBS finished course of instruction and reported to Officer Commanding 3/2nd West Lancs Field Ambulance to relieve Captain Cameron at LA CROIX LES CORNEZ. Lieut Col BROOK reported back to the 57th Division as Officer Commanding 2/3rd Wessex Field Ambulance. Lieut Col PARSONS returned to his own unit and handed over the duties of ADMS to Lieut Col BROOK. During the day enemy bombarded the back areas of the RUE de BOIS Section with gas shells of the new type, as winds are finding an HRMENTIERES. There is apparently a delayed action and it	

WAR DIARY
or
INTELLIGENCE SUMMARY.
(Erase heading not required.)

Army Form C. 2118.

Place	Date	Hour	Summary of Events and Information	Remarks and references to Appendices
CROIX DU BAC	24.7.17		The men suffered from sore eyes in dugouts in one place and felt no effects, while they were sound for their breakfast according to their own story. Later in the evening a telephone message was received from VI Corps to detail two Medical Officers for duty with the 5th ARMY. These to be found at the offices of A.D.M.S. 57th Division (G.12.a.9.9.) at 10 a.m. and received by Motor-ambulance at the Division to Headquarters 5th Army by two officers from 2nd Division. The two officers Captain NEILSON and Captain JAMES from 2nd Division, and Captains PINDER and WILLIAMS from 57th Division were detailed. There were 115 Casualties from the gas attack.	
	25.7.17		The two Medical Officers from 2nd Division and Captains PINDER and WILLIAMS departed from A.D.M.S. offices at 12.15 p.m. for 2nd ARMY. Lieut Col. PARSONS lunched at a Board convened by D.D.M.S. VI Corps. at ZELOBES, on two men of 1/5th West Riding Regt. to the Corps Employment Coy. at DARWIN who stood in Category A. Lieut Col PARSONS and the DADMS visited the 51st and 54th Casualty Clearing Stations to inquire into after effects on patients gassed in two bombardments by the enemy. The Officers Commanding of the Casualty Clearing Stations were found at the Stations evacuating all the cases of gas poisoning under instructions from	

Army Form C. 2118.

WAR DIARY
or
INTELLIGENCE SUMMARY.
(Erase heading not required.)

Place	Date	Hour	Summary of Events and Information	Remarks and references to Appendices
CROIX DU BAC	25.7.17		DMS. strong. The accuracy does not appear to be unsuccessful. Numbers appear to recover in 72 hours and thus relapse. The A/ADMS visited 2/3rd Wessex Field St Ambulances, and the DDMS visited stables of 413th Wessex and 3/2nd West Lancs Field St Ambulances. The northerly Brigade in front of ARMENTIERES carried out a raid on the enemy trenches. No words get of the night, our casualties all appear to have been in rear area. Lieut. ? Quartermaster BETHANY, 2/7th Kings Liverpool Regt., interviewed and recommended by A/ADMS. recommended to be transferred to BASE for Medical Board.	
	26.7.17		A/ADMS and DDMS visited all the Field St Ambulances Stations in the ARMENTIERES Section, and the Regimental Aid Posts. The town of ARMENTIERES had been badly shelled for some time and during the previous night. The house on the RUE de LILLE which had been used as an Advanced Dressing Station was visited, also the BRICKFIELD which is now being used as Advanced Dressing Station. This action of the Medical Officer in shifting from RUE de LILLE and leaving only one man to hold it was approved. The difficulty of the Advanced Dressing Station at BRICKFIELD is that it may easily be cut off from ingress and egress by shellfire, though the building itself is very good and capable of withstanding very heavy shellfire.	
	27.7.17		The A/ADMS visited DDMS at HINGES.	

WAR DIARY
or
INTELLIGENCE SUMMARY.
(Erase heading not required.)

Army Form C. 2118.

Place	Date	Hour	Summary of Events and Information	Remarks and references to Appendices
CROIX DU BAC	27.7.17		with regards to cases of dysentery and gas. Report asked for from Medical Officer in charge 2/4th N.LAN.Regt. D.A.D.M.S. visited the stables of the 3/2nd West Lancs Field Ambulance, and found the standings not in the condition required. A great deal of work had been done to improve them, but only small parts had been reset. The flooring floor uneven and likely to give trouble again very soon.	
	28.7.17		A/A.D.M.S. visited Field Ambulances, and interviewed G.O.C., D.A.D.M.S. visited the Advanced Dressing Station, LA CROIX LESGORNEZ, and the Regimental Aid Post at EATON HALL to see Medical Officer in charge 2/4 Loyal North Lancs Regt. in regard to 3 cases of dysentery. Water supply has been in use by considerable numbers of other troops. Report received from Medical Officer. These men were resevent in a draft on 14th instant and evacuated to hospital on 15th and 16th instant. D.A.D.M.S. visited stables in back areas. Considerable enemy artillery activity in ARMENTIERES. Early morning raid carried out by 2/5 Loyal North Lancs Regt., which had no casualties, no enemy seen.	
	29.7.17		2/4th Loyal North Lancs Regt. carried out a raid on enemy trenches, and surprised an enemy raiding party in no mans land. Hand to hand fighting ensued. Our	

WAR DIARY or INTELLIGENCE SUMMARY

Army Form C. 2118.

Place	Date	Hour	Summary of Events and Information	Remarks and references to Appendices
CROIX DU BAC.	29-7-17		Casualties 1 Officer and 37 other ranks, all returned to our lines. Enemy lefts 3 wounded prisoners in our hands, 2 of whom have since died. Enemy bombarded ARMENTIERES billeting area with gas shells in early morning. Four periods of 15 minutes each, shells rifted to two at the rate of 120 per minute. Bombardment very intense also high-explosives and shrapnel. The St Dorneds Dressing Station at ST JUDE was used as a collecting place for all cases, who were afterwards evacuated by Motor Ambulance Cars, and by motor lorry. The enemy shelled the town very persistently all day with shrapnel and high explosive. The main object of this bombardment seemed to be the RUE SADI CARNOT and immediate neighbourhood. The Brigade Headquarters at ARMENTIERES was inside the circle of bombardment and could not be reached on foot between the hours of 2 and 3·30 p.m. The St Dorneds Dressing Station at ST JUDE funds 600 cars through before 2 p.m. Lastly slight but going were leisurely. This afternoon to his same cars as used in previous attack on the night of July 20th and 21st. The St Dorneds Dressing Station at ST JUDE received a direct hit during the late afternoon. The casualties up to midnight were 47 officers, 1023 other ranks, and 187 civilians. DDMS visited Advanced Dressing Stations ST JUDE, and the new	

Army Form C. 2118.

WAR DIARY
or
INTELLIGENCE SUMMARY.
(Erase heading not required.)

Instructions regarding War Diaries and Intelligence Summaries are contained in F. S. Regs., Part II. and the Staff Manual respectively. Title pages will be prepared in manuscript.

Place	Date	Hour	Summary of Events and Information	Remarks and references to Appendices
CROIX DU BAC	29-7-17		Dressing Station Sick cases were evacuated by Motor Ambulances Cars, except 120 evacuated to LE NOUVEAU MONDE.	
	30-7-17	9 a.m.	Total casualties 47 Officers, 1064 other ranks, 804 Divisional 254 Corps attached. ARMENTIERES bombarded with gas shells again early morning. St JUDE hit by high explosive shells. The ADMS returned from leave, most of morning spent in getting in touch with work of two days during which he was away. In the afternoon the ADMS and the DADMS visited the Advanced Dressing Station St JUDE, which was being very badly shelled. Civilians there had a large number of casualties, 287 on previous day. The institute St JUDE was shelled several times during the afternoon, and had to be evacuated during the evening. During the day 233 people were evacuated from ARMENTIERES including 72 civilians. The night was comparatively quiet on ARMENTIERES. The ADMS and DADMS visited the St branches Dressing Station during the afternoon, and the 54? Casualty Clearing Station. 2nd and 4 Divisions attached on our north.	
	31-7-17		Everywhere fairly quiet. The Field Ambulances not so busy. It was able to keep in touch with the Advanced Dressing Stations at HOUPLINES and	

Army Form C. 2118.

WAR DIARY
or
INTELLIGENCE SUMMARY.
(Erase heading not required.)

Instructions regarding War Diaries and Intelligence Summaries are contained in F. S. Regs., Part II. and the Staff Manual respectively. Title pages will be prepared in manuscript.

Place	Date	Hour	Summary of Events and Information	Remarks and references to Appendices
CROIX DU BAC	31-7-17		The BRICKFIELD, one motor ambulance defaced by shell fire. Still a large number of troops being evacuated from ARMENTIERES, though the numbers have fallen off considerably	
			.... Colonel. A. Med. S.	
			A.D.M.S. 57th (W.L.) Division,	

Secret A

57th DIVISION
R.A.M.C. Operation Order No. 10.

Copy No. 15

Reference Map Sheet 36 - 1/40,000.

1. The 2/3rd Wessex Field Ambulance will take over the Main Dressing Station at ERQUINGHEM (H.4.d.1.5.), Advanced Dressing Stations at HOUPLINES (C.26.d.5.9.) and Rue de Lille, ARMENTIERES (I.1.d.5.8.) from 2/2nd Wessex Field Ambulance on Friday 6th July, 1917.

2. The 2/3rd Wessex Field Ambulance will detail a holding party to take over from the 2/2nd Wessex Field Ambulance at the RUE DE MESSINES (C.19.c.1.1.) and the MATERNITE HOSPITAL (B.30.c.6.3.) Friday 6th July 1917.

3. The 2/2nd Wessex Field Ambulance will take over from the 2/3rd Wessex Field Ambulance the Main Dressing Station at FORT ROMPU (H.7.d.6.3.), Advanced Dressing Stations at BOIS GRENIER (H.24.d.5.0.) and LA CROIX LESCORNEZ (H.26.c.8.4.) and Car Collecting Post at PORT A CLOUS (H.21.a.3.8.) on Friday 6th July, 1917.

4. Advance parties will proceed on Thursday the 5th July 1917.

5. Details to be arranged direct between commanding officers concerned.

6. The Transport will not move from their present locations.

7. Moves to be completed by 6.0 p.m.

8. Completion of moves to be notified to this office by wire.

9. ACKNOWLEDGE.

Headquarters,
4th July, 1917.

Colonel, A. Med. S.,
A.D.M.S., 57th Division.

Issued at 6.15 p.m.

Distribution :-

Copy No. 1 to H.Q. 57th Division.
2. -do-
3. O.C. 2/2nd Wessex Fd.Amb.
4. O.C. 2/3rd Wessex Fd.Amb.
5. O.C. 3/2nd W.Lan. Fd.Amb.
6. D.D.M.S. Xl Corps.
7. H.Q. 170th Infantry Bde.
8. H.Q. 171st Infantry Bde.
9. H.Q. 172nd Infantry Bde.
10. C.R.E. 57th Division
11. C.R.A. 57th Division.
12. O.C. 57th Divl.Signal Co.
13. O.C. 57th Divl.Train.
14. O.C. No. 2 M.A.C.

Copy No. 15 War Diary
16 War Diary
17 File
18 Spare
19 Spare.

SECRET.   **57th DIVISION.**   Copy No. 15.

R.A.M.C. Operation Order No.11.
****
Reference Map Sheet 36 –
1/40,000.

1. The 3/2nd West Lancs. Field Ambulance will take over the Main Dressing Station at FORT ROMPU (H.7.d.6.3.), Advanced Dressing Stations at BOIS GRENIER (H24.d.5.0.) and LA CROIX LESCORNEZ (H26.c.8.4.) and Car Collecting Post at PORT A CLOUS (H21.a,3,8.) from 2/2nd Wessex Field Ambulance on Wednesday 11th July, 1917.

2. The 2/2nd Wessex Field Ambulance will take over the quarters at present occupied by 3/2nd West Lancs. Field Ambulance at LE NOUVEAU MONDE (G.27.c.3.2.) on Wednesday 11th July, 1917.

3. The 2/2nd Wessex Field Ambulance will commence training on Thursday, 12th July, 1917.

4. Advance Parties will proceed on Tuesday, the 10th July, 1917.

5. Details to be arranged direct between the Commanding Officers concerned.

6. Moves to be completed by 6.0 p.m.

7. Completion of moves to be notified to this Office by wire.

8. ACKNOWLEDGE.

Headquarters,
8th July, 1917.

Colonel, A. Med. S.,
A.D.M.S., 57th Division.

Issued at 9-0 p.m.

Distribution :-

Copy No.	1	to H.Q. 57th Division.	Copy No.	15	War Diary.
	2	-do-		16	War Diary.
	3	O.C. 2/2nd Wessex Fd.Amb.		17	File.
	4	O.C. 2/3rd Wessex Fd.Amb.		18	Spare.
	5	O.C. 3/2nd W.Lan. Fd.Amb.		19	Spare.
	6	D.D.M.S. XI Corps.			
	7	H.Q. 170th Infantry Bde.			
	8	H.Q. 171st Infantry Bde.			
	9	H.Q. 172nd Infantry Bde.			
	10	C.R.E. 57th Division.			
	11	C.R.A. 57th Division.			
	12	O.C. 57th Divl.Signal Co.			
	13	O.C. 57th Divl.Train.			
	14	O.C. No. 2 M.A.C.			

C

MATTERS RECEIVING ATTENTION BY THE A.D.M.S., 57th DIVN. 9th JULY 1917.

1. Perusal of A.F's.A.36 for week ending 7th July. (2/3 Wx.& 3/2 W.L.F.A.
2. Perusal of yesterday's Orders, Intelligence Summaries, &c.
3. Letter regd. accum. of stores in Cas. Clg. Stations.
4. Letter regarding work and duties of Sect. of F.Amb. at Zelobes.
5. War Diary. Entry for July 8th.
6. Plan of day's work.
7. Arrangements, Correspondence, &c. discussed with D.A.D.M.S.
8. Primus Stoves from Brit. Red Cross Society for R.A.Posts.
9. R.A.M.C. men for Water Duties for 172 Mach. Gun Coy. Letters.
10. Medical Equipment--Dressings, &c. for 172 Machine Gun Coy. Letter.
11. Arrangements and room for P.B.Board tomorrow. Letter.
12. Medical Attendance and Equipment for 170th Bde. School.
13. Letter redg. conference at Bethune on 11th regarding San. Sect. work.
14. Perusal and scrutiny of Divl. Sick Evac. Return, and Daily States
    (A.F.W 3185) sent to D.M.S., D.D.M.S., & Divl. Hdqrs.
15. Letters. Case of Ent. F. in 2/6 K.L'pool Regt.
16. Med. & sanit. arrangements for Portuguese troops in Divl. area.
17. Transmission of eye cases in half car loads to Arques.
18. Capt. Williams, M.O. 2/9 K. 'pool Rgt. Migraine.
19. Third M.O. for P.B.Bd. at Erquinghem tomorrow.
20. Yesterday's casualties. No consid. increase from gas release operats.
21. Letter to O.C. 2/3 Wessex F.Amb. redg. requests for motor ambs. and
    map references.
22. Discussed question of closure of M.D.Stn. at Erquinghem as unsuitable
23. Retention of Officers with Vener. Diseases in M.D.Stns. of F.Ambs.
24. Operation Order No. 11. (Moves of 3/2 W.Lans. & 2/2 Wessex F.Ambs.)
    tomorrow.
25. Route march of 3/2 W.Lancs F.Amb. for today is cancelled owing to
    impending move of "B" Section.
26. Letter fr. Capt. Parkinson, evac. sick and now in London.
27. Letter on Chlorination. Circ. Memo. No. 40 issued with Army Orders
    to be called attention to in R.A.M.C. Orders.
28. Case of Capt. Race. Letter redg. to O.C. 2/2 Wx. F.Amb.
29. Distrib. of Wheeled Stretch Carriages. Letter to O.C. 2/2 Wx. F.Amb.
30. Interviewed D.A.A.G. redg. bad roads on motor amb. lines of evac.
31. Wrote out list of subjects for discussion with D.D.M.S. on 11th.
32. Car for O.C.Sanit. Section. Reasons against habitual granting of.
33. Note. Transport of wounded civilians to Hazebrouck and Poperinghe
    now very onerous.
34. Note redg. foul ditch at H 26 C 30-05.
35. Letter redg. verminous clothing issued at Divl. Baths.
36. Letters fr. M.O. i'c 2/10 K.L'pool Rgt. redg. shelling of his R.A.P.
37. Letter fr. M.O. i'c 2/5 K.L'pool Regt. redg. lending of stretcher bear
    bearers to adjoining units
38. Letter to O.C. 2/3 Wx. F.Amb. redg. requests for motor ambs.
39. Saw D.A.A.G. redg. gallant action by certain men in B Sect. 2/2 Wx.
    F.Amb.
40. Wrote D.D.M.S. redg. renewal of contract of T.C.R.A.M.C.Officers.
41. Wrote O's.C. Fd.Ambs. regd. duties of M.O's. i/c A.D.Stns.
42. Interviewed Pte. Willoughby, 2/3 Wx.F.Amb. candidate for Commission.
43. Wrote regarding verminour clothing at 172nd. Bde. School.
44. Visited Divl. Baths. Saw inspection of men for scabies.
45. Ditto. Examined underclothing being issued for vermin. (Dead only.)
46. Letter to F.Amb. Commanders redg. disposal of surplus instruments
    and dressings.
47. Letter to D.D.M.S. redg. motor amb. for O.C.San. Section.
48. Saw A.A.& Q.M.G. regd. rewards for acts of gallantry.
49. Ditto redg. lice on clothing issued at Divl. Baths.
50. Wrote F.Amb. O.'s.C. redg. Double Cyanide Guaze, Stretcher pillows an
    and surplus instruments.
51. Drafted letter to D.D.M.S. on self-inflicted v. accidental wounds
    and transfer to Special Penal Hospital.
52. Discussion with A.A. & Q.M.G. & D.A.Q.M.G. regarding use of the
    transport of med. units on general duties.
53. Discussion with A.A. & Q.M.G. redg. unsuitable place for M.D.Stn. at
    Erquinghem.
54. Signing of correspondence and perusal of new evening cdspce.
55. Letter fr. M.O.i/c 2/4 S.Lan. R. regarding Sanitary squad & pioneers.
56. Read today's Intelligence Summaries, &c.
57. Letter regarding return of Capt. Aspinall fr. Base.   /Powder.
58. Enquiry fr. M.O. i/c 285 Bde.R.F.A. redg. Lice prevention & N.C.I.
59. Enquiry regarding prevention of mosquiot   os & treatment of m. bites.

SECRET

Copy No. 15

57th DIVISION

R.A.M.C. OPERATION ORDER No. 12.

Reference Map Sheet 36 – 1/40,000.

1. The 2/3rd Wessex Field Ambulance will take over Main Dressing Station at FORT ROMPU (H.7.d.3.3.) from 3/2nd West Lancs. Field Ambulance on Tuesday, 17th July, 1917.

2. The 3/2nd West Lancs. Field Ambulance will establish Main Dressing Station at SAILLY (G.17.a.8.4.).

3. The Advanced Dressing Stations at BOIS GRENIER (H.24.d.5.0.) and LA CROIX LESCORNEZ (H.26.c.8.4.) will evacuate to Main Dressing Station at SAILLY (G.17.a.8.4.)

4. The Advanced Dressing Stations at HOUPLINES (C.26.d.5.9.) RUE DE LILLE, ARMENTIERES (I.1.d.5.8.) and RUE DE MESSINES (C.19.c.1.1.) will evacuate to Main Dressing Station FORT ROMPU (H.7.d.3.3.)

5. Advance parties will proceed on Monday 16th July, 1917.

6. Details to be arranged direct between Commanding Officers concerned.

7. Moves to be completed by 6.0 p.m.

8. Completion of moves to be notified to this office by wire.

9. ACKNOWLEDGE.

Headquarters,
16th July, 1917.

Colonel, A.Med.S.,
A.D.M.S., 57th Division.

Issued at........2.30....p.m.

```
Copy No. 1 to H.Q. 57th Division.
        2        do.
        3     O.C. 2/2nd Wessex Fd.Amb.
        4     O.C. 2/3rd Wessex Fd.Amb.
        5     O.C. 3/2nd West Lan.Fd.Amb.
        6     D.D.M.S. Xl Corps.
        7     H.Q. 170 Infantry Brigade.
        8     H.Q. 171st Infantry Brigade.
        9     H.Q. 172nd Infantry Brigade.
       10     C.R.E., 57th Division.
       11     C.R.A. 57th Division.
       12     O.C. 57th Divl. Signal Coy.
       13     O.C. 57th Divl.Train A.S.C.
       14     O.C. No.2.M.A.C.
       15     War Diary
       16     War Diary
       17     File
       18     Spare
       19.    Spare.
```

CONFIDENTIAL.

WAR DIARY.

OF A.D.M.S. 54TH DIVISION

from 1st August 1917 to 31st August 1917.

(VOLUME I.)

Army Form C. 2118.

WAR DIARY
or
INTELLIGENCE SUMMARY.
(Erase heading not required.)

Instructions regarding War Diaries and Intelligence Summaries are contained in F.S. Regs., Part II. and the Staff Manual respectively. Title pages will be prepared in manuscript.

Place	Date	Hour	Summary of Events and Information	Remarks and references to Appendices
CROIX DU BAC	1/8/14		In and last night 5th Division had 31 wounded. Artillery bombardment of ARMENTIERES moderating. Saw G.O.C. regarding O.C. 2/9 K'pool R. transferred to Base as unfit for service at the front. Total wounded 5th Division July = 1695. Wounded in MARCH = 166 APRIL " = 228 MAY " = 312 JUNE " = 622 JULY " = 1695	
			Visited Divisional Baths and Main Dressing Station of 31/2nd Wares Field Ambulance at SAILLY. Two Battalions viz. 1st LEICESTERSHIRE Regt. and 9th NORFOLK Regt. temporarily attached to 6 Division. 141st and 140th Brigades exchanging together thus:- 191 / 192 to 192 / 190 190 / 191	
	2/8/14		Visited Baths at SAILLY where MO i/c 2/5th to 2/6th K'pool Rgt. (less than 1000 left between both) inspecting men. Only 6 found other than quite fit. Visited M.D.S. 2/2nd Wessex Field Ambulance LE NOUVEAU MONDE.	

T2134. Wt. W708—776. 50000. 4/15. Sir J. C. & S.

Army Form C. 2118.

WAR DIARY
OR
INTELLIGENCE SUMMARY.
(Erase heading not required.)

Place	Date	Hour	Summary of Events and Information	Remarks and references to Appendices
CROIX DU BAC	3/9/18		Visited Advanced Dressing Station at NOUVEL HOUPLINES, walking from ARMENTIERES owing to wreckage littering the streets. The Advanced Dressing Station has been hit several times but is still quite habitable and indeed in fairly good order. Streets strewn with wreckage and blocked in many places by debris and shell craters. It is estimated that the enemy put 30,000 H.E. and gas shells into ARMENTIERES on 29th and 30th July. Many civilians still in the town; but large numbers were wounded in these days. 4/5th N. Lan R. were entering ARMENTIERES and filing to billets there - chiefly in cellars - this afternoon. I tried to get to Advanced Dressing Station at BRICKFIELD, but could not find any road not blocked by debris except for foot passengers. Visited Main Dressing Stations of 2/3 WESSEX and 3/2nd W. LANCS. FIELD AMBULANCES and Advanced Dressing Station of latter at LA CROIX RESCORNEZ. Reported from ETAPLES that many cases of Dysentery there. DDMS. XI Corps called and saw DADMS regarding extension and improvement of Main Dressing Stations at SAILLY and LE NOUVEAU MONDE. Heavy and continuous, or almost continuous rains	

WAR DIARY
INTELLIGENCE SUMMARY.
(Erase heading not required.)

Army Form C. 2118.

Place	Date	Hour	Summary of Events and Information	Remarks and references to Appendices
CROIX DU BAC	4/8/14		The last three days have rested the muddy conditions of last spring. Visited IV Corps Headquarters and submitted many points of administrative detail to DDMS. Corps Commander wishes 2/2nd WESSEX and 2/2nd W LANCS FIELD AMBULANCES with Main Dressing Stations at LE NOUVEAU MONDE and SAILLY to commence to make plans, roads &c. with a view to Conversion of their Main Dressing Stations into Corps Main Dressing Stations. DADMS visited Advanced Dressing Stations at BOIS GRENIER and Regimental Aid Posts FLAMENGRIE SUBSECTION (Subsidiary line) and EPINETTE SUBSECTION (SQUARE FARM) especially with regard to gas precautions. He also inspected Advanced Dressing Station of RUE DE BOIS SUBSECTION at FERME DESCOBANQUE which is rapidly giving way owing to rains &c.	
	5/8/14		DADMS visited ETAPLES and saw men evacuated recently gassed from 57th Division and Divisional Area. 980 cases admitted from Divisional Area to hospitals in ETAPLES. 3 or 4 deaths. Many mild cases, with eyes only affected, were doing well. Many who had eyes bandaged up. 52 Officers (from 57th Divisional Area) had been	

WAR DIARY
INTELLIGENCE SUMMARY.

Army Form C. 2118.

Place	Date	Hour	Summary of Events and Information	Remarks and references to Appendices
CROIX DU BAC	5/8/17 (Contd)		evacuated. Two cases were bad with laryngitis or bronchitis. Fatal cases showed gangrene of larynx or lung. Worst parts of skin mostly affected. Visited Advanced Dressing Station at LA CROIX LESCORNEZ and Main Dressing Station at SAILLY. CAPTAIN PLUMLEY, A.D.G. R.A.M.C. T.C. arrived as supplement and was posted to 2/2 WESSEX FIELD AMBULANCE. This makes fourth new Medical Officer since 30th July :- Captain H.P. HARPUR, Lieut. H.A. HALL, Lieut. P.A. HALL and Captain A.D.G. PLUMLEY. Owing to departure of Lieut. CLARKE, time expired, and evacuation of Captain ROBINSON and Captain PRACY (gassed) the Division is still, today, five Medical Officers short of establishment.	
	6/8/17		Last night, bombs dropped on 171st Brigade Headquarters near FLEURBAIX and at other places in neighborhood Brigade Major 171st Infantry Brigade, and 1 Clerk killed and five others wounded, only one Severely. We had about 15 casualties from enemy gas in ÉPINETTE SUBSECTION. Visited all Main Dressing Stations nightlying employment	

WAR DIARY
or
INTELLIGENCE SUMMARY.
(Erase heading not required.)

Army Form C. 2118.

Place	Date	Hour	Summary of Events and Information	Remarks and references to Appendices
CROIX DU BAC	6/8/19 (Contd.)		of men, distribution of ambulance cars to best advantage and other matters. Also visited 51. CASUALTY CLEARING STATION, MERVILLE. When saw recent and old (8 days) gassed cases - some gravely ill - and shell wound cases. Visited Advanced Dressing Station at LA CROIX LESCORNEZ and also Regimental Aid Post at EATON HALL. Saw Medical Officer i/c 2/8th K/ Pool Rest. established there. Elephant 'dug out' (entirely above ground) just commenced to be erected for R.A.M.C. Bearers stationed there.	
	7/8/19		New Regimental Aid Posts to be constructed at WELLINGTON and SHAFTESBURY AVENUES under authority D.G.M.S. Medical Officer is no longer on establishment of Divisional Train. D.A.D.M.S. visited Headquarters 285th BRIGADE R.F.A.	
	8/8/19		D.A.D.M.S. visited R.A.P's in FLAMENGRIE and RUE DE BOIS Subsectors. One Battalion of PORTUGUESE was held front line in BOUTILLERIE Subsector. Torrential rain in evening.	
	9/9/19		Saw three R.A.M.C. Candidates for commissions. Discussed many points of water supply, sanitary construction &c with O.C. 49th Sanitary Section	

WAR DIARY
or
INTELLIGENCE SUMMARY.
(Erase heading not required.)

Army Form C. 2118.

Place	Date	Hour	Summary of Events and Information	Remarks and references to Appendices
CROIX DU BAC	9/5/19 (Contd)		Whose area now includes that of the 51st Division. Lieut. L.M. GABLE, United States Medical Corps arrived for duty and medical training with this Division and was attached to 2/2nd Wessex Field Ambulance. D.A.D.M.S. inspected water carts of 295th Brigade R.F.A. During the last 19 days (July 22nd – 9th August inclusive) 163 Officers and 1562 Other Ranks have been admitted to Field Ambulances of this Division suffering from Gas Poisoning, the maximum number in one day being 43 Officers and 1042 Other Ranks on July 30th. Most of these cases were gassed by "Yellow Cross" Gas Shell which contains a compressed gas that has dischanotic action on conjunctiva (including corneal), pharynx, larynx, and bronchial tubes and causes dermatitis. Lt.Col. Q.M.S. JONES, R.A.M.C. (Senior Centre in Officer) visited Main Dressing Stations of all three Medical Units regarding returns, back transport returns of Dressing Stations, immunisation of feaces, &c.	
	10/5/19		D.M.S. First Army (Surg. Genl. H.N. THOMPSON) with D.A.D.M.S. First Army and D.D.M.S. XI Corps visited and inspected Main Dressing Stations	

WAR DIARY or INTELLIGENCE SUMMARY

Army Form C. 2118.

Place	Date	Hour	Summary of Events and Information	Remarks and references to Appendices
CROIX DU BAC	10/9/14 (contd)		At all three Field Ambulances of this Division and Advanced Dressing Stations at LA CROIX LESCORNEZ and BOIS GRENIER. Present also ADMS and DADMS. He chiefly dwelt on sanitary arrangements, supervision and provision of drugs, use of Thomas's Splints and training of personnel.	
	11/9/14		Running horses of Field Ambulances now to be reduced from 11 to 5. He by withdrawn living Horses of the Field Ambulances to Brigade Horsing & instead of Medical Officers centred Medical Units they are now to be Medical Officers commissioned Officers then replaced by a temporary Commissioned Officer. Information received that 10 Lines of Communication return Maharin (Primary) had occurred in troops of 6th Division (b un 140th Infantry Brigade) CORDONNERIE Subsection. DADMS visited Advanced Dressing Station	
	12/9/14		With Officer Commanding 2/3rd Wessex Field Ambulance visited Advanced Dressing Station BRICKWORK which has been much under Shellfire during the past three or four weeks. DADMS visited Advanced Dressing Station LA CROIX LESCORNEZ, Regimental Aid Post EATON HALL YM.O. rd. 1/25th K. L'pool Regt. regarding Undeana, and Main Dressing Station.	

Army Form C. 2118.

WAR DIARY
or
INTELLIGENCE SUMMARY.
(Erase heading not required.)

Place	Date	Hour	Summary of Events and Information	Remarks and references to Appendices
CROIX DU BAC	12/8/14 (contd)		3/2nd Wessex Field Ambulance, SAILLY. Projection cars are to be collected on Wednesdays for this Division and go to No. 4 Stationary Hospital, ARQUES, by Motor Ambulance Convoy Cars each Thursday.	
	13/8/14		Capt A BEVAN RAMC arrived from 54th Casualty Clearing Station for duty in front line for a fortnight. He is to go to take medical charge of the 2/5th N. Lan R. in motor to the Captain McKENZIE for 10 days to train Water Duties Corporals. Captain McKENZIE came to office to hear about Scheme of training. Captain CREGAN Sgt, RAMC attached Divisional R.E. awarded Military Cross for gallant and distinct conduct on ARMENTIÈRES on 29th and 30th July. Discussion (with DADMS) regarding advisability of retaining BRICKFIELD, near ARMENTIÈRES as Advanced Dressing Station seeing that Observation Post was about to be established thereby. Decided in favour of its retention meantime. Letter from Medical Officer, 2/10th K L'pool R., regarding unsatisfactory state of Advanced Dressing Station in Rue de Bois. Submission (r. WELLINGTON AVENUE)	

WAR DIARY
or
INTELLIGENCE SUMMARY.
(Erase heading not required.)

Army Form C. 2118.

Place	Date	Hour	Summary of Events and Information	Remarks and references to Appendices
CROIX DU BAC	13/8/17 (contd)		and regarding sanitation of ERQUINGHEM. Visited Divisional Baths and Sock Cty Disinfector (which has today gone to Workshop). Visited Main Dressing Station of 3/2 Wares Field Ambulance at SAILLY and inspected latrines, horses etc very fully. G.O.C. later, inspected Main Dressing Station of 3/0th Wessex Field Ambulance at LE NOUVEAU MONDE and especially baths and horses and expressed great satisfaction with all. DADMS visited Advanced Dressing Station, BOIS GRENIER; Regimental Aid Post FLAMENGRIE Subsection; Regimental Aid Post RUE DE BOIS Subsection at WELLINGTON AVENUE, BRICKFIELD. which huts and Johes therein; and Advanced Dressing Station BRICKFIELD. which huts and Johes emerated through LA VESSE only to roads having been broken up by shell fire.	
	14/8/17		Visited Advanced Dressing Station BOIS GRENIER, with Officer Commanding 3/2nd Wares Field Ambulance. Meeting in Office of Medical Officers i/c Troops in back area with view of readjustment of work. Discussed Sanitation of ERQUINGHEM with Medical Officer i/c 2/0th W/1000th R.	

WAR DIARY
INTELLIGENCE SUMMARY.
(Erase heading not required.)

Army Form C. 2118.

Place	Date	Hour	Summary of Events and Information	Remarks and references to Appendices
CROIX DU BAC	14/8/19 (contd)		Discussed with A.A. & Q.M.G. question of award of Military Crosses to Captain COSTELLO. D.D.M.S. came and talked over many matters. D.A.D.M.S. visited 3/2nd Wessex Field Ambulance Main Dressing Station.	
	15/8/19		Fog continuing track of broken showery weather. D.A.D.M.S. visited Advanced Dressing Station HOUPLINES and Regimental Aid Post TISSAGE DUMP. A.D.M.S. & G.O.C. inspected Main Dressing Station, horse lines and horses of 2/3rd (Wessex) Field Ambulance at FORT ROMPU in afternoon.	
	16/8/19		Routine inspections. Much being done to improve Main Dressing Station at SAILLY (3/2nd Wessex Field Ambulance) and to increase the accommodation there. XI Corps Commander presented Decorations and Medals at Divisional Headquarters this afternoon including Military Cross to Captain G.T. CREGAN RAMC attached Royal Engineers, Military Medal to Private ASLATT, 2/3rd Wessex Field Ambulance. Sergt. BOLT who also has been awarded the Military Medal has gone home to Cadet School.	

Army Form C. 2118.

WAR DIARY
or
INTELLIGENCE SUMMARY.
(Erase heading not required.)

Instructions regarding War Diaries and Intelligence Summaries are contained in F. S. Regs., Part II. and the Staff Manual respectively. Title pages will be prepared in manuscript.

Place	Date	Hour	Summary of Events and Information	Remarks and references to Appendices
CROIX DU BAC	14/9/17		Visited Reinforcement Camp and inspected all quarters. Accommodation for Officers very limited. Visited Field Ambulances in connection with return of surplus stretchers. Visited Divisional Baths regarding RAMC men employed there.	
	17/9/17		Visited DDMS XI Corps at Corps Headquarters regarding distribution of Medical Officers as shewn in weekly return, weekly tables of sickness, storage of dressings, change of personnel at Advanced Dressing Stations and sundry similar points. DADMS visited Advanced Dressing Station at BOIS GRENIER, Regimental Aid Post in course of construction at SHAFTESBURY AVENUE (FLAMENGRIE Subsection) and Main Dressing Station 3/2nd (Wales) Field Ambulance. ADMS interviewed A/CRE regarding enlargement of Advanced Dressing Station at LA CROIX LESCORNEZ and refuse pit and the construction of roads at all three Main Dressing Stations. Lieut. BEVAN, RAMC, lent to 59th Division for fortnight, was ordered to report	
	19/9/17		for duty with GUARDS DIVISION. He left today. I was disturbed that cases gassed on 20-21st July. In very many instances, have	

WAR DIARY
or
INTELLIGENCE SUMMARY.
(Erase heading not required.)

Army Form C. 2118.

Place	Date	Hour	Summary of Events and Information	Remarks and references to Appendices
CROIX DU BAC	19/8/14 (Contd.)		that had had secondary effects and that most cases have gone to ENGLAND. Visited Main Dressing Stations at FORT ROMPU and SAILLY, and Advanced Dressing Stations at LA CROIX LESCORNEZ &c. D.A.D.M.S. visited Advanced Dressing Station at BOIS GRENIER and FLAMENGRIE and RUE DE BOIS Subsections Regimental Aid Posts.	
	20/8/14		Visited all Main Dressing Stations & Field Ambulances. Spending 2½ hrs at LE NOUVEAU MONDE and seeing everything in detail especially transport. All in good order except for wurval, grease-traps and the like which require to be replaced.	
	21/8/14		Visited Main Dressing Stations especially regarding their roads. Selection of Medical Officers for submission as Medical Officer in Charge XI Corps School. Improvement of quarters &c. D.A.D.M.S. visited Posts and Dressing Stations of Right Subsection of 171st Brigade, 285th Brigade RFA, and Saw't Methead Officers. Move of Division into Training Area around BOMY "early in September" is announced.	

Army Form C. 2118.

WAR DIARY
or
INTELLIGENCE SUMMARY.
(Erase heading not required.)

Place	Date	Hour	Summary of Events and Information	Remarks and references to Appendices
CROIX DU BAC	22/8/14		Visited Divisional Reinforcement Camp, Divisional Baths and Main Dressing Stations at SAILLY and LE NOUVEAU MONDE. DADMS visited 285th Brigade RFA in connection with handing over medical charge of the Brigade temporarily to new Medical Officer. At night 9-10 pm enemy aeroplanes dropped 40 to 50 bombs in Divisional area. Nine casualties - two severe - in wagon lines of 285th Brigade RFA	
	23/8/14		Preparation commenced for arrangements of Office papers with a view to handing over to next Division. DDMS. XI Corps visited Main Dressing Station, LE NOUVEAU MONDE, expressing himself as still greatly dissatisfied with the Sanitary arrangements, the Main Dressing Station, SAILLY, where he commented favourably on marked improvements - horse standings and quarters generally; and Advanced Dressing Station, BOIS GRENIER with which he expressed himself as well pleased. Work of clearing out unrequired documents in Office being	

Army Form C. 2118.

WAR DIARY
or
INTELLIGENCE SUMMARY.
(Erase heading not required.)

Instructions regarding War Diaries and Intelligence Summaries are contained in F.S. Regs., Part II. and the Staff Manual respectively. Title pages will be prepared in manuscript.

Place	Date	Hour	Summary of Events and Information	Remarks and references to Appendices
CROIX DU BAC	23/8/17 (contd.) 24/8/17		actively proceeded with. Colonel C.S. WALLACE, consulting Surgeon 1st Army gave demonstration on use and application of THOMAS'S SPLINT at Main Dressing Station. LE NOUVEAU MONDE to Field Ambulance Commanders and Officers and other Ranks and Regimental Stretcher Bearers. Visited Advanced Dressing Station, BOIS GRENIER, Regimental Aid Post (FLAMENGRIE Subsector) and in Subsidiary line, new Regimental Aid Post in process of construction off SHAFTESBURY AVENUE, Bearer Post at WHITE CITY and Regimental Aid Post (RUE DE BOIS Subsector) at Wellington Avenue. The last Still very defective.	
	25/8/17		Routine. Preparations for move of Division to training area within a few weeks. Field Ambulances have their establishment now reduced to 8 Medical Officers in place of 9. 51st Division has to day 12 Medical Officers thus distributed:- Headquarters 1. 2. (A.D., & D.A.D.,M.S.) A/c R.A. & R.E.:- 4	

A6945 Wt. W11422/M1160 35,000 12/16 D. D. & L. Forms/C./2118/14.

Army Form C. 2118.

WAR DIARY
or
INTELLIGENCE SUMMARY.
(Erase heading not required.)

Place	Date	Hour	Summary of Events and Information	Remarks and references to Appendices
CROIX DU BAC	25/7/17 (Cont'd)		Distribution of M.O.s (continued).	
			I/c. Infantry 12	
			Main Dressing Stations - 2/2 Wessex Fd Amb. 3 (one does M.O. a/c Units)	
			2/3 Wessex Fd Amb. 4 (one does M.O. a/c Units)	
			3/2 Wanes Fd Amb. 3 (one does MO a/c Units)	
			Advanced Dressing Stations — 4	
			Rest — 5	
			Training — 1 (MO of USMC)	
			Temporarily with 5th Army — 2	
			At Dressing Station, ZELOBES — 2	
			The Dressing Station at ZELOBES receives sick and wounded of British Troops from the LA GORGUE Sector at present held by PORTUGUESE. The result is that there are at each Main Dressing Station a Field Ambulance Commander and 2 (or more case 3) other officers; one of whom in each case has medical charge of adjacent Units.	
	26/8/17		Visited Advanced Dressing Station, LA CROIX L'ESCORNEZ, and discussed details of extension with Medical Officer i/c (Major WILLIAMS) and	

WAR DIARY
or
INTELLIGENCE SUMMARY.

(Erase heading not required.)

Army Form C. 2118.

Place	Date	Hour	Summary of Events and Information	Remarks and references to Appendices
CROIX DU BAC	26/8/17 (contd.)		R.E. Officer (Lieut. GLADSTONE). Visited Regimental Aid Post, EATON HALL. Good. Spacious and intimately splinter-proof shelter for R.A.M.C. Bearers is being rapidly erected. R.A.M.C. personnel tents are to be directly under orders of Medical Officer at this Regimental Aid Post.	
	27/8/17		Hear that Regimental Aid Post, L'EPINETTE Subsection, heavily bombarded yesterday, so that Medical Officer thereat (Medical Officer i/c 2/5th N. Lan. Regt., Captain W.G. McKENZIE) had to move (as ordered by Officer Commanding his Unit) to Regimental Aid Post at AUCKLAND ROAD. D.A.D.M.S. in afternoon, visited Advanced Dressing Station at BRICKFIELD, CHAPELLE d'ARMENTIÈRES, Regimental Aid Post at SQUARE FARM, adjacent R.A.M.C. Posts, Regimental Aid Posts at AUCKLAND ROAD and TISSAGE DUMP and Advanced Dressing Station at HOUPLINES.	
	28/8/17		A.D.M.S. was present at minute and exhaustive inspection of transport of each Field Ambulance by Officer Commanding & Sgt. Inst. Tram. D.M.S. First Army foreshed at Conference of D.D.M.S. & A.D.M.S.	

WAR DIARY
INTELLIGENCE SUMMARY

Army Form C. 2118.

Place	Date	Hour	Summary of Events and Information	Remarks and references to Appendices
CROIX DU BAC	28/8/17 (Contd)		at No 33 Casualty Clearing Station, BETHUNE. He spoke on many topics particularly contribution of men from R.A.M.C to Infantry, "combing out" of men for Infantry from other sources, the duties and responsibilities of A.D's.M.S.; the distribution of "Thomas" Splints in Regimental Aid Posts and Dressing Stations; the measures to be taken against mosquitoes and the return made to G.H.Q. by each Medical Officer in the Expeditionary force. Captain H.S. GASKELL was today transferred for duty from 3/2nd West Lancs Field Ambulance to 57" Casualty Clearing Station and Captain D.F. HUNTER sent from that Casualty Clearing Station to replace him.	
	29/8/17		Steps from XI Corps that now Medical Boards are to be held in every area to examine M.T. A.S.C. men, men in Entrenching Companies, &c., to see if they cannot be categorised as "A". Attended meeting at D.D.M.S. Office XI Corps regarding this and other subjects. Inspected in detail Dressing Station	

WAR DIARY
INTELLIGENCE SUMMARY.
(Erase heading not required.)

Army Form C. 2118.

Place	Date	Hour	Summary of Events and Information	Remarks and references to Appendices
CROIX DU BAC	29/8/14 (contd)		Staffed by 'C' Section 3/2nd West Lancs Field Ambulance (Major E.b. ANDERSON Commanding) at ZELOBES. Officer Commanding 3/2nd West Lancs Field Ambulance (Lieut. Col. W MACDONALD) went on leave today. Visited Main Dressing Stations at SAILLY and LE NOUVEAU MONDE of 3/2nd West Lancs Field Ambulance and 2/2nd Wessex Field Ambulance; also Divisional Baths at SAILLY supervising issue of shirts with hearty technique in them	
	30/8/14		Presided all Medical Board at Main Dressing Station, SAILLY, (Major O.H. WILLIAMS other member), examining all men other than 'A' in Employments Companies, [itou? Companies &c. and all A.S.C. M.T. men] Sat from 10 am to 1 pm and 2 pm to 4:30 pm. Seeing 149 men in all.	
	31/8/14		Board as yesterday. A.D.M.S. and Major WILLIAMS at Main Dressing Station, SAILLY, Lieut. Col. C. PARSONS and Captain HARPUR at LA BROGUE. The last eight days have been very quiet from the point of view of evacuation of wounded — only 32 wounded	

Army Form C. 2118.

WAR DIARY
or
INTELLIGENCE SUMMARY.
(Erase heading not required.)

Instructions regarding War Diaries and Intelligence Summaries are contained in F. S. Regs., Part II. and the Staff Manual respectively. Title pages will be prepared in manuscript.

Place	Date	Hour	Summary of Events and Information	Remarks and references to Appendices
CROIX DU BAC	31/8/17 (contd)		57th Division in last eight days of August. Very rainy tempestuous weather from August 24th to 31st inclusive.	

J Y Dawn
............Colonel A. Med. S.
A.D.M.S. 57th (W.L.) Division.

Confidential

War Diary

of

A.D.M.S.   57th Division

from September 1st 1917 to September 30th 1917.

Army Form C. 2118.

WAR DIARY
or
INTELLIGENCE SUMMARY.
(Erase heading not required.)

Place	Date	Hour	Summary of Events and Information	Remarks and references to Appendices
CROIX DU BAC	Sept 1st		Boards for examining all men on Labour and Employment Companies. A.D.M.S. and Major WILLIAMS at Main Dressing Station SAILLY, Lieut. Colonel PARSONS and Captain HARPUR at LA GORGUE. 57th Division which was to have gone to Training Area, first Army (as Strong Reserve) early in September, is now not to go out for a week or two, and is to go to ST HILAIRE, instead of BOMY District.	
	2/9/17		A.D.M.S. visited Main Dressing Stations of three Field Ambulances and Advanced Dressing Stations at LA CROIX LESCORNEZ, inspecting the latter minutely. Work on its extension is to commence tomorrow.	
	3/9/17		A.D.M.S. presided at Monthly Board of P.B. men at Main Dressing Station, SAILLY. Learn that 38th (WELSH) Division is to take over from 57th Division about September 15th. 459 wounded of 57th Division admitted to Field Ambulances of Division in August.	
	4/9/17		Colonel A.G.THOMSON, A.D.M.S. and Lieut Colonel A.JONES, A/D.A.D.M.S. 38th Division came to 57th Divisional Headquarters with a view to taking over of 57th Lines by 38th Division next week. They were shown all Main Dressing Stations; also Regimental Aid Post EATON HALL, and Advanced Dressing Station LA CROIX LESCORNEZ. A.D.M.S.	

Army Form C. 2118.

WAR DIARY
or
INTELLIGENCE SUMMARY.
(Erase heading not required.)

Instructions regarding War Diaries and Intelligence Summaries are contained in F.S. Regs., Part II. and the Staff Manual respectively. Title pages will be prepared in manuscript.

Place	Date	Hour	Summary of Events and Information	Remarks and references to Appendices
CROIX DU BAC	4/9/17		Presided at Medical Board at SAILLY Main Dressing Station, to examine A.S.C. personnel with a view to transference of "A" men to Infantry. A.D.M.S. then visited Reinforcement Camp, wells and tanks at RUE des FIEFS, Regimental Aid Post at EATON HALL (2/8th King's Liverpool Regt. Medical Officer, Captain MORRISON in place of Captain FAULKNER on leave) new R.A.M.C. Post near EATON HALL, Regimental Aid Post near WYE FARM, (2/6th King's Liverpool Regt. Medical Officer, Captain PLUMLEY) and advanced Dressing Station at present in process of extension at LES CROIX LESGORNEZ.	
	5/9/17		Completed series of Medical Boards with a view to "combing out" category "H" men for Infantry. Yesterday and today examined 102 A.S.C. details of which 77 are found "A". A.D.M.S. showed Lieut. Colonel JONES, and Captain REYNOLDS, F.A. Officers 38th Division round front line of ARMENTIERES Section and part of BOIS GRENIER. During August there have been a number of cases of suspected Dysentery in the Division (11 of which are confirmed), and a number of cases of Pyrexia Ignota (10 in all): the general sickness rate is still however very low, and these cannot be said to be any "measuring dream".	
	6.9.17		A.D.M.S. visited VI Corps Headquarters, No. 8 Sanitary Section, BETHUNE,	

WAR DIARY
or
INTELLIGENCE SUMMARY.

Place	Date	Hour	Summary of Events and Information	Remarks and references to Appendices
CROIX DU BAC.	6/9/17		(Sewing disinfestation chambers etc.) Main Dressing Station LE NOUVEAU MONDE. Dressing Station ZELOBES, etc. DADMS. showed representatives of each of the Field Ambulances of the 38th Division round front line Regimental Aid Posts etc. in BOIS GRENIER, and FLEURBAIX Sections. Letter received through Divisional Headquarters that Colonels over 57 years and Lieut Colonels over 55 (in Army Medical Service) are to be returned. This applies only to Lieut Colonel PARSONS, Officer Commanding 2/2nd Wessex Field Ambulance in this Division at present, he being 56 years of age. Lieut Colonel BROOK attains the age of 55 years on 29th December 1917.	
	7/9/17		A.D.M.S. visited all Main Dressing Stations also Advanced Dressing Station at LA CROIX LESCORNEZ. I being administrative detail. also DMS. XI Corps visited Regimental Aid Posts at WYE FARM and EATON HALL accompanied by DADMS. Captain J.P. RACE, 2/2nd Wessex Field Ambulance is suffering from synovitis of knees, and is advised by DMS. 1st Army to be evacuated to Hull BASE. Captain KIDSTON, Medical Officer in charge 2/10th Kings Liverpool (Scottish) Regt. applies for transfer to 3/2nd West Lancs Field Ambulance, and the application is granted.	

Army Form C. 2118.

WAR DIARY
or
INTELLIGENCE SUMMARY.
(Erase heading not required.)

Instructions regarding War Diaries and Intelligence Summaries are contained in F. S. Regs., Part II. and the Staff Manual respectively. Title pages will be prepared in manuscript.

Place	Date	Hour	Summary of Events and Information	Remarks and references to Appendices
CROIX DU BAC	8/9/17		Seven cars of suspected Dysentery reported in Division for past week, of which two confirmed and one diffused bacteriologically. ADMS visited manure dumps in area. Arrangement of office documents with a view to the handing over of area and local papers to incoming Division.	
	9/9/17		Routine. ADMS visited Main Dressing Stations.	
	10/9/17		This day was chiefly devoted to elaborating details of the handing over of the Medical arrangements and sites in this area to the 38th Division, September 14/18. ADMS and A/DADMS 38th Division came to 57th Divisional Headquarters and arranged details. At 6-30 pm ADMS held a conference of Field Ambulances Commanders. Operation Order No.13 issued.	Appendix A.
	11/9/17		ADMS with DDMMS II Corps visited Regimental Aid Posts in BOIS GRENIER sector, namely WHITE CITY Brasserie Regimental Aid Post. Regimental Aid Post off SHAFTESBURY AVENUE (under construction). Regimental Aid Post (temporary) in subsidiary line near SHAFTESBURY AVENUE, and Regimental Aid Post at WELLINGTON AVENUE. Captain G.C. WILLIAMS returned to 57th Division from 59th Army included and Captain PINDER today. 57th Division has now 40 Medical Officers.	

Army Form C. 2118.

WAR DIARY
or
INTELLIGENCE SUMMARY.
(Erase heading not required.)

Place	Date	Hour	Summary of Events and Information	Remarks and references to Appendices
CROIX DU BAC	11/9/17		HQ Headquarters, 2; Regimental, 16; Field Ambulances, 22; also (within Divisional Area) 1. ADMS and A/DADMS, 38th Division again visited 57th Division and conferred with G.S.O.2 and ADMS, 57th Division regarding details of move.	
	12/9/17		ADMS and DADMS visited new (Training) areas to which the Division is to move next week; especially NORRENT FONTES. (Divisional Headquarters); LAIRES (Billet of 2/8th West Lancs Field Ambulance.), NEDONCHELLE (Billet of 2/2nd West Lancs Field Ambulance.) and ST HILAIRE (Billet of 2/10th Wessex Field Ambulance) and LIGNY-LEZ AIRES, where Captain HARPER Medical Officer in charge Advanced Posts is at present stationed. Officer works chiefly concerning arrangements for handing over Medical arrangements from 57th to 38th Division, and moves of former. Dated of Field Ambulances moves settled to Officer Commanding today.	
	13/9/17		ADMS visited Casualty Clearing Stations at MERVILLE – 51st and 54th - to which the 57th Divisional Field Ambulances have evacuated since May 23rd. Saw number of recently "gassed" men of 57th Division. Visited billets of 2/10th Kings Liverpool Regt (Scottish) at ERQUINGHEM. Further preparation for handing over made on departure.	
	14/9/17			

Army Form C. 2118.

WAR DIARY
or
INTELLIGENCE SUMMARY.
(Erase heading not required.)

Instructions regarding War Diaries and Intelligence Summaries are contained in F. S. Regs., Part II. and the Staff Manual respectively. Title pages will be prepared in manuscript.

Place	Date	Hour	Summary of Events and Information	Remarks and references to Appendices
CROIX DU BAC	15/9/17		A.D.M.S. visited A.D.M.S. 38th Division at ESTAIRES. A.D.M.S. 38th Division visited 57th Divisional Headquarters; and A.D.M.S. 57th Division visited ZELOBES and the 3 Field Ambulances of this Division – all these visits in connection with details of handing over from 57th to 38th Division and approaching move of former.	
	16/9/17		A.D.M.S. & A.D.M.S. 38th Division visited Advanced Dressing Station at HOUPLINES and BRICKFIELD and Regimental Aid and Bearer Post at TISSAGE, AUCKLAND ROAD, SQUARE FARM and LEITH WALK. D.D.M.S. 57th Division took him round Advanced Dressing Station and Regimental Aid Post in BOIS GRENIER Section and BOUTILLERIE Subsection. A.D.M.S. visited 2/2nd West Lancs Field Ambulance parties near RABOT (Sheet 36. B.20.c.2.5.) Received orders to instruct two Company Commanders, Medical Officers to proceed at once to England and report at BLACKPOOL for duty in INDIA or MESOPOTAMIA, two U.S.A. Medical Officers and to be posted in lieu. Instructed Captain HARPUR and Lieut. A.H. HALL accordingly.	
	17/9/17		Handed over office of A.D.M.S. CROIX DU BAC, and Medical Arrangements in Divisional Area to A.D.M.S. 38th Division today at 10 a.m. Proceeded to new Headquarters	

Army Form C. 2118.

WAR DIARY
or
INTELLIGENCE SUMMARY.
(Erase heading not required.)

Instructions regarding War Diaries and Intelligence Summaries are contained in F.S. Regs., Part II. and the Staff Manual respectively. Title pages will be prepared in manuscript.

Place	Date	Hour	Summary of Events and Information	Remarks and references to Appendices
NORRENT FONTES.	17/9/17		of 57th Division at NORRENT FONTES. Lieuts GREEN and OLIN, U.S. Medical Corps attached at NORRENT FONTES for duty and were posted to 2/3rd Wessex Field Ambulance. ADMS visited 2/2nd West Sussex Field Ambulance details at REBCQ Farm.	
	18/9/17		Captain HARPUR and Lieut H.H. HILL who are both proceeding to England today. Routine. ADMS visited our part of divisional area. Ambulances of Division moving into new area ex their Brigade Groups each halting at two stages on the way.	
	19/9/17		ADMS rode round part of new area. Visited 2/2nd Wessex Field Ambulance arrived today at BOURECQ. Very few and cramped accommodation of every sort and no building to any degree suitable for reception of patients. ADMS wrote to officer i/c DMS First Army LILLERS regarding 2 Medical Officers to be sent to 38th Casualty Clearing Station (LILLERS) and one for 10 days or so as Medical Officer in charge First Army Headquarters.	
	20/9/17		ADMS visited 2/2nd Wessex Field Ambulance at BOURECQ. Took foot gratings. Bem to be set out as Ward of Nuns Dressing Station and tents pitched on schools land - the schools to accommodate up to 20 sick.	

Army Form C. 2118.

WAR DIARY
or
INTELLIGENCE SUMMARY.
(Erase heading not required.)

Instructions regarding War Diaries and Intelligence Summaries are contained in F. S. Regs. Part II. and the Staff Manual respectively. Title pages will be prepared in manuscript.

Place	Date	Hour	Summary of Events and Information	Remarks and references to Appendices
NORRENT FONTES	20/9/17		Cars, etc. and part seen for admission and receiving Buses. ADMS visited 3/2nd West Lancs Field Ambulance just arrived at NEDONCHEL. Anxious to be accommodated in schoolroom. Billets in town. Recommendation admitted to be accommodated in schoolroom. Billets in town. Recommendation rather scanty but not unsatisfactory and no complaint made. DADMS visited 2/3 Wessex Field Ambulance at LAIRES and reports very satisfactorily of the accommodation there.	
	21/9/17		57th Division, except Artillery, now all in training area, and Field Ambulances are accompanying infy. Sick distribution and situated as follows. 2/2nd Wessex Field Ambulance (with 171st Brigade-group) at BOURECQ (J.1.c.h.5) (Sheet 36ª) no main HIRE-LILLERS road, with fair billets and accommodation for sick, partly in barns and partly modern canvas. 2/3rd Wessex Field Ambulance (with 172nd Brigade group) at LAIRES (X.28.L) on "BERGUENEUSE" Map 1:10000 with fair billets and accommodation for sick, under three own canvas. 2/2nd West Lancs Field Ambulance (with 170th Brigade Group) at NEDONCHELLE (B.7.c.9.9. Sheet 36ª) with accommodation for sick in school room and fair billets. Divisional Artillery are at present	APPENDIX B

Army Form C. 2118.

WAR DIARY
or
INTELLIGENCE SUMMARY.
(Erase heading not required.)

Place	Date	Hour	Summary of Events and Information	Remarks and references to Appendices
NORRENT FONTES.	21/9/17		moving to villages taken out of Infantry Training Show, and will probably require as Stations of Field Ambulances opened in this area to evacuate their own sick. ADMS visited 4/5th Loyal North Lancs Regt at RELY, 2/5th King's Own Royal Lancs Regt at LIGNY, 2/10th King's Liverpool Regt at FLECHIN and BONCOURT, 2/3rd Wessex Field Ambulance at LIERES. Captain W.G. McKENZIE came to get in touch with after service so as to become H/DADMS.	
	22/9/17		on September 21st where Captain EDMISTON goes on 10 days leave. Conference of Divisional Medical Officers at LIGNY-LES-AIRE at 8.A.M. Twenty-six present, including ADMS, DADMS, 3 Field Ambulances Commanders, 3 Medical Officers of United States Medical Corps, & Captain RAGE reporting sick with chronic synovitis of knees. Captain EVANS reporting sick with painful right arm due to old injury. Captain KIDSTON from Medical Officer in charge 2/10th King's Liverpool Regt: to 3/2nd West Lancs Field Ambulance to be replaced by Lieut P.H. HALL. All the 57th Division except Artillery now settled down. OC Field Ambulances as usually situated in their	
	23/9/17		in training areas	

Army Form C. 2118.

WAR DIARY
or
INTELLIGENCE SUMMARY.
(Erase heading not required.)

Instructions regarding War Diaries and Intelligence Summaries are contained in F.S. Regs., Part II, and the Staff Manual respectively. Title pages will be prepared in manuscript.

Place	Date	Hour	Summary of Events and Information	Remarks and references to Appendices
NORRENT FONTES.	23/9/17		Brigade group areas has been placed under of collecting soiled and distributing clean under clothing. ADMS visited 3/2nd West Lancs Field Ambulances and saw the work in progress also visited Medical Officers in charge 2/4th and 4/5th Loyal North Lancs Regt.	
	24/9/17		D.ADMS. went on leave. (September 25th October 5th) Captain W.G. McKENZIE came to office as A/DADMS.	
	25/9/17		ADMS visited 2/2nd Wessex Field Ambulances at BOURECQ. 57th Divisional Reinforcement Camp at BOURECQ, and 58th Casualty Clearing Station at LILLERS, asking Officer Commanding and dental surgeon; Captains PLACE and BENNETTE regarding dental arrangements for 57th Divisional cases, cases of neglected dentition etc. The latter to go to No. 1 Casualty Clearing Station at CHOCQUES. Later with Captain W.G. McKENZIE A/DADMS visited baths at FLECHINELLE where men of the 2/5th South Lancs Regt were bathing. 2/10th Kings Liverpool Regt at FLECHIN, where Lieut PAHALL has today replaced Captain N.W. KIDSTON who has been continuously on Medical charge of the unit since Sept 10th 1914 and who has been today transferred to 3/2nd West Lancs Field Ambulance, and there	

Army Form C. 2118.

WAR DIARY
or
INTELLIGENCE SUMMARY.
(Erase heading not required.)

Instructions regarding War Diaries and Intelligence Summaries are contained in F. S. Regs., Part II. and the Staff Manual respectively. Title pages will be prepared in manuscript.

Place	Date	Hour	Summary of Events and Information	Remarks and references to Appendices
NORRENT FONTES	25/9/17		Quarters in new Artillery Area to which Divisional R.S. march yesterday, namely Headquarters at BOMY, 286th Brigade R.F.A. at DELETTE, 285th Brigade R.F.A. at COYECQUE, and Divisional Ammunition Column at RECLINGHEM. A.D.M.S. interviewed Medical Officers (Captains COSTELLO, McHUGH and FINDLAY) in each case.	
	26/9/17		A.D.M.S. visited 3/2nd West Lancs and 2/3rd Wessex Field Ambulances with Captains McKENZIE. Captains RAGE reported evacuated to Base. D.M.S. XI Corps to interview Captains ARNOLD and Lieut P.A.HALL regarding re-engagement. Medical Officers to be sent for duty to 54th Casualty Clearing Station. Commendations and preparation of Recommendations for New Years Honours and Rewards. Two places allotted to R.A.M.C. in 57th Division (Captains).	
	27/9/17		MORRISON 2/3rd Wessex Field Ambulance proceeded today to 54th Casualty Clearing Station for temporary duty.	
	28/9/17		Day uneventful. Officers work light. Average sick light. Average for 10 days September 19th – 28th is 13.6. No specially prevalent disease. Units engaged on training. A.D.M.S. visited 2/2nd Wessex Field Ambulance.	

Army Form C. 2118.

WAR DIARY
or
INTELLIGENCE SUMMARY.
(Erase heading not required.)

Place	Date	Hour	Summary of Events and Information	Remarks and references to Appendices
NORRENT-FONTES	28/9/17		and 58th Casualty Clearing Station. Bright fine weather up last fortnight (anti-cyclonic type). Man of 2/5th King's Liverpool Regt. was bitten on 20th instant by dog which died from unknown cause on 26th. he is being sent to PARIS tomorrow for antirabic treatment at PASTEUR Institute.	
	29/9/17		ADMS visited DDMS XI Corps at Corps Headquarters HINGES and discussed incidence of venereal disease in 57th Division, issue of Thomas Splint, Training of James Officers, Field Ambulances Commanders and Superannuation, Winter programme of Operations, provision of Travelling Cookers and Usual Spreads for Sterile Stretchers, etc. Visited No 6 Sanitary Section at CHOCQUES and was shown several improvised and effective appliances. Visited 58th Casualty Clearing Station, Divisional Reinforcement Camps and Baths ST HILAIRE. Incidence of Venereal Cases in Division is low, and tends to diminish: thus March 19, April 10, May 12, June 15, July 7, August 11, September 4. Total about 30 months. 88, of which many contracted infection in England.	
	30/9/17		Captain EVAN'S evacuated sick to Base (Paresis of right arm after old injury) Division is thus reduced to RAMC (on U.S.M.G.) officers	

Army Form C. 2118.

WAR DIARY
or
INTELLIGENCE SUMMARY.
(Erase heading not required.)

Place	Date	Hour	Summary of Events and Information	Remarks and references to Appendices
NORRENT-FONTES	30/9/17		Thus distributed:-	
			Headquarters. 2.	
			Regimental 16.	
			Quartermasters 8.	
			Leave 7.	
			Detached duty 4.	
			Field Ambulances 9.	
			41.	
			Those temporarily detached are at 38th Casualty Clearing Station LILLERS (2); at 54th Casualty Clearing Station, MERVILLE (1); interim Medical Officer in charge First Army Headquarters at LILLERS (1). With only 3 Medical Officers (on an average) at each Field Ambulance and the others scattered over a wide district - Any scheme of training of Junior Medical Officers is impossible. Attended sports of 2/5 Bn: King's Liverpool Regt. and saw Stretcher Bearers Competitions. Captain W.G. McKENZIE judging.	

.... Colonel, A. Med. S.
A.D.M.S. 57th (W.L.) Division.

SECRET.   APPENDIX H   Copy No...18...

57TH DIVISION.

R.A.M.C. OPERATION ORDER No. 13.

M.3679/40.

Reference Map Sheet 36 –
1/40,000.

1. The Field Ambulances of the 57th Division will be relieved by the Field Ambulances of the 36th Division on 16/9/1917.

2. The 129th Field Ambulance will relieve the 2/2nd Wessex Field Ambulance at LE NOUVEAU MONDE, (G.27.c.3.2.).

3. The 130th Field Ambulance will relieve the 3/2nd West Lancs Field Ambulance at SAILLY, (G.17.a.8.4.).

4. The 131st Field Ambulance will relieve the 2/3rd Wessex Field Ambulance at FORT ROMPU, (H.7.d.6.3.).

5. Advance Parties of one Officer and 20 Other Ranks will arrive on 14/9/1917 at LE NOUVEAU MONDE, SAILLY and FORT ROMPU.

6. An Advance Party of one Officer and 10 Other Ranks will arrive at ZELOBES on 15/9/1917.

7. Handing over will be completed by noon on 16/9/1917.

8. Details will be arranged direct between the Commanding Officers concerned.

9. The Field Ambulances of the 57th Division will move from these stations with their respective Brigades who will issue the necessary orders.

10. Issue and receipt vouchers will be passed.

11. The Field Ambulances of the 57th Division will carry with them mobilization store equipment, wheeled stretcher carriages and the extra stores as laid down in G.R.O. 419, less 50 blankets.

12. The Field Ambulances of the 57th Division will hand over to the incoming units all Red Cross Stores, 4,000 Reserve Shell Dressings, 200 Reserve P.H.Helmets and 50 stretchers. Any surplus Anti-toxin Serum will be returned to Advanced Depot of Medical Stores.

13. An extra receipt for the 50 stretchers will be forwarded to this office.

14. Completion of handing over to be notified to this office by wire.

15. ACKNOWLEDGE.

J. F. Dowen
Colonel. A.Med.S.,
A.D.M.S., 57th Division.

10th Septr, 1917.

Issued at......10-0......p.m.

For distribution see overleaf. –

Copy No. ....

57TH DIVISION.

S.S.Ist. Operation Order No. 31.

Reference Map Sheet 36 - 1/40,000.

1. The Field Ambulances of the 57th Division will be relieved by the Field Ambulances of the 39th Division on 16/9/1917.

   Distribution –

   Copy No. 1. to H.Q., 57th Division.
   2.   -do-
   3.   D.D.M.S., XI Corps.
   4.   O.C., 2/2nd Wessex Field Amblce.
   5.   O.C., 2/3rd Wessex Field Amblce.
   6.   O.C., 3/2nd West Lancs. Fd Amblce.
   7.   H.Q., 170th Infantry Brigade.
   8.   H.Q., 171st Infantry Brigade.
   9.   H.Q., 172nd Infantry Brigade.
   10.   C.R.E., 57th Division.
   11.   C.R.A., 57th Division.
   12.   O.C., 57th Divisional Train, A.S.C.
   13.   O.C., 57th Divisional Signal Coy.
   14.   A.D.M.S., 39th Division.
   15.   O.C., 129th Field Ambulance.
   16.   O.C., 130th Field Ambulance.
   17.   O.C., 131st Field Ambulance.
   18.   War Diary.
   19.   File
   20.
   21.   Spare.

2. The Field Ambulances of the 57th Division will move from their stations with their respective Brigades the ....

10. Issue and receipt vouchers will be passed.

11. The Field Ambulances of the 57th Division will carry with them mobilization store equipment, wheeled stretcher carriage and the extra stores as laid down in G.R.O. 619, less 80 blankets.

12. The Field Ambulances of the 57th Division will hand over to the incoming units all Red Cross Stores, 4,000 Reserve Shell Dressings, 200 Reserve P.H.Helmets and 50 stretchers. Any surplus Anti-toxin Serum will be returned to Advanced Depot of Medical Stores.

13. An extra receipt for the 50 stretchers will be forwarded to this office.

14. Completion of handing over to be notified to this office by wire.

15th Septr. 1917.

Colonel, A.D.M.S.,
A.D.M.S., 57th Division.

Issued at .... M ....

Distribution are overleaf.

APPENDIX B.

A.D.M.S. 57th Division

WAR DIARY
or
INTELLIGENCE SUMMARY.

Army Form C. 2118.

ADMS 5-7 1917

Place	Date	Hour	Summary of Events and Information	Remarks and references to Appendices
NORRENT FONTES.	1/10/17		A.D.M.S. inspected quarters of 2/2nd Wessex Field Ambulance at BOURECQ, with Officers Commanding. Owing to depletion of Medical Officers of Divisions generally, only two at present with this unit viz. Officer Commanding and one other. Billets fairly comfortable. Hospital marquee canvas in arrear. Transport horses satisfactory. Excellent office in which I found two clerks at work. Unit is collecting and distributing clean clothing to other units in Brigade Group. Late A.D.M.S. visited 2nd duties of 2/8th Kings Liverpool (Irish) Regt: at FONTES. Billets airy but fairly crowded; mostly cleans and fresh despite contact farm midden. Many complain of cold, having only one blanket at night. Infectious Diseases have been low in Divisions, namely: February 37, March 81, April 27, May 21, June 16, July 17, August 15, September 21.	

Army Form C. 2118.

WAR DIARY
or
INTELLIGENCE SUMMARY.
(Erase heading not required.)

Instructions regarding War Diaries and Intelligence
Summaries are contained in F.S. Regs., Part II.
and the Staff Manual respectively. Title pages
will be prepared in manuscript.

Place	Date	Hour	Summary of Events and Information	Remarks and references to Appendices
NORRENT FONTES.	1/10/17.		of those in August and September.	
			7 were Malaria and 1 suspected Malaria. 8.	
			2 were Pneumonia. 2.	
			3 were Pulmon Tuberc. and 2. suspected Tuberculosis. 5.	
			1 was Dysentery and 12 suspected Dysentery 13.	
			2 were Measles. 2.	
			3 were Mumps and 2 suspected Mumps 5.	
			1 was Weils Disease 1.	
			36.	
	2/10/17.		A.D.M.S. visited baths at FLECHINELLE : a company of 2/4th South Lancs Regt. were using the article spray baths provided for the use of the troops; men's there. Visited also quarters of 2/10th Kings Liverpool Regt at FLECHIN.	
			A.D.M.S. visited 2/2/27 West Lancs Field Ambulance at NEDONCHELLE. Long	
	3/10/17.		interview with DMS Lieut Stong regarding various matters and Majors WILLIAMS and MCLAREN for hot as Surgeons a Casualty Clearing Station - Commands of Field Ambulances training of Field Ambulances etc.	

T2134. Wt. W708-776. 50,000. 4/15. Sir J. C. & S.

Army Form C. 2118.

WAR DIARY
or
INTELLIGENCE SUMMARY.
(Erase heading not required.)

Instructions regarding War Diaries and Intelligence Summaries are contained in F. S. Regs., Part II. and the Staff Manual respectively. Title pages will be prepared in manuscript.

Place	Date	Hour	Summary of Events and Information	Remarks and references to Appendices
NORRENT-FONTES.	4/10/17		Conference of Medical Officers of Division at LIGNY-LEZ-AIRE, especially regarding Subsidiary B.S.W.&C. Fund for Widows and Orphans of Divisional B.S.W.&C. Officers killed or died of disease on campaign. Two Medical Officers (Captains PINDER and WILKINSON) left today for temporary duty with No 61 Casualty Clearing Station at DOSINGHEM. D.D.M.S. 2nd B.N. under orders to move off tomorrow by march route to join 5th Sherwy. Division. it is understood, will follow on or about 24th October.	
	5/10/17		H.D.M.S. visited all three Field Ambulances, inspecting the 2/3rd Wessex Field Ambulances in some detail. Captain W.G. McKENZIE. A/D.A.D.M.S. visited R.H. units on the line of march regarding their medical arrangement today and subsequently. Captain EDMISTON. D.A.D.M.S. returned from leave late last evening.	
	6/10/17		F.M. Sir DOUGLAS HAIG. inspected the Division on very wet weather today. Brigade training, spots, competitions etc. being completed steadily an arrear of more recent weeks. During 18 days 4th Division has been in the Ypres, more leave has been regularly to H.Q. at FLECHINELLE (up to 800 a day): at ST HILAIRE	

Army Form C. 2118.

WAR DIARY
or
INTELLIGENCE SUMMARY.
(Erase heading not required.)

Instructions regarding War Diaries and Intelligence Summaries are contained in F.S. Regs., Part II. and the Staff Manual respectively. Title pages will be prepared in manuscript.

Place	Date	Hour	Summary of Events and Information	Remarks and references to Appendices
NORRENT-FONTES	6/10/17		(up to 500 a day); at LA TIRHAND (200 a day); and at LILLERS (600 a day). At 2000 a day, all had a bath every 8 days or so.	
	7/10/17		ADMS visited and inspected billets, stores, wards, etc. of 3/2/2nd West Lancs Field Ambulance at NEDONCHELLE. 'C' Section (with Major Sanderson and Captains & Kildare) out on Brigade training with 170th Infantry Brigade. Also in met Officer Commanding and Major Williams other detailed as heave.	
	8/10/17		ADMS visited DMS 1st Army regarding his intended inspection of 57th Divisional Field Ambulances tomorrow. As the Division is leaving the Army he will not now inspect. He has given orders for the 3 Medical Officers lent to 2/8th and 2/4th Casualty Clearing Stations to be returned to 57th Division.	
	9/10/17		Routine. DADMS. went walk to NE of POPERINGHE and saw 6 R.A. 57th Division Sketchy and engaged being under XIV Corps. DADMS. arranged for additional Medical Officers to be sent for duty with R.A. in view of scattered situation of 285th and 286th R.A. Brigades.	

T.J.134. Wt. W708-776. 50000. 4/15. Sir J. C. & S.

Army Form C. 2118.

WAR DIARY
or
INTELLIGENCE SUMMARY.
(Erase heading not required.)

Instructions regarding War Diaries and Intelligence Summaries are contained in F. S. Regs., Part II. and the Staff Manual respectively. Title pages will be prepared in manuscript.

Place	Date	Hour	Summary of Events and Information	Remarks and references to Appendices
NORRENT-FONTES.	10-10-17		Captain G. ANDERSON now at 58th Casualty Clearing Station, to proceed to Divisional R.A. as additional Medical Officer. Major O.H. WILLIAMS, 2/2nd West Lancs Field Ambulance now ordered to proceed for duty to No 22 Casualty Clearing Station. BRUAY. Reinforcement to be applied for in his stead. Lieut. GREEN U.S.M.O. returned to duty with 57th Division from 54th Casualty Clearing Station. A.D.M.S. visited G.H.Q., 2nd Echelons, office of D.G.M.S. and interviewed Major MARTIN, D.A.D.G. regarding proposed administrative changes.	
	11-10-17		Captain J.F. EDMISTON. D.A.D.M.S. to be transferred to 2/2nd Wessex Field Ambulance. DMS First Army is today ordering Captain KING. M.G. to report for duty as D.A.D.M.S. 57th Division. A.D.M.S. with Captain EDMISTON, and in presence of Battalions Medical Officers very carefully examined stretcher Bearers of 2/5th and 2/6th Kings Liverpool Regt. Returning also on duty, theoretical and practical knowledge very high. Marks 2/5th Kings Liverpool Regt 104/120. 2/6 Kings Liverpool Regt 101/120.	
	12.10.17		57th Division, are shortly which is already in line on XIV Corps area, are to pass from First Army XI Corps to Fifth Army XIV Corps. 170th Brigade	

Army Form C. 2118.

WAR DIARY
or
INTELLIGENCE SUMMARY.
(Erase heading not required.)

Place	Date	Hour	Summary of Events and Information	Remarks and references to Appendices
NORRENT FONTES	12.10.17		Groups – with 2/2nd West Lancs Field Ambulance to march on 14th instant; 172nd Brigade Group with 2/3rd Wessex Field Ambulance and 171st Brigade Group with 2/2nd Wessex Field Ambulance on 15th and 16th. Each group to march by road to RENESCURE area. Divisional Headquarters to close at NORRENT FONTES at noon on 15th and open thereafter at RENESCURE. Brigade groups ordered to move from RENESCURE area to PROVEN on bus area thereafter to ELVERDINGHE by road. Major O.H. WILLIAMS left Division today to No. 62 Casualty Clearing Station.	
	13.10.17		Notification received that Captains M.B. KING, R.A.M.C., medical Officer in charge 18th Yorks and Lancs Regt. is to report for duty with 57th Division (as DADMS) Captain J.F. EDMISTON transferred today to 2/1st Welsh Field Ambulance. ADMS proceeded today by car to ELVERDINGHE and 75 Sidings GUARDS Division saw ADMS 1 R.E. Division at present holds BOESINGHE Sector. No details to ADMS the evacuation arrangements at present in force on that Sector. ADMS through wires DDMS XIII Corps at ST. SIXTE. HQrs to tell the ADMS that the 35 Divisions were coming into the XIV Corps immediately	

WAR DIARY
or
INTELLIGENCE SUMMARY.

Army Form C. 2118.

Place	Date	Hour	Summary of Events and Information	Remarks and references to Appendices
WORRENT-FONTES.	13/10/17		and that the arrival of the 57th Division was uncertain. The Guards Division is holding a nominal front of about 1200 yards on the left of the Fifth Army front &b.-	
			[diagram showing Gds Div, 29th Div, XIV Corps, 1st French Army, Fifth Army, Second Army]	
	14.10.17		Heavy rains today and almost every day since October 4th. Roads very muddy and flat country much waterlogged. Captain M.B. KING, R.A.M.C. D.A.D.M.S. 29th Division today from 31st Division to take over duties of D.A.D.M.S. 57th Division vice Captain J.F. EDMISTON R.A.M.C. transferred to 20th Manch. Field Ambulance. Learns today that the immediate destination of the 57th Division though probably the XIII Corps is uncertain and it is not to join our Area. Guards Division will probably not have 17th Division. DDMS visited 3/2nd West Lancs Field Ambulance at NEDONCHELLE.	

Army Form C. 2118.

WAR DIARY
or
INTELLIGENCE SUMMARY.
(Erase heading not required.)

Instructions regarding War Diaries and Intelligence Summaries are contained in F. S. Regs., Part II. and the Staff Manual respectively. Title pages will be prepared in manuscript.

Place	Date	Hour	Summary of Events and Information	Remarks and references to Appendices
NORRENT-FONTES.	15:10:17		ADMS with Captain KING ADDAMS, visited 2/7" Kings Liverpool Regt at ESTREE BLANCHE, Batts of FLECHINELLE, 2/10" Kings Liverpool Regt of FLECHIN, 2/8" West Yorks Stretcher bearers at LAIRES and 3/2nd West Lancs Fields Ambulance at NEDONCHELLE.	
	16:10:17		Routine. There are very quiet days with often sunk down to about 10% of manœuvres. It is understood that V Divisional Headquarters moves to RENESCURE on 18th and to PROVEN on 19th. 172nd Brigade moves similarly on the same days and 170th and 171st Brigade groups arriving similarly so preceding days respectively. Further destination not yet known.	
	17.10.17		HDMS with ADMS visited 3/2 West Yorks Ambulance. Skirmisher visited B.H. FLECHINELLE, 2/10 Kings Liverpool Regt at FLECHIN where inspected Shelter Bearers, 170" Infantry Brigade with 2/8? West Lancs Field Ambulance. Left this area today.	
RENESCURE.	18.10.17		1/2 1 Mcfarlan Brigade and 57th Divisional Headquarters moved to RENESCURE. HDMS visited 3th Cavalry Clearing Station, HILLERS, and asked for Lieut OAKFIELD 2/7 A. Kings Liverpool Regt. dangerously wounded no bearing	

A6915 Wt. W14422/M1160 35,000. 12/16 D. D. & I. Forms/C./2118/14.

WAR DIARY or INTELLIGENCE SUMMARY.

(Erase heading not required.)

Army Form C. 2118.

Place	Date	Hour	Summary of Events and Information	Remarks and references to Appendices
RENESCURE	18.10.17		accident three days ago. ADMS visited II Corps Headquarters to see DDMS on future. Spent night at RENESCURE.	
PROVEN	19.10.17		Divisional Headquarters moved from RENESCURE to PROVEN 1727nd Infantry Brigade with 2/3rd Wessex Field Ambulance also. Troops conveyed by bus. 57th Division in North Camp PROVEN.	
	20.10.17		The 57th Division is to take over in a few days from the 34th Division now in line. The 2/2nd Wessex Field Ambulance arrived today in camp near PROVEN completing moves of Headquarters and Field Ambulances (with Brigade Groups) as an attached Field Field Ambulances of 57th Division are now stationed near PROVEN thus:— 2/3rd Wessex Field Ambulance Sheet 27. E.5.a.4.8. 2/3rd Wessex Field Ambulance Sheet 27. F.1.b.4.2. 3/2nd West Lancs Field Ambulance Sheet 20 x 21 C.9.b. ADMS visited last named and also Corps Headquarters. Majors ANDERSON and STOKES who were to have gone on leave tomorrow have had leave cancelled as DDMS considers some may be spare until after 57th Division starts an impending attack.	APPENDIX A

WAR DIARY
or
INTELLIGENCE SUMMARY.
(Erase heading not required.)

Army Form C. 2118.

Place	Date	Hour	Summary of Events and Information	Remarks and references to Appendices
PROVEN	20/10/17		2/3rd Mean Field Ambulances ordered to move tomorrow (advanced party tonight) to relieve No. 52 Field Ambulance at Sheet 19.X.30.c central. No personnel of 1 Tent Subdivision and 2 Medical Officers to go on temporary duty to No. 4 Casualty Clearing Station DOZINGHEM. Sheet 27 F 11 & 35.	
	21/10/17		F.D.M.S. visited Headquarters XV Corps and Headquarters 49th Division at Mille Sums with a view to taking over from 54th & 56th Field Ambulances the Advance Dressing Stations taken from 3/3rd Means and 3/3rd West Lanc. Field Ambulances to go forward and collect wounded to Officers Commanding 104th and 103rd Field Ambulances actively cooperating. Arrangement made by YSER Canal and under our Field Ambulance Commanders, then west of canal under arrangements made	
	22/10/17		D.A.D.M.S. visited Headquarters XIV Corps and Headquarters 81st Division regarding taking over from 54th on October 23-25. The 51st and 50th Divisions are expected to take over June 3rd & 4th Divisions the 50th Division on 24th 25th on night. Evacuation of wounded is to be as common. Officers Commanding 2/2 Mercer Field Ambulance with Lee It Mason conducted a M.O. from	

WAR DIARY or INTELLIGENCE SUMMARY.

Army Form C. 2118.

Place	Date	Hour	Summary of Events and Information	Remarks and references to Appendices
PROVEN	22/8/17		Bearer Divison as to his reformith. two evacuation east of DE'LYSER Canal.	
			ADMS and DADMS 50th Division reported to discuss details of co-operation in evacuation. Officer Commanding 3/3rd Wessex Field Ambulances obtained instructions.	
			ADMS in absence of Colonel PARSON'S. 11.00 officers and NCO's went up today to advance party specially. Officer Commanding 2/3rd West Lancs Field Ambulance Officer and NCO's went as advance party to MOUTON FARM but it was more officer's half evacuation have west of the canal as to be done by a Field Ambulance of 50th Division.	
	23/8/17		Issued 5/9 Y[eomanry] RAMC Operation Orders No 14. APPENDIX D	
			ADMS visited Headquarters 3/1st Wessex Field Ambulances and 3/3rd West Lancs Field Ambulance regarding duties of personnel ([illegible]) of 2/2nd Wessex Field Ambulance personnel with Bearer personnel	
	24/8/17		of the 2 Field Ambulances at 5/9 Y.D. unless required to PELISSIER FARM and dressing stations and Posts in front thereof today – about 90 by motor ambulance: about 260 by rail and transport by road. Officer Commanding and 4 medical officers accompanied the	

Army Form C. 2118.

WAR DIARY
OR
INTELLIGENCE SUMMARY.
(Erase heading not required.)

Place	Date	Hour	Summary of Events and Information	Remarks and references to Appendices
PROVEN	24.10.17		Visited Headquarters, 34th Division at WELSH FARM and thereafter attended Conference of A.D.Ms.S at office of D.D.M.S, XIV Corps.	
WELSH FARM	25.10.17		Headquarters, 59th Division proceeded from PROVEN (North Camp) to WELSH FARM (Sheet 28 N.W/B.14.C.2.2.) today, office of A.D.M.S. opening and closing at 8 a.m. Visited PELISSIER FARM, Headquarters of 2/2nd Wessex Field Ambulance which with Bearer Divisions of 2/3rd Wessex & 3/2nd West Lancs. Field Ambulances is doing evacuation of forward area. Interviewed Major Adams, at present commanding, regarding arrangements for tomorrow. Present location of Field Ambulances is :-	
			2/2nd Wessex Field Ambulance, PELISSIER FARM, Sheet 28/B.21.a.2.0.	
			2/3rd Wessex Field Ambulance, Sheet 19/X.30.c. central.	
			3/2nd West Lancs. Field Ambulance, PROVEN Sheet 19/X.24.a.6.8.	
			140th Brigade, 59th Division, attached at dawn. Ground could not be gained chiefly owing to	
	26.10.17		moving to Sheet 27/F.7. & 3.4.'	

Army Form C. 2118.

WAR DIARY
or
INTELLIGENCE SUMMARY.
(Erase heading not required.)

Place	Date	Hour	Summary of Events and Information	Remarks and references to Appendices
WELSH FARM	26/10/17		Weather and muddy state of terrain very intense. 10 Officers and 348 Other Ranks reported wounded: 6 Officers and 186 additional wounded reported early on 27th as having happened yesterday. D.A.D.M.S. spent whole day in forward evacuation area finding considerably defective liaison between Regimental Medical Officers and R.A.M.C. Bearer personnel.	
	27.10.17		Visited Headquarters 1/2 Wessex Field Ambulance at PELISSIER FARM. Both Main Dressing Station at SOLFERINO. Advanced Dressing Stations at FUSILIER (where I saw the Officer commanding 1/2 Wessex Field Ambulance who is officer in charge forward evacuations and discussed with him the evacuation arrangements of yesterday with whose success he is, on the whole satisfied) and CEMENT HOUSE where CAPTAINS EDMISTON and BACKHOUSE very busy in confined space; also visited Relay Posts at ST. JOHN and CORNER HOUSE (50th Division) and	

Army Form C. 2118.

WAR DIARY
or
INTELLIGENCE SUMMARY.
(Erase heading not required.)

Instructions regarding War Diaries and Intelligence Summaries are contained in F. S. Regs. Part II. and the Staff Manual respectively. Title pages will be prepared in manuscript.

Place	Date	Hour	Summary of Events and Information	Remarks and references to Appendices
WELSH FARM	27.10.17		Braver Post at PIG & WHISTLE, the latter and CEMENT HOUSE any confined places. Wieuville Swain firing intermittently and Drank tracks sometimes blocked, so that evacuation not any satisfactory today, though casualties not very numerous. In evening interviewed S.O.b., 57th Division regarding alleged defective liaison between Regimental and R.A.M.C. personnel in evacuation yesterday. Undertook to make full enquiry. The XI Corps Commander has awarded the Military	
	28.10.17		Medal to 4613441 Pte. E.R. Barrett, 73rd Wessex Field Ambulance and 459302 L/Cpl. H.J. French, 72nd Wessex Field Ambulance for gallant conduct in performance of duty. Attended conference of Brigadiers and Heads of Departments, 57th Division at Advanced Headquarters. Only two medical points discussed, namely failure to recover wounded lying in and in front of line, and defective liaison between	

WAR DIARY
or
INTELLIGENCE SUMMARY.

Army Form C. 2118.

Place	Date	Hour	Summary of Events and Information	Remarks and references to Appendices
WELSH FARM	28/10/17		Regimental and R.A.M.C. Bearer personnel Saw our Brigadier General, 170th Brigade and all 1t medical officers in this subject all allege practically no sustained communication and practically no assistance in evacuation from R.A.M.C. and auxiliary Bearer personnel. Required each to submit concise statement in writing. Interviewed D.M.S., Fifth Army at Fifth Army Headquarters. He gave verbal instruction regarding control of Wyschaete, Wierdreed Vinsebes and French feet.	
	29/10/17		The XIX Corps took over from the XIV Corps today at 2 p.m. Wounded admitted to Corps Main Dressing Station in last four days are as follows:- Noon 25th – Noon 26th 2 Officers 99 Other Ranks " 26th " 27th 9 " 302 " " 27th " 28th 9 " 277 " " 28th " 29th 10 " 131 " Total 25 809	

WAR DIARY
or
INTELLIGENCE SUMMARY.

(Erase heading not required.)

Army Form C. 2118.

Place	Date	Hour	Summary of Events and Information	Remarks and references to Appendices
WELSH FARM	29.10.17		In compliance with orders from Divisional Commander visited Head-quarters, 170th Infantry Brigade, and all four units of that Brigade, saw Brigadier and all 4 Medical Officers regarding numbers fit to go up to forward area on November 1st and into line on Nov: 3rd. After full and careful enquiry reported in interview that 1100 men were probably be fit for duty on dates as above. Visited Divisional Baths at Louthoze Church nr. PROVEN. Spray Baths which can deal with 150-150 men an hour.	
	30.10.17		D.A.D.M.S. visited Posts east of Advanced Divisional Headquarters. Issued memo on Evacuation in preparation for attack (in which 142nd Infantry Brigade will take part) at an early date. He reports considerable shell fire, probably occasioned by our attack on the night (XVIII Corps and Second Army). Evacuation of wounded proceeding satisfactorily.	APPENDIX "C"
	31.10.17		Operation Order No. 15 (R.A.M.C. 51st Division) drafted.	

Army Form C. 2118.

WAR DIARY
or
INTELLIGENCE SUMMARY.
(Erase heading not required.)

Place	Date	Hour	Summary of Events and Information	Remarks and references to Appendices
WELSH FARM	3.10.17		Interviewed B.D.C. regarding numbers in 170th Infantry Brigade available for attack, on November 6. Met Fifth Army commander at 57th Divisional Advanced Headquarters and outlined to him system of evacuation in area. After conference of Officer Commanding and second in command, 172nd Wessex field Ambulance and Medical Officers of 172nd Infantry Brigade regarding medical arrangements in new attack.	

J J Johnston
Colonel, A. Med. S.
A.D.M.S. 57th (W.L.) Division.

B.E.F.

SUMMARY OF MEDICAL WAR DIARIES FOR

57th Divn. 14th Corps, 5th Army.

19th Corps from 29/10/17.

To 2nd Army on 14/11/17.

WESTERN FRONT. Oct.- Nov. 1917.

A.D.M.S. Col. J.F. Dewar.
D.A.D.M.S. Capt. M.B. King.

SUMMARISED UNDER THE FOLLOWING HEADINGS.

Phase "D" 1. Passchendaele Operations July-Dec. 1917.

(b) Operations commencing 1/10/17.
Canadians attacked Passchendaele Oct. 30th.
Canadians took Passchendaele Nov. 6th.

1.

B.E.F.

57th Divn. 14th Corps, 5th Army.   WESTERN FRONT.
A.D.M.S. Col. J.F. Dowar.   Oct. 1917.

Phase "D" 1. Passchendaele Operations July Dec. 1917.

(b) Operations commencing 1/10/17.
Canadians attacked Passchendaele Oct. 30th.
Canadians took Passchendaele Nov. 6th.

1917.	Headquarters. At Proven.
Oct. 19th.	Moves and Transfer. 57th Divn. transferred from 11th Corps 1st Army to 14th Corps, 5th Army and moved to Proven.
20th.	Locations Field Ambulances:- 2/2nd Wessex Field Ambulance E.5.a.4.8. (Sheet 27)
	2/3rd Wessex Field Ambulance F.1.b.4.2. (Sheet 27)
	3/2nd W. Lancs. Field Ambulance. A.21.c.9.1. (Sheet 20)
21st.	Moves Field Ambulance. 2/3rd Wessex Field Ambulance to X.30 c. central (Sheet 19) and took over camp from 52nd Field Ambulance.
	Moves Field Ambulance Det. 2 and 1 T.S.D. of 2/3rd Wessex Field Ambulance to 4th Casualty Clearing Station Dozinghem.
24th-25th.	Military Situation: Medical Arrangements. Appendix B. (paras. 1-9) Attached. (Put back into Diary.)
25th.	Moves. To Welsh Farm B.14.c.2.2. (Sheet 28)
	Locations Field Ambulance. 2/2nd Wessex Field Ambulance Pellissier Farm B.21.a.2.0. (Sheet 28)
	2/3rd Wessex Field Ambulance X.30.c. central (Sheet 19)
	3/2nd W. Lancs. F.7.b.3.4. (Sheet 27)
26th.	Operation: Operations Enemy: Terrain. 170th Bde.

57th Div. 14th Corps, 5th Army.   WESTERN FRONT.
A.D.M.S. Col. J.F. Dewar.   Oct. 1917.
19th Corps from 29/10/17.

Phase "D" 1. (b) (Cont.)

1917.
Oct. 26th. (Cont.) Operations: Operations Enemy: Terrain. (Cont.)
57th Divn. attacked at dawn. Ground could not be gained owing to muddy state of terrain and intense enemy fire.
Casualties. 16 and 534 wounded.

27th. Evacuation. Not very satisfactory owing to Decauville Trains running intermittently and plank tracks becoming blocked also defective liaison between Regl. and R.A.M.C. personnel.
Casualties. Not very numerous.

28th. Decorations. Cpl. Garrett C.R. 2/3rd Wessex Field Ambulance awarded M.M.
L/Cpl. French H.A. 2/2nd Wessex Field Ambulance awarded M.M.

29th. Transfer. To 19th Corps.

B.E.F. 3.

57th Divn. 19th Corps, 5th Army.   WESTERN FRONT.
A.D.M.S. Col. J.F.Dewar.   Oct. 1917.
                                    Nov. 1917.

Phase "D" 1. Passchendaele Operations July-Dec. 1917.

    (b) Operations commencing 1/10/17.
        Canadians attacked Passchendaele Oct. 30th.
        Canadians took Passchendaele Nov. 6th.

1917.
Oct. 29th.   Transfer. To 10th Corps.

          Casualties. Admitted to C.M.D.S.

          Noon 25th- Noon 26th---   2 and 99 wounded.
          "   26th " 27th   9 and 302 wounded.
          "   27th " 28th.   10 and 277 wounded.
          "   28th " 29th.   4 and 131 wounded.

30th.   Evacuation Instructions. Appendix C. Attached.

      Appendices. B. R.A.M.C. Op. Order 14 d/ 25/10/17.
      C. Memo regarding Evacuation d/ 30/10/17.

B.E.F.

57th Divn. 14th Corps, 5th Army.   WESTERN FRONT.
A.D.M.S. Col. J.F. Dewar.   Oct. 1917.

Phase "D" 1. Passchendaele Operations July-Dec. 1917.

(b) Operations commencing 1/10/17.
    Canadians attacked Passchendaele Oct. 30th.
    Canadians took Passchendaele Nov. 6th.

1917.	Headquarters. At Proven.
Oct. 19th.	Moves and Transfer. 57th Divn. transferred from 11th Corps 1st Army to 14th Corps, 5th Army and moved to Proven.
20th.	Locations Field Ambulances:- 2/2nd Wessex Field Ambulance E.5.a.4.8. (Sheet 27)
	2/3rd Wessex Field Ambulance F.1.b.4.2. (Sheet 27)
	3/2nd W. Lancs. Field Ambulance. X.21.c.9.1. (Sheet 20)
21st.	Moves Field Ambulance. 2/3rd Wessex Field Ambulance to X.20 c. central (Sheet 19) and took over camp from 52nd Field Ambulance.
	Moves Field Ambulance Det. 2 and 1 T.S.D. of 2/3rd Wessex Field Ambulance to 4th Casualty Clearing Station Dozinghem.
24th-25th.	Military Situation: Medical Arrangements. Appendix B. (paras. 1-9) Attached.
25th.	Moves. To Welsh Farm B.14.c.2.2. (Sheet 28)
	Locations Field Ambulance. 2/2nd Wessex Field Ambulance Pellissier Farm B.21.a.2.0. (Sheet 28)
	2/3rd Wessex Field Ambulance X.30.c. central (Sheet 19)
	3/2nd W. Lancs. F.7.b.3.4. (Sheet 27)
26th.	Operation: Operations Enemy: Terrain. 170th Bde.

57th Divn. 14th Corps, 5th Army.   WESTERN FRONT.
A.D.M.S. Col. J.F. Dewar.   Oct. 1917.

19th Corps from 29/10/17.

Phase "D" 1. (b) (Cont.)

1917.
Oct. 26th. (Cont.)
Operations. Operations Enemy: Terrain. (Cont.)
57th Divn. attacked at dawn. Ground could not be gained owing to muddy state of terrain and intense enemy fire.
Casualties. 16 and 534 wounded.

27th.
Evacuation. Not very satisfactory owing to Decauville Trains running intermittently and plank tracks becoming blocked also defective liaison between Regl. and R.A.M.C. personnel.
Casualties. Not very numerous.

28th.
Decorations. Cpl. Garrett C.R. 2/3rd Wessex Field Ambulance awarded M.M.
L/Cpl. French H.A. 2/2nd Wessex Field Ambulance awarded M.M.

29th.
Transfer. To 19th Corps.

B.E.F. 3.

57th Divn. 1@th Corps, 5th Army.   WESTERN FRONT.

A.D.M.S. Col. J.F.Dewar.   Oct. 1917.

                                      Nov. 1917.

Phase "D" 1. Passchendaele Operations July-Dec. 1917.

    (b) Operations commencing 1/10/17.
        Canadians attacked Passchendaele Oct. 30th.
        Canadians took Passchendaele Nov. 6th.

1917.

Oct. 29th.   **Transfer.** To 19th Corps.

            Casualties. Admitted to C.M.D.S.

Noon 25th-	Noon 26th-		2 and 99 wounded.
" 26th	" 27th		9 and 302 wounded.
" 27th	" 28th.		10 and 277 wounded.
" 28th	" 29th.		4 and 131 wounded.

30th.   **Evacuation. Instructions.** Appendix C. Attached.

            Appendices. B. R.A.M.C. Op. Order 14 d/ 23/10/17.

            C. Memo regarding Evacuation d/ 30/10/17.

APPENDIX. A.

Date.	170th Brigade & 3/2nd West Lancs Field Ambce.	172nd Brigade & 2/3rd Wessex Field Ambce:.	171st Brigade & 2/2nd Wessex Field Ambce:.	57th Division Headquarters
October 17th Wednesday.	NEDONCHELLE to RENESCURE.			
October 18th Thursday.	RENESCURE to PROVEN	LAIRES to RENESCURE.		NORRENT-FONTES RENESCURE
October 19th Friday.		RENESCURE to PROVEN.	BOURECQ to RENESCURE.	RENESCURE to PROVEN
October 20th Saturday.			RENESCURE to PROVEN.	

SECRET.   Appendix "B."   Copy No............

57th. DIVISION.

R.A.M.C. OPERATION ORDER No. 14.

Reference Map Sheet 20/ 1/40,000
" " " 28/ 1/40,000

1. (a) The 50th. and 57th. Divisions will relieve the 34th. Division in the line between October 23rd. and October 25th.

   (b) The 57th. Division (less Artillery) will take over the Southern portion of the 34th. Divisional front from V.14.central to V.7.b.55.50. (both references approximate).

2. On completion of relief location of D.H.Q. will be WELSH FARM B.14.c.2.2. Advanced D.H.Q. will be CANAL BANK C.19.c.0.9.

3. (a) The 2/2nd. Wessex Field Ambulance will take over from 104th. Field Ambulance at PELISSIER FARM, B.21.a.2.0. Relief to be complete by 5-0 p.m. 24th. October.
   Advanced posts to be relieved by 3-0 p.m. 24th. October. Details of reliefs to be arranged by Officers Commanding concerned.

   (b) Officer Commanding, 2/2nd. Wessex Field Ambulance will be in charge of all evacuations taking place East of the Canal DEL'YSER.

4. The following posts will be taken over by 2/2nd. Wessex Field Ambulance.

   (a)   FUSILIER   C.13.c.1.3.
          GALLWITZ FARM   C.8.a.6.4.
          PIG & WHISTLE   U.28.b.4.3.
          Henley   C.3.central.
          LOUIS FARM   U.24.a.5.0.
          FERDAN R.A.P.   V.19.a.7.6.
          EAGLE TRENCH   U.23.b.4.4. (in conjunction with 50th. Division.)

   (b) A.D.S. CEMENT HOUSE will be taken over from 50th. Division by 5-0 p.m. 26th. October.

5. The 2/3rd. Wessex Field Ambulance less bearer division will remain at present headquarters and deal with local sick. The bearer division with two Officers will be attached to 2/2nd. Wessex Field Ambulance.

6. The 3/2nd. West Lancs. Field Ambulance less bearer division will relieve the 105th. Field Ambulance at PROVEN SCHOOL, details to be arranged between Officers Commanding concerned. The bearer division with two Officers will be attached to 2/2nd. Wessex Field Ambulance.

7. (a) The 2/2nd. Wessex Field Ambulance less transport will move by rail from PROVEN at a time to be notified later.

   (b) Transport will move by road passing the starting point F.1.c.4.0. at 9-0 a.m. 24th. October. Route:- 27/F.1.c.4.0. - East by NORTHERN CHEMIN MILITAIRE - TYRONE CROSS ROADS (20/S.26.c.2.7.)- SAN SIXT JUNCTION 28/A.2.a.6.8. - A.2.b.9.4. - S.27.a.2.0. - Bridge at S.28.c.5.9. - Plank Road S.28.d.9.5. - DE WIPPE CAMP - ONDANK CABARET (A.12.a.0.7.) - WOESTEN SWITCH from ONDANK CABARET to B.1.c.9.1. - ELVERDINGHE - thence by most direct routes to destinations.

   (c) The bearer divisions of 2/3rd. Wessex Field Ambulance and 3/2nd. West Lancs. Field Ambulance will move by rail with 2/2nd. Wessex Field Ambulance.

2.

8. The Motor Ambulance Cars of the 2/3rd. Wessex Field Ambulance less one Daimler and those of the 3/2nd. West Lancs. Field Ambulance less one Daimler and one Ford, will report at 6-30 a.m. 24th. October, to Officer Commanding, 2/2nd. Wessex Field Ambulance remaining under his orders until further notice.

9. A party of 200 men has been detailed by D.H.Q. as extra bearers in emergency.

10. Completion of reliefs will be notified to this Office.

11. A.D.M.S. Office will close at PROVEN at 8-0 a.m. 25th. October opening at same hour at WELSH FARM.

12. ACKNOWLEDGE.

M 4176/40.
Headquarters,
23rd. October, 1917.

Colonel, A. Med. S.,
A.D.M.S., 57th. Division.

Issued at...........5-15....p.m.

Distribution :-

Copy No. 1 to H.Q., 57th. Division.
        2   -do-
        3   D.D.M.S., XIV Corps.
        4   D.M.S., Fifth Army.
        5   O.C., 2/2nd. Wessex Field Ambulance.
        6   O.C., 2/3rd. Wessex Field Ambulance.
        7   O.C., 3/2nd. West Lancs. Field Ambulance.
        8   H.Q., 170th. Infantry Brigade.
        9   H.Q., 171st. Infantry Brigade.
      10   H.Q., 172nd. Infantry Brigade.
      11   A.D.M.S., 34th. Division.
      12   A.D.M.S., 50th. Division.
      13   Area Commandant, PROVEN.
      14   C.R.A., 57th. Division.
      15   C.R.E. 57th. Division.
      16   57th. Divisional Signal Co.
      17   O.C., 57th. Divisional Train, A.S.C.
      18   D.A.D.V.S., 57th. Division.
      19   A.P.M., 57th. Division.
      20   War Diary.
      21   War Diary.
      22   File.
      23   File.
      24   Spare.

Appendix "C"

MEMORANDUM REGARDING EVACUATION.

As certain difficulties were experienced in the evacuation of wounded on 26/10/1917, the following instructions are issued:

1. It is vitally important that bearer officers should personally keep in touch with Regimental Medical Officers and personally supervise the evacuation of wounded. They should be prepared to reinforce the Regimental Stretcher Bearers and, when necessary, to provide a complete relief for them.

   The work of the bearer officer is not complete so long as one case remains to be evacuated. It will be found advantageous to detail two bearer officers for duty in advance of the Advanced Dressing Station; one to supervise the clearing of relay posts and one to direct the evacuation in advance of the Regimental Aid Posts when necessary. For these reasons it is important that bearer officers have a sound working knowledge of the geography of the trenches in their area and that they should invariably and at the earliest possible moment make themselves familiar with it. Each bearer officer should also have a thorough knowledge of the available personnel at his disposal in order that there may be no hitch in bringing up reinforcements.

2. The handing over of stretchers must be carefully arranged so that wastage is kept down to a minimum.

   Each relay post must be supplied with a sufficient number to enable it to hand over an empty stretcher for each stretcher case received. This number can easily be estimated with a knowledge of
   (a) the number of squads in front; and
   (b) the distance between the squads in front and behind and the post in question.

3. Stretcher bearers must not be allowed to remain in a post after having brought in a case. They should return immediately.

4. A certain number of reliable N.C.O's should be detailed to assist the bearer officer in the supervision of evacuation and in the leading of bearers. These N.C.O's should not be included in bearer squads.

5. One or two runners should be at the disposal of each bearer officer in order to facilitate communication. These men should be detailed from tent sub-division personnel (so as not to deplete the bearers) and should be employed, for the time being, on no other duty.

6. Field Ambulance Officers should realize that their most important duty, during active operations, is the rapid evacuation of wounded; and that unnecessary dressing of cases is to be avoided.

   It must be borne in mind that, when there is a rush of work at an Advanced Dressing Station, dressings can seldom be aseptic and that all cases will receive due and efficient treatment at Corps Main Dressing Station or Casualty Clearing Station.

6. (Contd.) When dressing does not hinder evacuation, as in quiet periods, time may be spent on individual cases: but great harm is done by undertaking unnecessary measures and so causing congestion. For these reasons, only those cases should be dressed that urgently require or may be reasonably be expected greatly to benefit by such treatment : e.g., cases of haemorrhage or unsplinted fracture.

In Advanced Dressing Stations much more attention should be given to the combating of shock by the provision of blankets hot drinks and small doses of morphia when necessary than to dressing any cases that do not urgently require it.

30th Octr.1917.

Colonel, A. Med. S.,
A.D.M.S., 57th Division.

A.D.M.S. 57th Division

COMMITTEE FOR THE
MEDICAL HISTORY OF THE WAR
Date 17 JAN. 1918

Army Form C. 2118.

WAR DIARY
or
INTELLIGENCE SUMMARY.
(Erase heading not required.)

ADM 572

Place	Date	Hour	Summary of Events and Information	Remarks and references to Appendices
WELSH FARM	1.11.17.		A.D.M.S. visited XIX Corps Headquarters at ST. SIXTE; 170th Brigade Headquarters, near PROVEN and 2/5th & 4/5th N. Lan.R. interviewing Brigadier, Staff Captain and Medical Officers regarding number fit to go up into the line. The camps of this Brigade near PROVEN are deplorably muddy with no duck-boards, no ablution places and no proper cook houses; 14 men in each tent which has no tent bottom and no floors. Brasiers in marquees was provided for drying of clothes. A.D.M.S. visited baths at Chateau of LA COUTHOVE now handed over to the 16th Division. Visited 46th West Lancs. Fd. Ambulance at PROVEN school. Accommodation here in school buildings and tents for nearly 150 patients. Accommodation is fairly dried; many cases of trench feet, rheumatism and general Chinese patients. A.D.M.S. visited 2/3 Wessex Field Ambulance with Headquarters in poor farm buildings 2½ miles east of PROVEN. Here there is meagre accommodation for a very few patients in a farm: cases for the most part are evacuated at once to C.C.S. (DOZINGHEM group of C.C.S. is only 1 mile or so distant). Horse	

Army Form C. 2118.

WAR DIARY
or
INTELLIGENCE SUMMARY.
(Erase heading not required.)

Instructions regarding War Diaries and Intelligence Summaries are contained in F. S. Regs. Part II. and the Staff Manual respectively. Title pages will be prepared in manuscript.

Place	Date	Hour	Summary of Events and Information	Remarks and references to Appendices
WELSH FARM	1.11.17		Landings here are deplorably muddy. W&K. The 59th Division is to be relieved by the 14th Division on November 6th, 7th and 8th: going probably to RECQUES area. A.D.M.S. interviewed at 32nd West Lancs Field ambulance 6 Medical Officers arrived on 30th as reinforcements. Three of these are U.S. Medical Corps. W&K.	
	2.11.17		A.D.M.S. visited Advanced Divisional Headquarters and interviewed D.O.E. regarding ① Numbers in battalions of 170th Brigade fit to go into line. ② Defective condition in camps of 170th Brigade. ③ Defective evacuation of wounded on 26th October, and ④ Total wounded on 26th and succeeding days. A.D.M.S. attended conference at Office of D.D.M.S., XIX Corps. Present, D.D.M.S. and D.A.D.M.S., XIX Corps and A.D's.M.S., 18th, 50th, 35th and 59th Divisions. The subjects discussed included heating of motor ambulances, tent boards, Quartermaster's conference, inoculation,	

A.5834 Wt.W4973/M687 750,000 8/16 D. D. & L. Ltd. Forms/C.2118/13.

WAR DIARY or INTELLIGENCE SUMMARY.

Army Form C. 2118.

Place	Date	Hour	Summary of Events and Information	Remarks and references to Appendices
WELSH FARM.	2.11.17.		Compilation of A.F. W.3185, salvage of Medical material, combating of shock, etc. " " A.D.M.S. interviewed A.A. & Q.M.G. 14th Division regarding handing over to him on November 6th - 8th. A.D.M.S. issued Medical arrangements for evacuation of wounded at quiet period. Fourteen men arrived as R.A.M.C. Reinforcements. Scrutiny of the returns of wounded shown on A.F. W.3185 for October 25th, 26th, 27th, 28th, and 28th-29th show 25 Officers and 809 Other Ranks. Of these the great majority were wounded on October 26th 1917.	APPENDIX 'A'
	3.11.17.		54th Division are to be relieved on November 6th-8th, moving into RECQUES area: 142nd Brigade now in line: 141st Brigade in camps West of Canal. 140th Brigade in PROYEN area. D.A.D.M.S., 14th Division and O.C., 53rd Field Ambulance who is	
	4.11.17.		to take over charge of forward evacuation came to 54th Divisional Headquarters and arranged with A.D.M.S., 54th Division details of taking	

WAR DIARY
or
INTELLIGENCE SUMMARY.

Army Form C. 2118.

Place	Date	Hour	Summary of Events and Information	Remarks and references to Appendices
WELSH FARM	4/11/17		over on November 6th - 8th. Thereafter A.D.M.S, 57th Division went to D.D.M.S. who approves in general and authorises arrangements in detail directly between A.D's.M.S. concerned. The 53rd Field Ambulance will take over work of evacuation from forward area from 3/2nd Wessex Field Ambulance. The 52nd Field Ambulance will relieve the 51st Field Ambulance now at Corps Main Dressing Station, the latter proceeding to PROVEN school to take over from 3/2nd West Lancs. Field Ambulance. The 3/3rd Wessex Field Ambulance at X.30.c. central will leave a holding party of 1 officer and 8 other ranks. The Field Ambulances of the 57th Division will move thus — November 6th 3/3rd Wessex Field Ambulance less 1 officer and 8 other ranks to LOSTEBARNE.	
			" 7th 3/2nd Wessex Field Ambulance to BLANC PIGNON	
			" 8th 3/2nd West Lancs. Field Ambulance to LIGQUES	
			Issued Operation Order No 15 for move of Field Ambulances	APPENDIX 'B'.
5/11/17				

Army Form C. 2118.

WAR DIARY
or
INTELLIGENCE SUMMARY.
(Erase heading not required.)

Instructions regarding War Diaries and Intelligence Summaries are contained in F. S. Regs., Part II. and the Staff Manual respectively. Title pages will be prepared in manuscript.

Place	Date	Hour	Summary of Events and Information	Remarks and references to Appendices
WELSH FARM	5.11.17		*on November 7th and 8th* not	
	6.11.17		A.D.M.S. visited all field ambulances of 57th Division regarding move to RECQUES area on 7th and 8th. Personnel with limbered wagon and 1 water cart and horses going by rail, other transport by road (two days march). Move of field ambulances under Brigade arrangements. 2/2nd Wessex Field Ambulance moved today from PELISSIER FARM near ELVERDINGHE to LOSTBARNE, in RECQUES Area; personnel by rail, transport by road (2 days).	
	7.11.17			
	8.11.17		Headquarters, 57th Division moved from WELSH FARM (Advanced Headquarters from FUSILIER HOUSE, Canal Bank) near ELVERDINGHE to ZUTKERQUE, between ST OMER and CALAIS. 2/3rd Wessex Field Ambulance from near ST SIXTE to BLANC PIGNON, near ZUTKERQUE; and 3/2nd West Lancs Field Ambulance from PROVEN School to LICQUES (both in RECQUES Area), in each case personnel by rail, transport (two days march) by road. 2/3rd Wessex Field Ambulance sent 2 Officers (U.S. Medical Corps) and 1 O/R Subdivision (1 Q.O.R.) to 61st Casualty Clearing Station.	

WAR DIARY
or
INTELLIGENCE SUMMARY.

Army Form C. 2118.

Place	Date	Hour	Summary of Events and Information	Remarks and references to Appendices
ZUTKERQUE	9.11.17		ADMS visited 2/2nd Wessex Field Ambulance at LOSTEBARNE. Accommodation in empty cottages (good) for 30-40 patients. Accommodation for Officers and personnel generally very good. Sufficient repairs and alterations of outbuildings and adjacent farm. All shoes and mules will be under cover. Two new large motor ambulance cars recently received by this unit (as replacement of one deficiency) and one by 2/3rd Wessex Field Ambulance.	
	10.11.17		Casualties in 59th Divisional Field Ambulances in period 19.10.17 to noon 1.11.17 —	
				Killed	Wounded	missing
			2/2nd Wessex Field Ambulance	1	21	1
			2/3rd Wessex Field Ambulance	-	7	-
			3/2nd West Lancs Field Ambulance	1	12	-
			Total	2	40	1
			The one man missing is believed to have been killed and partially buried by a shell. Lieut W.D. MACKINNON, S.R. joined Division for duty and was posted to 2/3/3rd Wessex Field Ambulance.	
	11.11.17		ADMS visited 2/2md West Lancs Field Ambulance at LIEQUES. Accommodation for about 100 patients and all personnel in old and somewhat decayed chateau. This	

WAR DIARY or INTELLIGENCE SUMMARY.

Army Form C. 2118.

Place	Date	Hour	Summary of Events and Information	Remarks and references to Appendices
ZUTKERQUE	11-11-17		Visited Divisional Rest Stations, as well as Main Dressing Station of Field Ambulances, and to have a special scabies wash. Found that Rhets tens arising in midly wounded passed on most of the rhets tens: but today all are hung out into suitable places with boxes and standing up across different places in neighbourhood. Dentist 2/27 Major Teeth Wintimere at LOSTEBARNE. Also, all the huts have been got under cover. Investigated detail complaints of defective conditions between regimental medical personnel and R.A.M.C. those personnel on October 28th. over.	
	12-11-17		A.D.M.S. held inquiry regarding defective evacuations of wounded on October 28th. Lt-Colonel PARSONS, Major ADAMS, and Lieut. GABLE referring evacuations from Forward Stores, and Captains O'HAGAN, McKENZIE, and CAMERON (Medical Officers 10th Infantry Brigade). Transpired in course of estimation by Medical Officers. A.D.M.S. saw two men reported by Medical Officer as unfit for service at the front line.	
	13-11-17		A.D.M.S. delivered two lectures on subject of Trench Feet and to personnel attached to Officers and N.C.O.s of 2/5, 2/8 and 2/6 K.R.R. Is hoped Regt. subsequently Divisional Artillery came out of time and manured on this area yesterday. More.	

WAR DIARY
or
INTELLIGENCE SUMMARY

Army Form C. 2118.

Place	Date	Hour	Summary of Events and Information	Remarks and references to Appendices
ZUTKERQUE	14/11/17		A.D.M.S. visited 2/3rd Wessex Field Ambulance seeing accommodation for patients (up to about 30), samples of filth and food items. Also savings and care her troops get too much of leave, and meals. Delivered that address to Divisions of Sanitation to unit of 170th Infantry Brigade at BONNINGUES (2/4th R.Lanc.R.), AUDENFORT, (2/5th R.Lanc.R.) LICQUES, (4/5th R.Lanc.R.) and ALEMBON (1/5 K.Lanc.Rgt) respectively. Dufield – syllabus of training lectures to be given to N.C.Officers and Other Ranks. Noted Units that there were failed to the Doctors when the that the much Bn. off more Mpositive's officers attended conference of Brigade and Battalion Commanding...	
			A.D.M.S. held a Divisional Conference. Proceeded by motor to units of 172nd Infantry Brigade at REBERGUES (2/4 K.Lanc.R.), LUMBRES (2/10 K.L.R.), LISBOURG (2/10 K.L.R.), NIELLES (2/9 K.Lpool Rgt) and LANDRETHUN (4/5 K. Lanc Rgt) respectively – no...	
			A.D.M.S. visited 2/2nd West Lancs Field Ambulance at LICQUES. Stretcher... to about 100 patients. Station was sometimes in the building. Gave instructions... Next to the village of LICQUES. Visited by the Medics N.C.O Stretcher-vals KIDSTE BARNE Accommodation of resident inability no two small cottages also by...	

A 5834 Wt.W4973/M687 750,000 8/16 D.D. & L. Ltd. Forms/C.2118/13.

Army Form C. 2118.

WAR DIARY
or
INTELLIGENCE SUMMARY.
(Erase heading not required.)

Instructions regarding War Diaries and Intelligence Summaries are contained in F. S. Regs., Part II. and the Staff Manual respectively. Title pages will be prepared in manuscript.

Place	Date	Hour	Summary of Events and Information	Remarks and references to Appendices
ZUTKERQUE	16.11.17		ends on standing. Conference of Field Ambulances Commanders and Medical Officers at LOSTEARNE at 2.30 pm. Twenty fifteen present.	
	17.11.17		Submitted to Deputy Director Medical Headquarters report on fighting drawn and evacuation of wounded on October 26. ADMS paid visits to Field Ambulance Officers injured the field to Division on Military Subjects. Other Captain (on and Infant) DADMS attended a meeting and military talks of admin. (6 in all) to follow. Discussion.	
	18.11.17		ADMS proceeded on 14 days leave to United Kingdom. Lieut.-Colonel PARSONS, O.C. 2/2 Wessex Field Ambulance arrived at HQ Headquarters to take up duty as A/ADMS.	
	19.11.17		Major Adams, acting Officer Commanding 2/2nd Wessex Field Ambulances lectured junior Medical Officers on "Organisation of a division."	
	20.11.17		Inspected 2/3rd Wessex Field Ambulance with a view to the erection of litter staking.	
	21.11.17		DADMS lectured junior Medical Officers on "Duties of a regimental Medical Officer."	

WAR DIARY
or
INTELLIGENCE SUMMARY.
(Erase heading not required.)

Army Form C. 2118.

Place	Date	Hour	Summary of Events and Information	Remarks and references to Appendices
ZUTKERQUE	22/11/17		Inspected 2/2nd West Lancs Field Ambulances with reference to the treatment of scabies. Sister there have to be retained in the division. The question of accommodation is becoming acute.	
	23/11/17		Captain WHEATLEY. 2. i/c. 2/3rd Wessex Fields Ambulances was acting Junior Medical Officer on Rations and Supplies.	
	24/11/17		Officer Commanding 2/3rd Wessex Fields Ambulances was asked to increase his accommodation from 60 – 80 beds in view of the inadequate accommodation at the Divisional Rest Station at LIGUES.	
	25/11/17		DDMS XVIII Corps asked as adjust to be conducted on the incidence of diarrhoea which he considered receiving. Field Ambulances were asked to investigate the matter and report as soon as possible.	
	26/11/17		Captain EDMISTON R/Officer Commanding 2/03rd Wessex Fields Stretcher was retained junior Medical Officer on Correspondence.	
	27/11/17		Further instructions from DDMS XVIII Corps the Clayton Disinfector was returned to XIX Corps Rest Station. This D.R.S. Commanding 170th Bde asks states that experience in his battalion suggests that the entrenched area of White Oil Novels	

Army Form C. 2118.

WAR DIARY
or
INTELLIGENCE SUMMARY.
(Erase heading not required.)

Place	Date	Hour	Summary of Events and Information	Remarks and references to Appendices
ZUTKERQUE	27.11.17		to soften men's feet and render them more liable to foot affliction on the march. Admits rubbing without oil during "press".	
	28.11.17		Instructions received from D.D.M.S. XVIII Corps, that the XVIII Corps Skins Dept has opened at GRENOGE FARM. Msgs 27/40500. This will relieve congestion at the Divisional Rest Stations. Im w/fy to D.D.M.S. XVIII Corps. the Divisional Bath Column what that it is hoped to have all Baths Stationaries fitted with heating apparatus early in December.	
	29.11.17		Inspected baths at RECQUES, LICQUES and NIELLES. Lack of supervision was manifest at LICQUES and NIELLES. The issue of clean clothing is unsatisfactory. Submitted report to Division.	
	30.11.17		Complaint received about "Lacto" milk powder. Field Ambulances have been ^ ordered to report.	

Humphrey-Owany
Lieut-Colonel,
A/A. D. M. S., 57th Division.

November 30th 1917.

B.E.F.

SUMMARY OF MEDICAL WAR DIARIES FOR
57th Divn. 14th Corps, 5th Army.
19th Corps from 29/10/17.
To 2nd Army on 14/11/17.

WESTERN FRONT. Oct.- Nov. 1917.

A.D.M.S. Col. J.F. Dewar.
D.A.D.M.S. Capt. M.B. King.

SUMMARISED UNDER THE FOLLOWING HEADINGS.

Phase "D" 1. Passchendaele Operations July-Dec. 1917.

  (b) Operations commencing 1/10/17.
     Canadians attacked Passchendaele Oct. 30th.
     Canadians took Passchendaele Nov. 6th.

Nov. 1st.	Casualties R.A.M.C. Noon 24th Oct.- Noon 1st Nov.. 0 and 2 killed. 0 and 40 wounded, 0 and 1 missing. Trench Feet: Rheumatism. Many cases of trench feet and rheumatism owing to camp being in deplorably muddy condition with no duck boards. 14 men in each tent with no tent bottoms or straw.
2nd.	Medical Arrangements. Appendix A. (Paras. 1-3,5) Attached (Put back into Diary.)
7th- 8th.	Military Situation. Medical Arrangements. Appendix B. (Paras. 1-6) Attached. (Put back into Diary.)
8th.	Moves. To Zutkerque (Rest Area.) Moves Field Ambulance. 2/2 nd Wessex Field Ambulance to Lostbarne. 2/3rd Wessex Field Ambulance to Blanc Pignon.

B.E.F. 4.

57th Divn. 19th Corps, 5th Army.   WESTERN FRONT.
A.D.M.S. Col. J.F. Dewar.   Nov. 1917.
2nd Army from 14/11/17.

Phase "D" 1. (Cont.) (b)

1917.
Nov. 8th(Cont.)   Moves Field Ambulances (Cont.)
                  3/2nd W. Lancs Field Ambulance to Licques.
Nov. 8th.   Moves Field Ambulances Det. 2 and 19 2/3rd Wessex Field
                  Ambulance to 61st Casualty Clearing Station.
14th.   Transfer. To 2nd Army.
                  Appendices:-
                  A. Med. Arr. for evac. of W. during quiet period d/ 2/11/17.
                  B. R.A.M.C. Op. Order 15 d/ 5/11/17.

Nov. 1st.	**Casualties R.A.M.C.** Noon 24th Oct. - Noon 1st Nov.. 0 and 2 killed. 0 and 40 wounded, 0 and 1 missing. **Trench Feet: Rheumatism.** Many cases of trench feet and rheumatism owing to camp being in deplorably muddy condition with no duck boards. 14 men in each tent with no tent bottoms or straw
2nd.	**Medical Arrangements.** Appendix A. (Paras. 1-3,5) Attached
7th- 8th.	**Military Situation. Medical Arrangements.** Appendix B. (Paras. 1-6) Attached.
8th.	**Moves.** To Zutkerque (Rest Area.) **Moves Field Ambulance.** 2/2nd Wessex Field Ambulance to Lostbarne. 2/3rd Wessex Field Ambulance to Blanc Pignon.

57th Divn. 19th Corps, 5th Army.　　　WESTERN FRONT.
A.D.M.S. Col. J.F. Dewar.　　　Nov. 1917.
2nd Army from 14/11/17.

Phase "D" 1. (Cont.) (b)

1917.
Nov. 8th(Cont.)　Moves Field Ambulances (Cont.)
　　　　　3/2nd W. Lancs Field Ambulance to Licques.
Nov. 8th.　Moves Field Ambulances Det. 2 and 19 2/3rd Wessex Field Ambulance to 61st Casualty Clearing Station.
14th.　Transfer. To 2nd Army.
　Appendices:-
　A. Med. Arr. for evac. of W. during quiet period d/ 2/11/17.
　B. R.A.M.C. Op. Order 15 d/ 5/11/17.

Appendix "A"

57th. DIVISION.

MEDICAL ARRANGEMENTS.
for evacuation of wounded during quiet period.

Reference Map Sheet 28/ 1/40,000
                                20/ 1/40,000

1. **REGIMENTAL AID POST, LOUIS FARM (U.24.a.5.1.).**
   At this point there will be a number of R.A.M.C. bearers whose duty will be to carry down to the Relay Post at EAGLE TRENCH (U.23.b.4.4.). They may also be used by the Medical Officer in charge, ~~FEEDAN HOUSE (U.19.a.7.6.)~~ to keep up communications with the bearer officer in charge, PIG & WHISTLE, U.28.c.1.3., if no R.A.M.C. runner is available.

   LOUIS FARM

   C.H.2.

2. **RELAY POSTS, EAGLE TRENCH and PIG & WHISTLE**
   At each relay post there will be a number of R.A.M.C. bearers and also a supply of Stretchers, Blankets and Dressings. There will be an N.C.O. in charge of each relay post, whose duty will be to see that cases as they come in are rapidly evacuated and that stretchers and blankets are properly handed over.
   No dressing should be done at relay posts but what is absolutely essential. Dressings are kept in order to supply Regimental Medical Officers.

3. **ADVANCED DRESSING STATION, CEMENT HOUSE (U.28.c.1.3.).**
   (a) Here all necessary dressing will be done, under arrangements made by 50th. Division wounded will be given hot drinks, and evacuation will be by train (when available) to Corps Main Dressing Station, SOLFERINO FARM (B.23a.0.3.) Corps Walking Wounded Collecting Post, CHEAPSIDE (B.17.b.9.1.).
   (b) When trains are not available, Ford Cars for stretcher cases will run from CEMENT HOUSE to HUDDLESTONE CORNER (C.7.d.2.3.) at which point wounded will be transferred to Daimler Ambulances and taken to SOLFERINO FARM.
   (c) Walking wounded who cannot be accommodated on trains will be directed down TRACKS A & B to the COLLECTING POINTS, C.8.a.8.4. and C.8.a.8.0. (where tracks cross the road) where they will be met by Ambulance Cars and taken to CHEAPSIDE.
   All walking wounded finding their way to FUSILIER Advanced Dressing Station (C.13.c.1.3.) will be directed to CHEAPSIDE.
   (d) Officer Commanding, 2/2nd. Wessex Field Ambulance will arrange for the necessary notices to be erected at points C.8.a.8.4. and C.8.a.8.0., and also where necessary to ensure walking wounded finding their way from FUSILIER to CHEAPSIDE.

4. All requests by Regimental Medical Officers for extra bearers, stretchers, dressings, etc., must be in writing and sent by runner to Officer in charge PIG & WHISTLE.

5. Sick will be evacuated by Regimental Medical Officers in the same manner as wounded.
   Sick reporting at FUSILIER will be transferred, when necessary, to CANADA FARM (A.18.a.2.7.)

6. Officer Commanding, 2/2nd. Wessex Field Ambulance will establish an intermediate Relay Post near LANGEMARCK (U.23.c.) if he finds it advisable.

2nd. November, 1917.

                                          Colonel, A. Med. S.,
                                          A.D.M.S., 57th. Division.

DISTRIBUTION:-

Copies to:-

Headquarters, 57th. Division (2)
Headquarters, 170th. Infantry Brigade.
Headquarters, 171st. Infantry Brigade.
Headquarters, 172nd. Infantry Brigade.
D.M.S., Fifth Army.
D.D.M.S., XIX Corps.
A.D.M.S., 50th. Division.
A.D.M.S., 58th. Division.
O.C., 2/2nd. Wessex Field Ambulance.
O.C., 2/3rd. Wessex Field Ambulance.
O.C., 3/2nd. West Lancs. Field Ambulance.
M.O., 2/5th. R. Lanc. R.
M.O., 2/4th. N. Lan. R.
M.O., 2/5th. N. Lan. R.
M.O., 4/5th. N. Lan. R.
M.O., 2/5th. K. Lpool R.
M.O., 2/6th. K. Lpool R.
M.O., 2/7th. K. Lpool R.
M.O., 2/8th. K. Lpool R.
M.O., 2/9th. K. Lpool R.
M.O., 2/10th. K. Lpool R.
M.O., 2/4th. S. Lan. R.
M.O., 2/5th. S. Lan. R.
M.O., 285th. Bde. R.F.A.
M.O., 286th. Bde. R.F.A.
M.O., 57th. Divl. Amm. Colm.
M.O., 57th. Divisional R.E.
M.O., R.A. Wagon Lines.
D.A.D.V.S., 57th. Division.
A.P.M., 57th. Division.
G.R.A., 57th. Division.
O.C., 57th. Divisional Signal Co.
O.C., 57th. Divl. Train, A.S.C.
S.C.F., C/E.
S.C.F., Non C/E.
File (2)
War Diary. (2)

Appendix B.

Copy No. 16

57th. DIVISION.

R.A.M.C. OPERATION ORDER No. 15.

Reference Map Sheet HAZEBROUCK 5 A.

1. (a) The 57th. Division (less Artillery) will be relieved in the forward area by the 17th. Division (less Artillery) on the 6th., 7th., and 8th. November.
   (b) On relief, 57th. Division will concentrate in the RECQUES area.

2. The 2/2nd. Wessex Field Ambulance will hand over to the 53rd. Field Ambulance on the 7th. November. Advance parties from 53rd. Field Ambulance will arrive on the 6th. November. Relief to be complete by 9-0 a.m., 7th. November. Completion of relief to be reported to this Office.

3. (a) The 2/2nd. Wessex Field Ambulance plus attached personnel of 3/2nd. West Lancs. Field Ambulance will move under Brigade arrangements to the new area on the 7th. November.
   (b) The attached personnel of the 2/3rd. Wessex Field Ambulance will return to their unit on this date.

4. (a) The 3/2nd. West Lancs. Field Ambulance less personnel attached to 2/2nd. Wessex Field Ambulance, and the 2/3rd. Wessex Field Ambulance will proceed to the new area under Brigade arrangements on the 8th. November.

5. On arrival in the RECQUES area, the Field Ambulances will open to receive local sick.

6. Sick requiring evacuation will be sent to No. 13 Casualty Clearing Station, ARQUES, 14½ miles due East of RECQUES.

7. The A.D.M.S. Office will close at WELSH FARM at 10-0 a.m. on the 8th. November and open at ZUTKERQUE, at the same hour.

8. ACKNOWLEDGE.

Colonel A. Med. S.,
A.D.M.S., 57th. Division.

5th. November, 1917.

Issued at 7.15 p.m.

4. (b). The 3/2nd West Lancs. Field Ambulance will hand over to the 51st Field Ambulance on the night 7/8th November, 1917. Relief to be completed by 8-0am 8th November, 1917.

DISTRIBUTION -

Copy No. 1. to H.Q., 57th. Division.
       2.   -do-
       3.   D.D.M.S., XIX Corps.
       4.   D.M.S., Fifth Army.
       5.   O.C., 2/2nd. Wessex Field Ambulance.
       6.   O.C., 2/3rd. Wessex Field Ambulance.
       7.   O.C., 3/2nd. West Lancs. Field Ambulance.
       8.   H.Q., 170th. Infantry Brigade.
       9.   H.Q. 171st. Infantry Brigade.
      10.   H.Q., 172nd. Infantry Brigade.
      11.   C.R.E., 57th. Division.
      12.   C.R.A., 57th. Division.
      13.   O.C., 57th. Divisional Train, A.S.C.
      14.   O.C., 57th. Divisional Signal Company.
      15.   A.D.M.S., 17th. Division.
      16.   War Diary.
      17.   -do-
      18.   File.
      19.   Spare.
      20.   -do-
      21.   D.A.D.V.S., 57th Division.
      22.   A.P.M., 57th Division.
      23.   A.D.M.S., 50th Division.
      24.   A.D.M.S., 58th Division.

Medical Officer,

Course of
A short elementary lectures for junior Medical
Officers will be given shortly.
The Officers mentioned below will arrange to
lecture on the subjects stated before their names:-

SATURDAY, 17th November, 1917 - Lecture I - Introduction -
Army Methods - Discipline - Colonel T.F.DEWAR, T.D.,
A.D.M.S., 57th Division.

MONDAY, 19th November, 1917 - Lecture II - Constitution
of a Division - Duties of Various Departments -
Major H.C.ADAMS, 2/2nd Wessex Field Ambulance,
R.A.M.C.,TF.

WEDNESDAY, 21st November 1917 - Lecture III - Duties of
a Regimental Medical Officer - Captain M.B.KING,
M.C., D.A.D.M.S., 57th Division.

FRIDAY, 23rd November, 1917 - Lecture IV - Rations
and Supplies - Lieut. T.F.WHEATLEY, 2/3rd
Wessex Field Ambulance, R.A.M.C.,TF.,

MONDAY, 26th November, 1917 - Lecture V - Correspondence -
Captain J.F.DENISTON, 2/2nd Wessex Field
Ambulance, R.A.M.C.,TF,

WEDNESDAY, 28th November, 1917 - Lecture VI -
Horse Management - Lieut-Colonel H.Compton
Parsons, 2/2nd Wessex Field Ambulance, R.A.M.C.,TF.

The above Lectures will be given at the office
of A.D.M.S., 57th Division at 3-0pm on the days
specified.
All Medical Officers who have not completed
two months service in FRANCE will be present.
Any others who wish it may attend.

14/11/1917.

Captain,
D.A.D.M.S.,
for A.D.M.S., 57th Division.

COMMITTEE FOR THE
MEDICAL HISTORY OF THE WAR
Date 29 JAN 1918

Army Form C. 2118.

WAR DIARY
or
INTELLIGENCE SUMMARY.
(Erase heading not required.)

Place	Date	Hour	Summary of Events and Information	Remarks and references to Appendices
ZUTKERQUE	1-12-17		Warning orders received from Divisional Headquarters that the Division will move within a week to XIX Corps reserve Area, ROUSBRUGGE. This area is now occupied by the French.	
	2-12-17		Field Ambulances report on "Lacto" Milk Powder received. This powder appears to be unsatisfactory in many ways, being difficult to mix, leaving a sediment, giving an unpleasant taste and in some cases causing diarrhoea. Divisional Headquarters has been notified.	
	3-12-17		DADMS visited the XIX Corps Reserve Area with a view to seeing Field Ambulance sites. French troops are still in occupation of a portion of the new area.	
	4-12-17		R.S.M.G. relies received from 17th Division who will relieve us in the present area. The existing Field Ambulances at LOSTEBARNE will not be taken over by the 179 Division as only two of their Field Ambulances are coming to this area. Instructions received from DH2 for the move to XIX Corps Reserve.	
	5-12-17		R.S.M.G. Operation Order No 16 issued, also Medical Arrangements for the new area. Instructions received from XIX Corps that the A/D.M.S. will assume	Appendix A.3

Army Form C. 2118.

WAR DIARY
or
INTELLIGENCE SUMMARY.
(Erase heading not required.)

Instructions regarding War Diaries and Intelligence Summaries are contained in F.S. Regs. Part II. and the Staff Manual respectively. Title pages will be prepared in manuscript.

Place	Date	Hour	Summary of Events and Information	Remarks and references to Appendices
ZUTKERQUE	5.12.17		Field Ambulances will take over the French Hospital, ROUSBRUGGE as a Divisional Rest Station on December 12th, and the 2/2nd Wessex Field Ambulance take over the French Hospital WARYENBURG on the same date. The 3/2nd West Lancs Field Ambulances are detailed to proceed on 7th December direct to the French Hospital, HARINGHE. Colonel DEWAR returned from leave.	
	6.12.17		The transport of the 2/3rd Wessex Field Ambulance moved today to LEDERZEELE en route to the new area.	
	7.12.17		The personnel of the 2/3rd Wessex Field Ambulance proceeded by train to HERZEELE. Personnel and transport of 3/2nd West Lancs Field Ambulance left for HARINGHE, leaving an officer and 30 other ranks to carry on the Divisional Rest Station at LIGAULTS, until relief by 17th Division.	
ROUSBRUGGE	8.12.17		Personnel of 2/2nd Wessex Field Ambulance proceeded to the new area. The transport left yesterday. Move of Divisional Headquarters to ROUSBRUGGE. A.D.M.S. visited 3/2nd West Lancs Field Ambulance at HARINGHE. The French are still in occupation and the 3/2nd West Lancs Ambulance will not be able to receive sick for some days, owing to lack of accommodation.	
	9.12.17			

Army Form C. 2118.

WAR DIARY
or
INTELLIGENCE SUMMARY.

(Erase heading not required.)

Instructions regarding War Diaries and Intelligence Summaries are contained in F. S. Regs., Part II. and the Staff Manual respectively. Title pages will be prepared in manuscript.

Place	Date	Hour	Summary of Events and Information	Remarks and references to Appendices
ROUSBRUGGE	10.12.17		Arranged for sick of 170th Infantry Brigade to be sent to 2/2nd Wessex Field Ambulances. ADMS visited French Hospital at WAAYENBURG. Trenches still in occupation, but will probably leave by 16th.	
	11.12.17		DADMS inspected the Headquarter billets in ROUSBRUGGE. The sanitation leaves much to be desired. Efforts are being made to get buckets and latrine seats, but sanitary actions is short of latrines.	
	12.12.17		2/2nd Wessex Field Ambulance moved today from PORTSEA CAMP near PROVEN to Zuarkes (Hulh.de) Billets occupied as French Evacuation Hospital at WAAYENBURG, and opened to receive sick. 2/3rd Wessex Field Ambulance at HERZEELE. 3/2nd West Lancs Field Ambulance in former French Evacuation Hospital at HARINGHE, but not to be opened until French Hospital Authorities have vacated.	
	13.12.17		ADMS with A/DADMS. 18th Division, and Officer in charge Forward Evacuation BOESINGHE Sector (18th Division) visited that Bretts and Stretcher Bearers Dressing Stations and Relay Posts up to NEY FARM.	
	14.12.17		DADMS with Officer Commanding 2/2nd Wessex Field Ambulance, who is to be Officer in charge Forward Evacuation, visited our new front. ADMS attended	

Army Form C. 2118.

WAR DIARY
or
INTELLIGENCE SUMMARY.
(Erase heading not required.)

Instructions regarding War Diaries and Intelligence Summaries are contained in F. S. Regs., Part II. and the Staff Manual respectively. Title pages will be prepared in manuscript.

Place	Date	Hour	Summary of Events and Information	Remarks and references to Appendices
ROUSBRUGGE	14.12.17		G.O.C's Conference (Brigadiers &c) Discussed, inter alia, Evacuation of wounded in new Sector and French Foot Provisions Methods. Issued Operation Order No. 17.	Appendix B.
	15.12.17		Issued Medical Arrangements for evacuation of sick and wounded in new area. ADMS visited 3/2nd West Lancs Field Ambulance which is moving to CHEAPSIDE tomorrow.	Appendix C.
	16.12.17		DADMS visited French Hospital at CROMBEKE 2½ miles from ROUSBRUGGE which is being opened as Divisional Rest Station tomorrow. Division is at present short of one Medical Officer (41 out of 42). Of the 41, one is sick in England, one are on detached duty (Casualty Clearing Stations and the like) and usually 2-3 are home on leave! The result is that the available number is barely adequate.	
	17.12.17		ADMS visited Divisional Rest Station at CROMBEKE. Extensive but accommodation used till now as hutted by French Sisters. ADMS visited Corps Headquarters and saw DDMS regarding shortage of Medical Officers of Division.	

Army Form C. 2118.

WAR DIARY
or
INTELLIGENCE SUMMARY.
(Erase heading not required.)

Instructions regarding War Diaries and Intelligence Summaries are contained in F. S. Regs., Part II. and the Staff Manual respectively. Title pages will be prepared in manuscript.

Place	Date	Hour	Summary of Events and Information	Remarks and references to Appendices
ELVERDINGHE	18.12.17		Headquarters 57th Division moved from ROUSBRUGGE to ELVERDINGHE. 2 huts and offices in and around Chateau. ADMS visited Divisional Main Dressing Station at CHEAPSIDE, administered by 3/2nd West Lanc Field Ambulance.	
	19.12.17		ADMS visited 2/2nd Wessex Field Ambulance at BLEUET FARM.	
	20.12.17		ADMS visited 2/5th Kings Own Royal Lanc. Regt at "H" Camp near CORNISH CROSS. DADMS (Captain KING) went to England on 14 days leave, Captain CREGAN, Medical Officer in charge Divisional R.E. to act as his substitute.	
	21.12.17		Fourth day of extremely hard frost. Division threatened with extreme shortage of Medical Officers, Captain McRITCHIE having been given 6 weeks leave to go to Canada, Captain WOOD having been transferred to Lines of Communication. Captain HILLS been given charge of a Hospital Train, and Captain PLUMLEY declining to re-engage. ADMS visited Divisional Rest Station at CROMBEKE (staffed by 2/3rd Wessex Field Ambulance) afternoon, conference of Field Ambulances Commanders regarding shortage of Medical Officers and disposal of those available, trench methods of Trench Foot Prevention and distinguishing Badges for Field Ambulances Personnel. Decided to have a few of coloured cloth for each 2/2nd Wessex Field Ambulance, cherry, 2/3rd Wessex Field Ambulance, blue, and	

Army Form C. 2118.

WAR DIARY
or
INTELLIGENCE SUMMARY.
(Erase heading not required.)

Instructions regarding War Diaries and Intelligence Summaries are contained in F.S. Regs., Part II. and the Staff Manual respectively. Title pages will be prepared in manuscript.

Place	Date	Hour	Summary of Events and Information	Remarks and references to Appendices
ELVERDINGHE	21/12/17		3/2nd West Lancs Field Ambulance. Night yellow. Days to be khaki sos. A. Section. B. Section. C. Section.	
	22/12/17		A.D.M.S. accompanied by Lieut Colonel PARSONS, Officer Commanding 2/2nd visited Regimental Aid Post and Bearer Relay Post VEE BEND, Bearer Relay Post NEY FARM, Bearer Relay Post CAMONNE FARM, Bearer Relay Post SIGNAL FARM, Advanced Dressing Station GREEN MILL, Field Ambulance Headquarters BLEUET FARM. About fourteen cases of Trench Feet evacuated yesterday.	
	23/12/17		Diagram showing evacuation on this Sector. Field Ambulances of 57th Divisions now disposed as follows:- 2/2nd Wessex Field Ambulance BLEUET FARM 28/3 10.c.44. Evacuation from front line. 2/3rd Wessex Field Ambulance CROMBEKE 19/x 22 a 55. D.R.S. 3/2nd West Lancs Field Ambulance CHEEPS DE 22 B 17 K.9.2. M.D.S.	Appendix D.

A.5834 Wt.W4973/M687 750,000 8/16 D.D.& L. Ltd. Forms/C.2118/13.

Army Form C. 2118.

WAR DIARY
or
INTELLIGENCE SUMMARY.
(Erase heading not required.)

Instructions regarding War Diaries and Intelligence Summaries are contained in F. S. Regs., Part II. and the Staff Manual respectively. Title pages will be prepared in manuscript.

Place	Date	Hour	Summary of Events and Information	Remarks and references to Appendices
ELVERDINGHE	23.12.17		ADMS visited 2/2nd Wessex amb & 2/2nd West Lancs Field Ambulances and 2/5th South Lancs Regt. French Methods of Trench Feet Prevention to be begun by 57th Division at once.	
	24.12.17		Learn that the Divisions is to pass from XIXth to 1st ANZAC Corps and distributed orders on December 29th – January 3rd. ADMS drafted orders for introduction of French Camphor Method of Trench Foot Prevention for the Division. ADMS. visited 2/2nd and 2/3rd Wessex Field Ambulances. and saw DDMS at XIX Corps Headquarters. ADMS drafted and issued detailed instructions for performance of French Method of Trench Foot Prevention. (Copy) Under new transport orders issued by Divisional Headquarters at instance of XIX Corps, all transport is to be posted. 2/2nd Wessex Field Ambulance ordered by 171st Infantry Brigade to supply one G.S. wagon for non-medical transport. Represented to Division that this was in conflict with Geneva Convention. (2nd Field Service Manual, Medical Services ¶24 not B.) ADMS. visited 2/2nd Wessex Field Ambulance in connection with approaching conflict with Geneva Convention.	Appendix E
	26.12.17		moved to ARMENTIERES Sector. ADMS visited 2/10th K's foot R. and 2/4th Lancs R.	

A5834 Wt.W4973/M687 750,000 8/16 D. D. & L. Ltd. Forms/C.2118/13.

WAR DIARY
or
INTELLIGENCE SUMMARY.

Army Form C. 2118.

Place	Date	Hour	Summary of Events and Information	Remarks and references to Appendices
ELVERDINGHE.	26.12.17		regarding Trench Foot Precautions - now in force. ADMS interviewed DADMS 18th Division regarding details of exchange on December 29th - January 3rd. Drafts be issued Operation Orders No. 18. for the move.	Appendices F.
	27.12.17		ADMS with DDMS XIX Corps visited 2/10th Kings Liverpool Regt in camp at BOESINGHE and inspected their Trench Foot Preventive Arrangements. Late visited DADMS (in absence of ADMS) 58th Division. Advanced Dressing Station at GREEN MILL, 1st Division Relieved at CHARPENTIES and 2/2nd Wessex Field Ambulance and 3/2nd West Lancs Field Ambulance. Captain CREWS R.A.M.C. (T.C.) reported for duty.	
	28.12.17		ADMS attended conference held by Divisional Commander regarding mines intended to be undertaken on night of 30th December by 2 Companies 172nd Infantry Brigade. ADMS visited 3/2nd West Lancs Field Ambulance regarding Trench Foot cases.	
	29.12.17		ADMS with Officer Commanding 2/2nd Wessex Field Ambulance to STEENWERCK, where discussed details of taking over ARMENTIERES Sector from 3rd Australian Division with ADMS thereof and on to ERQUINGHEM where they were shown over quarters occupied by 10th Stationary Field Ambulance. Drafted Operation Order No. 19 for the move on days 1/10 to January 4th.	Appendices G.
	30.12.17		ADMS visited 2/2nd Wessex Field Ambulance and 3/2nd West Lancs Field Ambulance	

Army Form C. 2118.

WAR DIARY
or
INTELLIGENCE SUMMARY.
(Erase heading not required.)

Instructions regarding War Diaries and Intelligence Summaries are contained in F. S. Regs., Part II. and the Staff Manual respectively. Title pages will be prepared in manuscript.

Place	Date	Hour	Summary of Events and Information	Remarks and references to Appendices
ELVERDINGHE	30.12.17		regarding special Medical Arrangements for enemy tonight, and transport on approaching move. ADMS with Major General HALES, U.S. ARMY, and A.D.C. visited CRAONNE FARM, GREEN MILL and CHEAP SIDE, and demonstrated methods of evacuation in use in this Sector. Captain W.G.D. HILLS, RAMC left Division today for duty with 76 Hospital.	
	31.12.17		Of 18 regimental Medical Officers who came out with the Division in February only four now remain with their Units.	

December 21st 1917

J Johnston
................Colonel, A. Med. S.
A.D.M.S. 57th (W.L.) Division.

Appendix A

ADDENDA TO R.A.M.C. OPERATION ORDER NO. 16

i. The horse transport of the 3/2nd. West Lancs. Field Ambulance will move by road on December 8th. to the LEDERZEELE area, proceeding to the CANADA or the HARINGHE area on December 9th.

ii. Sufficient personnel will be left by the Officer Commanding, 3/2nd. West Lancs. Field Ambulance to carry on the Divisional Rest Station, LICQUES, until relieved.

(Sd.) H. COMPTON PARSONS,
Lieut-Colonel for Colonel, A. Med. S.,
5th. December, 1917.   A.D.M.S., 57th. Division.

SECRET

57th. DIVISION.

Copy No........18......

R.A.M.C. OPERATION ORDER No. 16.

Reference Map Sheet CALAIS 1³
1/100,000 and
Map Sheet HAZEBROUCK 5 A.
1/100,000

1. 57th. Division (less Artillery) will move to XIX Corps Reserve Area.

2. Field Ambulances are affiliated as follows :-

   3/2nd. West Lancs. Field Ambulance - 170th. Brigade.
   2/2nd. Wessex Field Ambulance - 171st. Brigade.
   2/3rd. Wessex Field Ambulance - 172nd. Brigade.

3. Field Ambulances will be relieved as follows :-

   2/3rd. Wessex Field Ambulance at BLANC PIGNON by the 53rd. Field Ambulance, 17th. Division.

   2/2nd. Wessex Field Ambulance at LOSTEBARNE by the 3/2nd. West Lancs. Field Ambulance, 57th. Division.

   3/2nd. West Lancs. Field Ambulance at LICQUES by the 52nd. Field Ambulance, 17th. Division.

   3/2nd. West Lancs. Field Ambulance at LOSTEBARNE by a holding party from 17th. Division.

4. Moves of Medical Units

   (a) The 2/3rd. Wessex Field Ambulance, less transport plus one limbered wagon and one water cart, will move by train on 7th. December, 1917 to the HERZEELE Area. The horse transport less one limbered wagon and one water cart will move by road on the 6th. December to the LEDERZEELE Area, proceeding to the HERZEELE Area on the 7th. December.

   (b) The 2/2nd. Wessex Field Ambulance less transport will move by bus on 8th. December to the PROOSDY Area. The horse transport will proceed by road on 7th. December to the LEDERZEELE Area, proceeding to the PROOSDY Area on 8th. December.

   (c) The 3/2nd. West Lancs. Field Ambulance less transport will move by road to the Field Ambulance site at LOSTEBARNE on the 8th. December arriving there not before 1-0 p.m.
   The unit will move by bus on the 9th. December to either the CANADA or the HARENGHE Area.

5. Train and bus arrangements and transport routes will be notified later.

6. There are no restrictions for moves to or from train and bus stations.

7. A distance of 500 yards will be maintained between Field Ambulances and other units on the road.

8. Only mobilization equipment and that authorised by General Routine Orders will be taken to the new area. Receipts will be taken for all stores etc., handed over to relieving Field Ambulances. Copies of receipts to be sent to this Office.

2.

9. Holding parties, as small as possible, will be left by each Field Ambulance until the relieving unit arrives.

10. Motor Transport will proceed under instructions of Officers Commanding, Field Ambulances.

11. Departure and completion of moves to be reported to this Office.

12. The A.D.M.S. Office will close at ZUTKERQUE at 10-0 a.m. December, 8th, and will re-open at the same hour at PROVEN.

13. Acknowledge.

H Compton Pinsury
Lt Col.
for Colonel, A. Med. S.,
A.D.M.S., 57th. Division.

5th. December, 1917.

Issued at........4-15......p.m.

DISTRIBUTION :-

Copy No. 1 to H.Q., 57th. Division.
    2   H.Q., 57th. Division.
    3   D.D.M.S., XIX Corps.
    4   D.M.S., Second Army.
    5   H.Q., 170th. Infantry Brigade.
    6   H.Q., 171st. Infantry Brigade.
    7   H.Q., 172nd. Infantry Brigade.
    8   O.C., 2/2nd. Wessex Field Ambulance.
    9   O.C., 2/3rd. Wessex Field Ambulance.
    10   O.C., 3/2nd. West Lancs. Field Ambulance.
    11   C.R.E., 57th. Division.
    12   C.R.A., 57th. Division.
    13   O.C., 57th. Divisional Train, A.S.C.
    14   O.C., 57th. Divisional Signal Company.
    15   D.A.D.V.S., 57th. Division.
    16   A.P.M., 57th. Division.
    17   A.D.M.S., 17th. Division.
    18   War Diary.
    19   -do-
    20   File.
    21   -do-
    22   Spare.
    23   -do-

SECRET

57th. DIVISION.   Appendix B   Copy No. 20
Dec. 1917

A.D.M.S. OPERATION ORDER No. 17.

                         Reference Map Sheet 19 S.E. 1/20,000
                                   -    -   - 20 S.E. 1/20,000
                                   -    -   - 20 S.W. 1/20,000
                                   -    -   - 28   1/40,000

1. (a) The 57th. Division (less artillery) will relieve the 18th. Division (less artillery) in the line between the 16th. and 18th. December, 1917.

   (b) On completion of relief the Divisional Boundaries will run as follows :-

       Southern Boundary.
   From V.7.b.4.4. down the BROEMBEEK to where it cuts the railway at U.17d.7.9. thence S.W. along the railway.

       Northern Boundary.
   U.10.d.2.9. - U.10.b.75.40. - U.11.a.0.4. - U.11.a.6.3. - U.5.d.8.3. CLARGES STREET (inclusive) to front line U.5.b.8.8.

2. Moves of Medical Units.

   (a) The 2/2nd. Wessex Field Ambulance will take over BLEUET FARM 28/B.10c.4.4. from the 55th. Field Ambulance on 17th. December, relief to be complete by 6-0 p.m. Advanced Posts will be relieved by 6-0 p.m. on 18th. December.
      On completion of relief Officer Commanding, 2/2nd. Wessex Field Ambulance will be responsible for the evacuation of wounded and sick from the line.

   (b) The 2/3rd. Wessex Field Ambulance will take over the French Hospital, CROMBEKE 19/X.22.a.central. from the 56th. Field Ambulance on 17th. December, relief to be complete by 6-0 p.m. An advanced party will be sent on 16th. December.
      On completion of relief the 2/3rd. Wessex Field Ambulance will open as the Divisional Rest Station.
      A holding party of 1 N.C.O. and 2 Other Ranks will be left at the French Hospital, ROUSBRUGGE.

   (c) The 3/2nd. West Lancs. Field Ambulance will take over the Divisional Main Dressing Station, CHEAPSIDE 28/B.17.b.9.2. from the 54th. Field Ambulance on 16th. December, relief to be complete by 6-0 p.m. An advanced party will be sent on 15th. December.

   (d) Details of reliefs will be arranged by Officers Commanding, Field Ambulances, concerned.

   (e) Moves of main bodies of personnel will be by train; moves of transport by road. Times and routes will be notified later.

3. Commencement and completion of reliefs will be reported to this office.

4. A.D.M.S. Office will close at ROUSBRUGGE at 8-0 a.m. and re-open at ELVERDINGHE CHATEAU at 10-0 a.m., 18th. December.

5. ACKNOWLEDGE.

                                                  Colonel, A. Med. S.,
14th. December, 1917.   A.D.M.S., 57th. Division.

Issued at............p.m.

DISTRIBUTION.

Copy No. 1 to H.Q., 57th. Division.
          2   H.Q., 57th. Division.
          3   D.D.M.S., XIX Corps.
          4   D.M.S., Second Army.
          5.   H.Q., 170th. Infantry Brigade.
          6.   H.Q., 171st. Infantry Brigade.
          7.   H.Q., 172nd. Infantry Brigade.
          8.   O.C., 2/2nd. Wessex Field Ambulance.
          9.   O.C., 2/3rd. Wessex Field Ambulance.
         10.   O.C., 3/2nd. West Lancs. Field Ambulance.
         11.   C.R.E., 57th. Division.
         12.   C.R.A., 57th. Division.
         13.   O.C., 57th. Divisional Train, A.S.C.
         14.   O.C., 57th. Divisional Signal Company.
         15.   D.A.D.V.S., 57th. Division.
         16.   A.P.M., 57th. Division.
         17.   A.D.M.S., 18th. Division.
         18.   A.D.M.S., 35th. Division.
         19.   A.D.M.S., 1st. Division.
         20.   War Diary,
         21.   -do-
         22.   File.
         23.   -do-
         24.   Spare.
         25.   -do-

Appendix G.   57th Div.
                Dec 1917.

MEDICAL ARRANGEMENTS.

A.D.M.S.
57th (W.L.) DIVISION
15-12-17.
M. 5109/HO.

Reference Map Sheet 19 S.E. 1/20,000
"   "   "   20 S.E. 1/20,000
"   "   "   20 S.W. 1/20,000
"   "   "   28   1/40,000

1. Sick and wounded will be dealt with as follows :-

    (a) From the line.
        The chain of evacuation will be

    Regimental Aid Posts   EGYPT HOUSE 20 S.W.4/U.12.b.2.9.
                            VEE BEND   do.   /U.11.d.2.6.

    Relay Posts   NEY FARM   do.   /U.16.a.3.7.
                            CRAONNE FARM   do.   /U.15.d.2.5.
                            SIGNAL FARM   do.   /U.21.c.2.0.

    Advanced Dressing   GREEN MILL   do.   /U.25.d.1.2.
    Station.

    Main Dressing Station   CHEAPSIDE   28/B.17.b.9.2.

        From Regimental Aid Posts cases will be conveyed by Field Ambulance Bearers to the Advanced Dressing Station via the Relay Posts.
        Stretcher cases will be conveyed by hand trolley from VEE BEND to GREEN MILL, thence by train to CHEAPSIDE.
        Conveyance is by hand carry in advance of VEE BEND.
        Field Ambulance Officers will be stationed at GREEN MILL and CRAONNE FARM.

    (b) From the support Brigade.
        Officer Commanding, 2/2nd. Wessex Field Ambulance, BLEUET FARM 28/B.10.c.4.4. will receive cases, and convey them to 2/2nd. West Lancs. Field Ambulance Main Dressing Station, CHEAPSIDE 28/B.17.b.9.2.

    (c) From the Reserve Brigade.
        Officer Commanding, 141st. Field Ambulance, 1st. Division, ZUIDHUIS FARM 20/S.28.b.central. will receive cases.

    (d) A squad R.A.M.C. and one Ambulance Car will be stationed at BOESINGHE CHATEAU 28/B.12.a.1.4., to deal with local casualties. A squad will also be stationed at ONDANK DUMP 28/A.11.b.2.5.

2. All requests for extra stretcher bearers for the line should be sent to the Officer in charge, CRAONNE FARM, GREEN MILL or BLEUET FARM, whichever is nearest. These requests must be in writing and state approximately number and map reference of cases requiring evacuation.

3. All requests for stretchers, blankets, splints, dressings etc., should be dealt with as in (2).

4. Field Ambulance Officers will keep in personal touch with the Regimental Medical Officers. This is absolutely essential.

5. No Regimental Medical Officer will change the location of his Aid Post without notifying the change to the nearest Field Ambulance Officer who will at once make known the new location to Officer Commanding, 2/2nd. Wessex Field Ambulance.

6. No cases will be dressed at CRAONNE FARM or GREEN MILL except those who may be reasonably expected to benefit by such treatment, such as cases of haemorrhage and unsplinted fractures.
        Every attention must be given to the prevention and combating of shock by the methods recommended in D.M.S., Second Army No. 18/59 circulated under my M.4796/65 dated 20/11/17.
        Tourniquets should be removed as soon as possible.

7. Sick who are likely to recover within 14 days will be sent to Divisional Rest Station.

8. Sick and wounded will be evacuated from Field Ambulances as laid down in D.M.S. Circular Memo. No. 50 and my MS.105 dated 5/12/17.

9. ACKNOWLEDGE.

[signature]

Colonel, A. Med. S.,
14th. December, 1917.   A.D.M.S., 57th. Division.

DISTRIBUTION.

Copies to:-

H.Q., 57th. Division.
D.D.M.S., XIX Corps.
D.M.S., Second Army.
H.Q., 170th. Infantry Brigade.
H.Q., 171st. Infantry Brigade.
H.Q., 172nd. Infantry Brigade.
O.C., 2/2nd. Wessex Field Ambulance.
O.C., 2/3rd. Wessex Field Ambulance.
O.C., 2/2nd. West Lancs. Field Ambulance.
C.R.E., 57th. Division.
C.R.A., 57th. Division.
O.C., 57th. Divisional Train, A.S.C.
O.C., 57th. Divisional Signal Company.
D.A.D.V.S., 57th. Division.
A.P.M., 57th. Division.
A.D.M.S., 18th. Division.
A.D.M.S., 35th. Division.
A.D.M.S., 1st. Division.
Senior Chaplain, C. of E.
Senior Chaplain, non C. of E.
War Diary.
All Regimental Medical Officers

Appendix D.

57th Div.
Dec. 1917.

DIAGRAM OF EVACUATION
ARRANGEMENTS.
57th DIVISION.
December 18th 1917.

EGYPT HOUSE.
R.A.P. & B.P.

Hand. Hand

VEE-BEND.

NEY FARM.
R.P.

TROLLEY LINE

CRAONNE FARM.
B.P.

Steenbeck R.   Broenbeek R.

SIGNAL FARM.
R.P.

GREEN MILL.
A.D.S.

LIGHT RAILWAY

CHEAPSIDE.
M.D.S.

MAC. CARS.
MAC. CARS.

CROMBEKE.
D.R.S.

C.C.Ss. (Various.

M 4972/67/1

Appendix E

DETAILED INSTRUCTIONS REGARDING FRENCH PREVENTIVE
TREATMENT OF TRENCH FOOT.

1. These notes are in amplification of those contained in IVth Army Standing Orders para 597 which were issued to all Medical Officers of the Division on 3/12/17 under my M 4972/67.

2. An order prescribing the immediate commencement of this treatment in the 57th Division was issued by Divisional Headquarters 24/12/17.

3. The material required is ¼ oz of the medicated powder per man per day and ¼ oz of the medicated soap twice weekly per man.

4. These materials will be prepared and supplied to units in proportion to their strength and in quantity sufficient to last half a week by the O.C. 2/2nd Wessex Field Ambulance at BLEUET FARM 28/B.10.c.4.4.

5. The O.C. 2/2nd Wessex Field Ambulance or an Officer deputed by him will supervise these preventive measures in their medical aspect so far as the Brigades in line and support, the Divisional Artillery and other units in the forward area are concerned.

6. The O.C. 3/2nd West Lancs. Field Ambulance at CHEAPSIDE 28/B.17.b.9.2. or an officer detailed by him will similarly supervise the arrangements in the Reserve Brigade Area.

7. The essentials of the method are :-

    (a) Maintaining cleanliness of the feet by washing with special soap

    (b) Powdering the socks with medicated powder.

8. Along with these special methods, careful attention must be given to the fitting of boots, the avoidance of restriction of the circulation and the supply of hot food and hot drinks when feasible.

9. The special soap is composed of :-

    Soft Potash Soap   1000 parts.
    Powdered Camphor   25 "
    Powdered Borax   100 "

It is made by heating the Potash Soap gently until it is liquid, stirring in the camphor and borax, then removing from the fire and stirring until the soap has set.

10. The powder is made of :-

    Talc   1000 parts.
    Camphor   25 "

11. The feet should first be washed in warm water with ordinary soap, then in hot water with the medicated soap. After being carefully dried the socks about to be put on are dusted with the medicated powder. This is done before going into the line.

12. When in the line, the socks will be changed once a day at least if conditions permit. That this may be done each man must take up a spare pair of socks and a sufficiency of medicated powder to dust over the feet, between the toes and into the socks. Before the powder is applied, the feet should be dried and rubbed from the toes upwards. Two men should do this for one another.

13. The Regimental Medical Officer and Battalion Chiropodist will supervise and direct the application of this treatment in their units. The Stretcher Bearers will also assist and will attend to minor cuts, sores, etc. on the feet.

14. The foot rubbing should be done quietly and firmly with both hands, should last for five minutes at least and should be done twice daily if possible. The powder should not be used for rubbing.

25/12/17.

Colonel, A. Med. S.,
A.D.M.S., 57th Division.

DISTRIBUTION :-

O.C. 2/2nd Wessex Field Ambulance.
O.C. 2/3rd Wessex Field Ambulance.
O.C. 2/2nd West Lancs. Field Ambulance.
All Regimental Medical Officers.
Headquarters, 57th Division - for information.

SECRET.   Appendix F   Copy No. 20

57th DIVISION.

R.A.M.C. OPERATION ORDER No.18.

Reference Map Sheet 19 S.E. 1/20,000.
" " " 28 1/40,000.

1. The 57th Division will be relieved by the 18th Division in the forward area.

2. The Field Ambulances will be affiliated to Brigade Groups for the move as follows:-

   2/3rd Wessex Field Ambulance - 171 Brigade Group.
   3/2nd W.Lanc. Field Ambulance - 170 Brigade Group.
   2/2nd Wessex Field Ambulance - 172 Brigade Group.

3. Field Ambulances will be relieved as follows:-

   (a). The 2/3rd Wessex Field Ambulance at CROMBEKE, Divisional Rest Station, (19/X.22.a.central), will be relieved by the 55th Field Ambulance. Advanced Party will arrive on 28/12/1917. Relief to be completed by 10-0am, 29/12/1917.

   (b). The 3/2nd West Lancs. Field Ambulance, CHEAPSIDE, Main Dressing Station, (28/B.17.b.9.2.), will be relieved by the 56th Field Ambulance. Relief to be completed by 9-0am, 31/12/1917.

   (c). The 2/2nd Wessex Field Ambulance at BLEUET FARM, (28/B.10.c.4.4.), and Advanced Posts, will be relieved by the 54th Field Ambulance between 1/1/1918 and 3/1/1918. Relief to be completed by 10-0am, 3/1/1918.

4. Moves of Field Ambulances.

   On completion of reliefs Field Ambulances will move to the new area under orders of Brigade Groups concerned.

5. Only mobilization equipment and that authorised by General Routine Orders will be taken to the new area. Receipts will be taken for all stores, etc., handed over to relieving Field Ambulances.

6. Details of reliefs will be arranged direct between Commanding Officers concerned.

7. Completion of reliefs and arrival in new area will be notified to this office.

8. A.D.M.S'. Office will close at ELVERDINGHE CHATEAU at 10-0am, 3/1/1918 and reopen at a place and time to be notified later.

9. ACKNOWLEDGE.

Headquarters,   Colonel A.Med.S.,
26/12/1917.   A.D.M.S., 57th Division.

Issued at 9-0 pm.

Distribution:- Copy No.1 H.Q., 57th Division.

DISTRIBUTION:-

Copy No. 1 to H.Q., 57th Division.
       2   H.Q., 57th Division.
       3   D.D.M.S., XIX Corps.
       4   D.M.S., ~~Second Army~~ Fourth Army.
       5   H.Q., 170th Infantry Brigade.
       6   H.Q., 171st Infantry Brigade.
       7   H.Q., 172nd Infantry Brigade.
       8   O.C., 2/2nd Wessex Field Ambulance.
       9   O.C., 2/3rd Wessex Field Ambulance.
     10   O.C., 3/2nd W.Lanc.Field Ambulance.
     11   C.R.E., 57th Division.
     12   C.R.A., 57th Division.
     13   O.C., 57th Divisional Train, A.S.C.
     14   O.C., 57th Divisional Signal Coy.
     15   D.A.D.V.S., 57th Division.
     16   A.P.M., 57th Division.
     17   A.D.M.S., 18th Division.
     18   A.D.M.S., 1st Division.
     19   A.D.M.S., 58th Division.
     20   War Diary.
     21   -do-
     22   File.
     23   -do-
     24   Spare.
     25   -do-

Appendix G.

SECRET.   57TH DIVISION.   Copy No...19...

R.A.M.C. OPERATION ORDER NO. 19.

Reference Map Sheet 36 NW.1/20,000.

1. On arrival in the 1st Anzac Corps Area, 57th Division (less Artillery) will relieve 3rd Australian Division (less Artillery) in the line.

2. Field Ambulances of 57th Division will relieve Field Ambulances of 3rd Australian Division as under:-

(a). 2/3rd Wessex Field Ambulance to proceed to STEENWERCK to relieve the 11th Australian Field Ambulance at A.23.a.9.9. on 31/12/1917.
Relief to be completed by 12-Onoon 1/1/1918.

(b). 3/2nd West Lancs. Field Ambulance to proceed to L'ESTRADE to relieve the 9th Australian Field Ambulance at A.24.c.9.5. on 2/1/1918.
Relief to be completed by 6-0pm.

(c). 2/2nd Wessex Field Ambulance to proceed to Y.M.C.A. Building, EROUINGHEM, H.4.d.central, to relieve the 10th Australian Field Ambulance at present evacuating in the Right Sector of the 1st A.& N.Z. Army Corps.
Relief to be completed by 10-0am on 4/1/1918.

3. Advanced Parties will be sent in each case.

4. Detailed arrangements for relief will be made by the Field Ambulance Commanders concerned.

5. A list of stores taken over from outgoing units will be forwarded to this office.

6. Completion of reliefs will be notified to this office.

7. A.D.M.S'. Office will close at ELVERDINGHE at 10-0am, 3/1/1918, and will re-open at 12-Onoon at STEENWERCK on the same date.

8. A C K N O W L E D G E.

Headquarters,   Colonel. A.Med.S.,
30/12/1917.   A.D.M.S., 57th Division.

Issued at 12-Onoon.

For distribution see over -

DISTRIBUTION :-

Copy No. 1 to H.Q., 57th Division.
        2   -ditto-
        3.   D.D.M.S., XIX Corps.
        4.   D.D.M.S., I A.& N.Z.Corps.
        5.   D.M.S., Fourth Army.
        6.   H.Q., 170th Infantry Brigade.
        7.   H.Q., 171st Infantry Brigade.
        8.   H.Q., 172nd Infantry Brigade.
        9.   Officer Cmdg, 2/2nd Wessex
                   Field Ambulance.
       10.   O.C., 2/3rd Wessex Field Ambulance.
       11.   O.C., 2/2nd West Lancs. Field Ambulance.
       12.   C.R.E., 57th Division.
       13.   C.R.A., 57th Division.
       14.   O.C., 57th Divisional Signal Coy.
       15.   O.C., 57th Divisional Train, A.S.C.
       16.   D.A.D.V.S., 57th Division.
       17.   A.P.M., 57th Division.
       18.   A.D.M.S., 3rd Australian Division.
       19.   War Diary.
       20.   -ditto-
       21.   File.
       22.   -do-
       23.   Spare.
       24.   -do-

CONFIDENTIAL.

War Diary
of
A.D.M.S., 57th Division.

from 1st January 1918 to 31st January 1918.

(Volume 1).

Army Form C. 2118.

WAR DIARY
or
INTELLIGENCE SUMMARY.
(Erase heading not required.)

Place	Date	Hour	Summary of Events and Information	Remarks and references to Appendices
ELVERDINGHE	1-1-18		With transport intermissions roads are very slippery. With transport intermissions have now continued for 14 days and the 39th Division now on move from BOESINGHE Sector to ARMENTIERES Sector. 171st Brigade Group with 2/3rd Wessex Field Ambulances completed journey yesterday. The Field Ambulance having proceeded to STEENWERCK. The 170th Brigade Group with 3/2nd West Lancs Field Ambulances are at present en route. The 172nd Brigade Group with 2/2nd Wessex Field Ambulances commences their move out today.	
	2-1-18		Move of 39th Division from BOSINGHE Sector to ARMENTIERES Sector continues. The 2/2nd Wessex Field Ambulance now handing over Evacuation of Wounded from the front to field Ambulances of 18th Division. A.D.M.S. visited Dressing Stations of 1st Division at CHARPENTIER cross roads where French Trench Foot Prevention are systematically at field along with Shirebody and well excellent results as it is claimed. A.D.M.S. visited advanced Dressing Station at GRENMILL and proceeded to Cheapside by light Railway line. A.D.M.S. fixed Headquarters XIX Corps.	
STEENWERCK	3-1-18		Clerks office at ELVERDINGHE Château at 10 a.m. and opened at STEENWERCK at noon. Tomorrow the 39th Division is on XV Corps with Headquarters at HINGES and takes ARMENTIERES Sector from the LYS to where the ARMENTIERES – WAVRIN Railway cuts the	

Army Form C. 2118.

WAR DIARY
or
INTELLIGENCE SUMMARY.
(Erase heading not required.)

Place	Date	Hour	Summary of Events and Information	Remarks and references to Appendices
STEENWERCK	3·1·18		ADMS visited and inspected the quarters of the 2/3rd Wessex Field Ambulances comfortably installed in spacious buildings in STEENWERCK and moving sub.	
	4·1·18		57th Division completed its move to new area. Brigades and units are thus located:—	
			Divisional Headquarters. — STEENWERCK H17. d.4.4.	
			170th Infantry Brigade. — CHAPELLE d'ARMENTIERES H.11.a.4.4.	
			171st Infantry Brigade. — ERQINGHEM H.4.d.3.6.	
			172nd Infantry Brigade. — STEENWERCK	
			2/2 Wessex Field Ambulance — ERQUINGHEM H.4.d.central	
			2/3 Wessex Field Ambulance — STEENWERCK A.28. a 9.9.	
			3/2 West Lancs Field Ambulance — L'ESTRADE A.30.b.2.9.	
			ADMS visited Headquarters of XV Corps at HINGES and saw DDMS regarding Medical arrangements, etc.	
	5·1·18		ADMS visited 3/2nd West Lancs Field Ambulance at L'ESTRADE. Conference by GOC Division and Brigadiers, etc. Submitted statement of Evacuation arrangements to DDMS Corps.	

Army Form C. 2118.

WAR DIARY
or
INTELLIGENCE SUMMARY.
(Erase heading not required.)

Place	Date	Hour	Summary of Events and Information	Remarks and references to Appendices
STEENWERCK	6-1-18		Issued "Medical Arrangements" for this area to all concerned. Sent letter to Field Ambulances Commanders regarding economy of fuel and material generally, prison, sterilisation of dressings, Thomas's Splints, Trench Feet Preventors and Officers Kits. Sent diagram of evacuation to DDMS XV Corps.	Appendices A. Appendix B
	7-1-18		ADMS visited 2/2nd Wessex Field Ambulance at ERQUINGHEM, 3/2nd West Lancs Field Ambulance at L'ESTRADE and BATERNITE Hospital ARMENTIERES as regards its suitability to form a Walking Wounded Collecting Post, and Divisional Baths ERQUINGHEM. Today met an miss the pump being in disrepair. Submitted note to Headquarters (G) as Evacuation from present Divisional front in the event of its being made on two — Divisional front.	
	8-1-18		Issued Orders RAMC. 57th Division. for 1-6/1/18. Captain KING D.A.D.M.S. returned from leave. Considerable rise in incidence of sick admitted to Field Ambulances and Divisional Rest Station chiefly identified to cases diagnosed P.U.O. and I.C.T. The Divisional Rest Station at STEENWERCK now full and short of stretcher and blankets. Routine.	
	9-1-18			
	10-1-18		D.D.M.S. XV Corps visited and inspected the Divisional Rest Station (2/2/3rd Wessex Field Ambulance) STEENWERCK: the Divisional Main Dressing Station	

Army Form C. 2118.

WAR DIARY
or
INTELLIGENCE SUMMARY.
(Erase heading not required.)

Instructions regarding War Diaries and Intelligence Summaries are contained in F. S. Regs., Part II. and the Staff Manual respectively. Title pages will be prepared in manuscript.

Place	Date	Hour	Summary of Events and Information	Remarks and references to Appendices
STEENWERCK	10-1-18.		(3/2 West Lancs Field Ambulance) L'ESTRADE: and the Headquarters of the 2/2nd Wessex Field Ambulance at ERQUINGHEM.	
	11-1-18.		ADMS visited baths at ERQUINGHEM. Maternity Hospital (regarding Walking Wounded Pat) at ARMENTIERES. Conference (regarding Baths) and of Medical Officers (19 present) at Headquarters 2/2nd Wessex Field Ambulance at ERQUINGHEM.	
	12-1-18.		Drafted memoranda on Treatment of "Scabies" and of "Sacred Cases". ADMS visited 3/2nd West Lancs Field Ambulance regarding accommodation therefor. Reported to DDMS XV Corps on Stretchers held by and required by Field Ambulances of Division and on employment of Category "B" men in Field Ambulances. Reports to DDMS XV Corps/ on cases of Trench Feet on periods January 1st – 15th (A) and January 5th – 12th (1). ADMS visited 171st Hospital CONVENT ARMENTIERES.	
	13-1-18.		ADMS with Officer Commanding 2/2nd Wessex Field Ambulance (Officer in charge evacuation) visited Advanced Dressing Station at HOUPLINES and BRICKFIELD Regimental Aid Posts at TISSAG DUMP, SQUARE FARM, and WELLINGTON AVENUE and Divn Rest Park at AUCKLAND ROAD.	

Army Form C. 2118.

WAR DIARY
or
INTELLIGENCE SUMMARY.
(Erase heading not required.)

Instructions regarding War Diaries and Intelligence Summaries are contained in F. S. Regs., Part II. and the Staff Manual respectively. Title pages will be prepared in manuscript.

Place	Date	Hour	Summary of Events and Information	Remarks and references to Appendices
STEENWERCK	13·1·18		Issued arrangements for Dental. Nose, Ear and Throat Cases.	
	14·1·18		ADMS. with DADMS commenced exhaustive inspection of 2/2nd West Lancs Field Ambulances at L'ESTRADE. Investigation by DDMS regarding 22 recent cases sent from 2/3rd Wessex and 2/2nd West Lancs Field Ambulances as I.C.T. which Officer Commanding 54th Casualty Clearing Station reports as being really "Trench Foot" of severe type.	
	15·1·18		Drafted schemes for disposal and treatment of Scabies and Cases in Division. Replied to DDMS that no Field Ambulance Officers RAMC in this Division deserve in my opinion to be returned to England. DADMS investigates cases reported as I.C.T. but really owe to front line conditions at BOESINGHE Sector. Report on this matter sent to DDMS. ADMS interviewed Divisional Commander regarding Trench Feet as above.	
	16·1·18		ADMS visited ARMENTIERES regarding Divisional Dressing Stations in 14 Boulevards Faidherbe and Town Majors regarding Baths. ADMS visited 2/2nd Wessex Field Ambulance and 2/2nd West Lancs Field Ambulance. Owing to temperature weather and heavy rains flooding very general. Sixty-one regulars an occasional	

Army Form C. 2118.

WAR DIARY
or
INTELLIGENCE SUMMARY.
(Erase heading not required.)

Instructions regarding War Diaries and Intelligence Summaries are contained in F. S. Regs., Part II. and the Staff Manual respectively. Title pages will be prepared in manuscript.

Place	Date	Hour	Summary of Events and Information	Remarks and references to Appendices
STEENWERCK	16-1-18.		returns are now rendered by this Office under first Strong and XV Corps. Gee list attached	Appendices C.
	17-1-18.		Further correspondence with DDMS XV Corps regarding general incidence of Sickness and Cases of Trench Feet. ADMS visited 2/3rd Wessex Field Ambulance regarding accommodation for sick officers and for venereal cases. ADMS visited 54th Casualty Clearing Station at MERVILLE. Reported to DDMS XV Corps 10 Medical Officers short (5 different Sick and 2 at School of Instruction). Tabulated Sick admissions and evacuations by Brigades of 57th Division, for period January 1st – 15th inclusive. Reported to DDMS XV Corps on causes of recent increase in sick incidences of the Division.	
	18-1-18		Large increase of sick admissions in 24 hours to 9.0 a.m. today. Total 92 of which 38 from 2/5th S. Lan R. and 27 of these Trench Foot acquired within last 60 hours or so. ADMS saw G.O.C. regarding this, then saw cases in 3/2nd West Lancs Field Ambulance, then with DADMS XV Corps visited Regimental Aid Post at Trisago Dump and saw three and at Battalion HQ at galgastes Medical Officer and Officer Commanding 2/5th South Lancs Regt. M.O. latter went to Parls 15+20 by EDMENDS AVENUE Communication Trenches water logged owing to flooring and 3 feet deep in muddy water in parts.	

A5834 Wt.W4973/M687 750,000 8/16 D. D. & L. Ltd. Forms/C.2118/13

Army Form C. 2118.

WAR DIARY
or
INTELLIGENCE SUMMARY.
(Erase heading not required.)

Instructions regarding War Diaries and Intelligence Summaries are contained in F. S. Regs., Part II. and the Staff Manual respectively. Title pages will be prepared in manuscript.

Place	Date	Hour	Summary of Events and Information	Remarks and references to Appendices
STEENWERCK	19-1-18		D.A.D.M.S. visited all front lines with special view to conditions likely to cause Trench Foot. A.D.M.S. visited 2/6th K. Liverpool Regt. and 3/2nd West Lancs Field Ambulances. A.D.M.S. saw Divisional Commander regarding Trench Foot.	
	20-1-18		A.D.M.S. visited A.D.M.S. 12th Division regarding Trench Foot Preventive measures: 2/2nd Wessex Field Ambulance: 2/10th Kings Liverpool Bn. Headquarters and Regimental Slab Vat at TISSAGE DUMP: gum-boot store and soup kitchen thereat. Baths in the Convent ARMENTIERES. Divisional Baths at ERQUINGHEM now flooded and only in Headquarters 2/6th Kings Liverpool Regt. MENISATE Camp regarding ears for clothing issues, and Headquarters 2/6th Kings Liverpool Regt. MENISATE Camp regarding Trench Foot Preventions. Reports to DDMS XV Corps on recent health of the Division, and on provision of Anti-Aircraft two to chiefcoats and fatigues.	
LILLERS	21-1-18		DADMS 57th Division accompanied DADMS XV Corps on visit of inspections attended conferences of DDsMS and ADsMS held by DMS First Army at of Trench Foot Prevention arrangements.	
	22-1-18		DMS First Army visited 2/3rd Wessex Field Ambulance and 3/2nd West Lancs Field Ambulance chiefly in regard to prevailing illness. Afterwards he discussed Trench Foot, Physique of Divisions, condition of Field Ambulances etc. with DGS Division and ADMS.	

Army Form C. 2118.

WAR DIARY
or
INTELLIGENCE SUMMARY.
(Erase heading not required.)

Instructions regarding War Diaries and Intelligence Summaries are contained in F. S. Regs., Part II. and the Staff Manual respectively. Title pages will be prepared in manuscript.

Place	Date	Hour	Summary of Events and Information	Remarks and references to Appendices
STEENWERCK	23/1/18		XV Corps Commander visited Policemen at ERQUINGHEM. DADIVS invited others.	
	24/1/18		Received private notices of detail of commerce of Divisions from 12 to 10 Battalion Commands. Three Infantry Brigades of three Battalions each - one Pioneer Battalion. ADMS visited 3/2nd West Lancs Field Ambulance regarding general condition there. ADMS had long interview with Divisional Commander regarding Trench Foot, recent schemes, general health and progress of the Division, suitability of Field Ambulance Commanders etc. Comparisons of wounded sick evacuation percentages since October show this Division suffers (very slightly) above the average. Signing statery notes on Trench Foot (17) and sick admission a.k. ADMS. ADMS visited 2/3rd Wessex and 3/2nd West Lancs Fields. saw D.O.C. concerning. Baths at ERQUINGHEM and Ambulances, turns out of the first Foot Treatment Centres. ARMENTIERES and various Battalions. Trench Feet only 2, to 9 a.m. today. Sick admissions and evacuations	
	26.1.18		cases sh. visited Battalion Foot Treatment T.Cents at 2/10th Kings Liverpool and 2/4 North Lancs Regts.	

WAR DIARY or INTELLIGENCE SUMMARY

Army Form C. 2118.

Place	Date	Hour	Summary of Events and Information	Remarks and references to Appendices
STEENWERCK	27-1-18		ADMS and AA/QMG visited Sewer Beef Store and Drying Room at SAPPHIRE FARM and TISSAGE DUMP. DADMS visited fuel area, Ins centre and FA ambulances with special reference to Sanitation. ADMS interviewed S.O.E.'s regarding relative risk evacuation rates of this to other Divisions, the lay of Medical Officers and transport Feet.	
	28-1-18		ADMS visited D.H.Q. at PONT de NIEPPE; No 2 Cav ARMENTIERES; and ERQUINGHEM and Fort washing centres. ADMS interviewed O.C. 170 and 171st Infantry Brigades regarding Medical Officers DADMS visited Camps at MENEGATE and HOLLEBECQUE.	
	29.1.18		ADMS visited and made general inspection of 2/2nd West Lancs Field Ambulance, M.D.S. LESTRADE and 2/3rd West Field Ambulance Divisional Rest Station STEENWERCK. ADMS attended G.O.C.'s conference on training of Divisional units and Field Brigade Front.	
	30.1.18		DADMS visited Headquarters of 2/2nd Warwick Field Ambulance in connection with an enterprise shortly to be undertaken by 172nd Infantry Brigade.	

Army Form C. 2118.

WAR DIARY
or
INTELLIGENCE SUMMARY.
(Erase heading not required.)

Instructions regarding War Diaries and Intelligence Summaries are contained in F. S. Regs., Part II. and the Staff Manual respectively. Title pages will be prepared in manuscript.

Place	Date	Hour	Summary of Events and Information	Remarks and references to Appendices
STEENWERCK	31.1.18		Royal Artillery and Infantry Brigade Admissions and Discharge figures for January 16th – 31st forwarded to Headquarters, copy attached (see Appendix D) A.D.M.S. visited 2/2nd Wessex Field Ambulance Unit (-with A.A.& Q.M.G.) 2/2nd West Lancs. Field Ambulance. A.D.M.S. also visited 2/8th K. Lpool Camp at WATERLANDS CAMP.	Appendix "D"
	31/1/18			

Y F Deuchi

.... Colonel, A. Med. S.

A.D.M.S. 57th (W.L.) Division.

A.D.M.S., 57th Div: No.M.5342/40.

Appendix A.

SECRET.

57th DIVISION.
MEDICAL ARRANGEMENTS.

Reference Map Sheet 36 NW, 1/20,000.

1. Sick and Wounded will be dealt with as follows:-

    From the Line.

    LEFT BRIGADE. — From TISSAGE Regimental Aid Post, C.27.b.7.6., by hand carriage to Advanced Dressing Station, NOUVEL HOUPLINES, C.26.b.8.1., thence by motor ambulance car to Main Dressing Station, ERQUINGHEM, H.4.d.central.

    and

    From SQUARE FARM Regimental Aid Post, I.9.c.8.5., by hand carriage to Advanced Dressing Station, BRICKFIELD, I.8.b.3.8., thence by motor ambulance car to Main Dressing Station, ERQUINGHEM, H.4.d.central.

    RIGHT BRIGADE. — From WELLINGTON AVENUE Regimental Aid Post, I.14.a.5.8., by hand carriage to Advanced Dressing Station, BRICKFIELD, I.8.b.3.8., thence by motor ambulance car to Main Dressing Station, ERQUINGHEM, H.4.d.central.

2. All requests for extra stretcher bearers for the line should be sent to the Officer in Charge, NOUVEL HOUPLINES or BRICKFIELD, whichever is nearer. Such requests must be in writing and state approximately number and map reference of cases requiring evacuation. Requests for stretchers, blankets, splints, dressings etc., should be dealt with similarly.

3. Field Ambulance Officers will keep in personal touch with the Regimental Medical Officers.

4. The 3/2nd West Lancs. Field Ambulance is open as a Main Dressing Station at A.30.b.2.9. Sick of units not in line will be evacuated direct thereto.

5. The 2/3rd Wessex Field Ambulance is open as a Divisional Rest Station at A.23.a.9.9.

6. SICK AND WOUNDED WILL BE DISPOSED OF BY FIELD AMBULANCES AS FOLLOWS:-

    (a). Sick and Wounded admitted to 2/2nd Wessex Field Ambulance will be passed on to the 3/2nd West Lancs. Field Ambulance, except urgent cases which may be evacuated direct to Casualty Clearing Station. Only the latter cases will be passed through A.&.D.Book of 2/2nd Wessex Field Ambulance.

    (b). Ordinary Sick and Wounded will be evacuated to No. 51, No.54 Casualty Clearing Station, MERVILLE, or Advanced Surgical Centre, ESTAIRES.

    (c). Venereal Cases will be evacuated as ordinary sick after the authority of the A.P.M. has been obtained.

    (d). Infectious Cases will be evacuated to No.7 General Hospital, MALASSISE.

- 2 -

(e). Self-Inflicted Wounds will be evacuated to No.58 Casualty Clearing Station, LILLERS.

(f). N.Y.D.N. Cases will be evacuated to No.39 (Special) Stationary Hospital, AIRE.

(g). Mild Skin Cases (boils, scabies, impetigo,) will be transferred to the Divisional Rest Station for treatment.

(h). Scabies (severe cases) up to 30 in number, will be transferred to 130th Field Ambulance, ESTAIRES, after application for vacancies has been made to this office.

(i). Eye Cases. Instructions will be issued later.

(j). Ear, Nose, and Throat Cases will be evacuated to No. 12 Stationary Hospital, ST POL.

(k). Dental Cases. Instructions will be issued later.

(l). Gassed Cases (serious) will be evacuated to the nearest Casualty Clearing Station.

(m). Gassed Cases (undoubted) will be evacuated as ordinary wounded.

(n). Gassed Cases (doubtful). Instructions will be issued later.

(o). Officers' Rest Station, ST POL. Applications for vacancies will be made to this office.

(p). Civilian Sick and Wounded will be evacuated to HAZEBROUCK after D.M.S. Instructions, para.74, have been complied with

NOTE. Wounded will be evacuated to Casualty Clearing Station, as possible, missing the Main Dressing Station if desirable. In such cases the necessary particulars for A.&.D.Book will be taken at the Advanced Dressing Station.

7. No.2 Motor Ambulance Convoy, MERVILLE, will clear sick and and wounded from Main Dressing Stations of this Division.

8. No. 1 Advanced Depot of Medical Stores, MERVILLE, will supply the Medical Units of this Division.

9. No. 3 Mobile Laboratory, MERVILLE, is available for use of this Division.

10. The Sanitary Section (No.49) for this area is situated at SAILLY.

Headquarters,
6/1/1918.

Colonel. A.Med.S.,
A.D.M.S., 57th Division.

DISTRIBUTION –

Copies to:-

H.Q., 57th Division.
D.D.M.S., XV Corps.
D.M.S., First Army.
H.Q., 170th Infantry Brigade.
H.Q., 171st Infantry Brigade.
H.Q., 172nd Infantry Brigade.
O.C., 2/2nd Wessex Field Ambulance.
O.C., 2/3rd Wessex Field Ambulance.
O.C., 3/2nd W.Lanc.Field Ambulance.
C.R.E., 57th Division.
C.R.A., 57th Division.
O.C., 57th Divisional Train A.S.C.
O.C., 57th Divisional Signal Coy.
D.A.D.V.S., 57th Division.
A.P.M., 57th Division.
All Regimental Medical Officers, 57th Division.
Senior Chaplain. (C.of E).
Senior Chaplain. (Non.C.of E).

Army Form C. 2118.

DIAGRAM OF EVACUATION OF WOUNDED.
ARMENTIERES SECTOR.

Appendix B.

A.	R.A.P. TISSAGE DUMP	36/C.27.b.7.6.
B.	R.A.P. AUCHLAND ROAD	36/I.4.a.6.4.
C.	R.A.P. SQUARE FARM	36/I.9.a.8.5.
D.	R.A.P. WELLINGTON Av.	36/I.14.d.5.8.
E.	A.D.S. N.HOUPLINES.	36/C.26.b.8.1.
F.	A.D.S. BRICKFIELD.	36/I.8.b.3.8.
G.	M.D.S. ERQUINGHEM.	36/H.4.d.central.
H.	M.D.S. L'ESTRADE.	36/A.30.b.2.9.
K.	D.R.S. STEENWERCK.	36/A.23.a.9.9.
L.	51st C.C.Station, ESTAIRES.	
M.	54th C.C.Station, ESTAIRES.	
N.	Other Special C.C.Ss. and Hospitals.	

- ---------- Hand Carriage of Stretchers.
- ooooooooo By Wheeled Stretcher Carriages.
- ~~~~~~~ Divl: Horse and Motor Amb: Cars.
- — — — Motor Amb: Convoy Cars.
- ++++++++ Trolley Lines.

WAR DIARY
or
INTELLIGENCE SUMMARY.
(Erase heading not required.)

Instructions regarding War Diaries and Intelligence Summaries are contained in F.S. Regs., Part II. and the Staff Manual respectively. Title pages will be prepared in manuscript.

Place	Date	Hour	Summary of Events and Information	Remarks and references to Appendices

Appendix G.

LIST OF RETURNS RENDERED BY A.D.M.S., 57th DIVISION.

DAILY RETURNS.

A.F. W.3185 - Daily State of Sick and Wounded.
Wire of Admissions, Evacuations, etc.
Portuguese Troops admitted to Fd. Ambs.
List of Sick Evacuations: Officers & O.Ranks.
Number of Gassed Cases admitted.
Deaths in Medical Units.
Casualties in personnel of Medical Units.

WEEKLY RETURNS.

Location of Units Report (Thursday) forecast for 6 am. Sunday.
Location and Strength of Units. Report.
Progress Reports - Improvements in accommodation,
    Horse Standings, etc.
Administrative State Report.
Return of Stragglers, Absentees, and Courts Martial.
Deaths from Shell Gas during week.
A.F. B.213 - Field State.
Timber cut in Woods devastated by Shell fire.
Weekly Return of Infectious Diseases.
Amendments to Nominal Roll of R.A.M.C. Officers.
A.F.B.2069 - Offence Reports.
Return of all cases dealt with under headings of
    Nervousness, Neurasthenia, Hysteria, etc.
Reinforcement Return.
Nominal Roll of R.A.M.C. Officers.
Statement of transfers to Rest Stations, numbers returned
    to duty, and deaths in Fd.Ambs. during week.
Sick of South African Native Labour Corps admitted to hospital.
Chinese Labourers evacuated to ARQUES.
Number of cases of Scabies and other Skin Diseases admitted to
    Field Ambulances during the week.
Commissions in Tank Corps - nominal roll of applicants.

MONTHLY RETURNS.

Return of Motor Vehicles in possession of Fd. Ambs.
Combatants slightly wounded & sick returned to duty.
Portuguese Troops treated in Field Ambulances.
Dental Mechanics - Privates R.A.M.C. qualified as such.
Particulars of all purchases from Civilians made by Fd. Ambs.
Roll of R.A.M.C. Officers attached to Regtl. Units.
Tentage Return.
Hutting Return.
Remount Demand - bi-monthly.
Timber requisitioned: - bi-monthly.
Commissions in Signal Service, roll of applicants.
Commission in Regular Army (Permanent) roll of applicants.
Inoculation Return.
Drugs and Dressings issued to Civilians.
Surpluses and deficiencies in Horsed Transport.
Motor Cars and Cycles on charge of Field Ambulances.
Horse Census Return.
Return showing number of O.Ranks with out leave to the U.K.
    for 12 mos., 15 mos., and 18 mos.
Roll of American Troops treated in Field Ambulances.
Schedule of Stores issued to American Troops.

MONTHLY RETURNS (continued.)

Return showing W.E. Strength of Medical Officers, and actual strength of Medical Officers of Units.
Nominal Roll of Field Ambulance Officers.
Statement of strength and categories of all R.A.M.C. O.Ranks in Division.
Wheeled Stretcher Carriages in possession of Fd. Ambs.
Casualties in Officers during month.
Positions of Field Ambulances, Advanced Dressing Stations, and A.D.M.S. Office.
Monthly Infectious Disease Return.
Number of civilians inoculated during month.
Statement shewing principal diseases for which patients were admitted to Field Ambulances.

OCCASIONAL RETURNS.

Notification of cases of Infectious Disease as they occur.
Change in Command of a Medical Unit.
Report on prevalence of any Infectious Disease.
Change in positions of Field Ambulances, Advanced Dressing Stations, and A.D.M.S. Office.
Number of Wounded remaining in Main Dressing Stations, Rest Stations, etc.(During active operations.)
Information regarding cases of Trench Foot.

APPENDIX "D"

NOTE OF ADMISSIONS TO AND EVACUATIONS FROM FIELD AMBULANCE OF UNITS OF 57th. DIVISION, Jan. 16 - 31 (Inclusive).

	Admissions.	Evacuations.
285th. Brigade R.F.A.	36	25
286th. Brigade R.F.A.	20	17
57th. Divl. Amm. Colm.	21	8
Total Royal Artillery =	77	50
2/5th. R. Lanc. R.	38	27
2/4th. N. Lan. R.	37	29
2/5th. N. Lan. R.	22	17
4/5th. N. Lan. R.	29	22
Total 170th. Infantry Bde. =	126	95
2/5th. K. Lpool R.	37	24
2/6th. K. Lpool R.	60	41
2/7th. K. Lpool R.	22	18
2/8th. K. Lpool R.	56	44
Total 171st. Infantry Bde. =	175	127
2/9th. K. Lpool R.	70	51
2/10th. K. Lpool R.	64	45
2/4th. S. Lan. R.	55	40
2/5th. S. Lan. R.	122	95
Total 172nd. Infantry Bde. =	311	231

31st. January, 1918.

Colonel, A. Med. S.,
A.D.M.S., 57th. Division.

Vol 13

140/2782

CONFIDENTIAL.

WAR DIARY.
of
A.D.M.S, 57th Division

from 1st February 1918 to 28th February 1918.

(Volume 1).

COMMITTEE FOR THE
MEDICAL HISTORY OF THE WAR.
Date 8 APR.1918

WAR DIARY or INTELLIGENCE SUMMARY.

Army Form C. 2118.

Place	Date	Hour	Summary of Events and Information	Remarks and references to Appendices
ST ENNERY	1-2-18		D.D.M.S. XV Corps inspected Medical units of the Division, and expressed a satisfactory opinion. O.C. Divisional Train inspected transport of 2/2nd Wessex Field Amb: on 31/1/18, expressing a highly satisfactory opinion. One half of the Medical units today expressing himself as fairly satisfied with their condition. D.A.D.M.S. went to front area in evening, nothing reported. Inspected in Ermance by 2/19 K Lpool Regt. 3 hrs notice given on the report (high officer) and four prisoners were taken.	
	2-2-18		A.D.M.S. visited quarters of 2/2nd Wessex Field Amb, and saw all men who would be rather than category "A". — A.D.M.S. visited Advanced Dressing Stations at HOUPLINES and BRICKFIELD, Regimental Aid Posts at TISSAGE DUMP, Battalion Headquarters of 2/10th Kings Liverpool Regiment, and 2/5th South Lancashire Regiment. Three gassed cases (chloric gas) with severe eye symptoms arrived at BRICKFIELD Advanced Dressing Station while A.D.M.S. was there. A.D.M.S. visited 2/10 Batn: a/c Foot treatment ointment.	

Army Form C. 2118.

WAR DIARY
or
INTELLIGENCE SUMMARY.
(Erase heading not required.)

Place	Date	Hour	Summary of Events and Information	Remarks and references to Appendices
STEENWERCK.	3.2.18		DDMS XV corps with DADMS (61st Division) visited Foot Treatment Centres at ERQUINGHEM, ARMENTIERES &c. A.D.M.S. addressed 172nd Brigade School on Prevention of Trench Foot. Wounded in 57th Division in January 12. - "P.U.O." still prevailing chiefly 56 cases of same admitted in January 1918.	
	4.2.18		A.D.M.S. visited 2/10th Kings (Liverpool Regiment) and 2/5th West Lancashire Field Ambulance &c. Division was rearranged in three Brigades of three Battalions each, and a 10th Pioneer Battalion. Sick admissions and evacuation rate considerably lower.	
	5.2.18		A.D.M.S. visited 2/10th Kings Liverpool in connection with training of Stretcher Bearers, and 2/5th Wessex Field Ambulance particularly regarding men not Category "A". D.A.D.M.S. visited left of the line, and made inquiry regarding medical arrangements for forthcoming enterprise.	
	6.2.18		A.D.M.S. with D.D.M.S. XV Corps visited Advanced Dressing Stations at HOUPLINES and BRICKFIELD, and all Regimental Aid Posts in line (TISSAGE DUMP) AUCKLAND ROAD, SQUARE FARM, and WELLINGTON AVENUE)	

WAR DIARY
or
INTELLIGENCE SUMMARY.

Army Form C. 2118.

Place	Date	Hour	Summary of Events and Information	Remarks and references to Appendices
STEENWERCK	6.2.18		ADMS afterwards, alone, went to Baths at ERQUINGHEM and went ARMENTIERES. ADMS held conference at 2/2nd Wessex Field Ambulance Headquarters of Officers Commanding Field Ambulances and Regimental Medical Officers (fourteen present). ADMS went to TISSAGE DUMP at 9.0 p.m. and saw wounded (12) of 2/4th Surrey Regiment being brought in and treated after Raid in which seven prisoners and a machine gun were taken.	
	7.2.18		Conference of A.D.Ms.S (12th, 58th and 57th Divisions) at office of DD.M.S, XV Corps. Headquarters – Discussed failure to obtain treatment, Disinfection in cases of Scabies and Boils, Shortage of Medical Officers, Alteration in Field Ambulance Establishment, etc. A.D.M.S discussed with G.O.C. cases of Trench Foot not so diagnosed in Division, but diagnosed as such on arrival at Clearing Station	
	8.2.18		A.D.M.S saw other than Category "A" men in 3/2nd West Lancashire Field Ambulance and inspected Scabies treatment etc. ADMS visited 2/5th Royal Lancaster Regiment, and 2/5th South Lancashire Regiment (Remains) in camps at HOLLEBEQUE and MENEGATE. Saw new United States Medical Corps Officers arrived last night (7/2/18) to division. ADMS wrote full report	

WAR DIARY
or
INTELLIGENCE SUMMARY.

Army Form C. 2118.

Place	Date	Hour	Summary of Events and Information	Remarks and references to Appendices
STEENWERCK	8-2-18		For G.O.C. on arrival of General Foot occurring Jan'y 8th - 15th Mondaine to exposure to frost near YPRES. A.D.M.S. received orders to evacuate 50 patients every third day to Casualty Clearing Station, which will be used as Corps Rest Station. Divisional Rest Station to be abolished.	
	9.2.18		Order received that 57th Division will be relieved by 38th Division in period February 13th – 16th. Command to pass on 16th. A.D.M.S. went to Advanced Dressing Station NOUVEL, HOUPLINES for period 9th – 11th February to relieve Medical Officer there, and study conduct of the station. Operation order No 20 issued.	
	10.2.18		A.D.M.S. saw Officer Commanding 2/2nd Wessex Field Ambulance regarding his move to LES PURESBECQUES. It is a poor place providing accommodation for fifteen to seventeen patients at most. A.D.M.S. visited Regimental Aid Post at TISSAGE DUMP and Reserve Post at AUCKLAND AVENUE with Medical Officer 2/8th Kings Liverpool Regiment.	See APPENDIX 'A'

Army Form C. 2118.

WAR DIARY
or
INTELLIGENCE SUMMARY.
(Erase heading not required.)

Instructions regarding War Diaries and Intelligence Summaries are contained in F. S. Regs., Part II. and the Staff Manual respectively. Title pages will be prepared in manuscript.

Place	Date	Hour	Summary of Events and Information	Remarks and references to Appendices
STEENWERCK	11.2.16		A.D.M.S returned to Divisional Headquarters. Bath accommodation in Divisional area can deal with 2,080 men daily namely ERQUINGHEM Baths 1,200 men, PONT DE NIEPPE Baths 480 men, and hornist Baths ARMENTIERES 400 men. In addition to these JESUS FARM Baths are to be ready about February 20th. These 1400 men can be bathed daily.	
	12.2.16		Orders received for MAJOR E.B. ANDERSON, 3/2nd West Lancashire Field Ambulance to report for duty to A.D.M.S. ABBEVILLE. A.D.M.S visited 3/2nd West Lancashire Field Ambulance and arrangement of Scabies cases. This unit is to move north 190th Infantry Brigade tomorrow, 13/2/19 16 to destination NORRENT FONTES.	
	13.2.16		3/2nd West Lancashire Field Ambulance moved today to ESTAIRES, en route for NORRENT FONTES. A.D.M.S. 38th Division called regarding handing over NORRENT FONTES. Details of medical arrangements discussed. A.D.M.S. sanction on 16/2/16. Return of medical Officers as unfit for service at front as reported by their Medical Officers.	

Army Form C. 2118.

WAR DIARY
or
INTELLIGENCE SUMMARY.

(Erase heading not required.)

Instructions regarding War Diaries and Intelligence Summaries are contained in F. S. Regs., Part II. and the Staff Manual respectively. Title pages will be prepared in manuscript.

Place	Date	Hour	Summary of Events and Information	Remarks and references to Appendices
STEENWERCK	14.2.18		2/2nd Wessex Field Ambulance moved today from ERQUINGHEM to LES PURESBECQUES near MERVILLE.	
	15.2.18		2/5th Wessex Field Ambulance moved today from STEENWERCK to ESTAIRES.	
MERVILLE	16.2.18		59th Divisional Headquarters moved to MERVILLE. Locations are now as follows:-	
			(Sheet 36A). A.D.M.S office, MERVILLE, K.29 central.	
			2/1st Wessex Field Ambulance LES PURESBECQUES. K.22.d.7.8	
			2/5th Wessex Field Ambulance ESTAIRES L.29.d.6.6	
			3/3rd West Lancashire Field Ambulance NORRENTFONTES N.30.c.0.0	
			A.D.M.S. inspected 2/2nd Wessex Field Ambulance billeted in farms around LES PURESBECQUES and Orenament livins and quarters near MERVILLE. Very scanty and poor accommodation for sick in barn attic up a ladder.	

Army Form C. 2118.

WAR DIARY
or
INTELLIGENCE SUMMARY.
(Erase heading not required.)

Place	Date	Hour	Summary of Events and Information	Remarks and references to Appendices
MERVILLE.	17.2.16		A.D.M.S. visited 2/3rd Wessex Field Ambulance, ESTAIRES. This unit has a main dressing station with capacity up to a maximum of 160 patients. The scabies cases are being treated on "Soft soap, Sulphur ointment, and 4 days without change" system. This unit has also the administration of the Advanced Surgical Centre, 54th Casualty Clearing Station. D.A.D.M.S. visited No. 8 Sanitary Section, BÉTHUNE in connection with comparative value of methods of delousing. A.D.M.S. to submit to Headquarters (B. Force), 57th Division a scheme for dealing with men in the Division generally.	
	18.2.16		Routine — Return to D.D.M.S. XI Corps showing the following numbers (a) detached from their units, and (b) available as bearers:-	
			Detached Available as Bearers	
			2/2nd Wessex Field Ambulance. 24. 70	
			2/3rd - do - 8. 40.	
			3/2nd West Lancashire Field Ambulance 27. 90.	

WAR DIARY
or
INTELLIGENCE SUMMARY.

(Erase heading not required.)

Army Form C. 2118.

Instructions regarding War Diaries and Intelligence Summaries are contained in F. S. Regs., Part II. and the Staff Manual respectively. Title pages will be prepared in manuscript.

Place	Date	Hour	Summary of Events and Information	Remarks and references to Appendices
MERVILLE	19.2.18		A.D.M.S visited and inspected 3/2nd West Lancashire Field Ambulance at NORRENT FONTES. Captain Edmiston commanding in absence of Lieut Colonel Macdonald on leave. D.A.D.M.S dropped a time for dealing with Returns in Divison especially as regards removal of Woman from station. D.D.M.S visited 2/2nd Wessex Field Ambulance at LES PURESBEC QUES.	
	20.2.18		D.A.D.M.S visited 2/3rd Wessex Field Ambulance at ESTAIRES. A.D.M.S attended conference of A.Ds.M.S. at Office of D.D.M.S. XV Corps - Discussed Medical arrangements of Defence Scheme, etc, etc.	
	22.2.18		A.D.M.S visited 2/2nd Wessex Field Ambulance and 2/3rd Wessex Field Ambulance. D.D.M.S. called in connection with Medical arrangements in event of retirement.	
	23.2.18		XV Corps Commander presented Military Cross and Military Medal in bands to Officers, N.C.Os and men of Royal Artillery and Royal Army Medical Corps who have received Military Crosses and Military Medals recently as immediate reward. From March 1st Division is to	

A.5834 Wt.W4973/M687 750,000 8/16 D.D. & L. Ltd. Forms/C.2118/13.

WAR DIARY
or
INTELLIGENCE SUMMARY.
(Erase heading not required.)

Army Form C. 2118.

Place	Date	Hour	Summary of Events and Information	Remarks and references to Appendices
MERVILLE	23.2.18		Received 86 names for leave (per day) which will mean 24 to Royal Army Medical Corps per week.	
	24.2.18		A.D.M.S reported to D.D.M.S, XV Corps on suggestion to establish Walking Wounded Collecting Post at or near ST FLORIS in event of hostile activity on XV Corps Front. In response to invitation to name Medical Officers in this Division whom A.D.M.S could recommend as Officer Commanding Motor Ambulance Convoy, A.D.M.S submitted to D.D.M.S XV Corps the names of Captains KIDSTON and EDMISTON.	
	25.2.18		A.D.M.S visited Corps Headquarters (XV*) and saw D.D.M.S regarding various matters. A.D.M.S visited Baths in MERVILLE. Captain SCHOLEFIELD ordered to report to 51st Casualty Clearing Station for duty. Instructions received that all three Field Ambulance Commanders of this Division are to proceed to England and report in writing to the War Office.	
	26.2.18		A.D.M.S attended conference at office of D.M.S, First Army of D.D's M.S and A.D's M.S regarding Corps Defence Scheme. Discussed Rail Station, Economy of Drugs, Dressings, Disinfectants, Periodical Inspection of men, Training of	

Army Form C. 2118.

WAR DIARY
or
INTELLIGENCE SUMMARY.
(Erase heading not required.)

Instructions regarding War Diaries and Intelligence Summaries are contained in F. S. Regs. Part II. and the Staff Manual respectively. Title pages will be prepared in manuscript.

Place	Date	Hour	Summary of Events and Information	Remarks and references to Appendices
MERVILLE	26.2.18		Field Ambulance Personnel when Medical Units are out of the line, etc. Thereafter, with D.D.M.S, A.D.M.S visited proposed site of Walking Wounded Collecting Post at ST FLORIS. D.A.D.M.S attended Staff Exercise held by XV Corps Commander at Corps Headquarters.	
	27.2.18		D.A.D.M.S attended Conference on Staff Exercise held yesterday. A.D.M.S visited Main Dressing Station at ESTAIRES, horse lines nearby of 2/3rd Fld Ambulance, and 2/6th and 8th King's Liverpool Regiments at PONT DE NIEPPE. Bathing arrangements and clothing spare for these units obtain in small factory. A.D.M.S so informed Headquarters of Division.	
	28.2.18		A.D.M.S attended Conference of A.D.M.S at office of D.D.M.S, XV Corps. Evacuation arrangements from troops from the Divisional Basis was the chief topic under consideration.	

28/2/1918.

J. F. Olsen .... Colonel A. Med. S.
A.D.M.S 57th (W.L.) Division.

SECRET. 57th. DIVISION. Copy No. 20

APPENDIX A

R.A.M.C. OPERATION ORDER No. 20

Reference Map Sheet HAZEBROUCK 5A

1. (a) 57th. Division will be relieved by 38th. Division during the period 13th. to 18th. February, 1918.

   (b) Command of the sector will pass to G.O.C., 38th. Division at 10-30 a.m. on 16th. February.

2. (a) Field Ambulances will be relieved as follows:-

   The 3/2nd. West Lancs. Field Ambulance at L'ESTRADE by the 130th. Field Ambulance on the 13th. instant relief to be complete by noon.

   The 2/2nd. Wessex Field Ambulance at ERQUINGHEM by the 131st. Field Ambulance on 14th. instant relief of Advanced Dressing Stations and bearer posts to be complete by 6-0 a.m.

   The 2/3rd. Wessex Field Ambulance at STEENWERCK by the 129th. Field Ambulance on 15th. instant relief to be complete by noon.

   (b) Details of reliefs will be arranged between Officers Commanding concerned.

   (c) Completion of reliefs will be notified to this Office.

3. Advanced parties of 1 Officer and 5 other ranks will be sent as follows:-

   From 3/2nd. West Lancs.   to NORRENT FONTES   on 12th. inst.
       Field Ambulance.

   From 2/2nd. Wessex Field   to LES PURESBECQUES on 13th. inst.
       Ambulance.

   From 2/3rd. Wessex Field   to ESTAIRES   on 13th. inst.
       Ambulance.

4. Field Ambulances will be affiliated as follows and will pass under the orders of their respective Brigades from the hours mentioned below.

   3/2nd. West Lancs. Field Ambulance - 170th. Brigade - Noon 13th. instant.
   2/2nd. Wessex Field Ambulance - 171st. Brigade - 6-0 a.m. 14th. instant.
   2/3rd. Wessex Field Ambulance - 172nd. Brigade - Noon 15th. instant.

5. (a) All equipment surplus to that authorised by Mobilization Store Table and G.R.O's. will be handed over to the relieving units.

   (b) Copies of receipts for all stores and equipment handed and taken over will be sent to this Office.

6. A.D.M.S. Office will close at STEENWERCK at 9-0 a.m. 16th. instant and re-open at 10-0 a.m. at MERVILLE.

7. Please acknowledge.

Headquarters.
10th. February, 1918.

Captain, D.A.D.M.S.,
for A.D.M.S., 57th. Division.

Issued at 2-30 p.m.

For distribution see over.

DISTRIBUTION :-

Copy No. 1 to H.Q., 57th. Division.
         2   -ditto-
         3   D.D.M.S., XV Corps.
         4   D.M.S., First Army.
         5   H.Q., 170th. Infantry Brigade.
         6   H.Q., 171st. Infantry Brigade.
         7   H.Q., 172nd. Infantry Brigade.
         8   O.C., 2/2nd. Wessex Field Ambulance.
         9   O.C., 2/3rd. Wessex Field Ambulance.
        10   O.C., 3/2nd. West Lancs. Field Ambulance.
        11   C.R.E., 57th. Division.
        12   C.R.A., 57th. Division.
        13   O.C., 57th. Divisional Signal Company.
        14   O.C., 57th. Divisional Train, A.S.C.
        15   D.A.D.V.S., 57th. Division.
        16   A.P.M., 57th. Division.
        17   D.M.G.O., 57th. Division.
        18   A.D.M.S., 38th. Division.
        19   A.D.M.S., 12th. Division.
        20   War Diary.
        21   -do-
        22   File.
        23   -do-
        24   Spare.
        25   -do-

CONFIDENTIAL.

WAR DIARY

of

A.D.M.S, 57th Division.

from 1st March 1918 to 31st March 1918.

Army Form C. 2118.

WAR DIARY
or
INTELLIGENCE SUMMARY.
(Erase heading not required.)

Instructions regarding War Diaries and Intelligence Summaries are contained in F. S. Regs., Part II. and the Staff Manual respectively. Title pages will be prepared in manuscript.

Place	Date	Hour	Summary of Events and Information	Remarks and references to Appendices
MERVILLE	1-3-18		A.D.M.S. reported to Headquarters, 57th Division and D.D.M.S. XV Corps that Division as now down Medical Officers short; removal of three Field Ambulances Commanders will make ten deficiency - 31 out of 41 - which is found to militate against efficiency, as well as making it difficult to grant leave. Reported also to Headquarters (with copy to D.D.M.S.) on continued high sick rate of the Division, and necessity for improved facilities for cleansing men, and freeing them from vermin. A.D.M.S. visited billets of 2/4th South Lancashire Regiment with D.D.M.S. XVth in connection with complaint of cold. Found billets very satisfactory, and no complaint of cold by men. A.D.M.S. with D.D.M.S. XV Corps also visited 2/3rd Wessex Field Ambulance, whose huts are now being taken down for transference to another site, and sites of Divisional Walking Wounded Collecting Post, and Advanced Dressing Stations at BEAUPRE and LESTREM, respectively. A.D.M.S. afterwards visited 3/2nd West Lancashire Field Ambulance at NORRENT FONTES, went over quarters and inspected unit on parade with Captain EDMISTON, acting Officer Commanding. Captain A.W.B. LOUDON,	

Army Form C. 2118.

WAR DIARY
or
INTELLIGENCE SUMMARY.
(Erase heading not required.)

Instructions regarding War Diaries and Intelligence Summaries are contained in F.S. Regs., Part II. and the Staff Manual respectively. Title pages will be prepared in manuscript.

Place	Date	Hour	Summary of Events and Information	Remarks and references to Appendices
MERVILLE	1-3-18		from 57th Casualty Clearing Station reported for duty as Officer Commanding 2/2nd West Lancashire Field Ambulance, vice Lieut Colonel MACDONALD.	
	2-3-18		Sick evacuations of 57th Division for week ending 28th February is 1.29%, about twice as high as any division (except Canadians) in First Army. A.D.M.S. wrote Field Ambulance Commanders (and very difficult to elicit) regarding evacuation of P.U.O. cases, and restriction of use of antipyretic drugs. Captain LOUDON proceeded to 2/2nd West Lancashire Field Ambulance today to take over command. Machine Gun Battalion now formed, and Medical Officer authorised by its establishment.	
	3-3-18		Lieut Colonel S.C. PARSONS left for England handing over command of the 2/2nd Wessex Field Ambulance temporarily to Major H.C. ADAMS. A.D.M.S visited Baths for troops in MERVILLE - ample capacity for present requirements. A.D.M.S. visited D.A.D.M.S. A.D.M.S. visited 2/3rd Wessex Field Ambulance, and attached Advanced Surgical Centre from 54 Casualty Clearing Station, which is now being used. A.D.M.S. visited 2/10th Kings Liverpool Regiment, and made general enquiries regarding sanitation and health.	

Army Form C. 2118.

WAR DIARY
or
INTELLIGENCE SUMMARY.
(Erase heading not required.)

Place	Date	Hour	Summary of Events and Information	Remarks and references to Appendices
MERVILLE	4.3.18		A.D.M.S visited 8th Kings Liverpool Regiment at BOUREC Q and 2/6th Kings Liverpool Regiment at ST HILAIRE making general enquiry regarding health and sanitation especially cleanliness of men, clothing and billets. D.A.D.M.S made similar enquiry regarding 9th Kings Liverpool Regiment at LE SARS. A.D.M.S also visited First Army Headquarters, and Portable Red Cross Store at HAM-EN-ARTOIS, and 2/2nd West Lancashire Field Ambulance at NORRENT-FONTES. A.D.M.S discussed with A.D.M.S First Army high and low examination rate in relation to Return strength (denominator). Reported to D.D.M.S, XV Corps on (1) Obedience, etiology and "PUO" in the Division, (2) Alternative sites of Divisional Dressing Station at LESTREM and BEAUPRE ; (3) (a) Treatment of Venereal cases before they can be evacuated from Field Ambulances, and (B) Inspection of men for Venereal Disease on their return from leave.	
	5.3.18		Captain P.T. RUTHERFORD, from 56th Division, reported from 56th Division for Command of 2/3rd Wessex Field Ambulance. A.D.M.S. visited 1/5th North Lancashire Regiment and 2/4th North Lancashire Regiment, both	

Army Form C. 2118.

WAR DIARY
or
INTELLIGENCE SUMMARY.
(Erase heading not required.)

Instructions regarding War Diaries and Intelligence Summaries are contained in F. S. Regs., Part II. and the Staff Manual respectively. Title pages will be prepared in manuscript.

Place	Date	Hour	Summary of Events and Information	Remarks and references to Appendices
MERVILLE	5.3.18		at PONT-DE-NIEPPE in regard to health of unit, sanitation, Blanketing, etc.	
	6.3.18		A.D.M.S. saw Divisional Commander regarding high sick admission and evacuation rate in the Division in last 18 days or so. A.D.M.S. visited 2/2nd and 2/3rd Wessex Field Ambulances, and newly formed 59th Divisional Machine Gun Battalion. At XV Corps Headquarters discussed Medical Officers of Division, sick rate of Division, Evacuation scheme, etc.) with D.D.M.S.	
	7.3.18		D.A.D.M.S. visited office of D.M.S. regarding sick evacuation percentages of this and other Divisions of the XV Corps. Long discussion on this subject with G.O.C. A.D.M.S. to issue an Order that transient cases of sickness should be kept in billets for some or two days if conditions are suitable.	
	8.3.18		A.D.M.S. saw G.O.C. further regarding Sick Admission and Evacuation Rates of the Division and is to replace 12th Division in line, FLEURBAIX Sector, March 16th-18th. New Medical Officer arrived from 12th Division and posted to 2/2nd Wessex Field Ambulance. Captain J.R.R.TRIST. S. Res. appointed to command 2/2nd Wessex Field Ambulance to take up duty tomorrow. A.D.M.S. visited Baths at MERVILLE (2) and ESTAIRES 2/4th South Lancashire Regiment, ESTAIRES, and visited NEUF BERQUIN	

WAR DIARY or INTELLIGENCE SUMMARY.

Army Form C. 2118.

Place	Date	Hour	Summary of Events and Information	Remarks and references to Appendices
MERVILLE	8.3.18		Went to site for Main Dressing Station.	
	9.3.18		Captain J.R.R.TRIST, S.R., formerly D.A.D.M.S., XV Corps came to take over command of 2/2nd Wessex Field Ambulance vice Lieut. Colonel PARSONS, transferred to England. A.D.M.S. submitted Medical Arrangements in connection with 64th Divisional Staff Exercise. A.D.M.S. visited 2/2nd West Lancashire Field Ambulance at NORRENT FONTES, 2/6th King's Liverpool Regiment at ST HILAIRE, and 8th King's Liverpool Regiment at BOUREC Q, also Office of D.M.S., First Army, regarding Major ADAMS application for transfer to Casualty Clearing Station, and Sick evacuation rates.	
	10.3.18		A.D.M.S. interviewed Captain J.R.R.TRIST, new Officer Commanding, 2/2nd Wessex Field Ambulance. 3/2nd West Lancashire Field Ambulance, and the 171st Brigade Group marched in fresh today from NORRENT FONTES to LE SARS. A.D.M.S. saw A.D.M.S., 12th Division and G.S.O. 2 (Headquarters,	
	11.3.18		CROIX-DU-BAC) regarding taking over from 12th Division area and front (BOIS GRENIER and FLEUR BAIX) on March 16th – 18th.	

WAR DIARY
or
INTELLIGENCE SUMMARY.

(Erase heading not required.)

Army Form C. 2118.

Place	Date	Hour	Summary of Events and Information	Remarks and references to Appendices
MERVILLE	11.2.18		A.D.M.S. visited Field Ambulance a/cs at FORT ROMPU (38A) and SAILLY (36A). A.D.M.S. visited and made general sanitary enquiry regarding 1/5th North Lancashire Regiment — PONT DE NIEPPE 2/5th North Lancashire Regiment — LE NOUVEAU MONDE 2/4th South Lancashire Regiment — ESTAIRES. Captain LONGLEY and 10 other Ranks sent, on orders, to 54 Casualty Clearing Station. Also Medical Officer to concentration camp, CALONNE. Another Medical Officer to go on inspection to Rendezvous for evacuation of civilians.	
	12.2.18		A.D.M.S visited 6 7th Batt. Machine Gun Corps, and reported on conditions there. A.D.M.S also visited 5/2nd West Lancashire Field Ambulance on NERVILLE-LE-SARS Road.	
	13.2.18		2/3rd Wessex Field Ambulance Headquarters, and Main Dressing Station at ESTAIRES shelled at 9.30am, one man killed, and three wounded, one severely. No patients injured, unit moved out	

Army Form C. 2118.

WAR DIARY
or
INTELLIGENCE SUMMARY.
(Erase heading not required.)

Instructions regarding War Diaries and Intelligence Summaries are contained in F. S. Regs., Part II. and the Staff Manual respectively. Title pages will be prepared in manuscript.

Place	Date	Hour	Summary of Events and Information	Remarks and references to Appendices
MERVILLE	13.3.18		promptly to Cross Roads just north of LA GORGUE (Sheet 36A/L 28. d. 5. 5) A.D.M.S visited them there. Personnel to be under canvas tonight. A.D.M.S visited 55 Casualty Clearing Station near STVENANT, but north of canal. Already 200 patients with accommodation for 100 more. Extended accommodation 600, plus 200 (Sick) plus 500 Convalescents.	
	14.3.18		A.D.M.S. visited 2/3rd Wessex Field Ambulance now in billets, and under canvas just west of ESTAIRES, and nearly of LAGORGUE. Sick accommodation in private houses satisfactory, except Scabies which are under canvas.	
	15.3.18		Conference of Brigadiers and Heads of Departments held by G.O.C. Division. Two American officers 1st/Lieutenants WOOD and MARCY arrived for duty with Division from 12th and 38th Divisions respectively. Both posted temporarily to 2/2nd West Lancashire Field Ambulance. A.D.M.S visited 2/2nd West Lancashire Field Ambulance at 7.30 a.m. A.D.M.S visited 2/3rd Wessex Field Ambulance in regard to new site on main ESTAIRES – NEUF BERQUIN road.	

Army Form C. 2118.

WAR DIARY
or
INTELLIGENCE SUMMARY.
(Erase heading not required.)

Instructions regarding War Diaries and Intelligence Summaries are contained in F.S. Regs., Part II. and the Staff Manual respectively. Title pages will be prepared in manuscript.

Place	Date	Hour	Summary of Events and Information	Remarks and references to Appendices
MERVILLE	16.3.18		A.D.M.S. visited and inspected working of Loden Lorry. Also visited billets of, and 'A' Battery Wagon Lines, 285th R.F.A. Brigade, and 2/3rd Wessex Field Ambulance, about to move to site on ESTAIRES - NEUF BERQUIN road. About six shells fired on MERVILLE between 12.0 noon and 1.0 pm today.	
	17.3.18		A.D.M.S. visited D.D.M.S. at XV Corps Headquarters regarding modification of Keerne Divisional Defence Scheme. A.D.M.S. with A.A. or Q.M.G., 57th Division visited Field Ambulances at DOULIEU, SAILLY, and FORT ROMPU and Advanced Dressing Stations at LES TROIS TOULETTES and LA CROIX LESCORNEZ that we are shortly to take over from 12th Division. A.D.M.S. visited 2/3rd Wessex Field Ambulance which moved yesterday from cross-roads, west, to site on NEUFBERQUIN ROAD, north-west of ESTAIRES.	
	18.3.18		G.O.C., 57th Division inspected all three Field Ambulances of the Division in a field north of MERVILLE. He expressed himself as very highly satisfied with the 2/2nd Wessex Field Ambulance, highly satisfied with the 3/2nd West Lancashire Field Ambulance, and fairly satisfied with the 2/3rd Wessex Field Ambulance. A.D.M.S. visited latter two units at their quarters later.	

Army Form C. 2118.

WAR DIARY
or
INTELLIGENCE SUMMARY.
(Erase heading not required.)

Instructions regarding War Diaries and Intelligence Summaries are contained in F. S. Regs., Part II. and the Staff Manual respectively. Title pages will be prepared in manuscript.

Place	Date	Hour	Summary of Events and Information	Remarks and references to Appendices
MERVILLE	18.3.18		Orders received for move of 57th Division to relieve 12th Division in the right sector of the XV Corps front March 19th - 23rd. Issued No M.S. 196 Operation Order 18/3/18 20	Appendix 'A'
	19.3.18		2/3rd Wessex Field Ambulance moved today from near ESTAIRES -on- NEUF BERQUIN Road to FORTROMPU. D.A.D.M.S visited HeadQuarters of 12th Division at CROIX-DU-BAC arranging details of exchange. A.D.M.S visited quarters of 2/2nd Wessex Field Ambulance at LES PURES BEC QUES. Major D.C.L. ORTON reported for duty with Division.	
	20.3.18		2/3rd Wessex Field Ambulance Main Dressing Station at FORTROMPU struck by shell yesterday afternoon. One patient wounded (not severely) and one Sergeant severely shaken. 3/2nd West Lancashire Field Ambulance moved from near MERVILLE to SAILLY today. A.D.M.S visited their Advanced Stations at SAILLY and FORTROMPU, Advanced Dressing Station at LA CROIX LESCORNEZ and quarters of 9th Kings Liverpool Regiment at ESTAIRES.	
CROIX DU BAC	21.3.18		2/2nd Wessex Field Ambulance moved from LES PURES BEC QUES near MERVILLE to DOULIEU. HeadQuarters 57th Division moved from	

WAR DIARY or INTELLIGENCE SUMMARY

Army Form C. 2118.

Place	Date	Hour	Summary of Events and Information	Remarks and references to Appendices
CROIX DU BAC	21.2.18		MERVILLE to CROIX DU BAC. Learned that each Division is shortly to be deprived of one Field Ambulance. A.D.M.S visited 3/3rd West Lancashire Field Ambulance, SAILLY. They had admitted 58 gassed cases and 14 wounded during the night and morning. Two cases of Trench Foot admitted to 2/3rd Wessex Field Ambulance from 2/5th Royal Lancaster Regiment today. On one case diagnosis altered to "I.C.T." by Officer Commanding Field Ambulance.	
	22.2.18		A.D.M.S visited 2/3rd Wessex Field Ambulance at FORT ROMPU, present and former Advanced Dressing Stations at AUX TROIS TOULETTES and BOIS GRENIER respectively and Regimental Aid Post of 2/5 2nd Royal Lancaster Regiment in SHAFTESBURY AVENUE chiefly in connection with two cases of Trench Foot in that Battalion. A third case of Trench Foot (in 9th Kings Liverpool Regiment) reported today. A.D.M.S wrote report on these cases for A.D.C, 57th Division and D.D.M.S, XV Corps. DADMS visited Advanced Dressing Station at LA CROIX LES CORNEZ, Regimental Aid Post at EATON HALL and front line in extreme right.	

Army Form C. 2118.

WAR DIARY
or
INTELLIGENCE SUMMARY.
(Erase heading not required.)

Place	Date	Hour	Summary of Events and Information	Remarks and references to Appendices
CROIX DU BAC	23.3.18.		Notification received that Field Ambulances of each Division to be reduced to two. A.D.M.S to report which he wishes to retain. A.D.M.S attended Conference of D.D.M.S and A.D.M.S at office of D.M.S, chiefly regarding anti-vermin measures, economy of rations, etc.	
	24.3.18		After consultation with G.O.C, A.D.M.S recommended that the Division retain the 2/2nd with all others, have to give up one Field Ambulance, should retain the 2/2nd and 2/3rd Wessex Field Ambulances, and have Captain KIDSTON transferred to 2/3rd Wessex Field Ambulance in place of Major ORTON transferred to 3/2nd West Lancashire Field Ambulance. A.D.M.S visited 2/2nd Wessex Field Ambulance a DOULIEU, where a large Sick Receiving Centre's for the whole Division is being built: accommodation for about 300 cases. A.D.M.S visited also the 3/2nd West Lancashire Field Ambulance at SAILLY.	
	25.3.18		10th/Lieutenant MONTGOMERY, M.O.R.C, U.S.A, arrived yesterday and posted to 2/2nd Wessex Field Ambulance. A.D.M.S discussed detached duties and site of Advanced Dressing Station for Advanced Dressing Station for left sector with D.D.M.S, XV Corps. A.D.M.S visited 3/2nd West Lancashire	

Army Form C. 2118.

WAR DIARY
or
INTELLIGENCE SUMMARY.
(Erase heading not required.)

Instructions regarding War Diaries and Intelligence Summaries are contained in F. S. Regs., Part II. and the Staff Manual respectively. Title pages will be prepared in manuscript.

Place	Date	Hour	Summary of Events and Information	Remarks and references to Appendices
CROIX DU BAC	25.3.18		Field Ambulance. Captain KIDSTON posted to 2/3rd Wessex Field Ambulance vice EDMISTON. Major ORTON posted to 2/2nd West Lancashire Field Ambulance to place EDMISTON posted to 3/2nd West Lancashire Field Ambulance. Section Commanders are now:— 2/2nd Wessex Field Ambulance 3/2nd West Lancashire Field Ambulance A Lieut Colonel TRIST Lieut Colonel RUTHERFORD. Lieut Colonel LOUDON B Major ADAMS, Major STOKES, Major ORTON. C Captain GIBBS, Captain KIDSTON. Captain EDMISTON	
	26.3.18		A.D.M.S. visited 2/3rd Wessex Field Ambulance and 3/2nd West Lancashire Field Ambulance	
	27.3.18		Conference of Medical Officers at 3/2nd West Lancashire Field Ambulance Main Dressing Station, SAILLY. Nineteen present including Field Ambulance Commanders (3), A.D.M.S. and D.A.D.M.S.	
	28.3.18		A.D.M.S. visited 2/2nd Wessex Field Ambulance at DOULIEU rapidly erecting a large hospital of Nissen huts and marquees ready to accommodate 200 patients. A.D.M.S. visited horse lines of 2/2nd Wessex Field Ambulance and 3/2nd West Lancashire	

Army Form C. 2118.

WAR DIARY
or
INTELLIGENCE SUMMARY.
(Erase heading not required.)

Instructions regarding War Diaries and Intelligence Summaries are contained in F. S. Regs., Part II. and the Staff Manual respectively. Title pages will be prepared in manuscript.

Place	Date	Hour	Summary of Events and Information	Remarks and references to Appendices
CROIX DU BAC	26.3.18		Field Ambulance, near CRUSE BEAU. Advanced Dressing Station at AUX TROIS TOULETTES shelled today (no casualties), and advanced Dressing Station left Sector moved accordingly to BOIS GRENIER. Captain LONGLEY left Division for 57 Casualty Clearing Station. 38th Division on left is leaving for south within the next few days.	
	29.3.18		A.D.M.S. visited Advanced Dressing Stations, Regimental Aid Posts &c in BOIS GRENIER Sector with Officer Commanding 2/3rd Wessex Field Ambulance. Information received that 57th Division is about to be relieved by 40th Division, and going south.	
	30.3.18		A.D.M.S. visited Advanced Dressing Station and Regimental Aid Posts FLEURBAIX Sector with Officer Commanding 2/2nd West Lancashire Field Ambulance. A.D.M.S arranged with D.A.D.M.S, 40th Division for relief of Medical Units, 57th Division by Medical Units, 40th Division on 1st April 1918. Issued Operation Order No 2 B.	APPENDIX "B"
	31.3.18		Issued Operation Order No 2 b.	APPENDIX "C"
			Notification received of promotion of Captain LOUDON to Lieut. Colonel March 19/1918	

Army Form C. 2118.

WAR DIARY
or
INTELLIGENCE SUMMARY.
(Erase heading not required.)

Place	Date	Hour	Summary of Events and Information	Remarks and references to Appendices
CROIX DU BAC	31.3.18		of Captain TRIST to Lieut: Colonel March 18th/1918, of Captain RUTHERFORD to Major commanding a section (obviously in error), and of Captain KIDSTON and EDMISTON to Acting Majors while commanding section of Field Ambulances. All detached details of Field Ambulances rejoined their units today. 1/35th Field Ambulance, 40th Division, arrived SAILLY yesterday and billeted there with 2/2nd West Lancashire Field Ambulance. A.D.M.S. saw Officer Commanding, 2/2nd West Lancashire Field Ambulance and visited 2/3rd Wessex Field Ambulance and 3/2nd West Lancashire Field Ambulance. A.D.M.S. also visited 2/6th King's Liverpool Regiment.	
	31/3/1918.			

J.J. Burn
Colonel. A. Med. S.
A.D.M.S. 57th (W.L.) Division.

SECRET   APPENDIX "A"

57th. DIVISION.   M.S. 196.

R.A.M.C. OPERATION ORDER No. 21.   Copy No.... 21

                         Reference Map Sheet 36 and 36a.

1. 57th. Division will relieve 12th. Division in the
   Southern Divisional Sector of XV Corps front on the 19th,
   20th, 21st, 22nd, and 23rd. March 1918.

2. The Reliefs of Field Ambulances will be as under :-

Unit to be relieved.	Station.	Unit relieving.	Date of relief.
38th Field Amb.	FORT ROMPU.	2/3rd. Wessex Field Ambulance.	19th March.
36th -do-	SAILLY.	3/2nd. W.Lancs.Field Ambulance.	20th March.
37th. -do-	DOULIEU.	2/2nd. Wessex Field Ambulance.	21st. March

   Details of reliefs will be arranged by Officers Commanding,
   Field Ambulances concerned.
   Completion of reliefs to be notified to this Office.

3. Field Ambulances will proceed by road, maintaining a distance
   of 500 yards between units on the march.

4. All stretchers and blankets surplus to Mob. Store Table and
   G.R.Os will be handed over to the incoming units. Copies
   of receipts for all stores taken over will be sent to this
   Office.

5. A.D.M.S. Office will close at MERVILLE at 9-0 a.m. on 21st.
   March and will re-open at CROIX DU BAC at 10-0 a.m.

6. Please acknowledge.

                                        Maurice King.
Headquarters,   Captain, D.A.D.M.S.,
18th. March, 1918.   for A.D.M.S., 57th. Division.

Issued at... 6-30 ...p.m.   P.T.O.

DISTRIBUTION :-

Copy No. 1 to H.Q., 57th. Division.
       2   -ditto-
       3   D.D.M.S., XV. Corps.
       4   D.M.S., First Army.
       5   H.Q., 170th. Infantry Brigade.
       6   H.Q., 171st. Infantry Brigade.
       7   H.Q., 172nd. Infantry Brigade.
       8   O.C., 2/2nd. Wessex Field Ambulance.
       9   O.C., 2/3rd. Wessex Field Ambulance.
     10   O.C., 2/2nd. West Lancs. Field Ambulance.
     11   C.R.E., 57th. Division.
     12   C.R.A., 57th. Division.
     13   O.C., 57th. Divisional Signal Company.
     14   O.C., 57th. Divisional Train, A.S.C.
     15   O.C., 57th. Battalion Machine Gun Corps.
     16   D.A.D.V.S., 57th. Division.
     17   A.P.M., 57th. Division.
     18   A.D.M.S., 38th. Division.
     19   A.D.M.S., 12th. Division.
     20   War Diary.
     21   -do-
     22   File
     23   -do-
     24   Spare
     25   -do-

APPENDIX "B"

57th. DIVISION.   M.S.210/4.
R.A.M.C. OPERATION ORDER NO. 22.   Copy No. 22

Reference Map Sheet 36 and 36a.

1. The 57th. Division is being relieved in the line by 40th. Division.

2. Field Ambulances will be relieved as follows :-

   2/3rd. Wessex Field Ambulance and 3/2nd. West Lancs. Field Ambulance by 137th. Field Ambulance on April 1st. Advanced Posts will be relieved as early as possible; relief to be complete by 4-0 p.m.

   2/2nd. Wessex Field Ambulance. by 135th. Field Ambulance on April 1st. relief to be complete by 4-0p.m.

3. Details of reliefs will be arranged by Officers Commanding, Field Ambulances concerned.

4. On completion of reliefs Field Ambulances will move as follows:-

   2/2nd. Wessex Field Ambulance.   to ESTAIRES Area.
   2/3rd. Wessex Field Ambulance.   to HAVERSKERQUE Area.
   3/2nd. West Lancs. Field Ambulance   to MERVILLE Area.

   Orders for these moves will be issued later.

5. The 2/3rd. Wessex Field Ambulance and 3/2nd. West Lancs. Field Ambulance should be prepared to move by noon April 1st., rear parties being left behind at FORT ROMPU and SAILLY if necessary.

6. Only equipment authorised in Mob. Store Table and G.R.Os. will be taken to the new area. All equipment in excess of above will be handed over to the relieving units and receipts obtained. Copies of receipts will be sent to this Office.

7. Please acknowledge.

Headquarters,   Colonel, A. Med. S.,
30th. March, 1918.   A.D.M.S., 57th. Division.

Issued at 10-0 p.m.

DISTRIBUTION:-

    Copy No. 1 to H.Q., 57th. Division.
           2   -ditto-
           3   D.D.M.S., XV Corps.
           4   D.M.S., First Army.
           5   H.Q., 170th. Infantry Brigade.
           6   H.Q., 171st. Infantry Brigade.
           7   H.Q., 172nd. Infantry Brigade.
           8   O.C., 2/2nd. Wessex Field Ambulance.
           9   O.C., 2/3rd. Wessex Field Ambulance.
          10   O.C., 3/2nd. West Lancs. Field Ambulance
          11   C.R.E., 57th. Division.
          12   C.R.A., 57th. Division.
          13   D.C.O., 57th. Division.
          14   O.C., 57th. Divisional Signal Company.
          15   O.C., 57th. Divisional Train, A.S.C.
          16   O.C., 57th. Battalion Machine Gun Corps.
          17   D.A.D.V.S., 57th. Division.
          18   A.P.M., 57th. Division.
          19   A.D.M.S., 34th. Division.
          20   A.D.M.S., 40th. Division.
          21   War Diary.
          22   -do-
          23   File.
          24   -do-
          25   Spare.
          26   -do-

APPENDIX "C"

57th DIVISION.   M.S.210/12.

R.A.M.C. OPERATION ORDER NO. 23.   Copy No. 13

Reference Map Sheet 36 and 36a.

1. Moves of Field Ambulances.

   (a) The 3/2nd W.Lancs. Field Ambulance will move from SAILLY to the MERVILLE area on April 1st, under orders of 170th Infantry Brigade.

   (b) The 2/2nd Wessex Field Ambulance will move by road from DOULIEU to the ESTAIRES area on April 1st, on completion of relief by 135th Field Ambulance. Billets will be arranged by 171st Infantry Brigade.

   (c) The 2/3rd Wessex Field Ambulance will move by road from FORT ROMPU to the HAVERSKERQUE area on April 1st, on completion of relief by 137th Field Ambulance. On arrival at HAVERSKERQUE the Field Ambulance will take over the billets vacated by a Field Ambulance of the 38th Division. These billets will not be available before 10 p.m.

2. On the march Field Ambulances will maintain a distance of 500 yards from other units, and 100 yards between Field Ambulance personnel and transport.

3. There are no restrictions as to routes taken by the 2/2nd and 2/3rd Wessex Field Ambulances.

4. On completion of moves Field Ambulances will pass into Brigade Groups as follows :-

   3/2nd W.Lancs. Field Ambulance - 170th Infantry Bde.
   2/2nd Wessex Field Ambulance   - 171st Infantry Bde.
   2/3rd Wessex Field Ambulance   - 172nd Infantry Bde.

5. Completion of moves will be notified to this Office by wire: map location of Field Ambulance Headquarters to be included in the wire.

6. A.D.M.S. Office will close at CROIX DU BAC at 10-0am April 2nd and will re-open at a time and place to be notified later.

7. Please acknowledge.

Headquarters,   Maurice King
  31st March, 1918.   Captain. D.A.D.M.S.,
                                   for A.D.M.S., 57th Division.
Issued at 6.15 p.m.

DISTRIBUTION:-

   Copy No. 1 to 57 Div. "G"
        2   57 Div. "Q"
        3.   H.Q., 170 Infantry Brigade.
        4.   H.Q., 171 Infantry Brigade.
        5.   H.Q., 172 Infantry Brigade.
        6.   O.C., 2/2nd Wessex Field Ambulance.
        7.   O.C., 2/3rd Wessex Field Ambulance.
        8.   O.C., 3/2nd W.Lanc.Field Ambulance.
        9.   A.D.M.S., 40th Division.
       10.   A.D.M.S., 38th Division.
       11.   D.D.M.S., XV Corps.
       12.   War Diary.
       13.   -do-
       14.   File.
       15.   Spare.

CONFIDENTIAL.

WAR DIARY,
of
A.D.M.S, 57th Division,

from 1st April to 30th April 1918.

Army Form C. 2118.

WAR DIARY
or
INTELLIGENCE SUMMARY.
(Erase heading not required.)

Instructions regarding War Diaries and Intelligence Summaries are contained in F. S. Regs., Part II. and the Staff Manual respectively. Title pages will be prepared in manuscript.

Place	Date	Hour	Summary of Events and Information	Remarks and references to Appendices
CROIX DU BAC	1.4.18		Field Ambulances of 57th Division moved by road in Brigade Groups to ESTAIRES, LES PURESBECQUES and HAYERSKERQUE (2/2nd West Lancashire Field Ambulance) (2/3rd Wessex Field Ambulance) respectively.	
LUCHEUX	2.4.18		Headquarters of Division moved from CROIX DU BAC via MERVILLE to LUCHEUX near DOULLENS by road. Brigade groups commenced to leave MERVILLE area in evening.	
	3.4.18		Brigade groups with Field Ambulances arrived in new area, and are in Third Army, VI Corps.	
	4.4.18		A.D.M.S. visited 2/2nd Wessex Field Ambulance and 2/2nd West Lancashire Field Ambulance at BREVILLERS (moving in evening to MONDICOURT and COULLEMONT respectively), 2/3rd Wessex Field Ambulance at SUS ST LEGER and Headquarters VI Corps at NOYELLE VION, D.D.M.S. Colonel H.A. HINGE, D.A.D.M.S. Major HEPPLETHWAITE. Medical units accommodated in huts of nissen type.	
COULLEMONT	5.4.18		2/2nd Wessex and 2/2nd West Lancashire Field Ambulances with the Brigade Groups changed positions in night. Field Ambulances of 57th Division are	

Army Form C. 2118.

WAR DIARY
or
INTELLIGENCE SUMMARY.
(Erase heading not required.)

Instructions regarding War Diaries and Intelligence Summaries are contained in F. S. Regs., Part II. and the Staff Manual respectively. Title pages will be prepared in manuscript.

Place	Date	Hour	Summary of Events and Information	Remarks and references to Appendices
COULLEMONT.	5.4.18		Now thus located:—	
			2/2nd Wessex Field Ambulance. POMMERA	
			2/3rd Wessex Field Ambulance. SUS-ST. LEGER.	
			3/2nd West Lancashire Field Ambulance. HUMBERCOURT	
			Units, especially 2/2nd Wessex and 3/2nd West Lancashire Field Ambulances, somewhat exhausted, having moved during two successive nights in darkness, rain and much mud. Divisions in GHQ or Army and VI Corps Reserve in positions south east of mud. Divisions are ready to relieve any of the VI Corps Divisions in line, viz:—	
			[diagram: triangle with 5th Division, 2nd Canadian Division, Guards Division, 32nd Division]	
	6.4.18		Headquarters of 57th Division arrived from LUCHEUX to COUTOURELLE and COULLEMONT. Sick being evacuated to No 6 Stationary Hospital, FREVENT. All quiet. All Divisional units resting and preparing. A.D.M.S. visited Field Ambulances and 2/6th Kings Liverpool Regiment. D.A.D.M.S. visited VI Corps Headquarters regarding general Medical arrangements.	

Army Form C. 2118.

WAR DIARY
or
INTELLIGENCE SUMMARY.
(Erase heading not required.)

Instructions regarding War Diaries and Intelligence Summaries are contained in F. S. Regs., Part II. and the Staff Manual respectively. Title pages will be prepared in manuscript.

Place	Date	Hour	Summary of Events and Information	Remarks and references to Appendices
COULLEMONT	7.4.18		Officer Commanding, 2/2nd West Lancashire Field Ambulance returned from leave. Saw all Medical Officers of Division on return Division. All quiet. A.D.M.S. visited A.D.M.S. Guards Division at BRETENCOURT. This division is holding entire sector of VI Corps Front. We went over Medical dispositions and evacuation arrangements, but it seems unlikely that the 57th Division will relieve Guards Division. A.D.M.S. visited Medical Units.	
	8.4.18		Division, except Headquarters moved southwards today. 2/2nd Wessex Field Ambulance with 171st Brigade from POMMERA to BEAUVAL. 2/3rd Wessex Field Ambulance with 172nd Brigade from SUS-ST-LEGER to FAMECHON. 2/2nd West Lancashire Field Ambulance with 170th Brigade from HUMBERCOURT to POMMERA. 57th Divisional Headquarters moved south from COUTURELLE and	
BEAUQUESNE	9.4.18		COULLEMONT to BEAUQUESNE. Division in 3rd Army Reserve, administered by IV Corps. 171st and 172nd Brigades standing fast. 170th Brigade moving, 2/2nd West Lancashire Field Ambulance going from POMMERA to AMPLIER. A.D.M.S. visited 2/3rd Wessex Field Ambulance at FAMECHON. A.D.M.S. saw O.C. 2/2nd Wessex Field Ambulance	

WAR DIARY
or
INTELLIGENCE SUMMARY.

Army Form C. 2118.

Place	Date	Hour	Summary of Events and Information	Remarks and references to Appendices
BEAUQUESNE	9.4.18		regarding boots which are very defective in a considerable proportion of cases	
	10.4.18		A.D.M.S. visited all three Field Ambulances, several Infantry Units and IV Corps Headquarters. Division warned to prepare to move at 2 hours notice.	
	11.4.18		Division standing by ready to move. A.D.M.S. visited 2/4 th North Lancashire Regiment regarding care of feet, boots and health generally. A.D.M.S. afterwards visited Headquarters, New Zealand Division (from whom it is thought we may take over the line) at BUS-EN-ARTOIS. 57th Division moved north in afternoon from BEAUQUESNE area to make room for French troops replacing Third Army. Divisional Headquarters from BEAUQUESNE to LUCHEUX: 2/2nd Wessex Field Ambulance with 171st Brigade Group from BEAUVAL to POMMERA; 2/3rd Wessex Field Ambulance with 172nd Brigade Group from PAMECHON to COULLEMONT; and 3/2nd West Lancashire Field Ambulance with 170th Brigade Group from HALLOY to SUS-ST-LEGER. Division passed from IV to X Corps. Sick evacuation rate today
LUCHEUX	12.4.18		reached 3.5% owing to move.	

Army Form C. 2118.

WAR DIARY
or
INTELLIGENCE SUMMARY.
(Erase heading not required.)

Place	Date	Hour	Summary of Events and Information	Remarks and references to Appendices
LUCHEUX	12.4.18		After standing by all day Division moved to PAS-EN-ARTOIS and neighbourhood in evening and night.	
PAS.EN-ARTOIS	14.4.18		Divisional troops now in bivouac and in part under canvas in woods near PAS. Conditions fairly dry, but very cold. Up to 27 men in tent. 2/10th Kings Liverpool Regiment, 2/2nd Wessex Field Ambulance etc., mostly in improvised wattle or blanket bivouac. Divisional Headquarters very crowded in PAS, which is much congested with French and English troops. Field Ambulances with their Brigade Groups, thus, 170th and 171st Brigades North East and South East of AUTHIE respectively, 172nd Brigade Group 1 mile East of PAS. (Divisional Royal Artillery left for FLEURBAIX Sector on April 2nd). A.D.M.S. attended conference of A.D.M.S. at Headquarters of D.D.M.S. IV Corps, MARIEUX. Divisional still in Third Army Reserve. Divisional Headquarters, Brigade Groups with	
	13.4.18		Field Ambulances did not move. A.D.M.S. visited 2/5th North Lancashire Regiment, 2/6th Kings Liverpool Regiment, 2/10th Kings Liverpool Regiment, 2/3rd Wessex and 3/2nd West Lancashire Field Ambulances etc. D.A.D.M.S. Captain N.B. KING. M.C. evacuated to Casualty Clearing Station yesterday P.U.O., and Lieut. Colonel P.T. RUTHERFORD with Information of death of above previous to-day. Division now eleven Medical Officers short but only 41.	

A5834 Wt.W4973/M687 750,000 8/16 D.D.&L. Ltd. Forms/C.2118/13.

Army Form C. 2118.

WAR DIARY
or
INTELLIGENCE SUMMARY.
(Erase heading not required.)

Instructions regarding War Diaries and Intelligence Summaries are contained in F. S. Regs., Part II. and the Staff Manual respectively. Title pages will be prepared in manuscript.

Place	Date	Hour	Summary of Events and Information	Remarks and references to Appendices
PAS.EN.ART.015	16.4.18.		Brigade groups all moved forward, 170th & 2/2nd West Lancashire Field Ambulance to COUIN, 171st with 2/2nd Wessex Field Ambulance to one mile east of PAS, and 172nd with 2/3rd Wessex Field Ambulance to HENU. A.D.M.S. visited 172nd Brigade Groups.	
	17.4.18.		O/C. Consultation with A.D.M.S., 62nd and 42nd Divisions and D.D.M.S. IV Corps. A.D.M.S. issued Medical Arrangements No. M.S. 219/3	APPENDIX "A"
	18.4.18.		Officer Commanding 2/3rd Wessex Field Ambulance (Lieut. Colonel P.T. RUTHERFORD) returned to duty from hospital. A.D.M.S. discussed arrangements for evacuation of wounded in event of Division becoming engaged with each Field Ambulance Commander in turn. A.D.M.S. visited all three Medical units.	
	19.4.18.		After consultation with A.D.M.S., 37th and 62nd Divisions regarding use of their Main Dressing Stations at AUTHIE MILL and PAS (Kimma Stall) respectively. A.D.M.S. issued Amendment to Medical Arrangements. A.D.M.S. visited 2/3rd Wessex and 2/2nd West Lancas. Field Ambulances regarding Medical arrangements, etc.	APPENDIX "B"
	20.4.18.		A.D.M.S. visited all three Field Ambulances, and discussed with Commanders remaining details of evacuation arrangements in connection	

WAR DIARY
or
INTELLIGENCE SUMMARY.

Army Form C. 2118.

Place	Date	Hour	Summary of Events and Information	Remarks and references to Appendices
PAS.EN.ARTOIS	20.4.18		with Defence Scheme. A.D.M.S. visited proposed Brigade Collecting Posts of 2/3rd Wessex Field Ambulance (one near St Amand) and 2/2nd West Lancashire Field Ambulance (two, south of SOUASTRE). A.D.M.S. discussed details of evacuation scheme with A.Do.M.S. 57th and 62nd divisions. 2/10th King's Liverpool (Scottish) Regiment left today to be amalgamated with 1/10th King's Liverpool (Scottish) Regiment, and 1st Royal Munster Fusiliers came in their place.	
	21.4.18		Conference in A.D.M.S. office attended by A.D.M.S. and Medical Officers, 57th Division, and also Medical Officers, 59th Division, addressed by Colonel H.M.W. GRAY, CB, Consulting Surgeon, Third Army, and Captain WALKER, Shock Specialist, Third Army. Units of D.D.M.S. IV Corps.	
	22.4.18		A.D.M.S. visited Headquarters, 57th Divisional Infantry Brigades and Field Ambulances in regard to Medical Arrangements in event of Brigades being ordered to counterattack.	
	23.4.18		Routine.— A.D.M.S. arranged with 57th Divisional Headquarters for supply of 6 officers and 150 Other Ranks (15 from each of 10 Battalions) as auxiliary bearers to reinforce R.A.M.C. in case of need.	

Army Form C. 2118.

WAR DIARY
or
INTELLIGENCE SUMMARY.
(Erase heading not required.)

Instructions regarding War Diaries and Intelligence Summaries are contained in F. S. Regs., Part II. and the Staff Manual respectively. Title pages will be prepared in manuscript.

Place	Date	Hour	Summary of Events and Information	Remarks and references to Appendices
PAS-EN-ARTOIS	24.4.18		Acting D.A.D.M.S. paid visit of inspection to front line, CHATEAU-DE-LA-HAIE switch, and rear line positions. A.D.M.S. visited Headquarters, IV Corps, and also D.D.M.S, IV Corps. Front quiet meantime.	
	25.4.18		Received four Medical Officers and nineteen other ranks R.A.M.C. as reinforcements. Medical Officer and nineteen other ranks returned from No 19 Casualty Clearing Station. A.D.M.S. visited Medical Units and several Infantry units.	
	26.4.18		Field Ambulances have now Officer Commanding and five other Medical Officers each. Division still in Third Army Reserve.	
	27.4.18		Routine. Division still in Third Army Reserve, in training. Sick rate low. Bathing and clean clothing issue proceeding briskly. A.D.M.S. visited D.D.M.S., IV Corps, and 2/2nd and 2/3rd Wessex Field Ambulances regarding administrative details.	
	28.4.18		Division and all its units stationary, all in training.	
	29.4.18		Warning order received to the effect that 57th Division relieves 42nd Division in the sector IV Corps Front. Line runs from Southwest of BUCQUOY L 2 c (sh 57D) to east of HEBUTERNE K 10 d.	

Army Form C. 2118.

WAR DIARY
or
INTELLIGENCE SUMMARY.
(Erase heading not required.)

Instructions regarding War Diaries and Intelligence Summaries are contained in F. S. Regs., Part II. and the Staff Manual respectively. Title pages will be prepared in manuscript.

Place	Date	Hour	Summary of Events and Information	Remarks and references to Appendices
PAS-EN-ARTOIS	30.4.18		A.D.M.S and A/D.A.D.M.S visited Main Dressing Station of 42nd Division at SOUASTRE, and Advanced Dressing Station at FONQUEVILLERS with A.D.M.S, 42nd Division. A.D.M.S issued preliminary orders to Field Ambulances to the effect that on May 4th – 6th. 2/2nd West Lancs Field Ambulance at SOUASTRE 2/3rd " " " " " FONQUEVILLERS 3/2nd West Lancs " " " " " COUIN.	

30/4/1918

J Newton

Colonel, A. Med. S.
A.D.M.S. 57th (W.L.) Division.

APPENDIX "A"

57th DIVISION.

SECRET.   A.D.M.S. 57th Div.No.MS 219/3.

MEDICAL ARRANGEMENTS

Reference Map Sheet 57D. 1/40,000.

The following preliminary medical arrangements are issued supplementary to 57th Division Order No. 81 dated 16/4/18.

1. At present Field Ambulances will remain closed. It is expected that a Corps Rest Station will be established at AUTHIE MILL after 19/4/18.

2. In the event of Brigades occupying positions as laid down in para. 6 of above quoted order –

   (A) Each Field Ambulance will establish with its bearer division a BRIGADE COLLECTING POST for the evacuation of casualties in the Brigade to which it is affiliated. This post will be in the proximity of BRIGADE BATTLE HEADQUARTERS.

   (B) The tent sub-divisions of each Field Ambulance will be held in reserve and at the disposal of D.D.M.S., Corps in readiness –

   (a) To supplement personnel of existing Dressing Stations,
           or
   (b) To establish an additional Station, as required, at AUTHIE or PAS.

3. Evacuation from REGIMENTAL AID POSTS to BRIGADE COLLECTING POSTS will be by hand carriage and wheeled stretcher carriages; from BRIGADE COLLECTING POSTS to DIVISIONAL DRESSING STATION by Divisional ambulance cars.

4. As soon as BRIGADE COLLECTING POSTS are established- Medical Officers in charge will effect liaison with (i) all Regimental Medical Officers in the Brigade and, (ii) with Brigade Headquarters.
   They will also furnish periodically direct to their Field Ambulance Commanders (for transmission to A.D.M.S.) the following :-

   (a) Situation Reports daily at 9.0 a.m. and 8.0 p.m. and at othertimes when occasion demands.
   (b) Casualty Reports daily at 8.0 am and 8.0 pm.

   All changes in location will be notified at once and revised map references supplied.

5. Each Field Ambulance Commander will furnish a Medical Situation Report to A.D.M.S. daily at 6.0 pm and more often when occasion demands. Special reference will be made to –

   (a) Numbers and nature of wounded.
   (b) Adequacy of evacuation.
   (c) Sufficiency of medical equipment and medical comforts.

6. A motor cyclist orderly will be provided - by the Motor Ambulance Convoy - at the DIVISIONAL DRESSING STATION to keep the Officer Commanding Motor Ambulance Convoy advised of -

   (a). Position of DIVISIONAL DRESSING STATION.
   (b). Numbers of wounded to be evacuated.

7. No active surgical treatment will be undertaken at BRIGADE COLLECTING POSTS. Evacuation should be as rapid as possible.

8. At DIVISIONAL DRESSING STATION no elaborate treatment will be undertaken. Dressings will not be disturbed if satisfactory but splints should be readjusted and hot drinks supplied. if necessary

9. Each BRIGADE COLLECTING POST will be provided with ample reserves of -

   (a). Dressings.
   (b). Stretchers.
   (c). Blankets.
   (d). Splints for the use of Regimental Medical Officers on demand.

   J F Dewar.

   Colonel. A.Med.S.,
17/4/1918.   A.D.M.S., 57th Division.

DISTRIBUTION -

   H.Q., 57th Division G.
   H.Q., 57th Division Q.
   D.D.M.S., IV Corps.
   D.M.S., Third Army.
   H.Q., 170th Infantry Brigade.
   H.Q., 171st Infantry Brigade.
   H.Q., 172nd Infantry Brigade.
   O.C., 2/2nd Wessex Field Ambulance.
   O.C., 2/3rd Wessex Field Ambulance.
   O.C., 3/2nd W.Lanc.Field Ambulance.
   C.R.E., 57th Division.
   O.C., 57th Divisional Signal Coy.
   O.C., 57th Divisional Train. A.S.C.
   O.C., 57th Bn. M.G.Corps.
   O.C., 2/5th N. Lan. R. (Pioneers).
   Senior Chaplain C.of E).
   Senior Chaplain (Non. C.of E).
   All Regimental Medical Officers, 57th Division.
   A.D.M.S., 37th Division.
   A.D.M.S., 42nd Division.
   A.D.M.S., 62nd Division.
   A.D.M.S., New Zealand Division.

APPENDIX "B"

SECRET

57th DIVISION

A.D.M.S. 57th Div.No.MS 221/6.

MEDICAL ARRANGEMENTS

Reference Map Sheet 57 D 1/40,000

Reference A.D.M.S. 57th Division No. M.S. 219/3 dated 17/4/18.

1. Map references of Brigade Collecting Posts -

    170th Inf. Bde. (a) Left.   D.28.d.5.3.
                     (b) Right   J.11.a.5.5.

    171st Inf. Bde.   I.12.a.2.2.

    172nd Inf. Bde.   D.15.b.6.2.

2. Evacuation of wounded from Brigade Collecting Posts will be as follows -

    Northern Section.   To Dressing Station at C.16.c.9.0.

    Southern Section.   To Dressing Station at I.15.b.2.7.

3. Complete records will be made and Anti Tetanic Serum administered at Brigade Collecting Posts.

4. Additional Stretchers and Blankets may be obtained from Motor Ambulance Convoy. A.D.M.S. must be advised of requisition of latter.

19/4/18.

Colonel, A. Med. S.,
A.D.M.S., 57th Division.

DISTRIBUTION -

To all recipients of Medical Arrangements issued under A.D.M.S. 57th Div. No.MS 219/3 dated 17/4/18.

C O N F I D E N T I A L.

WAR DIARY

of

A.D.M.S.

57th DIVISION.

from 1st May to 31st May, 1918.

Army Form C. 2118.

WAR DIARY
or
INTELLIGENCE SUMMARY.
(Erase heading not required.)

Instructions regarding War Diaries and Intelligence Summaries are contained in F. S. Regs., Part II. and the Staff Manual respectively. Title pages will be prepared in manuscript.

Place	Date	Hour	Summary of Events and Information	Remarks and references to Appendices
PAS EN ARTOIS	1.5.18		A.D.M.S. visited 42nd Divisional Headquarters and 1/1st East Lancashire Field Ambulance, both at COUIN, regarding taking over on May 5th, also 3/2nd West Lancashire Field Ambulance and 2/3rd Wessex Field Ambulance, and various regimental units.	
	2.5.18		A.D.M.S. walked from Advanced Dressing Station, FONQUEVILLERS with Officer Commanding, 1/2nd East Lancashire and 2/3rd Wessex Field Ambulance to Bearer Posts and Regimental Aid Posts at present held by 42nd Division. Captain J.T. HEFFERNAN, R.A.M.C. T.C. reported for duty from 16th Division. Lieutenant Quarter Master HAMILTON, 3/2nd West Lancashire Field Ambulance returned to duty from Base after illness. Captain W.J. McKENZIE, Acting D.A.D.M.S. went round front of 42nd Division this morning. Report from Officer Commanding 2/6th K. Shrop. R. regarding high sick incidence in this Battalion.	
	3.5.18		Orders for move of Division into line in place of 42nd Division received today. R.A.M.C. 57th Division Operation Order No 24 issued today regarding relief of 42nd Division Medical units by 57th Division.	APPENDIX "A"

Army Form C. 2118.

WAR DIARY
or
INTELLIGENCE SUMMARY.
(Erase heading not required.)

Place	Date	Hour	Summary of Events and Information	Remarks and references to Appendices
PAS-EN-ARTOIS	4.5.18		A.D.M.S. made exhaustive enquiry regarding high sick rate in 2/6th Kings Liverpool Regiment, attending morning sick parade and seeing men privately in afternoon.	
	5.5.18		Routine - Relief of 42nd Division by 57th Division commenced.	
COVIN.	6.5.18		Divisional Headquarters moved from PAS to COVIN and 57th Division took over line from 42nd Division. 3/2nd West Lancashire Field Ambulance remain at COVIN, 2/2nd Wessex Field Ambulance moved to SOUASTRE Main Dressing Station.	
	7.5.18		Medical arrangements now that Division is in line working smoothly.	
	8.5.18		A.D.M.S. visited 3/2nd West Lancashire Field Ambulance at COVIN and 2/2nd Wessex Field Ambulance at SOUASTRE, also Ambulance Post of 2/3rd Wessex Field Ambulance at BAYENCOURT. Captains SLACK and PARE, R.A.M.C., reported for duty yesterday, Captain KIER today. Division is now only one Medical Officer short of establishment.	
	9.5.18		A.D.M.S. visited Advanced Dressing Station, FONQUEVILLERS regarding evacuation arrangements. Two Brigades now in line with two Battalions	

WAR DIARY or INTELLIGENCE SUMMARY.

Army Form C. 2118.

Place	Date	Hour	Summary of Events and Information	Remarks and references to Appendices
COUIN.	9.5.18		In front and one in reserve viz :-	
			2/6th K.Lpool R.	2/7th K.Lpool R.	1st Regt Trench Mortar Battery	2/4 th S. Lan. R.	
			8th K.Lpool R.	9th K.Lpool R.	
	10.5.18		A.D.M.S. visited Advanced Dressing Station at FONQUEVILLERS and all Regimental Aid Posts on divisional front. Div. Artillery arrived from month. Considerable enemy shelling on enemy especially affecting 2/4 Lpool & 2/6th Lancs Regt.	
	11.5.18		D.A.D.M.S. returned to duty on recovery from P.U.O. in residence of D.D.M.S. Rouen.	
	12.5.18		3rd Gas case reported 16 hours chiefly in 2/4th Lpool & S. Lancs Regt., including Lieut J. ANNEY, U.S.M.C. M.O. of that unit. Total gassed cases passed through Field Ambulances up to 8 p.m. about 500 mostly mild. Eyes chiefly affected. B.Schools to tire chiefly 16 Yellow Cross gas. Gas shells also not part 16 Blue Cross gas.	
	13.5.18		A.D.M.S. visited A.D.S. at FONQUEVILLERS and M.D.S. at SOUASTRE. Gas shelling now among our ordinary evening amount only.	

Army Form C. 2118.

WAR DIARY
or
INTELLIGENCE SUMMARY.
(Erase heading not required.)

Instructions regarding War Diaries and Intelligence Summaries are contained in F. S. Regs., Part II. and the Staff Manual respectively. Title pages will be prepared in manuscript.

Place	Date	Hour	Summary of Events and Information	Remarks and references to Appendices
COUIN	13.5.16		Numbers at Spelling:—	
			3/yorks Div. Other troops	
			Offrs O.Ranks Offrs O.Ranks	
			at noon 11th to noon 12th 6 57. 3 128.	
			" 12th " 13th 21. 360. 1. 98.	
			2/4th Royal West Surrey Regt. left O.C., Adjutant, Medical Officer, Quartermaster, Transport Officer, and six junior Company Commanders — remainder, generally so far all cases seem not to be of severe degree.	
			D.A.D.M.S. returned to duty after illness.	
			A.D.M.S. visited 2/4th Royal North Lancs Regt. at request of G.O.C. to investigate their failure to go into the line last night. As a result of report their return to the line was delayed by one day.	
			A.D.M.S. attended Conference of A.D'sM.S. in IV Corps (6) at Offices of D.D.M.S. IV Corps.	
	15.5.16		A.D.M.S. again visited 2/4th Royal West Surrey Regt. (at Bazincourt Farm). Of about 500 on parade, quite a fifth show effects of nausea, gas attacks; but quite N.C.O. said we get as go into the line things will	

Army Form C. 2118.

WAR DIARY
or
INTELLIGENCE SUMMARY.
(Erase heading not required.)

Place	Date	Hour	Summary of Events and Information	Remarks and references to Appendices
COUIN	15.6.18.		Lieut WILKINS. R.A.M.C. arrived to replace Captain LUMLEY. Owing to growing sick list 12-13 Lieut. JANNEY & Captain MORRISON had had to be warned, and Major KIDSTON to visit on Field Ambulance.	
	16.6.18.		D.A.D.M.S. visited A.D.S. at FONQUEVILLERS and the R.A.P.s. Total passed back passed through Field Ambulances of this Division from 11th to noon 15th :- 64th Division Officers Other ranks. 32. 498. Other formations. Officers Other ranks. 8. 296. Total 469.	
	17.6.18		A.D.M.S. went to FONQUEVILLERS nr SOUASTRE chiefly to examine evacuation route; on way visited A.D.S. at SOUASTRE.	
	18.6.18		A.D.M.S. made an extended view of inspection of 3/2nd West London Field Ambulance	
	19.6.18.		Divisional draft stream again marked an unsteady slope with chiefly owing to incidence of scabies & pyrexia. A.D.M.S. discussed matter and prevention with Divisional Commandant.	

Army Form C. 2118.

WAR DIARY
or
INTELLIGENCE SUMMARY.
(Erase heading not required.)

Instructions regarding War Diaries and Intelligence Summaries are contained in F. S. Regs., Part II. and the Staff Manual respectively. Title pages will be prepared in manuscript.

Place	Date	Hour	Summary of Events and Information	Remarks and references to Appendices
COUIN	19.5.18		A.D.M.S. arranges for attachment of Medical Assistant Officers and 19 Other ranks to Field Ambulances of the Division for Instruction for instruction and experience. A.D.M.S. visits Corps Rest Station. Authorised (accommodation for 200) and Corps Headquarters.	
	20.5.18		D.M.S. Third Army visited 4/2nd West Lancs. Field Ambulance at COUIN. 2/2nd West Lancs. Field Ambulance at SOUASTRE and saw Divisional Commander regarding recovery of great coats. He states that a considerable number of men of the Division lost theirs 11-13th May 1918.	
	21.5.18		D.A.D.M.S. visits R.A.P's etc. M.O.1/c 2/1 Wayne of North Lancs. Regt. reports death of such and very first as result of man's gassing.	
	22.5.18		A.D.M.S. paid an extempore and full visit to 2/2nd West Lancs Field Ambulance. A.D.M.S. visited A.D.S. SOUASTRE and all R.A.P's with Major Station.	
	23.5.18		Two M.S. Medical officers attached for training. Chief consideration sanitation of R.A.P's and Evacuation Routes.	

WAR DIARY or INTELLIGENCE SUMMARY

Army Form C. 2118.

Place	Date	Hour	Summary of Events and Information	Remarks and references to Appendices
COUIN	24.5.18		A.D.M.S. discussed with Divisional Commandant arrangements on account of gas attack. He also visited 2/2nd N. Staff Ambulance regarding arrangements in charging gas Poisoning by Corps Chemical Adviser to Divisional Headquarters.	
	25.5.18		D.A.D.M.S. visited front regarding (1) alternative sites for A.D.S. in event of enemy's advance, (2) advance preparations for rear transport. A.D.M.S. visited 2/3rd N. Midland Field Ambulance at SOUASTRE and made general arrangement for attachment & move of outgoing R.A.M.C. personnel. A.D.M.S. commenced examination of all men of 7th Div. Employment Coy. with a view to raising "B" men to "A" category if possible. Sample out of 252 examined.	
	26.5.18		A.D.M.S. visited A.D.S. at FONQUEVILLERS and ascertained (in absence of an attack) on SOUASTRE-BIENVILLERS Road, the accommodation. M.O. i/c 2/1st N. LAN. R. at his R.A.P. & Lieut. French further's examination of 8th Employment Coy men.	
	27.5.18		D.A.D.M.S. visited A.D.S. at FONQUEVILLERS and R.A.P's. Making arrangements that 5th m. Div. will be relieved on the line by 42nd Division - June 4-6. S. 216 of 26 "A" not likely to become "A" gunfields became A.S.A. & 5 got attendance examination	

WAR DIARY
or
INTELLIGENCE SUMMARY.

Army Form C. 2118.

(Erase heading not required.)

Place	Date	Hour	Summary of Events and Information	Remarks and references to Appendices
BOVIN	28.5.18		A.D.M.S. attended Conference of A.Ds.M.S. at Offices of	
			D.D.M.S. MARIEUX. Major Adams 2/2nd Western Field Ambce to	
			be Divisional Sanitary Officer's experimentally for one month.	
			Ground Cases evac 11-24. (passed through field Ambce)	
			"Wm Regt. Offrs. 3.3 O.Rs Sick non Offrs. 8. Gun Shot Offrs. N.O.	
			O.Ranks 541. O.Ranks 251. O.Ranks 49.2	
			Total 5'4.3. Total 2.5.9 8.8.2	
29.5.18			D.A.D.V.S. visited R.A.P's.	
30.5.18			Deaths mule horses steady to rise. 3 days met	
			admission rate 30. 41.7%. Half of these admitted to Field	
			Ambulances are diagnosed "P.U.O." I accredit these with	
			recovered in identical with mutilated the German diagnoses. The chances	
			is apparently of epidemic, that is, infectious type.	
			Earliest printed Document issued & today at MARIEUX in	
			connection with	

WAR DIARY
or
INTELLIGENCE SUMMARY.

Army Form C. 2118.

(Erase heading not required.)

Place	Date	Hour	Summary of Events and Information	Remarks and references to Appendices
AVIN	31/5/18		medical arrangements. A.D.M.S. visited 59th Div. Wing at MARIEUX, saw outfits for stretcher on the Ball, and went round quarters with M.O.i/c. Also visited D.D.M.S. IX Corps at MARIEUX.	

31. 5. 18.

J.J.Dolan
Colonel, A. Med. S.
A.D.M.S. 57th (W.L.) Division.

Secret

57th DIVISION.   M.S.227/5.

R.A.M.C. OPERATION ORDER NO. 24.   Copy No .15.
================================
Reference Map Sheet 57D, 1/40,000.

1. 57th Division (less Artillery) will relieve 42nd Division (less Artillery) in Centre Sector IV Corps front on nights 5th/6th and 6th/7th May.

2. (a) 2/2nd Wessex Field Ambulance will relieve 1/3rd E.Lancs. Field Ambulance by noon 6/5/1918.
   (b) 2/3rd Wessex Field Ambulance will relieve 1/2nd E.Lancs. Field Ambulance by 1.0 a.m. 7/5/1918.
   (c) 3/2nd W.Lancs.Field Ambulance will relieve 1/1st E.Lancs. Field Ambulance by noon 6/5/1918.

3. (a) Advanced parties from each Field Ambulance will be attached to corresponding units of 42nd Division for 48 hours previous to relief. Such parties should be rationed for this period before proceeding.
   (b) All details of relief will be arranged direct between the Officers Commanding the Units concerned.
   (c) Completion of reliefs will be reported to this Office by using the code word "STRETCHER".

4. (a) All maps and plans will be taken over.
   (b) Field Ambulances will hand over all Field Ambulance arrangements (i) in case of manning of RED LINE and the CHATEAU DE LA HAIE Switch and (ii) in case of counter attacks.
   (c) Receipts (in duplicate) of all medical trench and area Stores taken over will be forwarded to reach this Office at 9 am. following the morning of relief.

5. All Divisional Ambulance Cars, bearers, wheeled stretcher carriages and 'walking wounded' notice-boards willbe placed at the disposal of Officer Commanding, 2/3rd Wessex Field Ambulance from 1.0 a.m. 7/5/1918 as required.

6. A.D.M.S. Office will close at PAS at 4 p.m. on 6th May and re-open at COUIN at the same hour.

7. Please acknowledge.

                                    W G McKenzie
                                    Capt. RAMC
                              for Colonel, A. Mod. S.,
Headquarters,   A.D.M.S., 57th Division.
3/5/1918.

Issued at 7.-0. p.m.
                        DISTRIBUTION:-
Copy No.1 to 57th Div. 'G'.
     2   57th Div. 'Q'
     3   H.Q., 170 Infantry Brigade.
     4   H.Q., 171 Infantry Brigade.
     5   H.Q., 172 Infantry Brigade.
     6   O.C., 2/2nd Wessex Field Ambulance.
     7   O.C., 2/3rd Wessex Field Ambulance.
     8   O.C., 3/2nd W.Lancs.Fld. Ambulance.
     9   A.D.M.S., N.Z. Division.
    10   A.D.M.S., 37th Div.
    11   A.D.M.S., 42nd Div.
    12   A.D.M.S., 62nd Div.
    13   D.M.S., Third Army.
    14   D.D.M.S., IV Corps.
  — 15 & 16. War Diary.
    17   File.
    18   Spare.

CONFIDENTIAL.

WAR DIARY.

of

A.D.M.S., 57th Divn.

From 1. 6. 18.   To 30. 6. 18.

Army Form C. 2118.

WAR DIARY
or
INTELLIGENCE SUMMARY.
(Erase heading not required.)

Instructions regarding War Diaries and Intelligence Summaries are contained in F. S. Regs., Part II. and the Staff Manual respectively. Title pages will be prepared in manuscript.

Place	Date	Hour	Summary of Events and Information	Remarks and references to Appendices
COUIN	1.6.18.		A.D.M.S. visited 3rd Canadian Stationary Hospital, DOULLENS, to which, for the most part, sick and wounded of this Division are being evacuated. Reconnoitrement at night that relief by 32nd Divisional front the night of June 4-6 in present in imminency of Division front.	Appendix A
	2.6.18.		A.D.M.S. visited Advanced Dressing Station, FONQUEVILLERS and all Regimental Aid Posts in O.C. 96th Field Ambulance who is O/C. Forward Evacuations. Shell very high. Account of dump arrangement of wounded figures in Division.	
	3.6.18.		A.D.M.S. inspected 3/2nd North Lancs Field Ambulance on parade. 3 Officers and 58 Other ranks on parade. 3 Officers and 109 Other ranks necessarily absent.	
	4.6.18.		D.A.D.M.S. visited R.A.P.s regarding improvement at BULLY POST and MATTHEWS POST.	
	5.6.18.		A.D.M.S. visited 2/5 N. LAN. R. regarding retirement of one officer Captn. W.H. MORRISON to be transferred from 2/3rd Western Field Amb.	Appendix B

Army Form C. 2118.

WAR DIARY
or
INTELLIGENCE SUMMARY.
(Erase heading not required.)

Instructions regarding War Diaries and Intelligence Summaries are contained in F. S. Regs., Part II. and the Staff Manual respectively. Title pages will be prepared in manuscript.

Place	Date	Hour	Summary of Events and Information	Remarks and references to Appendices
COUIN.			10 3/2nd W. James L. Amb.	mmb
	6.6.18		A.D.M.S. visited Armour Dressing Station at FONQUEVILLERS and all Regimental Aid Posts were inspected. 2/2nd W. Sandtn Anstel was at acting temporarily as Divisional Sanitary Officer (i.e. Senior Officer Detained Clothes on the one hand and Field Ambulance and Regimental Medical Officers on the other). A.D.M.S. investigated question of need of relieving M.O.s standing for more than deep augments. mm2	
	7.6.18		A.D.M.S. visited 206 Bde R.F.A. Headquarters in connection with retraining of one stretcher Bee Knight to no very satisfactory condition.	am2
	8.6.18		A.D.M.S. reported on retention of 1 stretcher from more win deep augments. Also visited Transport Lines of 2/3rd W. Green Lanes Ambee. D.A.D.M.S. visited Front line and side Posts. Daily admission and evacuation rates continue to be very high.	mm2

Army Form C. 2118.

WAR DIARY
or
INTELLIGENCE SUMMARY.
(Erase heading not required.)

Instructions regarding War Diaries and Intelligence Summaries are contained in F. S. Regs., Part II. and the Staff Manual respectively. Title pages will be prepared in manuscript.

Place	Date	Hour	Summary of Events and Information	Remarks and references to Appendices
COUIN.	9.6.18.		A.D.M.S. discussed with A.A.& Q.M.G. the cases of sickness in Division. Day out to be sponged with Creosote solution at Divisional.	amt
	10.6.18		A.D.M.S. visited Reserve Armour Dressing Station at SOUASTRE - BIENVILLERS Road; progress of erection satisfactory.	amt
	11.6.18		A.D.M.S. attended Conference of A.D.M.S. at Office of D.D.M.S. IV Corps.	amt
	12.6.18		A.D.M.S. visited and Opera air line and Advanced Dressing Station, FONQUEVILLERS with A.A.& Q.M.G. chiefly regarding Sanitation.	amt
	13.6.18.		Sick admissions have continued over of previous Divisions have been slight and are now getting satisfactorily. Sickness has chiefly been of nature of transient pyrexia aka Influenza but in our unit not true French Fever with relapses. Wounded admissions have recently been low. Division has of more than 38 days.	amt

A5834 Wt.W.4973/M687 750,000 8/16 D. D. & L. Ltd. Forms/C.2118/13.

Army Form C. 2118.

WAR DIARY
or
INTELLIGENCE SUMMARY.
(Erase heading not required.)

Instructions regarding War Diaries and Intelligence
Summaries are contained in F. S. Regs., Part II
and the Staff Manual respectively. Title pages
will be prepared in manuscript.

Place	Date	Hour	Summary of Events and Information	Remarks and references to Appendices
COUIN	13.6.18.		2/3rd Western F. Amb. to continue charge of Forward Evacuation. mm/	
	14.6.18.		A.D.M.S. visited 186th Bde. R.F.A., SAILLY-AUX-BOIS & saw Medical Officer re organising several matters. He also visited 2/6 N. Staff R. at COUIN and saw Medical Officer. A.D.M.S. inspected showers after Heam Plant – all in advanced condition. mm/	
	15.6.18.		A.D.M.S. visited Opening Lines with S.S.O. and saw Matrons doing disinfection and observed AUTHUILLE where the inspections and connection fire arcs of front entanglements with sitting up aqft. He also visited and inspected them in Dressing Station of and Western F. Amb. at SOUASTRE. mm/	
	16.6.18.		A.D.M.S. visited 2/2nd Western F. Amb. and inspected premises. mm/	
	17.6.18.		A.D.M.S. visited D.D.M.S. IV Corps and discussed administration generally with him. mm/	

Army Form C. 2118.

WAR DIARY
or
INTELLIGENCE SUMMARY.
(Erase heading not required.)

Instructions regarding War Diaries and Intelligence Summaries are contained in F. S. Regs., Part II. and the Staff Manual respectively. Title pages will be prepared in manuscript.

Place	Date	Hour	Summary of Events and Information	Remarks and references to Appendices
COUIN.	15.6.18.		A.D.M.S. visited supplying points with S.S.O. and inspected rations.	ADMS
	19.6.18		A.D.M.S. held a conference with Field Ambulance Commanders about various matters.	ADMS
	20.6.18.		A.D.M.S. visited Ambulances. Had interview with O.C. 3/2 W.F. amb. with reference to his taking over during absence of A.D.M.S. on leave.	ADMS
	21.6.18.		A.D.M.S. proceeded on leave to United Kingdom for 14 days. Lt. Col. A.W.B. LOUDON, O/C 3/2 W.F. amb. to be A/A.D.M.S. A/A.D.M.S. assumed duties on Dysentery by Asst. Advisor on Pathology Third Army - importance of mild cases as spreaders of infection indicated.	ADMS

A5834 Wt.W4973/M687 750,000 8/16 D. D. & L. Ltd. Forms/C.2118/13.

Army Form C. 2118.

WAR DIARY
or
INTELLIGENCE SUMMARY.

(Erase heading not required.)

Instructions regarding War Diaries and Intelligence Summaries are contained in F.S. Regs., Part II. and the Staff Manual respectively. Title pages will be prepared in manuscript.

Place	Date	Hour	Summary of Events and Information	Remarks and references to Appendices
COUIN	21.6.18.		2/Lt. W. Lane. T. Amb. to be centre for collecting cases of circumvision Dysentry.	
	22.6.18		A/ADMS visited 2/Lt. W. Lane. T. Amb. reference tapping in Dysentry and Diarrhoea cases, and cases for MAC Cars. Also visited Divional Reception Camp reference a requirement about treatment of those Officers which was shown to be quite groundless.	
	23.6.18.		A/ADMS visited Field Ambulances.	
	24.6.18.		A/ADMS visited area occupied Divional Reception Camp and made enquiries regarding reference Cookhouses (which is soon to be finished) Latrines urinals and foot-baths.	
	25.6.18		A/ADMS visited Corps Rest Station at AITHIE MILL reference admission from this Division. ADMS. New Zealand Division called in afternoon. Also visited COUIN Baths.	

Army Form C. 2118.

WAR DIARY
or
INTELLIGENCE SUMMARY.
(Erase heading not required)

Instructions regarding War Diaries and Intelligence Summaries are contained in F.S. Regs., Part II. and the Staff Manual respectively. Title pages will be prepared in manuscript.

Place	Date	Hour	Summary of Events and Information	Remarks and references to Appendices
COU N.	26.6.18.		and inspected training arrangements.	mm 2
			A/ADMS attended Conference at D.D.M.S. Office (IV Corps) re matter of special note. Also visited 2nd of the General Field Ambulance.	mm 2
	27.6.18		A/ADMS visited DEWAR POST on SOUASTRE — BIENVILLERS Road. A.D.M.S. New Zealand Division inspected all medical arrangements previous to taking over.	mm 2
	28.6.18.		A/ADMS visited VAUCHELLES and MARIEUX — to see which are to be taken over by Field Ambulances of this Division when it is relieved in turn by N. Zealand Div. The 3rd Field Ambulance of this Division is taking over Corps Rest Station at MT. RENAULT FARM. A/ADMS called at DDMS Office obone Order re reference relief, six lorries got out and sent to Field Ambulances. (R.A.M.C. Operation Order No. 26)	Appendix C. mm 2

Army Form C. 2118.

WAR DIARY
or
INTELLIGENCE SUMMARY.
(Erase heading not required.)

Place	Date	Hour	Summary of Events and Information	Remarks and references to Appendices
COUIN	29/6/18		A/A D.M.S. examined P. Brown 1st Brit. & LEE A. HADLEY M.O.R.C. (U.S.A.) reported for duty instruction; sent to join 1 Canad. Fd. Amb.	
	30.6.18		A/A.D.M.S. visited 3/2nd & 2/Lowl. Fd. Amb and saw O.C. 2nd W. Beaumont & Amb. reference nursing orderly Ambulance sick at MARIEUX. Discussed with O.C. number of cases of Influenza, but permission type; prophylactic treatment by means of nasal anointing to be tried.	MM2

30.6.18.

JW Lowdon
Lieut. Col. R.A.M.C.
A/A.D.M.S. 57th (W.L.) Division

SECRET.   M.S.261/4.

MEDICAL ARRANGEMENTS.

57th Division.

Ref.Maps 1/40,000, 57D.
1/100,000 Lens 11.

1. **LOCATIONS.**
   Headquarters of Field Ambulances.

   2/2nd Wessex Field Ambulance,   SOUASTRE,   D.22.c.6.3.
   2/3rd Wessex Field Ambulance,   SOUASTRE,   D.22.c.6.3.
   3/2nd W.Lancs. Fld.Ambulance,   COUIN,   J.1.b.6.7.

   Main Dressing Station,   SOUASTRE,   D.22.c.6.3.
   Advanced Dressing Station,   FONQUEVILLERS, E.21.d.1.6.

   BEARER RELAY POSTS.   GOMMECOURT POST,   E.28.c.8.1.
                          MATTHEWS POST,   K.5.a.5.4.
                          BULLY POST,   K.6.a.2.2.

   REGIMENTAL AID POSTS.

   Right Brigade.
   Right Battalion in Line, GOMMECOURT POST,   E.28.c.8.1.

   Left Battalion in Line,   MATTHEWS POST,   K.5.a.5.4.

   Reserve Battalion,   GOMMECOURT POST,   E.28.c.8.1.

   Left Brigade.
   Right Battalion in Line, BULLY POST,   K.6.a.2.2.

   Left Battalion in Line,   HIGH STREET,   K.6.d.3.4.

   Reserve Battalion,   RUM TRENCH,   E.29.a.8.7.

2. **EVACUATION ROUTES.**
   (a) Quiet Periods.
      (i) Stretcher Cases.
         (a) From R.A.P. K.6.d.3.4. by hand carry to BULLY POST, K.6.a.2.2. thence by carry to MATTHEWS POST K.5.a.5.4. thence by hand or wheeler (in fair weather) to GOMMECOURT POST E.28.c.8.1. thence by wheeler to A.D.S. FONQUEVILLERS, E.21.d.1.6.

         (b) From R.A.P. K.6.a.2.2. by carry to MATTHEWS POST, thence as in (a) above.

         (c) From R.A.P. E.29.a.8.7. to GOMMECOURT, thence by wheeler to GOMMECOURT POST, thence as in (a) above.

         (d) From A.D.S. FONQUEVILLERS E.21.d.1.6. by Divisional Motor Ambulances to M.D.S. SOUASTRE, D.22.c.6.3.

         (e) From MAIN DRESSING STATION to CASUALTY CLEARING STATION by No.21 M.A.C.

      (ii) Walking Cases.
         Walking Wounded will be evacuated by the same routes as lying wounded.

2.

(B) Active Operations.
   (i) Stretcher Cases.
      As in (A) (i) and also by tramway from K.5.a. and if necessary K.6.a. to E.28.c. Ambulance Cars may if necessary collect from GOMMECOURT POST, E.28.c.8.0.

   (ii) Walking Cases.
      Walking Wounded will proceed by the marked tracks through K.6.a., K.5.b., E.29., E.22., E.20., E.13. to the Advanced Walking Wounded Collecting Post at D.18.b.2.2.

3. Sick will be evacuated by the same routes as wounded.

4. All requests from Regimental Medical Officers for extra stretchers, blankets or bearers will be made in writing to M.O. i/c., A.D.S. stating (a) approximate number required and, (b) map reference of cases requiring evacuation.
   Field Ambulance Officers will keep in touch daily with Regimental Medical Officers.

5. DISPOSAL OF SICK AND WOUNDED.

   (a) Ordinary sick will be evacuated to :-

3rd. Canadian Stationary Hospital,	DOULLENS.
No. 3 Casualty Clearing Station.	GEZAINCOURT.
No. 29 -do-	GEZAINCOURT.
No. 56 -do-	GEZAINCOURT.

   (b) Cases suitable for C.R.S. will be sent by Horse Ambulance from D.R.S. at 10-0 a.m. daily.

   (c) Infectious. Infectious Cases will be sent to No. 21 Casualty Clearing Station at AUXI-LE-CHATEAU.

   (d) S.I. Wounds. S.I. Wounded Cases will be sent to No. 6 Stationary Hospital, FREVENT.

   (e) Venereal. Venereal Cases will be evacuated as ordinary sick after authority of A.P.M. has been obtained.

   (f) Dental Cases. Eight cases will be sent daily from the Division to see the Dental Surgeon at No. 29 C.C.S., GEZAINCOURT. While in the present area units will send names of Officers and Other Ranks requiring dental treatment to 3/2nd. West Lancs. Field Ambulance. A roster will be kept there and units will be notified when and where these are to report. At present only urgent cases are to be sent, and in every case the nature of the treatment required is to be stated.

   (g) Eye Cases. Names of Officers and Other Ranks requiring examination by the Ophthalmic Specialist will be sent to O.C., 3/2nd. West Lancs. Field Ambulance who will inform the unit when and where they will report.
      All ranks proceeding are to have full kit, pay books and one days' rations.
      The Ophthalmic Specialist is at 3rd. Army Ophthalmic Centre, No. 6 Stationary Hospital, FREVENT.

   (h) N.Y.D.N. Cases. N.Y.D.N. cases will be sent to No. 45 Casualty Clearing Station.

(i) SCABIES. Cases which are of so severe a nature that they cannot be treated at D.R.S. will be evacuated to C.C.S.

(j) FRENCH Sick and Wounded. French sick and wounded are to be evacuated in the ordinary way and are to be received at any post.

(k) INDIANS. Indians are to be evacuated in the same manner as white troops.

NOTES.
Additional Infantry Bearers.

In the event of Active Operations, the officer in charge of Forward Evacuations may call on Infantry Brigades for 150 men to act as reserve stretcher bearers in case of necessity.

Alternative Advanced Dressing Station.

In the event of a gas bombardment of FONQUEVILLERS the A.D.S. may be temporarily withdrawn to D.18.b.2.2.

Telephone.

Telephone is installed at A.D.S. and M.D.S.

Unfits.

Officers and Other Ranks considered unfit for work in the front line will be seen by the A.D.M.S. at his office (COUIN) by arrangement.

Maurice King Capt
for Colonel, A. Med. S.,
A.D.M.S., 57th Division.

1st June, 1918.

DISTRIBUTION:-

H.Q., 57th. Division 'G'.
H.Q., 57th. Division 'Q'.
D.D.M.S., IV Corps.
D.M.S., Third Army.
H.Q., 170th Infantry Brigade.
H.Q., 171st Infantry Brigade.
H.Q., 172nd Infantry Brigade.
O.C., 2/2nd Wessex Field Ambulance.
O.C., 2/3rd Wessex Field Ambulance.
O.C., 2/2nd W.Lancs. Field Ambulance.
C.R.E., 57th Division.
C.R.A., 57th Division.
D.A.D.V.S., 57th Division.
A.P.M., 57th Division.
O.C., 57th Divisional Signal Coy.
O.C., 57th Divisional Train.
O.C., 2/5th N. Lan. R. (P).
O.C., 57th Battn. Machine Gun Corps.
O.C., 57th Divisional Wing.
M.O., 57th Divisional Wing.
Senior Chaplain, C. of E.
Senior Chaplain, Non C. of E.
All Regimental Medical Officers, 57th Division.
A.D.M.S., 37th Division.
A.D.M.S., 42nd Division.
A.D.M.S., 62nd Division.
A.D.M.S., N.Z. Division.

SECRET.

> A.D.M.S.
> 57th (W.L.) DIVISION
> Date 5/6/18
> No. M.S. 261/12

B

57th DIVISION.
R.A.M.C. OPERATION ORDER NO. 25.   Copy No. 9

Reference Map Sheet 57D, 1/40,000.

1. The 1/1st East Lancs. Field Ambce., 42nd Division is vacating the site at J.1.b.5.7.

2. The 3/2nd West Lancs. Field Ambulance will take over this site on 7th June retaining its own site at J.1.b.6.7.

3. Details of taking over will be arranged between Officers Commanding, Field Ambulances concerned.

[signature]

Colonel A. Med. S.,
A.D.M.S., 57th Division.

5. 6. 18.

Distribution,-
```
Copy No. 1.   57th Division "G".
         2.   57th Division "Q".
         3.   D.D.M.S., IV Corps.
         4.   A.D.M.S., 42nd Division.
         5.   O.C., 2/2nd Wessex Field Ambulance.
         6.   O.C., 2/3rd Wessex Field Ambulance.
         7.   O.C., 3/2nd West Lancs. Field Ambce.
         8.   War Diary.
         9.   War Diary.
        10.   File.
```

SECRET.   57th. DIVISION.   Copy No. ....
         R.A.M.C. OPERATION ORDER NO. 26.   M.S. 280/5.
                    Reference Map Sheet 57D, 1/40,000
                                    LENS 11, 1/100,000

1. 57th. Division (less Artillery) will be relieved by New Zealand
   Division (less Artillery) in the Centre Sector of IV Corps front
   between the 1st. and 3rd. July.
   On relief 57th. Division will be Corps Reserve. Units will be in
   readiness to move at one hours' notice between 9-0 p.m. and 9-0
   a.m. and at two hours' notice between 9-0 a.m. and 9-0 p.m.

2. MOVES OF FIELD AMBULANCES.
   (a) The 2/2nd. Wessex Field Ambulance will be relieved at SOUASTR
   by the 1st. New Zealand Field Ambulance, VAUCHELLES, on the 1st.
   July; relief to be complete by 9-0 a.m. July 2nd. On relief the
   2/2nd. Wessex Field Ambulance will proceed to MONT RENAULT FARM
   (Lens 11/5.C.15.95.) and take over the Corps Rest Station there.

   (b) The 2/3rd. Wessex Field Ambulance will be relieved in the
   line by the 3rd. New Zealand Field Ambulance, AUTHIE, on the 2nd.
   July; relief to be complete by 9-0 a.m. July 3rd. On relief the
   2/3rd. Wessex Field Ambulance will proceed to VAUCHELLES and take
   over the accommodation vacated by the 1st. New Zealand Field
   Ambulance.

   (c) The 3/2nd. West Lancs. Field Ambulance will be relieved at
   COUIN by the 2nd. New Zealand Field Ambulance, MARIEUX, on the
   2nd. July; relief to be complete by 9-0 a.m. July 3rd. On relief
   the 3/2nd. West Lancs. Field Ambulance will proceed to MARIEUX
   and take over the site vacated by the 2nd. New Zealand Field
   Ambulance.

3. In each case Advanced Parties will report 24 hours before the time
   notified for the completion of relief. They will be rationed for
   that time.

4. (a) All Trench and Area Stores including Soda. Bicarb. for Anti-
   Gas Measures, Defence Schemes, Programmes of Work and Maps will be
   handed over.

   (b) A.D.M.S., New Zealand Division is arranging to hand over 3
   Operating and 10 C.S.L. Tents at VAUCHELLES and 4 Operating and 11
   C.S.L. Tents at MARIEUX in exchange for the Field Ambulance and
   Area Tentage at COUIN which will remain intact.

   (c) Copies of receipts for all Area and Trench Stores handed and
   taken over will be rendered to this Office by noon July 4th.

5. Details of reliefs will be arranged by Officers Commanding Field
   Ambulances concerned.

6. (a) Field Ambulances will move independently by road, maintaining a
   distance of 100 yards from other units on the march.

   (b) Lorries may be available for the move of the 2/2nd. Wessex Field
   Ambulance. Orders will be issued later.

7. Completion of reliefs will be notified to this Office by Despatch
   Rider.

8. A.D.M.S. Office will close at COUIN at 4-0 p.m. July 2nd., and
   open at AUTHIE, I.16.a.5.7. at the same hour.

9. ACKNOWLEDGE (Field Ambulances only).

Headquarters,   Lieut-Colonel, R.A.M.C.
28th. June, 1918.   A/A.D.M.S., 57th. Division.

                                                        P.T.O.

DISTRIBUTION :-

Copy No. 1 to 57th. Division, 'G'.
      2   57th. Division, 'Q'.
      3   H.Q., 170th. Infantry Brigade.
      4   H.Q., 171st. Infantry Brigade.
      5   H.Q., 172nd. Infantry Brigade.
      6   O.C., 2/2nd. Wessex Field Ambulance.
      7   O.C., 2/3rd. Wessex Field Ambulance.
      8   O.C., 3/2nd. West Lancs. Field Ambulance.
      9   A.D.M.S., N.Z. Division.
    10   A.D.M.S., 57th. Division.
    11   A.D.M.S., 42nd. Division.
    12   A.D.M.S., 62nd. Division.
    13   C.R.E., 57th. Division.
    14   C.R.A., 57th. Division.
    15   O.C., 57th. Divisional Signal Company.
    16   O.C., 57th. Battalion Machine Gun Corps.
    17   O.C., 2/5th. N. Lan. R.
    18   O.C., 57th. Divisional Train, A.S.C.
    19   D.A.D.V.S., 57th. Division.
    20   D.G.O., 57th. Division.
    21   A.P.M., 57th. Division.
    22   D.M.S., Third Army.
    23   D.D.M.S., IV Corps.
    24   War Diary.
    25   -do-
    26   File.
    27   -do-
    28   Spare.

Issued at............11-0...... p.m.

Confidential.

War Diary
of
A.D.M.S.
57th Division.
from 1.7.18. to 31.7.18.

Army Form C. 2118.

WAR DIARY
or
INTELLIGENCE SUMMARY.
(Erase heading not required.)

Instructions regarding War Diaries and Intelligence Summaries are contained in F. S. Regs., Part II. and the Staff Manual respectively. Title pages will be prepared in manuscript.

Place	Date	Hour	Summary of Events and Information	Remarks and references to Appendices
COUIN	1.4.18		A/A.D.M.S made sanitary inspection of Couin Baths, Coigneux Vitrysous manure dumps in Rossignol Farm — Couin — Vallers. A/A.D.M.S made out sanitary arrangements for new area used to new area — Authie.	Appendix A.
AUTHIE	2.4.18		A/A.D.M.S called on D.D.M.S. IV Corps re-opening Corps Rest Station etc.	
	3.4.18		A/A.D.M.S visited 5/2nd W Lanc. F Amb at Clincamps; D'ould IV Corps, and 2/3 N Midland F Amb at Vauchelles.	
	4.4.18		A/A.D.M.S visited 2/2nd N Mid F Amb and reference sites accommodation etc. D.A.D.M.S visited positions in neighbourhood and at Vauchelles.	
	5.4.18		A/A.D.M.S visited 2/6th and 2nd S. Mid F. Spec. R sanitation fair. Jones were to correct. — 14 — 19 men per tent. Stove Stovepipes being made.	
	6.4.18		A.D.M.S., S.Y.D. returned from 14 days leave and resumed duty.	

Army Form C. 2118.

WAR DIARY
or
INTELLIGENCE SUMMARY.
(Erase heading not required.)

Instructions regarding War Diaries and Intelligence Summaries are contained in F.S. Regs., Part II. and the Staff Manual respectively. Title pages will be prepared in manuscript.

Place	Date	Hour	Summary of Events and Information	Remarks and references to Appendices
AUTHIE	7/7/18		Divisional now to divisional officers' reports. Young GERHMAN U.S. M.O.R.C. joined for duty today and was posted to the 3/1st N.Z. Fld. Amb. Draft of 17 men and 3 officers joined 3/1st or to my independent unit. A.D.M.S. visited 3/2 N.Z. F.Amb. at MARIEUX. Find no cause for complaint. 230 patients currently residing in tentarium from N.Z. Division are mainly of accident. A.D.M.S. also visited M.D.S. of 2/3 N.Z. Fld. F. Amb. at VAUCHELLES. Has recommendation rather fragmentary, but is being rapidly improved.	
	8/7/18		A.D.M.S. visited 2/3 N.Z. Fld. F.Amb. at MONT RENAULT FERME on hill 9 found about 12 K[?]. S.W. of Doullens. There, he found generally satisfactory and no space to be written in to an X Corps R.A. station. He is to train 10 July with unit personnel for 2nd, if military measures subsequently	

16 f.M.
A5834 Wt. W4973/M687 750,000 8/16 D. D. & L. Ltd. Forms/C.2118/13.

WAR DIARY
or
INTELLIGENCE SUMMARY.

Army Form C. 2118.

(Erase heading not required.)

Place	Date	Hour	Summary of Events and Information	Remarks and references to Appendices
AUTHIE	9/4/18		ADMS visited Bricks near AUTHIE and arr. 2/6th 1st Apert R. at BOIS on MARIEMENT and now at new regiment as empty for grants not received. Remainder is to be transferred to Brus.	
	10/4/18	9 AM	Engineer of Second officer in Office (20 present) ADMS visited 3/2nd F. Amb. & Amb.	
	11/4/18		Visited 3/2nd F. Amb. at MARIEUX and inspected gun site on return. DADMS present. About 128 sick are accommodation in marquees and sheds ADMS ventilated	
	12/4/18		2/5" N.Z.A.R Camp in CUIN.	
	13/4/18		ADMS visited Div. H.Q's and inspected many of 2/8 Employment Coys evacd to Home "A" Cois evacd IX Corps R. P. from to MONT RENAULT FARM stopped and reinspected by 2/3 NZ Gen v Amb. and sent to NZ Hosp. (Authie) totaling supply 200 patients.	

WAR DIARY or INTELLIGENCE SUMMARY

Army Form C. 2118.

Place	Date	Hour	Summary of Events and Information	Remarks and references to Appendices
AUTHIE	14/7/18		Rest.	
PAS en ARTOIS	15/7/18		87th Dismounted transports moved from AUTHIE to PAS. 17th Inf Bn/8th Gordons LOUVENCOURT to HENU. Order promoted rest of move.	
	16/7/18		A.D.M.S. visited 2/5 W.LAN.R regarding medical arrangements. 87th Division now in V Corps Reserve. Executive arrangements in hands of Brigadier Khing. "Battle pontoon" arranged.	
	17/7/18		A.D.M.S. and Div Commander visited transports of 2/2nd W. Kent & Amb, 2/3rd Wessex & Amb and 3/2nd W. Lanc. & Amb. Sick admissions rate now very low: average 14% for upward July 3-18 inclusive. Reinforcements at present large. 12 chemical officers on leave at present.	
	18/7/18		Reports from Sanitary Section shew that the chlorine is not being found in Pté Cantl of this Division: enquiry seems to show that this is practically at best, due to defective quality of Chlorine of Lime.	

Army Form C. 2118.

WAR DIARY
or
INTELLIGENCE SUMMARY.
(Erase heading not required).

Instructions regarding War Diaries and Intelligence Summaries are contained in F. S. Regs, Part II. and the Staff Manual respectively. Title pages will be prepared in manuscript.

Place	Date	Hour	Summary of Events and Information	Remarks and references to Appendices
PAS.	20/4/18		The Sanitary Section having reported the water in many Divisional of R.E. Carts contains no free Chlorine, DADMS visited all water filling points in Divisional Area. ADMS visited 2/6 13 Spot Rgt, 8th M Spot Rgt, 2/5 W Land Rgt and 2/ff of Land Rgt regarding sanitation and medical arrangements.	
	21/4/18		DADMS visited O.C. Sanitary Sect. regarding production of wells and protection of protection at W.P. filling points. Administrative meeting regarding evac; chlorination, Medical Officers correspondence, medicine offered than to ORs. Complaint regarding Sanitary delivered.	
	22/4/18		ADMS visited new DDMS II Corps. Cor Getham at Corps Headquarters. Discussed accessory of Corps R.P. station at Mont Rouidet Farm. Ambulances regarding Annual Surgical Contents all lowered. Comment on Massieres, irregular use of Motors.	

Army Form C. 2118.

WAR DIARY
or
INTELLIGENCE SUMMARY.
(Erase heading not required.)

Place	Date	Hour	Summary of Events and Information	Remarks and references to Appendices
DHS	28.7.16		Ambulance Cars etc. Also visited 1/2nd W. Riding & Puch amb 2/3rd Wessex & Coll at Harrionrut, Vaucelles. Review morning over staff 54th Div. went never 42nd Division on my Rt. Sector of Corps front. July 30 - Aug 1.	
	24.7.16		ADMS with DDMS visited and made extensive inspection of Corps Coll stn at Warloy. Rumbetrhem evacuation by 1/2 Nord the Amb. Present accommodation 220 beds. It is proposed to enlarge site by erecting 20 marquees taking 8.2610 patients on each. Capt O/C Bulloch returned to the Division yesterday after recovery from minor illness. ADMS made enquiries regarding situation.	
	25.7.16		28 samples of water taken from 54th Div & III Bn. early July 9-14. ADMS visited ADMS 42nd Division at Authie regarding Nr Engineer of night medical of III Corps front forms 42nd Division	

A5834 Wt.W4973/M687 750,000 8/16 D. D. & L. Ltd. Forms/C.2118/13.

WAR DIARY
or
INTELLIGENCE SUMMARY

Army Form C. 2118.

Place	Date	Hour	Summary of Events and Information	Remarks and references to Appendices
P.A.S.	July 20-Aug 1 16/7/18		Also visited Headquarters of 59th D.A.C. Conference of Medical Officers (17 present) Chlorination of water, medical attendance of horse units; excellence; Major H.O. Adams gave demonstration and lecture on surgical methods at R.A.P.'s and A.D. Stations.	
	24/7/18		With Lieut. Col. Lauriston, O.C. 1/3 N. Lanc. F. Amb., A.D.M.S. visited A.D. Stations, R.A.P.'s and B.R.P's on Pilckem Sector of IX Corps Front which 59th Division is expected shortly to take over from 42nd Division. Latter learnt that the relief had been postponed, the 59th Divn. having become B.H.Q. of Reserve Divisional.	
	28/7/18		A.D.M.S. visited 1/5 N. Ant R. regarding elimination of scabies amongst them. Memoranda reports to Division on surface chlorination. Issued congratulatory letters to Medical Officers and Medical Chlorinators etc, orderly of Medical Officers with result. Units. Reports on Distribution, etc.	

Army Form C. 2118.

WAR DIARY
or
INTELLIGENCE SUMMARY.
(Erase heading not required.)

Place	Date	Hour	Summary of Events and Information	Remarks and references to Appendices
PAS.	28/7/18.		A.D.M.S. also visited 2/3rd Field Amb. Bit. ought moved orders for move of all their Ambulance trains on relief by corresponding Units of the 63rd (R.N.) Division.	Appendix B
	29/7/18		A.D.M.S. attended Conference of A.D.M.S. of VI Corps. DDMS presiding at B.A.C. and S.V.D. Discussion on Board of dean related treatment of Yellow Cross Gas Cases.	
			57th Div. Hdqrs moved from PAS-EN-ARTOIS to BOUQUEMAISON.	
			2/2nd Wessex Ft Amb from MONT RENAULT FARM to SUS-ST-LEGER.	
			2/3rd Wessex Ft Amb from VAUCHELLES to SAULTY.	
			3/2nd W. Lanc. Ft Amb. from MARIEUX to HAUTVISEE.	
			ADMS attended Conference held by G.O.C. 57th Division at BOUQUEMAISON	
BOUQUEMAISON	30/7/18	10 A.M.	57th Division to take over front from 12th Canadian Brigade of 4th Canadian Division, roughly Searpe. 2nd Canadian Brigade of 1st Canadian Division holding front Searpe, that is about an front 5	

Army Form C. 2118.

WAR DIARY
or
INTELLIGENCE SUMMARY.
(Erase heading not required.)

Instructions regarding War Diaries and Intelligence Summaries are contained in F. S. Regs., Part II. and the Staff Manual respectively. Title pages will be prepared in manuscript.

Place	Date	Hour	Summary of Events and Information	Remarks and references to Appendices
BUQUOY MAISON ROUGE	30/4/18		ARRAS. Also visited ADMS 4th Canadian Division at MAROEUIL (where also saw A/ADMS 52nd Division. ADMS 1st Canadian Division at ETRUN and DDMS XVII Corps newly established at DUISANS. As a result visited 57th Div. RAMC O. and O.C. 28. 3/2nd Western & Ambs moved today from SVS.ST.LEGER & Y Camp nr ETRUN 2/3rd Western & Ambs " " " SAULTY. 16 " " 3/2nd W. Lanc. & Amb " " " HAUTE VISEE " WANQUETON. ADMS visited all above and arranged details of staffing our respectively of evacuation with O.C. of each N. Lanc. & Amb	Appendix C.

Army Form C. 2118.

WAR DIARY
or
INTELLIGENCE SUMMARY.

(Erase heading not required.)

Place	Date	Hour	Summary of Events and Information	Remarks and references to Appendices
HERMANVILLE	31.8.18.		With Lt.Col. ANDERSON, O.C. 13th Canadian F.Amb., O.C. 2/2nd W.Lanc. F.Amb., and Major MORRISON, commanding "C" SECTION the reg. ADMS visited M.D.S. at ST. CATHERINES, ARRAS, ST. NICHOLAS A.D.S. at CHALK QUARRY, L'ABBAYE and R.A.P.s at CAM VALLEY and CASTLE ROAD. Revised medicine arrangements for XVII Corps.	

J. P. Burton
Colonel. A. Med. S.
A.D.M.S. 57th (W.L.) Division.

SECRET.   M.S. 280/12.

MEDICAL ARRANGEMENTS.
57th. DIVISION.

Ref. Map Sheet 57D, 1/40,000.
"   "   "   LENS 11, 1/100,000

1. **LOCATIONS.**

   Headquarters of Field Ambulances :-

   2/2nd. Wessex Field Ambulance.   Corps Rest Station,
                                         MONT RENAULT FARM,
                                         LENS 11/S.C.15.85.

   2/3rd. Wessex Field Ambulance.   VAUCHELLES,
                                         57D/I.33.a.1.8.

   3/2nd. W. Lancs. F. Ambulance.   MARIEUX,
                                         57D/H.24.d.9.7.

2. **DISPOSAL OF SICK AND WOUNDED.**

   (a) From Units at AUTHIE, ST. LEGER and BOIS DE WARNIMONT by
       horse ambulance to 3/2nd. West Lancs. Field Ambulance at
       MARIEUX.
       From Units at VAUCHELLES and LOUVENCOURT by horse
   (b) ambulance to 2/3rd. Wessex Field Ambulance at VAUCHELLES.
       Time and points of call to be arranged between Officers
       Commanding, Field Ambulances and Medical Officers concerned.

   (b) C.R.S. Cases. These will be sent to 3/2nd. West Lancs.
       Field Ambulance at MARIEUX, where they will stay overnight.
       Thence they will be taken at 10-0 a.m. daily to Corps Rest
       Station by M.A.C. Cars which will wait and bring back men
       returning to their units, to MARIEUX, whence they will be
       distributed.
       Cases for Corps Rest Station will take one days' rations
       with them from 3/2nd. West Lancs. Field Ambulance.

   (c) C.C.S. Cases. These will be evacuated by Field Ambulance
       Cars to :-

       No. 3 Canadian Stationary Hospital,   DOULLENS.
            3 Casualty Clearing Station,   GEZAINCOURT.
           29 Casualty Clearing Station,   GEZAINCOURT.
           56 Casualty Clearing Station,   GEZAINCOURT.

   (d) Cases of Diarrhoea and Dysentery will be sent to 3/2nd.
       West Lancs. Field Ambulance at MARIEUX.

   (e) Scabies. Cases of so severe a nature that they cannot be
       treated in Field Ambulance will be sent to C.C.S.

   (f) Infectious. Infectious cases will be sent to No. 21
       Casualty Clearing Station at WAVANS.

   (g) S.I. Wounds. S.I. Wounded Cases will be sent to No. 46
       C.C.S., FILLIEVRES in Field Ambulance Cars.

   (h) Venereal. Venereal Cases will be evacuated as ordinary
       sick after authority of A.P.M. has been obtained.

   (i) Dental Cases. Ten cases will be sent daily from the
       Division to see the Dental Surgeon at No. 29 C.C.S.,
       GEZAINCOURT. While in the present Area units will send
       names of Officers and Other Ranks requiring dental treat-
       ment to 3/2nd. West Lancs. Field Ambulance. A roster will
       be kept there and units will be notified when and where
       these are to report. At present only urgent cases are to
       be sent and in every case the nature of the treatment
       required is to be stated.
       OFFICERS will be seen by appointment at No. 3 Canadian
       Stationary Hospital.

(j) Eye Cases. Names of Officers and Other Ranks requiring examination by the Ophthalmic Specialist will be sent to O.C., 3/2nd. West Lancs. Field Ambulance who will inform the unit when and where they will report.
All Ranks proceeding are to have full kit, pay books and one days' rations.
The Ophthalmic Specialist is at Third Army Ophthalmic Centre, No. 43 C.C.S., FREVENT.

(k) N.Y.D.N. Cases. N.Y.D.N. Cases will be sent to No. 45 Casualty Clearing Station.

(l) Indians. Indians are to be evacuated in the same manner as White Troops.

(m) Nephritis. Cases of Nephritis in their earliest stages are to be sent to No. 6 Stationary Hospital, FREVENT, in Field Ambulance Cars.

(n) Unfits. Officers and Other Ranks considered unfit for work in the front line will be seen by the A.D.M.S. at his Office, AUTHIE, by arrangement.

A.W.B. Loudon.
Lieut-Colonel, R.A.M.C.,
A/A.D.M.S., 57th. Division.

Headquarters,
1st. July, 1918.

Distribution:-

H.Q., 57th. Division, 'G'.
H.Q., 57th. Division, 'Q'.
D.D.M.S., IV Corps.
D.M.S., Third Army.
H.Q., 170th. Infantry Brigade.
H.Q., 171st. Infantry Brigade.
H.Q., 172nd. Infantry Brigade.
O.C., 2/2nd. Wessex Field Ambulance.
O.C., 2/3rd. Wessex Field Ambulance.
O.C., 3/2nd. West Lancs. Field Ambulance.
C.R.E., 57th. Division.
C.R.A., 57th. Division.
D.A.D.V.S., 57th. Division.
A.P.M., 57th. Division.
O.C., 57th. Divisional Signal Company.
O.C., 57th. Divisional Train, A.S.C.
O.C., 2/5th. N. Lan. R.
O.C., 57th. Battalion Machine Gun Corps.
O.C., 57th. Divisional Reception Camp.
M.O., 57th. Divisional Reception Camp.
Senior Chaplain, C. of E.
Senior Chaplain, Non. C. of E.
All Regimental Medical Officers.
A.D.M.S., N.Z. Division.
A.D.M.S., 42nd. Division.
A.D.M.S., 37th. Division.
A.D.M.S., 62nd. Division.

SECRET.   57th. DIVISION.   M.S. 288/8.
   R.A.M.C. OPERATION ORDER No. 27.   Copy No. 26
                                       Reference Map Sheets 57D, 1/40,000
                                                            51C, 1/40,000

1. 57th. Division will be transferred to VI Corps on July 29th. and be in G.H.Q. Reserve in the LUCHEUX Area.

2. (a) 63rd. Division (less Artillery) is being transferred to G.H.Q. Reserve in IV Corps Area on July, 29th. and will take over all billet, camps and tents of 57th. Division.

   (b) All Defence Schemes, Maps, and programmes of work will be handed over to advanced parties of 63rd. Division.

3. MOVES OF FIELD AMBULANCES.

   (a) 2/2nd. Wessex Field Ambulance will hand over the Corps Rest Station at MONT RENAULT FARM and will proceed to SUS-ST-LEGER, being clear of the road junction T.11.c.8.0. before 1-30 p.m. On arrival the unit will be billeted by 171st. Infantry Brigade.

   (b) 2/3rd. Wessex Field Ambulance will hand over the site at VAUCHELLES and will proceed to SAULTY under orders of 172nd. Infantry Brigade.

   (c) 3/2nd. West Lancs. Field Ambulance will hand over the Divisional Rest Station at MARIEUX and will proceed to HAUTE-VISEE under orders of 170th. Infantry Brigade.

4. (a) Only equipment authorised by Mob. Store Table and G.R.Os. will be taken.

   (b) Receipts, in duplicate, for all Area Stores handed over will be sent to this Office by 12 noon July, 31st.

5. A.D.M.S. Office will close at PAS at 11-0 a.m., 29/7/18 and re-open at BOUQUEMAISON at 1-0 p.m.

6. PLEASE ACKNOWLEDGE (Field Ambulances only).

                                    J J Cewan
                                Colonel, A. Med. S.,
                           A.D.M.S., 57th. Division.

28th. July, 1918.

Issued at 9-30 P.M.

DISTRIBUTION :-

Copy No. 1 to H.Q., 57th. Division 'G'.
         2   H.Q., 57th. Division 'Q'.
         3   H.Q., 170th. Infantry Brigade.
         4   H.Q., 171st. Infantry Brigade.
         5   H.Q., 172nd. Infantry Brigade.
         6   O.C., 2/2nd. Wessex Field Ambulance.
         7   O.C., 2/3rd. Wessex Field Ambulance.
         8   O.C., 3/2nd. West Lancs. Field Ambulance.
         9   A.D.M.S., N.Z. Division.
        10   A.D.M.S., 37th. Division.
        11   A.D.M.S., 42nd. Division.
        12   A.D.M.S., 63rd. Division.
        13   C.R.E., 57th. Division.
        14   C.R.A., 57th. Division.
        15   O.C., 57th. Divisional Signal Company.
        16   O.C., 57th. Bn. M.G. Corps.
        17   O.C., 2/5th. N. Lan. R. (p).

Copy No. 18 to O.C., 57th. Div. Train   Copy No. 19 to D.A.D.V.S., 57 Div
        20   D.G.O., 57th. Division.   21   A.P.M., 57th. Divn.
        22   D.M.S., Third Army.   23   D.D.M.S., IV Corps.
        24   D.D.M.S., VI Corps.   25   War Diary.
        26   War Diary.   27   File.
        28   File.   29   Spare.

SECRET.   57th Division.   M.S.288/11.
          R.A.M.C. OPERATION ORDER NO. 28.   Copy No. 24
                        Reference Map Sheets 51B, 1/40,000
                                      Lens 11, 1/100,000.

1. INFORMATION.
          The 57th Division will relieve portions of the 1st and 4th Canadian Divisions on July 31st and August 1st.

2. MOVES.
          2/2nd Wessex Field Ambulance will relieve the 12th Canadian Field Ambulance, 1 mile N.E. of AGNEZ LES DUISANS and will establish the Divisional Rest Station. Relief to be complete by noon 1/8/18.
          2/3rd Wessex Field Ambulance will relieve the 3rd Canadian Field Ambulance at HAUTE - AVESNES. Relief to be complete by noon 1/8/18.
          3/2nd West Lancs Field Ambulance will relieve 13th Canadian Field Ambulance at ST CATHERINES taking over the Main Dressing Station at G.15.a.1.5. and the Advanced Dressing Stations at H.14.b.6.2. and H.13.b.4.7. and all Posts (N. and S. of the River SCARPE) on the Divisional Front. Relief to be complete by 8 a.m. 1/8/18.

          All details of relief to be arranged between the Field Ambulance Commanders concerned.

3. EVACUATION.
          Maps and details of present scheme of evacuation will be handed over by Canadian Field Ambulances.

4. REPORTS.
          Completion of relief will be notified as soon as possible to this office by use of the code word ' CLEAR '.

5. RECEIPTS.
          Receipts (in duplicate) of (1) all Trench and Area Stores, (2) Medical Stores, taken over will be forwarded to this office by noon 2/8/18.

6. ACKNOWLEDGE (Field Ambulances only).

                                            J.F.Ewen.
                                            Colonel, A.Med.S.
30/8/18.   A.D.M.S., 57th Division.

Issued at... 9.15. p.m.

DISTRIBUTION :-
Copy No. 1. to H.Q., 57th Division 'G'
       2.   H.Q., 57th Division 'Q'
       3.   H.Q., 170th Infantry Brigade.
       4.   H.Q., 171st Infantry Brigade.
       5.   H.Q., 172nd Infantry Brigade.
       6.   O.C., 2/2nd Wessex Field Ambulance.
       7.   O.C., 2/3rd Wessex Field Ambulance.
       8.   O.C., 3/2nd W.Lancs. Field Ambulance.
       9.   A.D.M.S., 1st Canadian Division.
      10.   A.D.M.S., 4th Canadian Division.
      11.   A.D.M.S., 52nd Division.
      12.   C.R.A., 57th Division.
      13.   C.R.E., 57th Division.
      14.   O.C., 57th Divisional Signal Company.
      15.   O.C., 57th Bn. M.G.Corps.
      16.   O.C., 2/5th N.Lan.R. (P)
Copy No. 17 to O.C., 57th Div. Train.   Copy No. 18 to D.A.D.V.S., 57 Div
       19. D.G.O., 57th Division.   20 A.P.M., 57th Division
       21. D.M.S., First Army.   22. D.D.M.S., XVII Corps.
       23. War Diary.   24. War Diary.
       25. FILE.   26. FILE.

Confidential

War Diary
of
A.D.M.S.
57th Division

From – August 1st to August 31st
1918

Army Form C. 2118.

WAR DIARY
or
INTELLIGENCE SUMMARY.
(Erase heading not required.)

Instructions regarding War Diaries and Intelligence Summaries are contained in F. S. Regs., Part II. and the Staff Manual respectively. Title pages will be prepared in manuscript.

Place	Date	Hour	Summary of Events and Information	Remarks and references to Appendices
HERMAVILLE	1.8.18		3/2nd W. Lanc. F. Amb. 1/2 Forward movement 3/2nd Divisional opened from today. H.Q. ST.CATHERINE, ARRAS 3/2nd W.Lanc.F.Amb. opening Divisional Rest Station at .... c/o AGNEZ-LES-DUISANS. Captain WO McKENZIE, MC, A/DADMS went up hill and visited above Dressing Stations, etc.	
	2.8.18		A.D.M.S. visited 2/3rd W.Lanc. F. Amb. (resting & training) at HAUTE AVESNES. Visited 3/2nd W.Lanc.F.Amb opening a 5Yth O.R.S. in AGNEZ les DUISANS in extension of units used at C.C. Stn(?) R.R. retirement in March 1918. Much renovation required. Visited D.D.M.S. XVII Corps at DUISANS regarding equipment of D.R.S. and lavatory and scale of field Ambulances. 54th Div. H.Q. moved today from HERMAVILLE is FRUN. Division now holds line covering ARRAS. Two Brigades north of SCARPE, and one south as in diagram.	

Army Form C. 2118.

WAR DIARY
or
INTELLIGENCE SUMMARY.
(Erase heading not required.)

Instructions regarding War Diaries and Intelligence Summaries are contained in F.S. Regs., Part II. and the Staff Manual respectively. Title pages will be prepared in manuscript.

Place	Date	Hour	Summary of Events and Information	Remarks and references to Appendices
			142 Infy Brigade	
			141 Infy Brigade	
			143 Infy Brigade	
			Reserve Reserve / Support / Support Support / Line Line / Enemy front line	
ARRAS	3.8.17		A.D.M.S. visited (1) M.D. Stn of 3/2nd W.Lanc. F. Amb. at ST CATHERINES and inspected it minutely. Entrance and partly good accommodation. (2) 2/5. N.LAN.R. in ARRAS. (3) RAPs of 2/1.N.LAN. in ST SAUVEUR (4) ADS of 3/2nd Division to which latter evacuates. (5) POSTS (RAMC) near BLANGY. (6) RAP of 2/6.N. Front A. at QUARRIES. (7) RAP of 1/5. N.LAN.R. in RAILWAY TRIANGLE and (8) ADS at L'ABBAYETTE.	
	4.8.17		DADMS. visited 2/5. R.LANC. R. regarding case of diphtheria and visited RAPs south of River SCARPE. ADMS visited 3/2 W.Lan F.Amb. Issued medical arrangements	Appendix A

Army Form C. 2118.

WAR DIARY
or
INTELLIGENCE SUMMARY.
(Erase heading not required.)

Place	Date	Hour	Summary of Events and Information	Remarks and references to Appendices
ARRAS	5/8/18		A.D.M.S. visited 2/5th Western F. Amb. at HAUTE AVESNES and 2/2nd Western F Amb. at AGNEZ les DUISANS. Latter unit is steadily getting n new unit of their.	
	6.8.18		A.D.M.S. visited M.D.S. of 2/1st W. N. Amb. at ST. CATHERINE and Transports Posts of same Units at ANZIN. Also visited Divl. Baths at ANZIN and ST. CATHERINE, ARRAS.	
	7/8/18		A/D A.D.M.S. visited 2/2 nd and 2/5 th Western F Amb. Divisionals Arrangements of yet Dis. visited yesterday. A.D.M.S. visited 2/2 nd Western F Amb. regarding administrative matter; visited Divisional Rest Camp and saw Medical Officer.	Appendix B
	8/8/16		A.D.M.S. visited all the medical Units Orders to supply Medical Officers to R.A.M.C. School of Instruction. This will entail seven return on Field Staff romans.	

Army Form C. 2118.

WAR DIARY
or
INTELLIGENCE SUMMARY.
(Erase heading not required.)

Instructions regarding War Diaries and Intelligence Summaries are contained in F.S. Regs., Part II. and the Staff Manual respectively. Title pages will be prepared in manuscript.

Place	Date	Hour	Summary of Events and Information	Remarks and references to Appendices
ETRUN	9.8.18		ADMS visited DDMS XVII Corps at Headquarters. Accompanied on inspection of DR stn (3/2nd Western F. Amb) Returned more recent inspection of 2/3rd Wessex F. Amb at HAUTE AVESNES.	
	10.8.18		Conference of ADsMS XVII Corps at Corps Headquarters. DUISANS. Officers DDMS. ADMS Rep Divisions (30) Cav & (51) Regts (63) of Corps. Discussion formation of Corps School for sanitary instruction of Walking wounded Collecting Coys, Reinforcements of Units 2/2nd Wessex F. Amb Werquignal.	
	11.8.18		ADMS gave full visits to OC of 2/Bde RFA Cambrian reported to Dainville M.D.S. with weakly sanitary conditions.	
	12.8.18		ADMS visited M.D.S. ST. CATHERINE, ADS QUARRIES, and LAFAYETTE R.A.Ps, QUARRIES, LE POINT DU JOUR, and MED POST, ST. NICHOLAS South O.C. 3/2nd W. Lowl. F. Amb.	

A5834 Wt.W4973/M687 750,000 8/16 D.D.&L. Ltd. Forms/C.2118/13.

Army Form C. 2118.

WAR DIARY
or
INTELLIGENCE SUMMARY.
(Erase heading not required.)

Place	Date	Hour	Summary of Events and Information	Remarks and references to Appendices
ETRUN	13/8/18		A.D.M.S visited 2/2nd Western F. Amb. seeing (1) Transport (2) details cases in detail. Also visited 54th Divl. Reception Camp and the	
	14.8.18		D.D.M.S XVII Corps. About Discussed transport repair equipment Dick arrangements re Major IRELAND, Regimental Surgeon, 91st American Division (received warning over night 91st Div. has 170 day OBs (i.e. was too Brigaded of 91st Div of the drafts) women re relieved by two Brigades of 51st Division on or about August 25. A.D.M.S visited Dist. Butler at AGNEZ-lez-DUISANS (at which time being used by American Troops). Divisional clothing store, and Decr Ammun Column at GOUVRES. A/ADMS went around front line this morning.	
	15/8/16		A.D.M.S went round 54th Divisional front R.A.P's etc, with Major IRELAND, M.O.R.C, USA. Received front few men now sick. Operation Order No. 29	Appendix C

WAR DIARY or INTELLIGENCE SUMMARY

Army Form C. 2118.

Place	Date	Hour	Summary of Events and Information	Remarks and references to Appendices
ETRUN			In connection with impending move of 2nd Division — len	
			140 Brigade are relieved by 51st Division, visited D.D.M.S XVII Corps	
			2/1st and 2/3rd Western F. Amb. now sites of posts at LIGNY-ST. FLOCHEL	
			and A.D.M.S 51st Division at MAROEUIL. Issued amendments to	
			Operation Order.	
	17.8.18		142 Brigade moving relieved today to ST.POL area	
			2/3rd Western F. Amb. by road to LIGNY-ST.FLOCHEL to open near head	
			of Corps Rail station. Also visited 2/2nd W. Lanc. F. Amb and	
			2/2nd Western F. Amb, especially regarding their move on 19th.	
	18.8.18		A.D.M.S visited 2/2 Mercer Fd Ambce. (A.R.S. AGNEZ-LES-DUISANS)	
			and saw many patients awaiting evacuation. Visited A.D.M.S 56th Division (Highland)	
			Division at MARIEUX regarding details of relief.	
	19.8.18		A.D.M.S attended Conference of A.D.s M.S. (15, 51, 57, 56, 157) at Office	
			of D.D.M.S. XVII Corps at DUISANS. Discussed final arrangements.	

WAR DIARY
or
INTELLIGENCE SUMMARY

Army Form C. 2118.

Place	Date	Hour	Summary of Events and Information	Remarks and references to Appendices
	19.8.18		Supervised dental arrangements. Corps medical arrangements re 2nd visit of 1st Anzac Div. which arrived on day erected. CO 9th etc. at LIGNY-ST-FLOCHEL to 17th. Two ample marquee reservations (about 80 marquees) which about to be erected. In warehouse (now 86 marquees) latrines sinks, non-existent, cookhouses, bath shelters, places, latrines sinks, non-existent, incomplete or ended. 4th Aust. Div. moves to hay from ETRUN to CHELERS and 17 to ST Pôle to neighbouring area under 2nd Anzac D. Corps at FREVILLERS and 2/3 Md. Sd. Ambs at HOUVELIN.	
	20.8.18		ADMS visited the Aust D Amb at FREVILLERS. Busy yrs army to keep 876 cases in opening limb. ADMS visited the H Q. D. Ambs at HOUVHN. Precipit in burn to keep 8-14 each in a barn defences for the purpose. Also visited 1/2 Anzac D. Amb. at LIGNY & FLOCHEL offering to-day no Corps Rest Station under Corps arrangement. Corps M.C.I. arrangements — very complete. Received.	

A5834 Wt. W4973/M687 750,000 8/16 D.D. & L. Ltd. Forms/C.2113/13.

WAR DIARY
or
INTELLIGENCE SUMMARY.

Army Form C. 2118.

Place	Date	Hour	Summary of Events and Information	Remarks and references to Appendices
	August		A.D.M.S. visited 7/3 Thoros. at Aubee at LIGNY. rapidly admitting patients in large flat fashion. Inspected transport of unit. Also visited 2/2 Thoros. d. Aubee, and 2/2 W.L. D. Aut., arranging with latter for move of 2nd Division with 2.8.3 medical officers to AUBIGNY. 8uch. received orders that Division moving forth with VI Corps. 3rd Army from to-night. 171st Inf. Bde (and 2/3 WL 2b. Aub) 173rd Inf Bde. with 2/2 Thoros bde. Aubee moving to-night. 2nd & XVII Corps has ordered 2/3 Thoros. d. Aut. to be ready to move at once. Leaving one Cabs Echelon to 33. C.C.S. near by.	
	4.8.16.		7/2 Thoros. d. Aubee now at HAUTEVILLE, 2/2 Wh. d. Aubee at GIVENCHY-LES-NOBLE Wood. Visited 2/2 W. D. Aut. at LIGNY. likely moving to-day. 1st MARLUS - BERNAVILLE Area, Division probably moving forth to-night. A.D.M.S. rides VI Corps this probably (later, is now in VI Corps H.Q. Army) receives medical arrangements	

WAR DIARY or INTELLIGENCE SUMMARY

Army Form C. 2118.

Place	Date	Hour	Summary of Events and Information	Remarks and references to Appendices
	7.8.16		ADMS visited 2/3 Wessex S.B. Ambce. at HAUTEVILLE & 2/1 W.R. St Ambce at GR-LES NOBLE to which places there were sent fortnight. 3/1st Air place FAR reserve. Issued note VI corps Reserve area near PREVENT. H.Q. to REBREUVE. 2/3 Wessex S. Amb leaves 10 men joined 10 p.m. last night. AGNY – ST-FLOUCHEL to REBREUVIETTE and 3/2 Wessex S. Amb moved in night to INVERGNY and 3/2 W.R. St Ambce to RUE-ST-LEGER. Each St. Ambulance is now in its "normal" Brigade group. 3/-:	
			10th Inf. Bde. — 2/1 W.R. St. Ambce.	
			17 1st — do — 2/2 Wessex St. Ambce.	
			17 2nd — do — 2/3 — do —	
	8.8.16		Sgt Sir H.R. Arenes K Prominent. Road visited VI corps H.Qrs at LUCHEAUX. to find that knowen was leaving at noon into XVII corps 1st Army. Also visited XVII corps H.Qrs at FOSSEUX (to which it was to move that day) and saw D.A.M.S. 2/3 Wessex	

A 5834 Wt. W4973/M687 750,000 8/16 D.D & T & L. Ltd. Forms(C2:118/13).

Army Form C. 2118.

WAR DIARY
or
INTELLIGENCE SUMMARY.
(Erase heading not required.)

Instructions regarding War Diaries and Intelligence Summaries are contained in F. S. Regs., Part II and the Staff Manual respectively. Title pages will be prepared in manuscript.

Place	Date	Hour	Summary of Events and Information	Remarks and references to Appendices
	7.8.18		Field Amb'ce moved to-day with Brigade Group from HAUTE-VISÉE to BAYINCOURT and in evening to GOUY. They have marched as follows:— Aug 5th 10pm to Aug 6th 3 am — ½ mile; 6/3 10am to Aug 6th 2pm — 1 "; 6th 8 am to Aug 6th 8pm — 16 "; 6th 7 pm to 6th 9 pm — 3 ". Total 38.	
	25.8.18		17th conj. Left Poles moving forward & corner with 2/2 N. Lanc. St. Amber — ment alternated from SUC-ST-LÉGER to BASSEUX. Moved to Amber for IVERGNY to GOUY-EN-ARTOIS. About miles total XVII Corps and 2/3 Division St. Amber now administering Corp. Rest Stn at GOUY. Very busy day with preparations for early action.	
	26-8-18		A.D.M.S. visited A.D.M.S. 56th Division. 56th Amber Hqtrs & M.D.S. & XVII Corps front — both 52" 56th Division trying to rapid advance of XVII Corps & Corps on left & right; 59th Division preparing to move forward. Issued orders to 2/2 N.K. Fd. Amber and	

WAR DIARY or INTELLIGENCE SUMMARY

Army Form C. 2118.

Place	Date	Hour	Summary of Events and Information	Remarks and references to Appendices
BLAIRVILLE	26.8.18		2/5th K.O.Y.L.I. formed D. Ambee. & moved forward at 8 a.m. from to BLAIRVILLE.	
	27.8.18		2/4th K.O. moved forward. O.C. advanced H.Qrs. to Bretencourt, then Blairville Quarries and then to near MERCATEL. Load H.Qrs. to BARGEUX. 2/5 Yorks. L.I. Ink. and 2/4 K. Lancs. St. Ambre. from BLAIRVILLE. FICHEUX, the formed Lathy near A.D.S. from 2nd & 3rd London Field Ambulance. 3rd Division at night. A.D.M.S. visited 2/2 Horse Inf. and 2/5 Yorkes St. Ink. at BLAIRVILLE early and at FICHEUX at dusk (8pm). Also visited R.A.M.C. at XVII Corps H.qrs. FUSSEUX (moving to BRETONCOURT). 2/5th Horse St. Ambre at GOUY — else very busy with sick, mostly wounded, including German P.W. & — 2/4 K. Lancs Operation Order No. 3 of. Sgt. Kidd. going into line in night — A.D.S. APPENDIX D.	
	28.8.18		Sgt. Sm in H.R. in Mercatel: very Headqrs moved early from BARGEUX to BLAIRVILLE QUARRIES. 2/2 Horse St. Ambee. Place moved	

WAR DIARY
or
INTELLIGENCE SUMMARY

Army Form C. 2118.

Place	Date	Hour	Summary of Events and Information	Remarks and references to Appendices
	2/9/18		Fm FICHEUX, X HENIN-SUR-COJEUL with R.S. Sn (?) in front of HENIN and on finishing line near CROISILLES. A.D.M.S. visited see of these. 11/2 Inf Bde easily attained its objective & encountered nil opposition; met M.G. wounds, Lang popular fight. Evacuation satisfactory at X from R.S.A.A.M. A.D.M.S. visited from R.D.S. proceeding satisfactorily.	
	29.8.18		A.D.M.S. visited Advanced M.D.S. when five separate scenarios of wounded from guns & head were satisfactory for evacuation of yesterday afternoon. Regimental Bearers ready to carry back from R.A.P. A.D.M.S. saw OC of Thames St Ambce and OC 5/L.N. Lanc. Field Ambce. Stated his activities infantry A.D.M.S. visited A.D. Dressing St at Henin — HINDENBURG LINE. Arrangements fairly satisfactory but no congestion of wounded. Visited C.R.S. (3/3 Thames Ambce) at GOUY.	

Army Form C. 2118.

WAR DIARY
or
INTELLIGENCE SUMMARY.
(Erase heading not required.)

Place	Date	Hour	Summary of Events and Information	Remarks and references to Appendices
	Aug 30th		ADMS appeared early to Advanced H.Q. Tel ADMS to HENIN and HINDENBERG A.D.Sn. are going smoothly. Arranged for evacuation of A.D.S in front of rank put of CROISILLES – FONTAINES-LES-CROISILLES and new formed. New line of evacuation to be by CROISILLES - HENIN road. Corps M.O. Gribini meets to BOIRY - BECQUERELLE.	
" 31st		Troops in fighting to day. road inside new Advance Dressing and Car Collecting Post at CROISILLES and FONTAINE-LES-CROISILLES. See new Medical arrangement issued to day. Received Divisional Order Appendix E that 171st Infantry Brigade would attack at 5.30 a.m. to-morrow.	

31.8.18.

.... Colonel, A. Med. S.
A.D.M.S. 57th (W.L.) Division.

SECRET

APPENDIX "A"

M.S. 288/24.

MEDICAL ARRANGEMENTS.

57th. Division.

Ref. Maps 51 C, 1/40,000
51 B, 1/40,000
LENS 11, 1/100,000

1. **LOCATIONS.**

   Headquarters of Field Ambulances:-

2/2nd. Wessex F. Amb.	AGNEZ LES DUISANS,	L.1.c.5.5.
2/3rd. Wessex F. Amb.	HAUTE-AVESNES,	E.22.d.8.7.
3/2nd. W.Lanc.F. Amb.	ST. CATHERINE,	G.15.a.1.5.

MAIN DRESSING STATION	ST. CATHERINE,	G.15.a.1.5.
ADVANCED DRESSING STATIONS	L'ABBAYETTE,	H.14.b.6.2.
(Reserve)	QUARRIES,	H.13.b.4.7.
DIVISIONAL REST STATION,	AGNEZ LES DUISANS,	L.1.c.5.5.
CAR COLLECTING POST,	QUARRIES,	H.13.b.4.7.

   REGIMENTAL AID POSTS.

Left Brigade.	H.16.a.5.6.
Centre Brigade.	H.15.b.3.1.
	H.13.b.4.7.
Right Brigade.	H.19.b.3.2.
	G.29.d.9.4.

   CASUALTY CLEARING STATIONS.

No. 7 Casualty Clearing Station,	LIGNY ST. FLOCHEL.
No. 33 Casualty Clearing Station,	LIGNY ST. FLOCHEL.
No. 42 Casualty Clearing Station,	AUBIGNY.

   SANITARY SECTIONS.

   Forward Area - No. 1 Canadian San. Section, H.Q. - Hopital St. Jean, ARRAS.

   Back Area - No. 2 Canadian San. Section, H.Q. - TILLOY les HERMANVILLE.
   No. 5 Canadian San. Section, H.Q. - MAROEUIL.

2. **METHOD OF EVACUATION.**
   (A) North of River Scarpe.

   (i) From Regimental Aid Posts by hand carry and wheeled stretcher to the A.D.S., L'ABBAYETTE, H.14.b.6.2.

   (ii) From A.D.S., L'ABBAYETTE, H.14.b.6.2. (a) during night - by Divisional Motor Ambulance to Main Dressing Station, ST. CATHERINE, G.15.a.1.5; (b) During day - by wheeled Stretcher to Car Collecting Post, QUARRIES, H.13.b.4.7. thence to Main Dressing Station, ST. CATHERINE, G.15.a.1.5. by Divisional Motor Ambulances.

   (iii) From Main Dressing Station to Casualty Clearing Station by No. 8 M.A.C.

   (B) South of River Scarpe.

   From Regimental Aid Post, RAILWAY TRIANGLE, H.19.b.3.2. by Wheeled Stretcher (or Divisional Motor Ambulance by night) over River Scarpe at BLANGY, thence by Ambulance Car to Main Dressing Station, ST. CATHERINE, G.15.a.1.5.

3. Sick will be evacuated by the same routes as wounded.

-2-

4. All requests from Regimental Medical Officers for extra stretchers, blankets or bearers will be made in writing to M.O. in charge, Advanced Dressing Station, stating (a) approximate number required and (b) map reference of cases requiring evacuation.

Field Ambulance Officers will keep in touch daily with Regimental Medical Officers.

5. DISPOSAL OF CASES.

WOUNDED.

All seriously wounded and those requiring immediate operation, which should include all fractures of the lower extremity, to No. 42 Casualty Clearing Station.

Slightly wounded to Nos. 7 and 33 Casualty Clearing Stations and head wounds fit to travel to No. 33 Casualty Clearing Station.

Self Inflicted Wounds to No. 12 Stationary Hospital, ST. POL.

Gas Cases (Severe) to No 33 and No. 7 C.C.S. Group.
Gas Cases (Slight) to Divisional Rest Stations.

SICK.

(a) Serious Cases to Nos. 33 and No. 7 C.C.S. Group by Field Ambulance Cars.

(b) Slight Cases (i.e. likely to be fit for duty in 14 days) to Divisional Rest Station.

(c) N.Y.D.N. Cases to Divisional Rest Station first, for subsequent disposal to No. 1 C.C.S., WAVRANS.
Officer Commanding, Divisional Rest Station will notify O.C., M.A.C. the number of cases for transfer by 9-0 a.m. daily.

(d) Scabies Cases will be treated in Divisional Rest Station.

(e) Infectious Cases to No. 12 Stationary Hospital by M.A.C. Officers Commanding, Field Ambulance to notify M.A.C. when a case requires transfer; M.A.C. will arrange time of transfer.

Evacuations of sick from Divisional Rest Station will be carried out daily by M.A.C. Cars. Officer Commanding, Divisional Rest Station will notify numbers to M.A.C. by 9-0 a.m. daily.

Eye Cases (Acute) to No. 22 Casualty Clearing Station, PERNES by M.A.C. at any time by notification by Officer Commanding, Field Ambulance.

Eye, Ear, Nose, throat and dental arrangements to be notified later.

(f) Venereal Cases will be evacuated as ordinary sick after authority of A.P.M. has been obtained.

NOTES.

Additional Infantry Bearers.

In the event of active operations the Officer in Charge of Forward Evacuations may call on Infantry Brigades to supply 6 Officers and 144 Other Ranks to act as Auxiliary Stretcher Bearers.

Unfits.

Officers and Other Ranks considered unfit for work in the front line will be seen by the A.D.M.S. at his Office in the Chateau Grounds, ETRUN, by arrangement.

J. H. Dewar
Colonel, A. Med. S.,
A.D.M.S., 57th. Division.

2nd. August, 1918.

N.B.
1. Eye, Ear, Nose and Throat Cases for examination will be sent to 2/2nd Wessex Field Ambulance on the day previous to the allotted day and sent by Motor Amb. Convoy Cars to the Special Casualty Clearing Station referred to in Paras. (i) and (j).
2. Nominal rolls, in duplicate, will accompany the cases showing Division and Corps from which they came, and in the case of Ear, Nose and Throat, in accordance with pro forma given in D.M.S. First Army No.1531 dated 10/12/17. (Issued to F.Ambs. Under my M.2356/40/1 dated 5/8/1918.)
3. Each case is to be in possession of his A.B.64 and the result of the examination will be entered on last page.
4. The cars conveying the patients will remain at the C.C.S. to take the cases back. Should it be necessary to detain cases overnight the required number of cars will be retained.
5. Patients will take their kit, and one day's rations will be carried by patients, orderlies, and car drivers.
6. Officer Commanding, 2/2nd Wessex Field Ambulance will notify O.C.M.A.C. by 8 pm. the day previous to the allotted days of the number of cases for collection on the following morning.

NOTES.

Additional Infantry Bearers.

In the event of active operations the officer in charge of Forward Evacuations may call on Infantry Brigades to supply 6 Officers and 144 Other Ranks to act as Auxiliary Stretcher Bearers.

Unfits.
Officers and Other Ranks considered unfit for work in the front line will be seen by the A.D.M.S. at his Office in the Chateau Grounds, ETRUN, by arrangement.

Colonel, A. Med. S.,
A.D.M.S., 57th Division.

6/8/1918.

Distribution :-
H.Q. 57th Division 'G' and 'Q'.
H.Q. 170th Infantry Brigade.
H.Q. 171st Infantry Brigade.
H.Q. 172nd Infantry Brigade.
O.C. 2/2nd Wessex F. Amb.
O.C. 2/3rd Wessex F. Amb.
O.C. 3/2nd W.Lanc.F. Amb.
A.D.M.S. 52nd Division.
A.D.M.S. 56th Division.
Senior Chaplain, D.C.G's Dept.
Senior Chaplain, P.C's Dept.
C.R.E. 57th Division.
C.R.A. 57th Division.
O.C. 57th Divisional Signal Coy.
O.C. 57th Battn. M.G. Corps.
O.C. 2/5th N. Lan. R. (P)
O.C. 57th Div. Train.
O.C. 57th M.T. Coy.
D.A.D.V.S., 57th Div.
A.P.M., 57th Division.
R.M.O's 57th Division.
O.C. 57th Div.Reception Camp.
O.C. No. 8 M. A. C.
D.G.O., 57th Division.
M.O. 57th Div.Reception Camp.
D.M.S., First Army.
D.D.M.S., XVII Corps.

5. DISPOSAL OF CASES.

   Sick - continued.

   (f) Evacuations of sick from Divisional Rest Station will be carried out daily by M.A.C. Cars. Officer Commanding, Divisional Rest Station will notify the numbers to M.A.C. by 9 am. daily.

   (g) Venereal Cases will be evacuated as ordinary sick after authority of A.P.M. has been obtained.

   (h) Dental cases.
   A. Officers. Medical Officers i/c Units will arrange dental appointments for officers direct with O.C. Canadian Dental Centre - AGNEZ LES DUISANS, L.1.c.5.5.

   B. Other Ranks.
   (1) Medical Officers i/c Units will submit to O.C. 2/2nd Wessex Field Ambulance a nominal roll of men requiring dental treatment, in every case specifying No., Rank, Name, and Nature of treatment required. A roster will be kept by Officer Commanding 2/2nd Wessex Field Ambulance and Units will be notified when such men should report.
   (2) A Dental Officer from 57th C.C.S. will undertake treatment of 57th Divisional cases at the Divisional Rest Station (L.1.c.5.5.) at 10 am. on Tuesdays, Thursdays and Saturdays.
   (3) Not more than 30 cases will be sent to see the Dental Officer on any one day, and every man will take with him A.F. B. 256 (in duplicate, signed by the M.O.) specifying nature of treatment required.
   (4) Cases for evacuation will be sent to No.7 and No.33 C.C.S's.
   (5) Simple extractions will be carried out by Medical Officers.

   (i) Eye Cases. (A) Acute :-
   Eye cases (acute) will be sent to No.22 Casualty Clearing Station, PERNES, by M.A.C. at any time by notification by Officer Commanding, Field Ambulance.

   (B) Ordinary :-
   Officers will be sent to No.22 C.C.S., PERNES, on Saturdays at 9 am.
   Other Ranks will be sent to No.22 C.C.S. PERNES, on Thursdays at 9 am.

   10 Vacancies per week is allotted to the Division. This also includes Corps Troops.

   (j) Ear, Nose and Throat Cases.

   Officers will be sent to No.12 Stationary Hosp. ST.POL on Saturdays at 9 am.
   Other Ranks will be sent to No.12 Staty. Hospital ST.POL on Thursdays at 9 am.

   3 vacancies (to include Corps Troops) are allotted to the Division per week.

- 2 -

METHOD OF EVACUATION (Continued.)

(ii) From A.D.S., L'ABBAYETTE, H.14.b.6.2. (a) During night - by Divisional Motor Ambulance to Main Dressing Station, ST.CATHERINE, G.15.a.1.5.; (B) During day - by wheeled stretcher to Car Collecting Post, QUARRIES, H.13.b.4.7., thence to Main Dressing Station, ST. CATHERINE, G.15.a.1.5. by Divisional Motor Ambulance.

(iii) From Main Dressing Station to Casualty Clearing Station by No.8 M.A.C.

(B) South of River Scarpe.

From R.A.P. Railway Triangle (H.19.b.3.4.).

(a) During night - By Divisional Motor Ambulance to Main Dressing Station , ST.CATHERINE, G.15.a.1.5., crossing the river at BLANGY.

(b) During day - By hand carry along west side of Railway embankment across the river to the QUARRIES, H.13.b.4.7. thence by Motor Ambulance Car to Main Dressing Station, ST. CATHERINE, G.15.a.1.5.

3. Sick will be evacuated by the same routes as wounded.

4. All requests from Regimental Medical Officers for extra stretchers, blankets, or bearers will be made in writing to M.O. i/c Advanced Dressing Station, stating (a) approximate number required and (b) map reference of cases requiring evacuation.

Field Ambulance Officers will keep in touch daily with Regimental Medical Officers.

5. DISPOSAL OF CASES.

WOUNDED. All seriously wounded and those requiring immediate operation, which should include all fractures of the lower extremity , to No. 42 Casualty Clearing Stn.
Slightly wounded to Nos. 7 and 33 Casualty Clearing Stations, and head wounds fit to travel to No.33 Casualty Clearing Station.

Self Inflicted Wounds to No.12 Stationary Hospital, ST.POL.

Gas Cases (severe) to No.33 and No.7 C.C.S. Group.
Gas Cases (slight) to Divisional Rest Station.

SICK.

(a) Serious cases to No .33 and No.7 C.C.S. Group by Field Ambulance Cars.

(b) Slight cases (i.e. likely to be fit for duty in fourteen days) to Divisional Rest Station.

(c) N.Y.D.N. Cases to Divisional Rest Station first, for subsequent disposal to No.1 C.C.S., WAVRANS. Officer Commanding, Divisional Rest Station will notify O.C. M.A.C. the number of cases for transfer by 9 am. daily.

(d) Scabies cases will be treated in Divisional Rest Station.

(e) Infectious cases to No.12 Stationary Hospital by M.A.C. Officers Commanding, Field Ambulances to notify O.C., M.A.C. when a case requires transfer; M.A.C. will arrange time of transfer.

SECRET.   M.S.288/25.

MEDICAL ARRANGEMENTS.

57th Division.

Ref. Maps. 51 C. 1/40,000.
           51 B. 1/40,000.
           LENS 11 1/100,000.

1. LOCATIONS.

Headquarters of Field Ambulances:-

2/2nd Wessex F.Amb.	AGNEZ LES DUISANS,	L.1.c.5.5.
2/3rd Wessex F.Amb.	HAUTE-AVESNES,	E.22.d.8.7.
3/2nd W.Lancs.F.Amb.	ST. CATHERINE,	G.15.a.1.5.

MAIN DRESSING STATION	ST CATHERINE.	G.15.a.1.5.
ADVANCED DRESSING STATIONS	L'ABBAYETTE,	H.14.b.6.2.
(Reserve)	QUARRIES,	H.13.b.4.7.
DIVISIONAL REST STATION.	AGNEZ LES DUISANS,	L.1.c.5.5.
CAR COLLECTING POST.	QUARRIES,	H.13.b.4.7.

REGIMENTAL AID POSTS.

Left Brigade.	Line,	H.16.a.5.6.
	Support,	H.14.a.0.9.
Centre Brigade.	Line,	H.15.b.3.1.
	Support,	H.13.b.5.5.
Right Brigade.	Line,	H.19.b.3.4.
	Support,	G.29.d.9.4.

NOTE:- R.A.M.C. Bearers are stationed at the 3 R.A.P's of the Battalions holding the Line

R.A.M.C Posts.   G.24.a.5.6.
                              G.23.b.9.3.

CASUALTY CLEARING STATIONS.

No. 7 Casualty Clearing Station,	LIGNY ST. FLOCHEL.
No.33 Casualty Clearing Station,	LIGNY St. FLOCHEL.
No.42 Casualty Clearing Station,	AUBIGNY.

SANITARY SECTIONS.

Forward Area - No. 1 Canadian San. Section, H.Q. - Hopital St. John, ARRAS.

Back Area   - No. 2 Canadian San. Section, H.Q.,- TILLOY les HERMAVILLE.
              No. 5 Canadian San. Section, H.Q. - MAROEUIL.

ADVANCED DEPOT MEDICAL STORES.

No. 33 Advanced Depot Medical Stores, SAVY.

MOBILE LABORATORIES.

No. 2 Mobile (Bacteriological) Laboratory.	AUBIGNY.
No. 6. " (Hygiene) Laboratory.	AUBIGNY.

2. METHOD OF EVACUATION
(a) North of River Scarpe.

(q) (1) From Regimental Aid Posts by hand carry and wheeled stretcher to the A.D.S., L'ABBAYETTE. H.14.b.6.2.

APPENDIX "B"

ADDENDUM TO MEDICAL ARRANGEMENTS, 57th DIVISION
ISSUED UNDER M.S.288/25, dated 8. 8. 1918.

At 9.am on 7. 8. 18. the 42nd C. C. S. will close: at the same hour No. 57 C. C. S. will open at MINGOVAL for the reception of cases seriously wounded.

SECRET.   57th. DIVISION.   APPENDIX "C"   M.S. 296/5.
                  R.A.M.C. OPERATION ORDER NO. 29.
                           Reference Map Sheet LENS, 11, 1/100,000.
                                              Copy No.........
   1.   INFORMATION.

        (a) 57th. Division (less 170th. Infantry Brigade Group) will
            be relieved in the line between August 16th. and August
            19th. by 51st. Division.

        (b) For purposes of relief the 2/2nd. Wessex Field Ambulance
            and 3/2nd. West Lancs. Field Ambulance will be included
            in 171st. Infantry Brigade Group and the 2/3rd. Wessex
            Field Ambulance in 172nd. Infantry Brigade Group.

        (c) Movements of personnel will take place by light railway
            or bus. Transport will proceed by road. Further
            details will be issued subsequently.

        (d) On completion of relief the Division will concentrate
            as follows :-

                Div. H.Q.   CHELERS.
                                           ROELLECOURT.
                Div. Artillery.   ST. MICHEL.
                                           OSTREVILLE.
                                           MONCHY LE BRETON.
                171st. Inf. Bde. Group.   MAGNICOURT.
                                           ORLENCOURT.
                                           LA THIEULOYE.
                                           TINQUES.
                172nd. Inf. Bde. Group.   FREVILLERS.
                                           BAILLEUL AUX CORNAILLES.
                2/5th. N. Lan. R. (P).   MARQUAY.
                57th. Bn. M.G. Corps.   LIGNY ST. FLOCHEL.

        2/2nd. Wessex Field Ambulance.)
        3/2nd. W. Lanc. F. Ambulance.) will be stationed at HOUVELIN,
        and 2/3rd. Wessex Field Ambulance at FREVILLERS and
        thereafter will be under Brigade Arrangements.

   2.   RELIEFS.

        (a) 3/2nd. West Lancs. Field Ambulance will be relieved at
            ST. CATHERINE by 10-0 a.m. on 18th. August by 1/2nd.
            Highland Field Ambulance.
            2/2nd. Wessex Field Ambulance will be relieved at the
            Divisional Rest Station at AGNEZ LES DUISANS by 10-0 a.m.
            on the 18th. August by the 2/1st. Highland Field
            Ambulance
                Details of relief to be arranged between Field
            Ambulance Commanders concerned.
            2/3rd. Wessex Field Ambulance site will not be taken over
            by 51st. Division. The Ambulance will be prepared to
            move at 8-0 a.m. on the 17th. August.

        (b) Completion of reliefs will be reported to this Office
            by use of the code word "FINIS".

        (c) All maps will be handed over to relieving units.

        (d) Receipts (in duplicate) of all (a) Ordnance, (b) Medical
            and (c) Trench and Area Stores will be forwarded to
            reach this Office by noon 19/8/18.

        (e) A.D.M.S. Office will close at ETRUN at 9-0 a.m. 19/8/18
            and open at CHELERS at the same hour.

                                              W.G. McKenzie
                                          for Capt. A/DADMS
                                              Colonel, A. Med. S.,
   15th. August, 1918.   A.D.M.S., 57th. Division.

                                                              P.T.O.

Issued at....9-0........ p.m.

DISTRIBUTION:-

Copy No. 1 to H.Q., 57th. Division, 'Q'.
       2   H.Q., 57th. Division, 'G'.
       3   H.Q., 170th. Infantry Brigade.
       4   H.Q., 171st. Infantry Brigade.
       5   H.Q., 172nd. Infantry Brigade.
       6   O.C., 2/2nd Wessex Field Ambulance.
       7.   O.C., 2/3rd Wessex Field Ambulance.
       8.   O.C., 3/2nd W.Lancs.Field Ambulance.
       9.   A.D.M.S., 15th Division.
     10.   A.D.M.S. 51st Division.
     11.   A.D.M.S., 52nd Division.
     12.   A.D.M.S., 56th Division.
     13.   C.R.A., 57th Division.
     14.   C.R.E., 57th Division.
     15.   O.C., 57th Divisional Signal Coy.
     16.   O.C., 57th Battn. M. G. Corps.
     17.   O.C., 2/5th N. Lan. R. (P).
     18.   O.C., 57th Divisional Train.
     19.   D.A.D.S.S., 57th Division.
     20.   D.G.O., 57th Division.
     21.   A.P.M., 57th Division.
     22.   D.M.S., First Army.
     23.   D.D.M.S., XVII Corps.
     24.   War Diary.
     25.   War Diary.
     26.   File.
     27.   File.
     28.   Spare.

SECRET.   M.S.302/28.

APPENDIX "D"

R.A.M.C. 57th Division Operation Order No. 30.
==

Ref.Map Sheet 51.B. 1/40,000

1. 57th Division will relieve 52nd Division on 27/28th August, relief being carried out as far as possible by day.

   2/2nd Wessex Field Ambulance will take over the A.D.S's of 2nd and 3rd Lowland Field Ambulances at N.33.c.7.5. and T.3.a.5.2. or such other sites as may have replaced these.

2. The bearers of the 3/2nd West Lancs Field Ambulance will be available to augment the bearer Division of 2/2nd Wessex Field Ambulance.

3. Transport of these will remain at FICHEUX.

4. 2/3rd Wessex Field Ambulance will remain at GOUY at Corps Rest Station.

5. At midnight 27/28th August A.D.M.S. Office (Advanced) will open at M.34.d.8.3.
   A.D.M.S. Office (Rear) will remain at BASSEUX until further notice.
   Correspondence relating to Operations will be addressed "A.D.M.S.(Advanced)".
   Routine correspondence to "A.D.M.S.(Rear)".

6. Acknowledge (Field Ambulances only).

Colonel,
(sd) T.F.DEWAR, A.Med.S.
A.D.M.S., 57th Division.

27/8/18.

Distribution :-

    Headquarters, 57th Division 'G'.
    Headquarters, 57th Division 'Q'.
    Headquarters, 170th Infantry Brigade.
    Headquarters, 171st Infantry Brigade.
    Headquarters, 172nd Infantry Brigade.
    O.C., 2/2nd Wessex Field Ambulance.
    O.C., 2/3rd Wessex Field Ambulance.
    O.C., 3/2nd W.Lancs. Fd. Ambulance.
    O.C., 57th Divisional Train.
    A.D.M.S., 52nd Division.
    A.D.M.S., 56th Division.
    A.D.M.S., 2nd Canadian Division.
    D.D.M.S., 17th Corps.
    D.M.S., Third Army.

APPENDIX "E"

SECRET.   M.S.302/56.

PROVISIONAL MEDICAL ARRANGEMENTS, 57th DIVISION.

Ref. Map Sheet, 51C.
1/40,000.

1. The Regimental Aid Posts of Battalions in line are as follows :-
    U.8.b.7.4.
    U.9.a.3.4.
    U.8.b.1.8.

2. Car Collecting Post at FONTAINE - LES - CROISILLES, U.2.c.5.4.
   Car Collecting Post on FONTAINE - CROISILLES Road, T.18.c.9.7.

3. Advanced Dressing Station,   CROISILLES,   T.17.c.9.4.

4. Corps Main Dressing Station, BOIRY-BECQUERELLE,   T.1.c.3.8.

5. The Officer Commanding, 2/2nd Wessex Field Ambulance, with Headquarters at CROISILLES, T.17.c.9.4., is Officer i/c Forward Evacuation.

6. Office of A.D.M.S. (Advanced) is in HENINEL,   N.28.c.8.4
   - do -   (Rear) at BLAIRVILLE QUARRY, R.34.d.5.2.

7. Evacuation Routes. From Regimental Aid Posts to Car Collecting Post by hand carry: thence to A.D.S. by Motor Ambulance Car or wheeled stretcher carriage: thence to Corps Main Dressing Station by Field Ambulance motor by alternative roads: thence to Casualty Clearing Station at BAC - DU - SUD by M.A. Convoy.

8. Walking wounded as above: except that from Corps Main Dressing Station they go by lorry to Corps Rest Station, GOUY (2/3rd Wessex Field Ambulance) and thence by Light Rly.

9. Regimental Medical Officers must immediately report in writing all changes in the situation of their R.A.P's. to the Advanced Dressing Station or Officer i/c Bearers: he, in turn, will maintain touch continuously with the Regimental Medical Officer.

10. Application for additional bearers, stretchers, blankets, splints or dressings to be made in writing to Advanced Dressing Station or Bearer Officer.

J.F.Dewar

Colonel, A. Med. S.,
A.D.M.S., 57th Division.

31/8/18.

P.T.O.

Distribution :-

Headquarters, 57th Division 'G'.
Headquarters, 57th Division 'Q'.
Headquarters, 170th Infantry Brigade.
Headquarters, 171st Infantry Brigade.
Headquarters, 172nd Infantry Brigade.
O.C. 2/2nd Wessex Field Ambulance.
O.C. 2/3rd Wessex Field Ambulance.
O.C., 3/2nd W.Lancs.Fld. Ambulance.
D.A.D.V.S., 57th Division.
A.P.M., 57th Division.
Gas Officer, 57th Division.
Senior Chaplain, P.C's Dept.
Senior Chaplain, D.C.G's Dept.
A.D.M.S., 1st Can. Division.
A.D.M.S., 52nd Division.
A.D.M.S., 58th Division.
A.D.M.S., 63rd Division.
O.C. 9 Infantry Battalions.
M.Os.all Regimental Units.
O.C., 57th Divisional Train.
O.C., 57th Battn. Machine Gun Corps.
O.C., 57th Signal Coy.
O.C., 2/5th N. Lan. R. (P).
C.R.A., 57th Division.
C.R.E., 57th Division.
D.D.M.S., XVII Corps.
D.M.S., Third Army.

DISTRIBUTION :-

Copy No. 1 to H.Q., 57th Division 'G'.
    2   H.Q., 57th Division 'Q'.
    3   H.Q., 170th Infantry Brigade.
    4   H.Q., 171st Infantry Brigade.
    5   H.Q., 172nd Infantry Brigade.
    6   O.C., 2/2nd Wessex Field Ambulance.
    7   O.C., 2/3rd Wessex Field Ambulance.
    8   O.C., 3/2nd W.Lancs Field Ambulance.
    9   A.D.M.S., 52nd Division.
   10   A.D.M.S., 56th Division.
   12   Senior Chaplain, D.C.G's Dept.
   13   Senior Chaplain, P.C's Dept.
   14   C.R.E., 57th Division.
   15   C.R.A., 57th Division.
   16   O.C., 57th Div'l Signal Company.
   17   O.C., 57th Bn. M.G.Corps.
   18   O.C., 2/5th N.Lan.R. (P).
   19   O.C., 57th Divisional Train.
   20   D.A.D.V.S. 57th Division.
   21   D.G.O., 57th Division.
   22   A.P.M., 57th Division.
   23   O.C., 57th Div'l Reception Camp.
   24   M.O.i/c., 57th Div'l Reception Camp.
   25   O.C., 57th M.T.Company.
   26   O.C., No. 8 M.A.C.
   27   ALL R.M.O's 57th Division.
   28   D.M.S., First Army.
   29   D.D.M.S., XVII Corps.

Confidential

September 1918

War Diary

of

A.D.M.S. 57th Division

from 1st Sept- to 30th Sept

1918

VOL. 19.

Army Form C. 2118.

WAR DIARY
or
INTELLIGENCE SUMMARY.
(Erase heading not required.)

Place	Date	Hour	Summary of Events and Information	Remarks and references to Appendices
Late Brill / BLAIRVILLE	1/9/18	—	A.D.M.S. visited A.D.Ss. & Car Collecting Post re Croisilles very few. Received orders that attack to be renewed at 6 p.m. by 57th Division probably to be relieved by (63rd R.N.) Division right of left 3/8th. Later orders received to the effect that 57th Div with Canadian Corps on left + 52nd Division were attack at 5 a.m. 2nd and that 63rd Div. were push through carry on.	
"	2/9/18		Great attack started A.R.E.C. at 6 a.m. Steady but not excessive work during the night. Advance rapid so that by 10 a.m. 63rd Division passing through fighting line. In the afternoon A.R.M.S. visited Corps Rest Station (2/3 Monmouth Ambce.) at GOUY — 600 700 patients.	
"	3/9/18	—	Quiet day. Brigades to of 57th Division were withdrawn for re-organisation. 2/2 Wessex Fd. Ambce and Vehicles collected at CROISILLES, except one Officer 100 men at foot at HENDE COURT. Later attacks effecting and when of 2/3 Monmouth Fd Ambce and 2/2 W Lancs Field Ambulance will	

A5834 Wt. W4973/M687. 750,000 8/16 D. D. & L. Ltd. Forms/C.2118/13.

WAR DIARY or INTELLIGENCE SUMMARY

Army Form C. 2118.

Place	Date	Hour	Summary of Events and Information	Remarks and references to Appendices
BLAIRVILLE S 9 B			Have no notes embodied returned to their units. D.A.D.M.S returned from leave (1 month). Sick admissions continue rather high. August extremely low. Wounded figures (from A.F. W3185) for ten days up to noon yesterday.	

	Officers	Other Ranks
9 am Aug 28th to noon Aug 29th	12	240.
" 29th " " 30th	9	326.
" 30th " " 31st	5	145.
" Aug 31st " " Sept 1st	1	63.
" Sept 1st " " 2nd	—	—
" 2nd " " 3rd	3	104.
	4	144
	34	1047

There were no evacuations of cases admitted through Canadian Field Ambulances, all but 19 of 94 counted in R.A. of Division.

57th Division relieving us on P.M. A.D.M.S. discussed with Div't Commandant on detail the evacuation of wounded Aug 28—Sept 2nd inclusive.

4.9.18.

WAR DIARY or INTELLIGENCE SUMMARY

Army Form C. 2118.

Place	Date	Hour	Summary of Events and Information	Remarks and references to Appendices
BLAIRVILLE H.Q 18.	5.9.18.		The suggested Advanced Dressing Station might have moved forward more quickly. A.D.M.S. visited 2/2nd W.Staff. F.Amb. and discussed the same subject with a view of improving the arrangements in future. 57th Division settling in west; Brigade reorganizing. A.D.M.S. visited approximately 15,000. Fighting strength (Inf.) approx 6,000. A.D.M.S. visited C.P.S Pte. Station (2/3rd Western F.Amb.) GOUY. 900 patients here. Planned scheme of evacuation of Papelhart 57th Div. wounded return to 63rd Divisional line (in front of CAMBRAI) on Sept 7-8th. A.D.M.S. visited Advanced Headquarters 2/2nd O.C. 2/2nd Western F.Amb. regarding details of relief. A.D.M.S. attended conference of A.D'sM.S. at office of D.D.M.S. XVII Corps. BRETONCOURT at which operating details of evacuation were discussed for next advance. French (New O.C. 2/2nd Western F.Amb.) their Operation Order 1.	Appendix # A 3
	6.9.18		Battalion moved 3½" Div. Operation Order No 31.	Appendix #

Army Form C. 2118.

WAR DIARY
or
INTELLIGENCE SUMMARY.
(Erase heading not required.)

Place	Date	Hour	Summary of Events and Information	Remarks and references to Appendices
BLAIRVILLE			In short, men furnished are given effects as : viz (1) about attachment of Bearer Officers to Infantry Brigades (1 to each); and (2) amount of reporting return (a) Advance Dressing Stations and (b) Forward Evacuation.	
	7.9.18.		I received arrangement as accompanying Operation Order Appendix B. A.D.M.S. 57th Div. visited A.D.M.S. 63rd Division BLAIRVILLE 06031. reporting strength and relief. Also visited Corps of Field Ambulance GOUY where O.C. 2/3rd N. Midd. F. Amb. unaware with what was in forward. Co/2nd V Lanc. F. Amb gave orders to move from FICHEUX to CROISILLES and advanced Divisional headquarters which is to move	
QUEANT	8.9.18.		forwards from near HENINEL to east of QUEANT. Divisional Headquarters moved forward to near QUEANT. ADMS from near HENINEL (advance) and BLAIRVILLE QUARRIES (rear) to within 800 yards west of QUEANT. Headquarters 2/1st Wessex F. Amb. and	

WAR DIARY
or
INTELLIGENCE SUMMARY.

(Erase heading not required.)

Army Form C. 2118.

Instructions regarding War Diaries and Intelligence Summaries are contained in F. S. Regs., Part II. and the Staff Manual respectively. Title pages will be prepared in manuscript.

Place	Date	Hour	Summary of Events and Information	Remarks and references to Appendices
NEAR QUEANT	8.9.18		3/2nd N. Zealand F. Amb. at CAGNICOURT shelled last night and this morning. 3/2nd N. Zeal. F. Amb. moving to existing ex German Hospital, QUEANT tonight. ADMS visited 3/2nd N. Zeal. F. Amb. at CAGNICOURT. They are moved to extend to CROISILLES tomorrow. ADMS visited 2/2nd N. Zea. F. Amb. Officer Comdg. states all sites of enemy hospital at QUEANT unit busy on repair work. 3/2nd N. Zea. F. Amb. have returned to CROISILLES. 1/1st Inf. Bn. looking where Corps Limit — all stores transferred via him. ADMS visited RAP's 2/6th and 2/4th 18th Hnd Rover INCHY E. N. ARTOIS 1/4th Inf. Bn. taking over from 1st Canc. Guards Division on night tonight.	
	10.9.18		6pm Divisional Boundary extended Northwards last night. Comparatively little hostile activity on Divisional frontal present. 26 wounded sent back to day b.	

Army Form C. 2118.

WAR DIARY
or
INTELLIGENCE SUMMARY.
(Erase heading not required.)

Place	Date	Hour	Summary of Events and Information	Remarks and references to Appendices
Near QUEANT.	10.9.18		Arrangements for dental treatment of Divisional troops are now in anticipation; they are constantly changing, and rarely convenient to those principally concerned. The arrangements which generally in the New Zealand Division by which a dental surgeon with equipment forms an inalienable part of the Divisional Establishment is worthy of imitation in British Divisions. Their patter in the American system with mine dental officers per Division who do everything including and surgeon work when required and who accompany detachment into the line for that purpose. The system of manrie returns in the B.E.F. suffers from lack of uniformity and information. In the various Armies were seen and the general Corps intently different returns (hither in regard to list of returns and nature and form of each) are required from A.D'M.S' of Divisions. This appears even to such matters as	

WAR DIARY
INTELLIGENCE SUMMARY.
(Erase heading not required.)

Army Form C. 2118.

Place	Date	Hour	Summary of Events and Information	Remarks and references to Appendices
QUEANT	27.9.18		Inspections carried out this morning when the conditions in each Army area were identical of producing a great movement and great quantity of dust and enemy planes flew this morning which seemed ground in nothing but intense personal protections. 140th and 141st Cdns notified enemy INCHY-EN-ARTOIS and CANAL DU NORD this evening at 6.15. Army circulars requested, special arrangements made to cope with these. A.D.M.S. visited Advanced Dressing Station of 2/2nd M Amb. QUEANT. They admitted 147 wounded from 6 p.m. to 6 a.m. — 94 sitting and 53 lying cases. (140 Bn 34 + 15 = 82 ; 141 Bn 24 + 36 = 95) and about 40 stretcher cases to 11 a.m. Evacuation reported satisfactory no enemy expected. Sugar wounded German also treated.	
	28.9.18		A.D.M.S. visited 2/2nd Western F. Amb. QUEANT and 3/2nd M. F. Amb.	

J. Amb.

Army Form C. 2118.

WAR DIARY
or
INTELLIGENCE SUMMARY.
(Erase heading not required.)

Instructions regarding War Diaries and Intelligence Summaries are contained in F. S. Regs. Part II. and the Staff Manual respectively. Title pages will be prepared in manuscript.

Place	Date	Hour	Summary of Events and Information	Remarks and references to Appendices
QUEANT	13.9.18		near CROISILLES. Learn that 52nd Division to be relieved by 53rd Division on 16-17th. Arranged with A.D.M.S. 52nd Division for relief of Field Ambulances & Evacuation (2/2nd W. Essex Fd. Amb.) to be completed by 5p.m. on 16th.	Appendix III
M.Q.H.	15.9.18		Seen R.A.M.C. Officers about O.R.2. A.D.M.S. views Sec 18 Army Reorganising reinforcements. Hear that Capts and Quartermasters H. Ruddy, 2/1st W. Essex Fd. Amb. has been granted six months leave on business grounds. 2/2nd W. Essex Fd. Amb. moved from QUEANT to near CROISILLES in 141st Bde Group.	
	16.9.18		52nd Division on relief by 53rd Division moved into lay out. Headquarters from QUEANT to BAVINCOURT. 170th Inf Bde with 2/1st W. Lanc. Fd. Amb. to GOUY AUX. 141st Inf Bde with 2/2nd W. Essex Fd. Amb.	
BAVINCOURT	17.9.18			

Army Form C. 2118.

WAR DIARY
or
INTELLIGENCE SUMMARY.

(Erase heading not required.)

Instructions regarding War Diaries and Intelligence Summaries are contained in F. S. Regs., Part II. and the Staff Manual respectively. Title pages will be prepared in manuscript.

Place	Date	Hour	Summary of Events and Information	Remarks and references to Appendices
DAVINCOURT	14/9/18		1st SAVILY Area, and 142nd Inf Bde is BAILLEULMONT — BAILLEULVAL Area. A.D.M.S. visited 2/3rd Western F. Amb. administering Corps Rest Station at GOUY. Captain FINDLAY, Medical Officer i/c 57th D.A.C. reported to duty from Hospital. Place on recovery from illness.	
	16.9.18		A.D.M.S. visited all Divisional Field Ambulances, 1/6th N. Fus R.P. at BARLY and Divisional Baths at SAULTY and BARLY.	
	19.9.18		Since admission rate which has been unusually low since Aug 1st has been higher Sept 15-19 probably a result of long marches in the field without rest or change. Number figures (admitted to other Dressing Stations from 5 Yorks Division) for period Aug 20 – Sept 19 is inclusive have been as follows:— Aug 20 – 27 y/m " 28 – 31 m Sept 1 – 3 m " 4 – 11 m " 12 – 15 m " 16 – 19 m	469 509 y/m 349 452 1st C.C

WAR DIARY
or
INTELLIGENCE SUMMARY.
(Erase heading not required.)

Army Form C. 2118.

Instructions regarding War Diaries and Intelligence Summaries are contained in F. S. Regs., Part II. and the Staff Manual respectively. Title pages will be prepared in manuscript.

Place	Date	Hour	Summary of Events and Information	Remarks and references to Appendices
BAVINCOURT	20-9-18		Conference of Medical officers in A.D.M.S. Office this afternoon.	
			Twenty-one M.O.'s present. A.D.M.S. visited Corps Rest station (7/3rd N Sean. Field Ambulance) GOUY-EN-ARTOIS. 5/2 N.M. Sean. t. Amb. is moving from GOUY-EN-ARTOIS to BLAIRVILLE.	
	21-9-18		A.D.M.S. visited Divisional BAILLEULVAL and GOUY; 1/3rd W. Sean. t. Amb. at Hautes; and 1st Uffordbander Hut. at BAILLEUL MONT. 1st Lieut. (A.P.M.) MORE USA. reported for duty after dismal (reinforcement). Attry Captain G.E. ANDERSON arrived as reinforcement. Division now has Several officers deficient.	
		2.30 p.m	A.D.M.S. visited 2/5 N S D. Sean. Div. regarding hospd. Requirements, fitting etc. Also visited 1/3rd W. Seaman t. Amb. (C.R. Sn.) GOUY, and saw all cases of trench nephritis. Received preliminary instruction regarding operation to commence shortly gently shared by Canadian XVII Corps & VI Corps.	

WAR DIARY
or
INTELLIGENCE SUMMARY.

Army Form C. 2118.

Place	Date	Hour	Summary of Events and Information	Remarks and references to Appendices
	23.9.18		ADMI worked H/Qrs Bn. J. Sand et jour and 2/Lt N Luck (B) at ST LEGER and 1/2 Manor St Aubre, at BLAIRVILLE.	APPENDIX D
	24.9.18		ADMI issued draft Tactical arrangement. Annexes immediate engagement in retail with BR 1/2 Manor St Aubre. ADMI visited BAILLEUVAL and Bn Hrs re. 1/2 Manor St. Aub. & 3/R N.F. St. Aubree moved forward to day to L. QUEANT. ADM group as 1/2 Manor S. Aub regarding details of counter attacks of N.O. re, ADM visits 1/2 Michael St. Aubree. et BLAIRVILLE and later D.A.&M. to Division.	
	25.9.18		A.D.M. visited 1/2 Manor & Aubre at OUY. Issued instruct arranged for attack to resume 1/2 Manor & Aubre and 1/2 Michael St. Aub, moved yesterday to LAGNICOURT. ADMI visited 1/2 Manor & Aub. at LAGNICOURT. Rationed Headquarters.	

Place	Date	Hour	Summary of Events and Information	Remarks and references to Appendices
K.9.A			moved from Barracks to QUÉANT. Pushed forward to ? Guns through their depth to compress at 5.30 am. 9 officers & ? men through 63 Division (with 1st Otago) at 10.70 am. S/o Herron & Lieut. and S/o Shane & Anker. Toward up the attack to near LOUVERVAL when the Battle Hd 5 men killed and 7 wounded. As Herron became sick on with Hinchman by sick pass at 10 am. At 11 am a ? attack moved to BOURSIES when S/o Herron the killed when Shane & Lieut on (covering) ? on the BAPAUME-CAMBRAI Road. Menses & Ahd in Resembling Post in the BAPAUME-CAMBRAI Road met the Lind Br Tup. Ahd muntes them placed & Great attack forward at R.O.S.	APPENDIX "E"
K.9.B			attack of 9th Division having been held up yesterday am seemed to day at 5.30 am. Shortly by 17th & 19th Inf Brigades Rhd under R.O.S. of BOURSIES at noon and with

Army Form C. 2118.

WAR DIARY
or
INTELLIGENCE SUMMARY.
(Erase heading not required.)

Instructions regarding War Diaries and Intelligence Summaries are contained in F. S. Regs., Part II. and the Staff Manual respectively. Title pages will be prepared in manuscript.

Place	Date	Hour	Summary of Events and Information	Remarks and references to Appendices
	28.9.18		A.D.M.S. XVII Corps went in P.M. near AMNEUX. Tony for remainder through. No News of Unit. Moving in the afternoon to H.Qtrs. at in CAMBRAI-BAPAUME Rd - about 3/4 mile E of enemy at E.29.c.9.5.8. Rec'd Ord'r H'ters with A.D.M.S. Office moved up 7pm from RUZANT to E of Syned. D.17.a.8.2.	
	29.9.18		A.D.M.S. visits the various D.routes in CAMBRAI BAPAUME Rd. Very few casualties, difficulty when experienced in keeping touch with Bearer Officers, 47th & 78 F.A. Rd & walks 3/2 Bearer & Ambces ADS by Canal when it was crossed by BAPAUNE-CAMBRAI Road	
	30.9.18		A.D.M.S. visited 34 Rcvng & Ambce which had gone in H.Q.S. by BAPAUME-CAMBRAI Rd. past N of FONTAINES-NOTRE-DAMES. Road turned 1/2 Bearer & Amb. was back at Canal DE L'ESCAUT. just N of CANTAING. Rear divisional Hangueles from zone	

Army Form C. 2118.

WAR DIARY
or
INTELLIGENCE SUMMARY.
(Erase heading not required.)

Instructions regarding War Diaries and Intelligence Summaries are contained in F. S. Regs., Part II. and the Staff Manual respectively. Title pages will be prepared in manuscript.

Place	Date	Hour	Summary of Events and Information	Remarks and references to Appendices
	30.9.18		To LYNX trench by BEAUNE - CAMBRAI road, thence from BOURSIES to FONTAINE.	

y.g.Burton
..........Colonel, A. Med. S
A.D.M.S. 57th (W.L.) Division.

SECRET.   Copy No. 30

57th DIVISION R.A.M.C. OPERATION ORDER NO. 31.   M.S. 306/4.

Ref.Map Sht.51B.& 51C.,
1/40,000.

1.   57th Division (less Artillery) will relieve 63rd Divn. (less Artillery) in the line on 7/8th September. The Divisional Front extends from E.14.a.8.0. to W.26.c.3.0.

2.   The O.C., 2/2nd Wessex Field Ambulance, will be in charge of evacuation of all cases from the forward area up to the Advanced Dressing Station. He will have at his disposal all the bearer personnel of the Field Ambulances of the Division, all the horse ambulance wagons and wheeled stretcher carriages. His Headquarters will be at the Collecting Post if in advance of Advanced Dressing Station.

3.   The Officer Commanding, 3/2nd W.Lancs.Field Ambulance, with his Tent Division will have charge of the Advanced Dressing Station. At his disposal will be placed all the motor ambulance cars of the Division except two which will be retained by the O.C. 2/3rd Wessex Field Ambulance for use at the Corps Rest Station. The O.C. 3/2nd W.Lancs. Field Ambulance will also have at his disposal on application to No.15 Motor Ambulance Convoy, at Corps Main Dressing Station, two lorries to be used between the Advanced Dressing Station and the Corps Main Dressing Stn.

4.   The O.C., 2/3rd Wessex Field Ambulance with his Tent Division will continue in charge of the Corps Rest Station, GOUY.

5.   Under the O.C. 2/2nd Wessex Field Ambulance, a Bearer Officer and R.A.M.C. Personnel will be attached to each Brigade; and to each Infantry Battalion 4 R.A.M.C. Bearers and 1 Runner.

6.   When so ordered by the Division, Auxiliary Bearers (6 Officers and 144 Other Ranks) will be distributed as follows :- 1 Officer and approximately 24 Other Ranks to work with each Brigade. The remaining 3 Officers and 72 Other Ranks in Reserve.

7.   Detailed arrangements for evacuation of wounded to be issued by O.C. 2/2nd Wessex Field Ambulance: and details of relief by him and by the O.C. 3/2nd W.Lancs.Field Ambce. respectively of the 150th (R.N.) Field Ambulance to be arranged between the Commanding Officers directly concerned.

8.   Office of A.D.M.S. will be at V.20.c.6.8. after 10 am. on 8th September, by which hour the relief will be complete.

9.   Receipts, in duplicate, of all stores handed or taken over will be forwarded to this Office by 9 am. 10th Septr.

10. Field Ambulances will acknowledge.

J F Dewar.

Colonel, A. Med. S.,
A.D.M.S., 57th Division.

6/9/18.

Issued at 11.30 pm.   P.T.O.

2.

Distribution :-

Copy No. 1.   Headquarters, 57th Divn. 'G'.
         2.   Headquarters, 57th Division 'A'.
         3.   Headquarters, 170 Inf. Brigade.
         4.   Headquarters, 171 Inf. Brigade.
         5.   Headquarters, 172 Inf. Brigade.
         6.   O.C., 2/2nd Wessex Field Ambulance.
         7.   O.C., 2/3rd Wessex Field Ambulance.
         8.   O.C., 3/2nd W.Lancs.Field Ambulance.
         9.   O.C., 2/5th N. Lan. R. (P).
        10.   O.C., 57th Battn. M. G. Corps.
        11.   O.C., 57th Divl. Train.
        12.   S.S.O., 57th Division.
        13.   O.C., 57th Divisional Signal Coy.
        14.   C.R.A., 57th Division.
        15.   C.R.E., 57th Division.
        16.   D.A.D.V.S., 57th Division.
        17.   D.A.P.M., 57th Division.
        18.   D.G.O., 57th Division.
        19.   O.C., 57th Div. M.T. Coy.
        20.   O.C., 57th Div. Reception Camp.
        21.   O.C., No.15 M. A. C.
        22.   A.D.M.S., Guards Division.
        23.   A.D.M.S., 1st Can. Division.
        24.   A.D.M.S., 33rd Division.
        25.   A.D.M.S., 52nd Division.
        26.   A.D.M.S., 56th Division.
        27.   A.D.M.S., 63rd Division.
        28.   D.D.M.S., XVII Corps.
        29.   D.M.S., Third Army.
        30.   War Diary.
        31.   War Diary.
        32.   File.
        33.   File.
        34.   Spare.
        35.   Spare.

M.S.206

AMENDMENT TO 57th. DIVISION R.A.M.C. OPERATION ORDER No. 31
DATED 6th. September, '18.

Para. 8.   For V.20.c.6.8. read D.7.a.5.7.

7th. September, '18.

Colonel, A. Med. S.,
A.D.M.S., 57th. Division.

SECRET.   M.S. 305/5. B

MEDICAL ARRANGEMENTS

Issued in connection with 57th Division Order No.120
and 57th Div.R.A.M.C. Operation Order No.31 both
dated 6th Septr.1918.

Ref. Maps Sheet 57C and 51B.   7th September, 1918.

1. Location of Medical Posts - Forward Area.

    (a) Regtl. Aid Posts.   D.18.d.
                                       E. 1.c.

    (b) Collecting Post.   V.22.d.2.3.

    (c) Advanced Dressing Station.   V.15.a.8.5.

    (d) Corps Main Dressing Stn.   U.25.central.

2. METHOD AND ROUTE OF EVACUATION.

    (a) Lying & Sitting cases. From R.A.P. to Car Collecting Post by hand carriage. Thence to A.D.S. by motor ambulance car, horse ambulance, or wheeled stretcher carrier. From A.D.S. to C.M.D.S. by Unit ambulance car or lorry, thence by M.A.C. cars to Casualty Clearing Station.

    (b) Walking Cases. By same route as above to Corps Main Dressing Station, thence by light railway to Corps Rest Station for entrainment to C.C.S.. Horse Ambulances will assist in the conveyance of walking wounded as much as possible.

    (c) Directing Posts. The Officer i/c Forward Evacuation will take all possible steps to indicate to bearers and walking wounded the routes to be followed to the Collecting Post and Advanced Dressing Station respectively, placing directing posts or notices where necessary.

3. EVACUATION. O.C., 3/2nd W.Lancs. Field Ambulance will be in
    (a)   charge of Advanced Dressing Station and will be responsible for the circulation of motor ambulance cars to the Car Collecting Post as required by the O.i/c Forward Evacuation.
    (b)   The O.C., 2/2nd Wessex Field Ambulance will be responsible for the evacuation from the R.A.Ps. and forward area generally to the Advanced Dressing Station.
    (c)   To each Brigade is attached a Brigade Bearer Officer to maintain liaison and superintend evacuation of the wounded of that Brigade.

4. SITES FOR FUTURE MEDICAL POSTS. O.C. 2/2nd Wessex Field Ambulance will be responsible for the selection of suitable sites for Medical Posts as the situation demands, informing this Office and Brigade Bearer Officers immediately of such changes.

5. LIAISON. Communication will be maintained between Regtl. Medical Officers, Officers i/c Bearers, and Advanced Dressg. Station by means of runners.

6. A.T.SERUM. A.T.S. ¼ W. is to be given at the Advanced Dressing Station.

7. MORPHIA. To be given hypodermically. The dose and hour must be recorded on the tally or Field Medical Card.

Sheet 2.

8. STRETCHERS AND BLANKETS.

   (a) There is a Corps dump of Stretchers and Blankets at the Corps Main Dressing Station. Demands for extra blankets and stretchers, etc., should be made initially on O.C. 3/2nd W.Lancs.Field Ambulance at the Advanced Dressing Station, who, in turn, will apply to this Office for further supplies. In the case of extreme urgency, however, O.C.3/2nd W.Lancs. Field Ambulance can obtain 50 Stretchers and 100 blankets on application direct to Corps Main Dressing Station.

   (b) The utmost care must be taken by all concerned that the return flow of stretchers and blankets (towards the line) is adequately maintained: so that Medical Officers and bearers in front are never without a sufficient supply.

9. STRETCHER SLINGS. Each bearer should be in possession of a stretcher sling: it should be marked with his name and number and never pass out of his keeping.

10. MEDICAL COMFORTS.
    (a) O.C., 3/2nd W.Lancs. Field Ambulance will arrange for the supply of medical comforts, hot soups, etc., whenever possible, at the Advanced Dressing Station. These are solely for the use of wounded.
    (b) The O.C. 2/2nd Wessex Field Ambulance will arrange for the supply of hot liquid - preferably tea - at the various relay posts including that beside the R.A.P.

11. SPLINTS AND TALLY BOOKS.
    (a) An adequate supply of Thomas' and the various splints will be maintained at R.A.Ps. and at the Advanced Dressing Station.
    (b) Regimental Medical Officers must ensure that they are possessed of an ample supply of tallies, both plain and red-edged.

12. RECORDS, RETURNS, ETC.
    (a) Field Medical Cards will be made out for all patients at the Adv.Dressing Station, but no A.& D.Books kept.

    (b) All official records of Admissions & Discharges will be made at the Corps Main Dressing Station by the Divisional Clerks. These clerks will render A.F.W.3185 for this Division daily, which will be collected under arrangements made by this Office. The greatest care must be taken to ensure that the correct rank, name and unit of every officer are given, and, in the case of death, the precise date.
    (c) O.C. 2/2nd Wessex Field Ambulance will render a situation report to this Office made up to 2 pm. and 9 pm. daily, in accordance with the pro forma recently issued to him.
    (d). Notifications of admissions and disposals will be sent as early as possible to all units concerned.

13. Office of A.D.M.S. - D.7.b.central (Sh.57 C.)

14. Field Ambulances will acknowledge.

J F Dewar

Colonel, A. Med. S.,
A.D.M.S., 57th Division.

Distribution - see over

DISTRIBUTION :-

    Headquarters, 57th Division 'G'.
    Headquarters, 57th Division 'A'.
    Headquarters, 57th Division 'Q'.
    Headquarters, 170th Inf. Brigade.
    Headquarters, 171st Inf. Brigade.
    Headquarters, 172nd Inf. Brigade.
    O.C., 2/2nd Wessex Field Ambulance.
    O.C., 2/3rd Wessex Field Ambulance.
    O.C., 3/2nd W.Lancs.Fld. Ambulance.
    A.D.M.S., Guards Division.
    A.D.M.S., 1st Can. Division.
    A.D.M.S., 33rd Division.
    A.D.M.S., 52nd Division.
    A.D.M.S., 56th Division.
    A.D.M.S., 63rd (R.N.) Division.
    Senior Chaplain, D.C.G's Dept.
    Senior Chaplain, P.C's Dept.
    C.R.A., 57th Division.
    C.R.E., 57th Division.
    O.C., 57th Divl.Signal Coy.
    O.C., 57th Battn. M. G. Coy.
    O.C., 2/5th N. Lan. R.
    O.C., 57th Divl. Train.
    S.S.O., 57th Division.
    D.A.D.V.S., 57th Division.
    D.G.O., 57th Division.
    D.A.P.M., 57th Division.
    O.C., 57th Divl. Reception Camp.
    O.C., 57th Divl. M. T. Coy.
    O.C., No.15 M. A. C.
    All Regimental Medical Officers.
    D.D.M.S., XVII Corps.
    D.M.S., Third Army.

M.S.306/8.

Amendment No.1. to Medical Arrangements, 57th Division,
issued under M.S. 306/5 dated 7th Septr.1918.

Para.1 (c). Advanced Dressing Station: for 'V.15.a.8.5.'
read '2/2nd Wessex Field Ambulance,
D.1.d.8.6.'

Para.2 (b) is cancelled and the following substituted:-

Walking Cases. By same route as above to
Corps Main Dressing Station,
thence to Casualty Clearing Station,
BAC-DU-SUD. Horse ambulances will assist
in the conveyance of walking wounded as
much as possible.

Para.5 (a) EVACUATION. For 'O.C.3/2nd W.Lancs.Field
Ambulance' read 'O.C., 2/2nd Wessex Field
Ambulance.'

Para.8 (a) STRETCHERS & BLANKETS. For 'O.C. 3/2nd
W.Lancs.Field Ambulance' read 'O.C.,2/2nd
Wessex Field Ambulance.'

Para.10 (a).MEDICAL COMFORTS. For 'O.C., 3/2nd W.Lancs.
Fd. Ambulance' read 'O.C. 2/2nd Wessex Field
Ambulance'.

Para.13. Office of A.D.M.S. For 'D.7.b.central
Sh.57 C.) read 'D.7.a.5.7..(Sh.57.6.)'

Maurice King, Major.
for Colonel, A. Med.S.,
9th Septr.1918.   A.D.M.S., 57th Division.

To all recipients of Medical Arrangements issued under
M.S. 306/5 dated 7th. September, 1918

SECRET.   Copy No.......

57th DIVISION R.A.M.C. OPERATION
ORDER No. 32.   M.S. 306/16.

                                    Ref. Map Sht. 57C. N.E. 1/20,000 and
                                         LENS 11. 1/100,000.

1.   57th Division (less Artillery) will be relieved in the line
on 15/16th and 16/17th September by 52nd Division (less Artillery).
        On relief 57th Division (less Artillery) will move by march
route to the neighbourhood of ECOUST and NOREUIL Area preparatory
to entraining for the Corps Reserve Area.   Bivouac Areas will
be notified separately by "Q".

2.   On completion of the move the Division will concentrate in
the following area:-

        GOUY-EN-ARTOIS - BEAUMETZ - BARLY - BAILLEULVAL - BELLACOURT -
        BAILLEULMONT - BAVINCOURT - LA HERLIERE - SAULTY.

        Distribution of Area will be notified separately by "Q".

3.   Infantry reliefs will take place as under -

(a)   On night 15/16th September, 170th Infantry Brigade in the
        MOEUVRES SECTION will be relieved by 155th Infantry Brigade.
        Route QUEANT - NOREUIL.

(b)   On September 16th and night September 16/17th 171st Infantry
        Brigade in Divisional Reserve will be relieved by 156th
        Infantry Brigade.   Route QUEANT - NOREUIL.

(c)   On night 16/17th September, 172nd Infantry Brigade in the
        INCHY SECTION will be relieved by the 157th Infantry Brigade.
        Route QUEANT - NOREUIL.

4.   Moves of Field Ambulances.-

(a)   The 2/2nd Wessex Field Ambulance will be relieved by the
        1/1st Lowland Field Ambulance, relief to be complete by
        2 p.m. 16th September, and will move to the new area under
        orders from 171st Infantry Brigade.

(b)   The 3/2nd W. Lanc. Field Ambulance will move without relief
        under orders of 170th Infantry Brigade.

(c)   The 2/3rd Wessex Field Ambulance will remain at the Corps
        Rest Station, GOUY.

5.   O.C., 2/2nd Wessex Field Ambulance will arrange details of
relief direct with O.C., 1/1st Lowland Field Ambulance and will
hand over all Area Stores, programmes of work, and maps of area.

6.   O.C., 2/2nd Wessex Field Ambulance will return to their
Units the attached personnel and vehicles of 3/2nd West Lancs.
Field Ambulance by midnight 15th September, and all attached
vehicles on completion of relief.
        Attached personnel of the 2/3rd Wessex Field Ambulance may
be retained until arrival in the new area.

7.   Field Ambulances will move only with equipment authorised
by M.S. Table and G.R.Os.

8.   Receipts for all stores handed over will be forwarded to
this office by 18th September.

9.   Completion of relief will be notified to this office by
O.C., 2/2nd Wessex Field Ambulance.

2.

10. A.D.M.S. Office will close at D.7.a.5.7. at 10 a.m. 17th September and open at BAVINCOURT at 11 a.m.

11. Field Ambulances will acknowledge.

y ✗ Dillwan.

Colonel A. Med. S.,
A.D.M.S., 57th Division.

15. 9. 18.

Issued at 10.30 a.m.

Distribution.-

Copy No. 1. Headquarters, 57th Division "G".
2. Headquarters, 57th Division "Q".
3. Headquarters, 170th Infantry Brigade.
4. Headquarters, 171st Infantry Brigade.
5. Headquarters, 172nd Infantry Brigade.
6. O.C., 2/2nd Wessex Field Ambulance.
7. O.C., 2/3rd Wessex Field Ambulance.
8. O.C., 3/2nd W. Lancs Field Ambulance.
9. O.C., 2/5th N. Lan. R. (P).
10. O.C., 57th Bn. M. G. Corps.
11. O.C., 57th Divl. Train.
12. S.S.O., 57th Division.
13. O.C., 57th Divl. Signal Coy.
14. C.R.A., 57th Division.
15. C.R.E., 57th Division.
16. D.A.D.V.S., 57th Division.
17. D.A.P.M., 57th Division.
18. D.G.O., 57th Division.
19. O.C., 57th Divl. M.T. Coy.
20. O.C., 57th Divl. Reception Camp.
21. O.C., No. 15 M.A.C.,
22. A.D.M.S., Guards Division,
23. 2nd Canadian Division,
24. A.D.M.S., 33rd Division,
25. A.D.M.S., 52nd Division,
26. A.D.M.S., 63rd Division,
27. D.D.M.S., XVII Corps,
28. D.M.S., Third Army,
29. War Diary,
30. War Diary,
31. File.
32. File.
33. Spare.
34. Spare.
35. Headquarters, 57th Division "A".

SECRET.   M.S.316/3.

OUTLINE OF MEDICAL ARRANGEMENTS FOR THE EVACUATION OF WOUNDED DURING ACTIVE OPERATIONS.

1.   Each Field Ambulance will provide 5 R.A.M.C. for each Battalion of its affiliated Brigade. These men will report before their Battalion goes into the line and will be the first link in the chain of evacuation from the R.A.P.

2.   (a) Each Field Ambulance will in addition provide 1 Officer and 50 other ranks for its affiliated Brigade. This party will report to Brigade Headquarters when ordered by this office and will maintain the evacuation of wounded from R.A.P. to Collecting Post or Advanced A.D.S. as the case may be.

        (b) All remaining available R.A.M.C. other ranks will report to the Officer in charge forward evacuation at a place and time to be selected by him.

3.   The 3 Infantry Brigades will between them find 6 Officers and 144 other ranks to act as auxiliary Stretcher Bearers. They will report to the Officer in charge forward evacuation at zero minus 12 hours at a place to be selected by him. Their duty will be to reinforce the R.A.M.C. bearers when required.

4.   The Officer Commanding 2/2nd Wessex Field Ambulance will be in charge of forward evacuation and will be responsible for the evacuation of wounded to the Advanced Dressing Station.

        2 Medical Officers will be detailed to assist him in addition to the R.A.M.C. Brigade Bearer Officers and the Infantry Officers in charge Auxiliary Bearers.

        All the motor and horsed ambulances and wheeled stretcher carriages of the Division will be at his disposal less those required by Officer Commanding Corps Rest Station and Officer Commanding Advanced Dressing Station.

5.   The Officer Commanding 3/2nd W.Lancs Field Ambulance will be in charge of the Advanced Dressing Station with 3 Medical Officers and 2 Tent Sub-Divisions.

6.   The Officer Commanding 2/3rd Wessex Field Ambulance will continue in charge of the Corps Rest Station.

7.   2 Medical Officers and 1 Tent Sub-Division (including 4 Clerks) will be required for duty at the Corps Main Dressing Station.

                                            y y Dewar.
                                        Colonel, A.Med.C.
24/9/18.   A.D.M.S., 57th Division.

DISTRIBUTION.

Headquarters, 57th Division (2)
Headquarters, 170th Infantry Brigade.
Headquarters, 171st Infantry Brigade.
Headquarters, 172nd Infantry Brigade.
OsC all Infantry Battalions.
C.C., 57th Bn. M.G.Corps.
O.C., 2/5th N. Lan. R. (P).
D.D.M.S., XVII Corps.
A.D.M.S. 63rd Division.
A.D.M.S. 52nd Division.
A.D.M.S. Guards Division.
A.D.M.S. 4th Canadian Division.
O.C., 2/2nd Wessex Field Ambulance.
O.C., 2/3rd Wessex Field Ambulance.
O.C., 3/2nd W.Lancs. Fd. Ambulance.(4)

SECRET.   M.S. 313/12.

MEDICAL ARRANGEMENTS.

Issued in connection with A.D.M.S., 57th Division
No. M.S. 313/3 dated 24. 9. 18.
****

Ref. Maps Sheet 57C.N.E.; 1/20,000.
    Map "M" (2/2nd Wessex F. Amb.
       and 3/2nd W. Lanc. F. Amb.
          only.)   25th Sept., 1918.

1.   On a date and at a time which will be notified later, XVII Corps in conjunction with Canadian Corps and VI Corps will resume the attack.

2.   Objectives are shown as follows on Map "M":-

   (a) First objective in RED, to be captured by 52nd & 63rd Divs.
   (b) Second objective in BROWN, to be captured by 63rd Div.
   (c) Third objective in BLUE, to be captured by 57th Div.

3.   The hour of departure from the second objective will be approximately zero plus 290 minutes.

4.(a)   The Officer Commanding, 3/2nd W. Lanc. F. Amb. will reconnoitre in the neighbourhood of J.6. and K.1. with a view to establishing an Advanced Dressing Station there. Exact map reference will be sent to this office, to O.C., No. 15 M.A.C., and to O.C., 2/2nd Wessex F. Amb. as soon as decided.

   (b) Officer Commanding, 3/2nd W. Lanc F. Amb. will be responsible for the evacuation to Corps Main Dressing Station. Two lorries will be attached to him by Officer Commanding, No. 15 M.A.C.

   (c) He will be responsible for the supply to Officer Commanding, 2/2nd Wessex F. Amb. of stretchers, blankets, dressings, and medical comforts.

   (d) He will keep in touch, through Officer Commanding, 2/2nd Wessex F. Amb. with the military situation, with a view to moving forward when advisable.

   (e) He will keep Officer Commanding, 2/2nd Wessex F. Amb., Officer Commanding, No. 15 M.A.C., and this office informed of any change in location of the Advanced Dressing Stations.

   (f) He will render a situation report to this office at 12 noon and 8 p.m. daily.

5.(a)   The Officer Commanding, 2/2nd Wessex F. Amb. (Officer in charge, Forward Evacuation) will be responsible for the evacuation of wounded to the A.D.S.

   (b) He will make every use of light railways, and push his motor ambulances as far forward as possible.

   (c) He will indicate the route of evacuation from Regimental Aid Posts to Advanced Dressing Station as far as possible by suitable signs.

   (d) He will keep in close touch, through his Brigade Bearer Officers, with Regimental Medical Officers and superintend the supply of stretchers, blankets, dressings, etc. to the Regimental Aid Posts.

   (e) He will keep Officer Commanding, Advanced Dressing Station informed of the military situation, and assist him in the choice of a site, should the Advanced Dressing Station be moved forward.

(f) He will replace casualties in Regimental Medical Officers.

(g) He will render a situation report to this office at 12 noon and 9 p.m. daily.

6. Regimental Medical Officers will assist Brigade Bearer Officers to keep touch with Regimental Aid Posts. No Regimental Medical Officer will move his Regimental Aid Post without notifying Bearer Officer of his Brigade of his new location and leaving a reliable guide behind to conduct bearer squads to the new site.

7. Regimental Medical Officers needing extra bearers will inform their Brigade Bearer Officer of the fact, in writing, stating number and map reference of casualties.
    approx.

8. Casualties occurring west of the first objective may be evacuated through the existing posts of the 52nd Division a list of which is attached:-

    (a) Regimental Aid Posts.   (E.13.d.8.8.
                                 (D.18.d.2.6.
                                 (E.19.a.8.3.
                                 (E.19.a.1.9.

    (b) Bearer Relay Posts.   (D.17.d.3.8.
                                 (D.18.c.5.8.
                                 (D.18.d.2.6.
                                 (E.19.a.8.3.
                                 (E.19.a.1.9.

    (c) Collecting Post.   (D.17.d.5.5.

9. Officer Commanding, No. 15 M.A.C. will be at the Corps Main Dressing Station, J.25.central.

10. Field Ambulances will acknowledge.

Maurice Uiney Major

for Colonel A. Med. S.,
A.D.M.S., 57th Division.

25. 9. 18.

Distribution:-

H.Q., 57th Division "G".   H.Q., 57th Division "Q".
H.Q., 170 Inf. Bde.   H.Q., 171 Inf. Bde.
H.Q., 172 Inf. Bde.   O.C., 2/2nd Wessex F. Amb.
O.C., 2/3rd Wessex F. Amb.   O.C., 3/2nd W. Lanc. F. Amb.
A.D.M.S., 63rd Division.   A.D.M.S., 52nd Division.
A.D.M.S., Guards Division.   A.D.M.S., 4th Can. Division.
Senior Chaplain, D.C.G's. Dep.   Senior Chaplain, P.C's. Dep.
C.R.E., 57th Division.   C.R.A., 57th Division.
O.C., 57th Div. Sig. Co.   O.C., 57th Bn. M.G. Corps.
O.C., 2/5th N. Lan. R. (P).   O.C., 57th Division Train.
S.S.O., 57th Division.   D.A.D.V.S., 57th Division.
D.G.O., 57th Division.   D.A.P.M., 57th Division.
O.C., 57th Div. Rec. Camp.   O.C., 57th Div. M.T. Co.
O.C., No. 15 M.A.C.   D.M.S., Third Army.
All R.M.Os., 57th Division.   D.D.M.S., XVII Corps.

Vol 21

160/3323

War Diary
of
A.D.M.S.
57th Division
from 1st October to 31st October 1918

Oct 1918 16

Army Form C. 2118.

WAR DIARY
or
INTELLIGENCE SUMMARY.
(Erase heading not required.)

Instructions regarding War Diaries and Intelligence Summaries are contained in F.S. Regs., Part II. and the Staff Manual respectively. Title pages will be prepared in manuscript.

Place	Date	Hour	Summary of Events and Information	Remarks and references to Appendices
NEAR CANAL DU NORD	1.10.18		A.D.M.S. visited 2/2nd W. Rid. F. Amb. near Canal and 3/2nd W. Lanc. F. Amb. at Advanced Dressing Station near FONTAINES-NOTRE-DAME. Attack being pressed on PROVILLE. Casualties admitted to A.D.S. chiefly 62nd and 63rd Div.	
	2.10.18		190 in Bn attacked. Wounded admitted in 1/s. N.L.N.R. Wounded of 57th Division admitted to C.M.D. Stn in last five days of September. Sept. 26. 1 Sept 29. 244. " 27. " 30. 64. " 28. 183. A.D.M.S. visited 3/2nd W. Lanc. F. Amb. A.D.S. near FONTAINES-NOTRE-DAME just South of BAPAUME-CAMBRAI ROAD. Met DDMS XVII Corps there. Also visited advanced H.Q. of 2/2nd W. Rid. F. Amb. and saw retaining Posts E of Canal on CANTAING ROAD	
	3.10.18		Attended Conference of ADMS (62nd 64th & 63rd Divs) at Office of DDMS XVII Corps. LOUVERVAL. Visited 3/2nd W. Lanc. F. Amb. Meeting Current. [illegible] North. 11 am. Wet Lieut LAMBETH. M.O.R.C., U.S.A. attached us supp'ty S.R.Gibbs and Lieut LAMBETH. M.O.R.C., U.S.A. attached Officer I/c 9th Fd. Sport Pl. A.D.M.S. visited	
	4.10.18		Fighting on XVII Corps front quieter.	

Army Form C. 2118.

WAR DIARY
or
INTELLIGENCE SUMMARY.
(Erase heading not required.)

Instructions regarding War Diaries and Intelligence Summaries are contained in F. S. Regs., Part II. and the Staff Manual respectively. Title pages will be prepared in manuscript.

Place	Date	Hour	Summary of Events and Information	Remarks and references to Appendices
	4.10.18		2/2nd Western F. Amb. arrived D.S. (car collecting O.Rs) and 2/3rd W. Lanc. F. Amb. (A.D.S.) whereas new G.O.C. 142nd Inf. Bde. Names in text.	
	5.10.18		Quiet day. Major ADAMS, 2/2nd Western F. Amb., wounded, now Rev. SHOVEL, C.F. attached 2/2nd Western F. Amb. killed by shrapnel. G.O.C. 141st Inf. Bde and C.R.E. wounded.	
	6.10.18		47th Div. relieved 62nd Div. in line on night of O.C. 5-6. By extending front 16 south 141st Bde. now one deps 142nd Bde. (in rear of 53rd Div.) in reserve. Rearrangements of reconcinochement to meet latered front and new air parts. 63rd Div. 16 pass through line of 3rd Div. and attack tomorrow. 142 Bde moving to cover left flank. 142 Bde night flank conforming. Issued Operation	
	7.10.18		CAMBRAI turned N.E. at hour tomorrow. 140 Bde. moving to cover left flank of 142 Bde right flank conforming. Issued Operation Order No. 34. Visited NOYELLES regarding evacuation in projected operation.	"A"
	8.10.18		A.D.M.S. visited A.D.S. at ANNEUX. Line of evacuation at CANTAING, NOYELLES, etc interviewing Bearer Officers of 140th and 142nd Bdes.	

Army Form C. 2118.

WAR DIARY
or
INTELLIGENCE SUMMARY.
(Erase heading not required.)

Instructions regarding War Diaries and Intelligence Summaries are contained in F.S. Regs., Part II. and the Staff Manual respectively. Title pages will be prepared in manuscript.

Place	Date	Hour	Summary of Events and Information	Remarks and references to Appendices
	8.10.18		O i/c Evacuation all going well intermittently and morning. Attempts began at 04.20 today and progress rapidly. Casualties 65th Division about 65 to 85 sick and wounded. Visited A.D.S. ANNEUX at night. Very few wounded arriving.	
	9.10.18		A.D.M.S. informed 57th Divn to rapidly concentrating transport and artillery to more into new movement, that after 140th and 143rd Bdes moving on frontier in this article 24th Div gone in. Visited CAMBRAI which is now full of British troops. Almost every house gutted and in ruins. Also visited 143rd and 140th Bde Bearer Officers to ADS and now LA MERLIERE farm. 57th Div is rapidly moving out of the line; their ambulances in 57th Divn in Corps Rest.	
	10.10.18		Bus group. Medical Officers and R.A.M.C. personnel at Corps Rest Station and Convoy Clearing Station being returned to Divn. Dummy return of Septr 28 to Oct 9 in infantry wounded admitted to Corps Rest Station. 140th Bde. 345 / 141st " 196 / 142nd " 415 / 2/5 M.G.P. 10 / 54 M.G.C. 5.8.	

Army Form C. 2118.

WAR DIARY
or
INTELLIGENCE SUMMARY.
(Erase heading not required.)

Instructions regarding War Diaries and Intelligence Summaries are contained in F. S. Regs., Part II. and the Staff Manual respectively. Title pages will be prepared in manuscript.

Place	Date	Hour	Summary of Events and Information	Remarks and references to Appendices
	11.10.14		51st Div. withdrawn from line and concentrating near a view to entrainment for BARLIN area south of BETHUNE.	"B"
BARLIN	12.10.14		Division arr. from N.E. of CAMBRAI to just S. of BETHUNE on I Corps, First Army. Headquarters BARLIN.	
	13.10.14		Division to relieve 44th Division XI Corps, Fifth Army on night 14/15 of XI Corps front N.E. of BETHUNE and N. of LA BASSÉE. Visited A.D.M.S. 44th Division at RIEZ BAILLEUL and arranged details of relief. Visited DDMS XI Corps at BUSNES. Issued Operation Order No. 35 and Medical arrangement.	
L'EPINETTE	14.10.14		51st Division moved North. Headquarters to L'EPINETTE near LESTREM. Division to relieve 44th Division an hour in front of LILLE one day later than was originally arranged.	
	15.10.14		A.D.M.S. visited D.D.M.S. XI Corps at BUSNES. Relief of 44th Division by 51st Division taking place from today.	
	16.10.14		A.D.M.S. visited 2/2nd W. Lan. F. Amb. at D.R. Stn. south of LESTREM. One hand general post service LESTREM, another half a mile N. and S. of R. LAWE Canal for cases of P.U.O., diarrhoea, and scabies only.	

A 5834 Wt. W4973/M687 750,000 8/16 D. D. & L. Ltd. Forms/C.2118/13.

WAR DIARY
or
INTELLIGENCE SUMMARY.

Army Form C. 2118.

Place	Date	Hour	Summary of Events and Information	Remarks and references to Appendices
L'EPINETTE, LION			A.D.M.S. visited 3/2nd W.Lanc. F. Amb. at M.D.S. LAVENTIE.	
		14.0M	D.A.D.M.S. visited forward area and found 3/2nd Division much forward. Headquarters from L'EPINETTE to PROMELLES.	
			141 and 142 Bled on LILLE so 441 → 442 →	
			140. Blue on Reserve	
			A.D.S. pushed on from PROMELLES to (1) FIN DE LA GUERRE: and (2) la VERT BALLOT. LILLE found to have been evacuated by enemy. Blue move in by of Enskina South enclosing it and picking entrances to City. 2/2nd Queen F. Amb. moved to 3/2nd W.Lanc. F. Amb. at LAVENTIE, becoming D.R.S. instead of M.D.S. No wounded in Division lines.	
	18.10.18.		Division advancing unstopped much South of LILLE which the enemy has evacuated. 3/3rd W.Lanc. F. Amb. moving from PONT CANTELAU to HELLEMMES, 3/2nd William F. Amb. moving from FROMELLES to PONT CANTELAU, 3/2 nd W. Lanc. F. Amb. to FROMELLES.	

Army Form C. 2118.

WAR DIARY
or
INTELLIGENCE SUMMARY.
(Erase heading not required.)

Instructions regarding War Diaries and Intelligence Summaries are contained in F.S. Regs., Part II. and the Staff Manual respectively. Title pages will be prepared in manuscript.

Place	Date	Hour	Summary of Events and Information	Remarks and references to Appendices
ENGLOS	19/10/18		Division remains in Corps. West, east & west of LILLE without opposition, with 59th Division on left and 94th Division on right. 3/5th N. Som. F. Amb. (Adv. Drsg. Stn.) moving to "Halte" on LILLE-TOURNAI ROAD, South East of TRESSIN.	
PETIT RONCHIN	20/10/18		3/2nd No. Lanc. F. Amb. moving today to PONTE CANTELAU on N.W. of LILLE: 3/2nd Wessex F. Amb. to HELLEMMES, East of LILLE. 3/3rd Wessex F. Amb. from previous stations S/IN on LILLE-TOURNAI ROAD. 141 Inf Bde advancing slowly toward SCHELDT CANAL and heights of MONT AUBERT beyond, and engaging retiring enemy. Divisional Headquarters moved today to WILLEMS. 141 Bde engaging enemy established in woods west of Carnie and east of BLANDAIN. A.D.S. moved to distillerie in BLANDAIN. Headquarters of 3/5th Wessex F. Amb. remaining in SIN. 3/3rd No. Som. F. Amb. moved to TRESSIN and remaining closed. 3/2nd Wessex F. Amb. remaining at HELLEMMES. BLANDAIN frequently shelled	
WILLEMS	21/10/18		all day and A.D.S. not hit. Six cases on system from M.G. fire.	

A5834 Wt.W4973/M687 750,000 8/16 D.D. & L. Ltd. Forms/C.2118/13.

Army Form C. 2118.

WAR DIARY
or
INTELLIGENCE SUMMARY.
(Erase heading not required.)

Instructions regarding War Diaries and Intelligence Summaries are contained in F. S. Regs., Part II. and the Staff Manual respectively. Title pages will be prepared in manuscript.

Place	Date	Hour	Summary of Events and Information	Remarks and references to Appendices
WILLEMS.	22.10.18.		A.D.M.S visited A.D.S at BLANDAIN and R.A.P.s behind line. About 35 wounded in 24 hours.	
	23.10.18.		A.D.M.S visited 2/3rd Western F. Amb. A.D.S at BLANDAIN, and Headquarters at SIN. 2/2nd W. Lanc. F. Amb with Main Dressing Station at TRESSIN, and 2/2nd Western F. Amb. at HELLEMMES now closed. Demand now on line of CANAL making no appreciable advance. Two clearing Officers Surgeon Lieuts. CORRY and BUCHANAN, sent from Royal Navy to Army arrived today, and were posted to 2/2nd W. Lanc. F. Amb. Major ADAMS returned to 2/2 nd Western F. Amb. on staff on recovery from wounds - viz, as a reinforcement. 142 nd Inf. Bde. returning 141st Inf. Bde. in line tonight. Casualties - 30 yesterday on Divisional Frontage on a wide frontage at present. Situated before 2/2nd W. Lanc. F. Amb. to return suitable accommodation in M.D.S. TRESSIN. A.D.M.S visited A.D.S at	
	24.10.18			
	25.10.18.		BLANDAIN. D.A.D.M.S visited 1st R.M.V.N.S. FUS. regarding occurrence of Dysentery.	

WAR DIARY or INTELLIGENCE SUMMARY.

Army Form C. 2118.

Place	Date	Hour	Summary of Events and Information	Remarks and references to Appendices
WILLEMS	26.10.18.		Situation decidedly as before. Very few casualties; there are being attended in alternate days at 1,500 a day, and clean evacuating is being done. 3/2nd W. Lanc. F. Amb. have opened M.D.S. at TRESSIN in Château.	
	27.10.18.		A.D.S. in Schoolhouse at BLANDAIN being kept wheeler getting into fair shape though inadequate enough for workings. 3/1st W. Lanc. F. Amb. are now moved to Convent in same village. A.D.M.S. visited it. Building very spacious. Also visited Divisional Baths at TEMPLEUVE and found still they are not carrying on owing to lack of water. Also visited 1/2 W. Lanc. F. Amb. at TRESSIN, 14 patients.	"C."
	28.10.18.		3rd Division to be relieved in line by 49th Division on Oct 30-31st. Issued Operation Orders for relief.	
	29.10.18.		A.D.M.S. visited 1/1st W. Lanc. F. Amb. where their spare men from one Convent, BLANDAIN which was considerably damaged by shellfire getting to house over Station. Units to be relieved by 3rd Divison Field Ambulances on 31st.	

Army Form C. 2118.

WAR DIARY
or
INTELLIGENCE SUMMARY.

(Erase heading not required.)

Instructions regarding War Diaries and Intelligence Summaries are contained in F. S. Regs., Part II. and the Staff Manual respectively. Title pages will be prepared in manuscript.

Place	Date	Hour	Summary of Events and Information	Remarks and references to Appendices
WILLEMS	30.10.18		Division carrying out of line stations and moving its quarters in eastern outskirts of LILLE. 47th Division relieving.	
	31.10.18		Divisional Headquarters moved from WILLEMS to MONS EN BAROEUL. Opened in East end and South East end outskirts of LILLE. Attended Conference of A.D.Ms.S at Office of D.D.M.S XI Corps yesterday. Discussed Venereal Disease Prophylaxis, Administrative control of Influenza etc	
	31.10.18.			

J F Olver
.... Colonel, A. Med. S.
A.D.M.S 57th (W.L.) Division.

SECRET.
　　　　　　　　　　　　　　　　　　　　　　　　　　　S.318/25.

57th DIVISION, R.A.M.C, OPERATION ORDER No. 34.

Reference Map Sheets 57C.NE. 1 in 20,000,
57B.NW. 1 in 20,000,

1. 57th Division will take part in an attack on 8th October with 63rd Division on its right. The role of 57th Division is to form a defensive flank facing north to secure the left flank of 63rd Division.

2. The attack will be carried out by 170th Infantry Brigade.

3. The objective of 170th Infantry Brigade will be a line drawn through G.3.1.2.9, G.4.a.0.8, and along the trench to G.4.b.central.

4. 172nd Infantry Brigade simultaneously with attack of 170th Infantry Brigade will throw its right forward so as to connect with 170th Infantry Brigade at about A.27.d.2.0.

5. A. Officer Commanding, 2/2nd Wessex Field Ambulance will be in charge of forward evacuation of wounded.
   B. Officer Commanding 3/2nd West Lancs. Field Ambulance will be in charge of the Advanced Dressing Station and will select a suitable site, in conjunction with the Officer Commanding 2/2nd Wessex Field Ambulance.

6. Corps Main Dressing Station will open on the 8th October at F.19.c.

7. A. The Advanced Dressing Stations of the 2nd and 63rd Divisions will be situated in NOYELLES, so the formation of a third A.D.S. there is contra indicated.
   B. The stream of wounded should be diverted to the bridge at F.29.b.central, as far as the situation allows.

8. Zero hour will be 8430 hours.

9. Field Ambulances will acknowledge.

　　　　　　　　　　　　　　　　　　　　Maurice King
　　　　　　　　　　　　　　　　　　　　Colonel, A.M.d.S,
　　　　　　　　　　　　　　　　　　A.D.M.S, 57th Division.

7/10/1918.
Issued at 1200 hours

Distribution :-
Copy No. 1. Headquarters, 57th Division,'G'.
2. Headquarters, 57th Division,'Q'.
3. A.D.M.S, 63rd Division.
4. A.D.M.S, 2nd Division.
5. D.D.M.S, XVII Corps.
6. O.C, 2/2nd Wessex Field Ambulance.
7. O.C, 2/3rd Wessex Field Ambulance.
8. O.C, 3/2nd West Lanc. Field Ambulance.

SECRET.   Copy No. _____

                    57th DIVISION R.A.M.C. OPERATION ORDER,
                                   No. 35.
                    ------------------------   M.S.319/2.

                                        Reference Map BETHUNE Combined Sheet,
                                                36.S.W. 1 in 20,000.
                                                36.   1 in 40,000.

1.   The 57th Division (less Artillery) is relieving the 47th (London)
        Division in the right divisional sector of the line on the 14th,
        15th and 16th October.

2.   Field Ambulance Reliefs :-
        (a). The 2/3rd Wessex Field Ambulance will relieve the 5th London
             Field Ambulance in the Forward area on the 14th and 15th October;
             relief to be complete by 1200 hours, 15th October.
        (b). The 3/2nd West Lancs. Field Ambulance will take over the Main
             Dressing Station from the 4th London Field Ambulance on the 14th and
             15th October, relief to be complete by 1200 hours, 15th October.
        (c). The 2/2nd Wessex Field Ambulance will take over the Divisional
             Rest Station from the 6th London Field Ambulance on 15th and 16th
             October, relief to be complete by 0900 hours, 16th October.

3.(a). Details of relief will be arranged between Officers Commanding
        Field Ambulances concerned.

  (b). Completion of reliefs will be notified to this office at once.

4.   All surplus and Corps stores and maps of the area will be taken over
        and copies of receipts forwarded to this office in duplicate by
        16th October.

5.   Moves of Field Ambulances :-
        (a). The 2/3rd Wessex Field Ambulance will move under orders of
             172nd Infantry Brigade to the support area (FROMELLES - LE
             MAISNIL) on the 14th October, thence independently.
        (b). The 3/2nd West Lanc. Field Ambulance will move under orders of
             170th Infantry Brigade to the FOSSE-BOUT-DEVILLE area on the 14th
             October; thence independently to the Main Dressing Station.
        (c). The 2/2nd Wessex Field Ambulance will move under orders of
             171st Infantry Brigade on the 15th October as far as the fork in
             BETHUNE/E.6.a, and thence independently to the Divisional Rest
             Station.

6.   A.D.M.S. office will close at L'EPINETTE, R.13.b. at 1800 hours on
        16th October, and reopen at RIEZ BAILLEUL at the same hour.

7.   Field Ambulances will acknowledge.

                                                Maurice King Major
                                                /- Colonel, A.Med.S,
Issued at 2130 hours.   A.D.M.S, 57th Division.
    13/10/1918.

DISTRIBUTION :-

Copy No. 1 to H.Q., 57th Division, 'G'.
          2   H.Q., 57th Division, 'Q'.
          3   H.Q., 170th Infantry Brigade.
          4   H.Q., 171st Infantry Brigade.
          5   H.Q., 172nd Infantry Brigade.
          6   O.C., 2/2nd Wessex Field Ambulance.
          7   O.C., 2/3rd Wessex Field Ambulance.
          8   O.C., 3/2nd West Lanc.Field Ambulance.
          9   A.D.M.S, 47th Division.
         10.   A.D.M.S, 59th Division.
         11.   A.D.M.S, 74th Division.
         12.   C.R.E, 57th Division.
         13.   C.R.A, 57th Division.
         14.   O.C, 57th Divl.Signal Company.
         15.   O.C, 57th Bn.M.G.Corps.
         16.   O.C, 2/5th N.Lan.R. (P).
         17.   O.C, 57th Divisional Train.
         18.   S.S.O, 57th Division.
         19.   D.A.D.V.S, 57th Division.
         20.   D.G.O, 57th Division.
         21.   D.A.P.M, 57th Division.
         22.   O.C, 57th Divl.Reception Camp.
         23.   O.C, 57th Div.M.T.Company.
         26.   D.M.S, Fifth Army.
         27.   D.D.M.S, 1st Corps.
         28.   D.D.M.S, 11th Corps.

SECRET.   M.S.319/3.

MEDICAL ARRANGEMENTS, 57th DIVISION.
R.A.M.C.
(Published with 57th Division/Operation Order No.35).

Reference Map Sheets 36   1 in 40,000.
                      36.S.W.1 in 20,000.
                      BETHUNE.1 in 40,000.

1. LOCATIONS.

    A.D.M.S. Office.   RIEZ BAILLEUL.

    2/2nd Wessex Field Ambulance. LESTREM, R.15.d.3.3.
    2/3rd Wessex Field Ambulance. TWO TREE FARM, N.2.c.central.
    3/2nd West Lanc.Field Ambce. LAVENTIE,   M.9.b.6.9.

    Regimental Aid Posts.
       Right Brigade.   Left Brigade.   Support Brigade.
       O.20.a.6.7.   O.9.d.3.8.   O.13.a.4.5.
       O.13.d.1.6.   O.1.b.8.8.   O.7.c.3.1.
       O.13.e.9.9.   O.7.a.5.2.   N.22.d.8.8.

    Bearer Relay Post.   2/3rd Wessex Field Ambulance, O.13.b.4.7.

    Advanced Dressing Station. 2/3rd Wessex Field Ambulance. N.24.b.6.9

    Walking Wounded and Rechauffement Station.
                        2/3rd Wessex Field Ambulance.   N.23.c.5.

    Main Dressing Station.   3/2nd West Lanc.Field Ambulance.
                                 LAVENTIE,   M.9.b.6.9.

    Divisional Rest Station. 2/2nd Wessex Field Ambulance.
                                 LESTREM.   R.9.c.central.

    Divisional Diarrhoea Centre. 2/2nd Wessex Field Ambulance.
                                 LESTREM,   R.15.d.3.3.

2. Each Field Ambulance will attach 5 other ranks to each battalion of its affiliated brigade by 1200 hours, 15th October.
   These men will remain with battalions while the Division is in the line and will be used to convey casualties from Regimental Aid Posts.
   They will be under the command of the battalion Medical Officer for the period.

3. Regimental Medical Officers will keep Officer Commanding, 2/3rd Wessex Field Ambulance notified of the location of their Regimental Aid Posts.

Maurice King, Major
for Colonel, A.Med.S,
A.D.M.S, 57th Division.

13/10/18.

DISTRIBUTION :-

    Copy No. 1 to H.Q., 57th Division 'G'.
            2.   H.Q., 57th Division 'Q'.
            3.   H.Q., 170th Infantry Brigade.
            4.   H.Q., 171st Infantry Brigade.
            5.   H.Q., 172nd Infantry Brigade.
            6.   O.C, 2/2nd Wessex Field Ambulance.
            7.   O.C, 2/3rd Wessex Field Ambulance.
            8.   O.C, 3/2nd West Lanc.Field Ambulance.
            9.   A.D.M.S, 47th Division.
           10.   A.D.M.S, 58th Division.
           11.   A.D.M.S, 74th Division.
           12.   Senior Chaplain, D.C.G's Dept,
           13.   Senior Chaplain, P.C's Dept,
           14.   C.R.E, 57th Division.
           15.   C.R.A, 57th Division.
           16.   O.C, 57th Divisional Signal Co.
           17.   O.C, 57th Div.M.G.Corps.
           18.   O.C, 2/5th N.Lan.R. (P).
           19.   O.C, 57th Divisional Train.
           20.   S.S.O, 57th Division.
           21.   D.A.D.V.S, 57th Division.
           22.   D.G.O, 57th Division.
           23.   D.A.P.M, 57th Division.
           24.   O.C, 57th Div.Reception.Camp.
           25.   O.C, 57th Div.M.T.Company.
           26.   All R.M.O's, 57th.Division.
           27.   D.M.S, Fifth Army.
           28.   D.D.M.S, 1st Corps.
           29.   D.D.M.S, 11th Corps.

SECRET.

R.A.M.C. OPERATION ORDER NO. 36.
57th. Division.

M.S. 325/5.
Copy No. 29

Reference Map Sheets 36 & 37, 1/40,000.

1. 57th. Division will be relieved by 47th. Division in right Divisional Sector of XI Corps between October 30th. and November 2nd.

2. FIELD AMBULANCE RELIEFS

   (a) 2/2nd. Wessex Field Ambulance will not be relieved meantime.

   (b) 2/3rd. Wessex Field Ambulance will be relieved by 5th. London Field Ambulance, relief to be complete by noon 31/10/18.

   (c) 3/2nd. West Lancs. Field Ambulance will be relieved by 4th. London Field Ambulance, relief to be complete by 6-0 a.m. 1/11/18.

3. (a) Details of reliefs will be arranged by Officers Commanding Field Ambulances concerned.

   (b) Completion of reliefs and moves will be notified to this Office.

4. (a) All Corps and Area Stores, programmes of work, 1/20,000 maps and a copy of 5th. Army and other local Medical Arrangements will be handed over to relieving units.

   (b) Copies of receipts will be forwarded to this Office by November 2nd.

5. MOVES OF FIELD AMBULANCES

   (a) The 2/2nd. Wessex Field Ambulances will remain at present location and will pass into 171st. Infantry Brigade Group at noon 30/10/18.

   (b) The 2/3rd. Wessex Field Ambulance will pass into 172nd. Infantry Brigade Group at noon 31/10/18 and will move under Brigade Orders.

   (c) The 3/2nd. West Lancs. Field Ambulance will pass into 170th. Infantry Brigade Group at 0600 hours 1/11/18 and will move under Brigade Orders.

6. A.D.M.S. Office will close at 1000 hours and open at MONS EN BAROEUL at 1200 hours November 1st.

7. Field Ambulances will acknowledge.

J.F.Dewar
Colonel, A. Med. S.,
A.D.M.S., 57th. Division.

29th. October, 1918.
Issued at 1900 hours.

P.T.O.

DISTRIBUTION :-

Copy No. 1. to H.Q., 57th. Division, 'G'.
         2.   H.Q., 57th. Division, 'Q'.
         3.   H.Q., 170th. Infantry Brigade.
         4.   H.Q., 171st. Infantry Brigade.
         5.   H.Q., 172nd. Infantry Brigade.
         6.   O.C., 2/2nd. Wessex Field Ambulance.
         7.   O.C., 2/3rd. Wessex Field Ambulance.
         8.   O.C., 3/2nd. West Lancs. Field Ambulance.
         9.   A.D.M.S., 47th. Division.
        10.   A.D.M.S., 59th. Division.
        11.   A.D.M.S., 74th. Division.
        12.   C.R.E., 57th. Division.
        13.   C.R.A., 57th. Division.
        14.   O.C., 57th. Divisional Signal Company.
        15.   O.C., 57th. Bn. M.G. Corps.
        16.   O.C., 2/5th. N. Lan. R. (P).
        17.   O.C., 57th. Divisional Train
        18.   S.S.O., 57th. Division.
        19.   D.A.D.V.S., 57th. Division.
        20.   D.G.O., 57th. Division.
        21.   D.A.P.M., 57th. Division.
        22.   O.C., 57th. Divisional Reception Camp.
        23.   O.C., 57th. Divisional M.T. Coy.
        24.   D.M.S., Fifth Army.
        25.   D.D.M.S., XI Corps.
        26.   O.C., No. 25 M.A.C.
        27.   File
        28.   -do-
        29.   War Diary.
        30.   -do-
        31.   Spare.

WAR DIARY
of
A.D.M.S.,
57th DIVISION.

From:- 1st November, 1918.

To:- 30th November, 1918.

Army Form C. 2118.

WAR DIARY
or
INTELLIGENCE SUMMARY.
(Erase heading not required.)

Instructions regarding War Diaries and Intelligence Summaries are contained in F.S. Regs., Part II. and the Staff Manual respectively. Title pages will be prepared in manuscript.

Place	Date	Hour	Summary of Events and Information	Remarks and references to Appendices
LILLE.	1.11.18.		A.D.M.S. visited 2/2nd W. Lanc. T. Amb. opening a Corps Hospital for Influenza in Lycée Fenelon, Lille.	
	2.11.18		A.D.M.S. visited divisional units of Division 2/2nd W. Lanc. T. Amb. with 6th Pyrenées Field Ambulance attached is treating sick local sick and will provide accommodation for 25-35 at HELLEMMES: 2/3rd W. Lanc. T. Amb. at FAUBOURG DES FIVES is opening an annexe home—accommodation for 40-50 patients; 2/2nd W. Lanc. T. Amb. in LYCEE FENELON LILLE can now admit 20 Officers and 120 Other Ranks.	
	3.11.18		ADMS visited Divisional Baths, HELLEMMES about 1,000 can be bathed daily. Clean underclothing being issued. 2/2nd W. Lanc. T. Amb. open in LYCEE FENELON for 20 Officers and 120 Other Ranks.	
	4.11.18		[signature] Rashart	
	5.11.18			
	6.11.18		Conference of 5*Y.A. Division Medical Officers in LYCEE FENELON, LILLE. 19 present. A.D.M.S. afterwards accompanied DDMS XI Corps in inspection of XI Corps Influenza Centre, LYCEE FENELON accommodation about 140 for Influenza and no sharp beds. [signature]	

WAR DIARY or INTELLIGENCE SUMMARY

Army Form C. 2118.

Instructions regarding War Diaries and Intelligence Summaries are contained in F. S. Regs., Part II. and the Staff Manual respectively. Title pages will be prepared in manuscript.

(Erase heading not required.)

Place	Date	Hour	Summary of Events and Information	Remarks and references to Appendices
MON EN BAROEUL	7/11/18		Influenza still very prevalent but not appreciably on increase. A.D.M.S. visited 2/3rd W. Riding & Amb. Main Dressing Station HELLEMMES now very efficient. Distribution 236th & 238th Field Amb. FAUBOURG DES FIRES and Divisional Baths. Proposed Headquarters for April for October 1918.	
	8/11/18		A.D.M.S. visited 54th Divisional Receive Camp and 2/1st W.L.A.N.R. 167 patients at about this time. Influenza numbers still about the same. Gathering Centre. Gathering Centre.	
	9/11/18		A.D.M.S. visited all Field Ambulances and Divisional Baths. 167 patients in XI Corps.	
	10/11/18		Influenza now starting to diminish. DADMS (Major KING, R.A.M.C.) being granted leave (P.U.O.)	
	11/11/18		Recent information apparent that Armistice terms accepted by Germany. French R.A. Bath at BREUCQ.	
	12/11/18		Going through a lung. A.D.M.S. visited third Field Ambulance In view of the Armistice taking place 1100 hours yesterday all are not Settled by enquiring	

Army Form C. 2118.

WAR DIARY
or
INTELLIGENCE SUMMARY.

(Erase heading not required.)

Place	Date	Hour	Summary of Events and Information	Remarks and references to Appendices
MONS & BARROEUL	12.11.18		Enrolment of 218 Employment Coy for moving of category. Inspected 2/5 N. Midn F. Amb now 3/2 nd W. Lanc. F. Amb. Road reconce 2/3 rd N. Midn F. Amb and merged 71 F. Lanc F. Amb.	
	13.11.18		Discount with and DDMS XI Corps. Arrangements to be kept in Reserve to be moved to LA MADELAINE as soon as "Reproved". 2/2 nd W. Lanc F. Amb to move to LA MADELAINE to them "Reproved". 2/2 nd W. Lanc F. Amb to "Curiere".	
			to thence by ASILLES and VENARDS etc. to HELLEMMES & LA M + D GLEING. 2/2 nd W. Lanc F. Amb moved from HELLEMMES LA M + D GLEING Reconce tomorrow of post Reconce of 2 nd W. Lanc F. Amb and	
	14.11.18		3/2 nd W. Lanc F. Amb of Rachum Camps for Refuge Rel. of West Army XI Corps with 2/ 4 and 1/2 Division pushed away from Lepers to Hombourg. ADMS on Long 2/5 nd Nestre & Amb at Repon Conf W.O. Rachum Camps LA MADELAINE chiefly they wear Italians and	

A 5834 Wt. W4973/M687 750,000 8/16 D. D. & L. Ltd. Forms/C.2118/13.

Army Form C. 2118.

WAR DIARY
or
INTELLIGENCE SUMMARY.
(Erase heading not required.)

Instructions regarding War Diaries and Intelligence Summaries are contained in F. S. Regs., Part II. and the Staff Manual respectively. Title pages will be prepared in manuscript.

Place	Date	Hour	Summary of Events and Information	Remarks and references to Appendices
NAIVYS WOOD cm BAROEUL N.N.M.			Fourth prisoners, and 3/2nd H.Q. 2nd & 2nd at LILLE. ADMS visited 3/5th H.Q. 4 2nd. FAUBOURG DES FIVES Divisional moving in present station.	
	19.11.18		39th Division moving in and located Boards Batteries and R.E. which are forward as in near TOURNAI, having returned. Troops in Joining 3/2nd H.Q. 2nd at LA MADELEINE, ASILE DES VEILLARDS, Repaired Personnel (HQ Reception Camp), admitting very varying numbers (up to 16,400) daily: 3/3rd H.Q. 2nd at FAUBOURG DES FIVES retaining up to 10 to 15 Duties and other attendants. 3/2nd H.Q. 2nd. in LYCEE FENELON, LILLE receiving men chiefly of Intransigent personnel Corps Area (Offrecommune) up to 80 cases. Condition generally very quiet and satisfactory.	
	20.11.18 21.11.18 22.11.18		No incident. Warning order received last Division moving South Nov. 30th - Dec. 3rd. to ARRAS-DUISANS-AUBIGNY Area. Is about	

Army Form 2118.

WAR DIARY
or
INTELLIGENCE SUMMARY.
(Erase heading not required.)

Instructions regarding War Diaries and Intelligence Summaries are contained in F. S. Regs., Part II. and the Staff Manual respectively. Title pages will be prepared in manuscript.

Place	Date	Hour	Summary of Events and Information	Remarks and references to Appendices
MONS EN BAROEUL	23/11/18		Reconnaissance of road & railway between ARRAS and LILLERS. Meeting of Asst Director and Executive Officers, ADMS and DADMS to discuss activity of their Amb. Evacuation scheme.	
	24/11/18		Visited 1/2nd Western F. Amb. at LA MADELEINE. About 410 Repats. & Refs. at their centres. This Unit moves to 9/2nd Western F. Amb. hospital at Refugee Camp, ASILE DES VIELLARDS, LA MADELEINE to their Ambulance annexe to FIVES	
	25-11-18 26-11-18 27-11-18 28-11-18		Patients.	
			No change in situation. Divisions preparing to proceed by road & rail to area W of ARRAS	
	29-11-18 30-11-18		Division units now preparing for move to South.	"A"

30th of November, 1918.

J.J. Owen
Colonel A. Med. S.
A.D.M.S. 57th (W.L.) Division.

'A'

SECRET.   M.S. 333/1.

R.A.M.C. OPERATION ORDER   Copy No. 30
        No. 37.
     57th DIVISION.

Ref. 1/100,000 Sheets
    TOURNAI.
    HAZEBROUCK.
    LENS.

1. 57th Division will march to the ARRAS Area commencing
    30th November, 1918.

2. Field Ambulances will not be relieved.

3. Field Ambulances will move under orders of their
    affiliated Infantry Brigades.

4. Completion of moves will be at once notified to this
    Office.

5. A.D.M.S. Office will close at MONS-EN-BAROEUL at
    1000 hours and re-open at DUISANS at 1400 hours on
    2nd ~~November~~, 1918.
        December.

6. Field Ambulances will acknowledge.

                                        J.F. Dewar

                                    Colonel A. Med. S.,
29. 11. 18.   A.D.M.S., 57th Division.

Issued at 1400 hours.

DISTRIBUTION:-

Copy No. 1. H.Q., 57th Div. "G".   No. 17. O.C., 57th Div. Train.
        2.   H.Q., 57th Div. "Q".   18. S.S.O., 57th Div.
        3.   H.Q., 170 Inf. Bde.   19. D.A.D.V.S., 57th Div.
        4.   H.Q., 171 Inf. Bde.   20. D.G.C., 57th Div.
        5.   H.Q., 172 Inf. Bde.   21. D.A.P.M., 57th Div.
        6.   O.C., 2/2nd Wessex F. Amb.   22. O.C., 57th D. Rec. Gp.
        7.   O.C., 2/3rd Wessex F. Amb.   23. O.C. D.M.T. Co.
        8.   O.C., 3/2nd W. L. F. Amb.   24. D.M.S., First Army.
        9.   A.D.M.S., 57th Div.   25. D.D.M.S., XI Corps.
        10. A.D.M.S., 59th Div.   26. O.C., No. 25 M.A.C.
        11. A.D.M.S., 15th Div.   27. File.
        12. C.R.E., 57th Div.   28. File.
        13. C.R.A., 57th Div.   29. War Diary.
        14. 57th Div. Sig. Co.   30. War Diary.
        15. O.C., 57th Bn. M.G.C..   31. Spare.
        16. O.C., 2/5th N. Lan. R. (P).

C.

SECRET. M.S. 333/2.

PROVISIONAL MEDICAL ARRANGEMENTS, 57th DIVISION,
issued in connection with
R.A.M.C. 57th Division Operation Order 37.

Reference Map Sheets 1/100,000
   TOURNAI,
   HAZEBROUCK,   29th November, 1918.
   LENS.

1.   During the move to the ARRAS Area Field Ambulances will collect the sick from their affiliated Brigade Groups.

2.   Officer Commanding 3/2nd West Lancs. Field Ambulance will in addition be responsible for the collection of sick from the Divisional Artillery Group, under arrangements to be made mutually.

3.   Infantry Brigade Groups are constituted as follows :-

170th Bde. Group.	171st Infantry Bde. Group.
170th Inf. Bde.	171st Inf. Bde.
502nd Fd.Coy.R.E.	421st Fd. Coy. R.E.
No.3 Sect. D.A.C.	2/5th N. Lan. R. (P).
Mob. Vet. Sect.	2/2nd Wessex F. Amb.
3/2nd W.Lanc. F. Amb.	No.2 Coy. Train.
No.3 Coy. Train.	

172nd Infantry Bde. Group.
   172nd Inf. Bde.
   505th Fd. Coy. R.E.
   57th Battn. M.G.C.
   2/3rd Wessex F. Amb.
   Reception Camp Details.
   No.4 Coy. Train.

4.   Divisional Artillery Group is constituted as follows :-

      57th Div. Artillery Group :-

            57th Div. Arty. (less No.3 Sect. D.A.C.)
            No.1 Coy. Train.

5.   Cases needing evacuation may be sent to the Casualty Clearing Stations named in my M.S. 333 dated 27th and 28th November, 1918.

                                    Maurice King, Major
                               for Colonel, A. Med. S.,
29/11/18.   A.D.M.S., 57th Division.

                                                       P.T.O.

Copy No. 1. H.Q., 57th Division "Q".
2. H.Q., 57th Division "G".
3. H.Q., 170th Inf. Brigade.
4. H.Q., 171st Inf. Brigade.
5. H.Q., 172nd Inf. Brigade.
6. O.C., 2/2nd Wessex F. Amb.
7. O.C., 2/3rd Wessex F. Amb.
8. O.C., 2/2nd W. Lanc. F. Amb.
9. A.D.M.S., 47th Division.
10. A.D.M.S., 59th Division.
11. A.D.M.S., 15th Division.
12. C.R.E., 57th Division.
13. C.R.A., 57th Division.
14. 57th Div. Sig. Co.
15. 57th Bn. M. G. Corps.
16. O.C., 2/5th N. Lan. R. (P).
17. O.C., 57th Div. Train.
18. S.S.O., 57th Division.
19. D.A.D.V.S., 57th Division.
20. D.A.C., 57th Division.
21. D.A.P.M., 57th Division.
22. O.C., 57th Div. Reception Camp.
23. O.C., 57th Div. M. T. Co.
24. D.M.S., First Army.
25. D.D.M.S., XI Corps.
26. O.C., No. 25 C.C.S.
27. Senior Chaplain, D.C.G's Dept.
28. Senior Chaplain, P.C's Dept.
29. File.
30. File.
31. War Diary.
32. War Diary.
33. Spare.
34. Spare.
35 to)
51.   ) All Regimental Medical Officers.

War Diary
of
A.D.M.S.
57th Division

from 1.12.18. to 31.12.18.

WAR DIARY
or
INTELLIGENCE SUMMARY.

(Erase heading not required.)

Army Form C. 2118

Place	Date	Hour	Summary of Events and Information	Remarks and references to Appendices
MONS EN BAROEUL	1.12.18		3/2 N/Lan. F. Amb. left LILLE for ESCOBECQ, 1st stage of march to DUISANS.	PLR
	2.12.18		3/2 N/Lan. completed march to DUISANS at 1400 hrs. Divisional Headquarters moved to DUISANS.	PLR
			2/2 N/Western F. Amb. left FIVES on the 1st stage of their march to DUISANS.	
DUISANS	3.12.18		2/3 N/Lan F. Amb. left FIVES on the 1st stage of their march to DUISANS.	PLR
			1/2 N/Lan F. Amb. completed march from FIVES and arrived at ANZIN	
			N.A.D.M.S. visited the 1/1 N.Lan. R. at AGNEZ-lez-DUISANS	PLR
			" " 2/1 R.Lanc. R. " "	
			" " 1/5 N.Lan. R. " "	
			" " 3/2 N/Lan. F. Amb. at C.C.S. Site, DUISANS	
	4.12.18		2/3rd N/Western F. Amb. completed march and are located at MAROEUIL	PLR
			... ancient Turn Ambulance site. It is intended to move 3/2 N.Lanc F. Amb. Divisional Rest Station at DUISANS with accommodation of 200	
			if the ill and no more at the gate the necessary accommodation was found	
			necessary to send 2/3 N/Western F. Amb. to MAROEUIL where they will be	

Place	Date	Hour	Summary of Events and Information	Remarks and references to Appendices
DOISANS			ode to start them and besides made out the family compositor. Convoluterns lines one also intents all shot with.	FJR
			A/ADMS. visited 9/2nd N. Zealand F. Amb at AWZIN. Constructional works are proceeding in order to get the personnel comfortable. Both on site is expected that they will be able to receive and treat a certain amount of sick	
	9.12.16		A/ADMS. along with DADMS. visited the Billets of 141st Brigade in ATRAS and a report was duly sent in to Sy Div. Headquarters to the effect that:-	RJR
			(a) General awnings
			(b) Some rooms not waterproof
			(c) Some stables had stone floors.
			and recommendations that they be found upon as the owners of these not being government, it was decided to repair and "patch up" these billets. It has since the record got these billets with stone floors the mentioned.	

Army Form C. 2118

WAR DIARY
or
INTELLIGENCE SUMMARY.
(Erase heading not required.)

Place	Date	Hour	Summary of Events and Information	Remarks and references to Appendices
DUISANS	8/12/16		ARRAS SANITATION (No 10 Sanitary Section)	GFR
			Present system in vogue at the present time is Barrack system in 38 proof barracks. At present there is an insufficiency, but O.C. No 10 Sanitary Section is arranging to increase this strength.	
			Major ADAMS - 3/2nd Western t. Amb.	
			Capt. STONEHOUSE 3/2nd W. L. Gen. t. Amb.	
			Capt. WILKINSON 3/3rd Western t. Amb.	
			orders as reports to ADASTRAL HOUSE forwarded. They leave on Saturday for Embarkation at CALAIS on Sunday. Captain Stonehouse had already proceeded on leave when the order arrived; a telegram was sent to him home asking him to report at Divn immediately.	
	6.12.16.		A/ADMS. attended Ambulating parade and by Divisional Commander. Despot Despatch of group 29 of Canteens. We were trained to issue working capital to fr. 20,000 and divide up immediately the morning balance between Divisional Divisions.	GFR

Army Form C. 2118

WAR DIARY
or
INTELLIGENCE SUMMARY.

(Erase heading not required.)

Instructions regarding War Diaries and Intelligence Summaries are contained in F. S. Regs., Part II. and the Staff Manual respectively. Title pages will be prepared in manuscript.

Place	Date	Hour	Summary of Events and Information	Remarks and references to Appendices
	6.12.15		A/ADMS visited 2/3 Wessex & D. med. on. the afternoon	OJR
			With aspirin therapy supplied and lectured re measles, scabies & other contagious diseases.	
	7.12.15		A/ADMS visited 1/3 No. Midlands 9 to Report and inspect on attending to Y Emer. Evacuation fronts off Ramur	OJR
			Visited Dugout	OJR
	8.12.15		A/ADMS visited Baths at ABNEZ-LES-DUISANS and MAROEUIL.	OJR
			I then went over and gave orders re moving to the face that Bullets are milling. Engineers are busy and still expect that one of the mines is an unexploded in Dragoon WTMS visited 2/3 N. Essex & Ounce.	
			A/ADMS visited 1/2 N. Essex & 2nd as arranged at CROIX-C	PJR
	10.2.15		No K. C. C. S. stated he understand 20 patients could be kept on at D.R.S. for convenience of the Division. All arrangements re. returning men going with hospitalised troops are classed in with him, final arrangement are as to correspondence of patients to be made fit future.	

Army Form C. 2118

WAR DIARY
or
INTELLIGENCE SUMMARY.
(Erase heading not required.)

Instructions regarding War Diaries and Intelligence Summaries are contained in F. S. Regs., Part II. and the Staff Manual respectively. Title pages will be prepared in manuscript.

Place	Date	Hour	Summary of Events and Information	Remarks and references to Appendices
DUISANS	1/12/18		A/A/D/MS arrived & took over at MAT DE VIL. There were no returns from units till one of [illegible] the morning [illegible]	OK
	2/12/18		[illegible]	OK
	3/12/18		Visited Units SCMEZ-LES-DUISANS. Bombing range [illegible]	OK
			100 men being trained each hour of [illegible] for them [illegible] attended. 4/7 RWF, 4/4 repairs [illegible] at MAROEUIL [illegible]	
			Moving Round by buses [illegible] un [illegible] at least seen [illegible] visited 4/5" Wessex & Rant at MAROEUIL.	
	4/12/18		[illegible]	OK
	5/12/18		[illegible]	OK
	6/12/18		Payment of [illegible]	OK
	7/12/18		[illegible] Amount paid 140 + 23 = HR.	OK
	8/12/18		[illegible]	OK
	9/12/18		A/A/D/MS marked up Battery 136 Bde RFA [illegible] [illegible] Bund	OK
	/12/18		[illegible]	OK

Army Form C. 2118

WAR DIARY
or
INTELLIGENCE SUMMARY.
(Erase heading not required.)

Instructions regarding War Diaries and Intelligence Summaries are contained in F. S. Regs., Part II. and the Staff Manual respectively. Title pages will be prepared in manuscript.

Place	Date	Hour	Summary of Events and Information	Remarks and references to Appendices
DUISANS	21.12.18		A/A D.M.S visited Batgt at MAROEUIL. Joining Orders completed.	PLR
	22.12.18		Routine. A.D.S visited 2/3 Western F. Amb.	FMR
	23.12.18		Routine — nothing of note.	OLR
	24.12.18		A/A.D.M.S visited 2/3 from AGNEZ-LES-DUISANS & 3/2nd N. 20m. F. Amb.	OLR
	25.12.18		A/A.D.M.S visited 2/2 N.Z.2ans F. Amb. and 4/1st Western F. Amb.	OLR
	26.12.18		Routine	OLR
	27.12.18		A/A.D.M.S visited 2/3rd Western F. Amb and 9th F. Amb at R	OLR
	28.12.18		Major King visited S.K. P.O.W Camps — Onissy — Gy — Highest rate amm P.O.W.'s have TRENCH FEET — frost bite. Some unrest that there are slow return, otherwise in good condition. Both much improved.	FLR
			Visited 13 Bde D.D.M.S. XI Corps.	
	29.12.18		Routine.	ELR
	30.12.18		A/A.D.M.S visited 2/1st Western F. Amb and 2/3rd N. Western F. Amb at R.	EL
	31.12.18		Routine.	AJ

31.12.18.

Lewis Newton Hyne
Lieut. Colonel R.A.M.C
A/A.D.M.S. 54th Division

WAR DIARY.
of
A.D.M.S., 57th DIVISION

from 1st January, 1919.

to 31st January, 1919.

BOX 2839

Army Form C. 2118.

WAR DIARY
or
INTELLIGENCE SUMMARY.
(Erase heading not required.)

Instructions regarding War Diaries and Intelligence Summaries are contained in F. S. Regs., Part II. and the Staff Manual respectively. Title pages will be prepared in manuscript.

Place	Date	Hour	Summary of Events and Information	Remarks and references to Appendices
DUISANS	1.1.19		Duisans Road.	
	2.1.19		Duisans Road.	
	3.1.19		A/A.D.M.S. visited 2/5th Wiltshire F. Amb. D.A.D.M.S. visited Bands at Bagneux-sur-Duisans.	
	4.1.19		A/A.D.M.S. attended D.D.M.S. Conference at XI Corps H.Q.	
	5.1.19		A.D.M.S. returned from leave and relieved Lt.Col. P.T. RUTHERFORD A/A.D.M.S.	
	6.1.19		A.D.M.S. visited all units in area and inspected by G.O.C. on Jan 7th and 9th. Arrangements for demobilization without seriously occupying much movement of individual Medical Officers previously demanded.	
	7.1.19		A.D.M.S. attended B.O.C. 54th Division as himself sick. D. of 4/5 Wiltshire F. Amb. at MAROEUIL. I hope turn out fairly soon. Am to visit 2/C and see what demobilization arrangements of unit. O.C. and own to attend CB medical advancement in the different areas while troops …	

Place	Date	Hour	Summary of Events and Information	Remarks and references to Appendices
DUISANS	8/1/19		(2) of 3/2 N Firs F Amb. at MARQUEVILLE. Supplementary personnel and stores Rec'd. There will be those [?] sent out next quarter. Unit running night throughout are [?] is prominent. The S.O.C.'s view is unfortunate. Some few casualties every day and are to be managed. A.D.M.S. visited 3/2 N.M. [?] Amb. near DUISANS and inspected arrangements for evacuation of wounded by E.O.C. tomorrow. The Unit has Divisional Rec Station with accommodation for 80-120. 40 patients in at present. Visited 3/2 N.M. [?] Amb in afternoon regarding arrangements for receiving [?]. Two C.R.E. meetings with [?] are [?] accommodation for movement of forces starting.	
	9/1/19		A.D.M.S. accompanied G.O.C. 4 Division of 3/2 N.Div. F. Amb or afternoon around Div. [?] areas examining quarters, etc., with view to accommodation for troops in new C.B.S areas. AGNEZ-LES-DUISANS	

Army Form C. 2118.

WAR DIARY
or
INTELLIGENCE SUMMARY.
(Erase heading not required.)

Instructions regarding War Diaries and Intelligence Summaries are contained in F. S. Regs., Part II and the Staff Manual respectively. Title pages will be prepared in manuscript.

Place	Date	Hour	Summary of Events and Information	Remarks and references to Appendices
DUISANS	10.1.19		A.D.M.S. visited XI Corps Headquarters LABUSSIERE regarding duties & not accept for a month from Jan 15th.	
	11.1.19		A.D.M.S. visited 3/2nd N.Z.Amb. 3 Amb. Divisional Boot at MAROEUIL and ACHEZ LEZ DUISANS. D.D.M.S. Corps re a journey on January 18th.	
	12.1.19		Demobilisation arranged & now with usual show assembling early.	
	13.1.19 } 14.1.19			
	15.1.19		A.D.M.S. visited office of D.A.D. R(P) at ARRAS.	
	16.1.19		A.D.M.S. visited 51st Divisional quarters of removal of units. 3/2 and 3/6 N.Z.Amb. & Amb. de chivis de Minor Diverging Station. Orders went to go to 3/2 N.Z.Amb. & Amb.	
	17.1.19		A.D.M.S. instructed all active units, Divisional Boot, also four D.M.S. units August at 3/2 & N.Z.Boot & Amb. & Rev. new H.Q. N.Z. Div. at Divisional Boot.	

WAR DIARY
or
INTELLIGENCE SUMMARY.

(Erase heading not required.)

Army Form C. 2118.

Place	Date	Hour	Summary of Events and Information	Remarks and references to Appendices
DUISANS	18.1.19		A.D.M.S. visited Headquarters and spoke to O.C. 9/2nd N. Lanc. F. Amb.	
	19.1.19		A.D.M.S. visited Headquarters Kent Army VALENCIENNES and discussed question of known Quintana, Punate or Medical Officers, illness and surgical ailments at once D.M.S.	
	20.1.19		A.D.M.S. (Col. T.F. DEWAR, C.B., T.D. A.M.S.) visited 3/2nd N. Lanc. F. Amb and 3/3rd N. Lanc. F. Amb. at HANQUETIN and MAROEUIL respectively and were attached funeral Col. DEWAR handed over command of R.A.M.S. of Division to Col. A.M. BLOWDEN, O.M., 3/2. N.O. Lanc. F. Amb. and Lieut. Col. 54th Division.	
	21.1.19		3/2nd and 3/3rd N. Lanc. F. Amb. closed no occurrences since evacuation. 3/2nd N.O. Lanc. F. Amb. will meet the visit of the whole division. Evacuations to be carried out at the pier.	
	22.1.19.		Instructional meeting from D.D.M.S. VI Corps that demobilisation of R.A.M.C. Lantern Lecturer by D.G.M.S.	
	23.1.19.		Received Form 24th Command Technical Lectures Nurses & Field Ambulance	

Army Form C. 2118.

WAR DIARY
or
INTELLIGENCE SUMMARY.
(Erase heading not required.)

Instructions regarding War Diaries and Intelligence Summaries are contained in F. S. Regs., Part II. and the Staff Manual respectively. Title pages will be prepared in manuscript.

Place	Date	Hour	Summary of Events and Information	Remarks and references to Appendices
DUISANS	23.1.19.		D.D.M.S. asks for a return, stating to whom it be entrusted	
	24.1.19.		Return.	
	25.1.19.		Lieut. Col. RUTHERFORD, O.C. 2/3 Western F. Amb. motored over today ammanster on the order of A.D.M.S.	
	26.1.19.		Return.	
	27.1.19.		He is arrived which the 2/3 area and 2/8 Western F. Amb. mice. Paid into 1/2 & W. Lanc. F. Amb. reps. is attempting of 100. Demobilisation of east 2/3 W. Lanc. F. Amb. completes to carry out provisions with staff of the whole field Ambulances, now maintained. Capt(A/Major) H.H. MORRISON has been	
	28.1.19.		return from military service where not no receipt of Lieut. Col. V. Burleigh R.A.M.C. Captain 2/8. CREGAN. 2/3 Western F. Amb., is placed as the 2/3 W. Lanc. F. Amb. from today. Captain	
	29.1.19.		A. The Lewis RAMC has been discharged since 16.1.19.	
	30.1.19.		D.O. of X Corps who motored in here 21.1.19. that more essentials	

Army Form C. 2118.

WAR DIARY
or
INTELLIGENCE SUMMARY.

(Erase heading not required.)

Instructions regarding War Diaries and Intelligence Summaries are contained in F. S. Regs., Part II. and the Staff Manual respectively. Title pages will be prepared in manuscript.

Place	Date	Hour	Summary of Events and Information	Remarks and references to Appendices
DIVISANS.	30.1.19. 31.1.19.		first claim carried to strength for a month. A/A.D.M.S. visited 3/9. P. of W. Coy. Prisoners forwarded to D.D.M.S. XI Corps.	
	31.1.19.		Lucial J. Rutherford Lieut. Colonel A/A.D.M.S. 57th Division.	

War Diary
of
A.D.M.S. 57th Division.
from
1st February, 1919.
to
28th February, 1919.

WAR DIARY
or
INTELLIGENCE SUMMARY.

(Erase heading not required.)

Army Form C.

Instructions regarding War Diaries and Intelligence Summaries are contained in F. S. Regs., Part II. and the Staff Manual respectively. Title pages will be prepared in manuscript.

Place	Date	Hour	Summary of Events and Information	Remarks and references to Appendices
Lucient	1-2-19		Major King, M.O. to 2nd Sp. Division proceeds to the U.K. on 14 days leave. Staff. Clerk R.me. Murphy 7/4th Bn N. Fus R. to no. J. Ce.f. sick.	
	2-2-19		Routine - Rehabilitation allotment received from 2nd and XI Corps for divisional R.A.M.C. for month of February under 105.	
	3-2-19		W/H/7747. G miles 7/2. Planet Succ Ambulance Rehabilitation allotment succeed by A.D.M.S. XI Corps a new one being issued.	
	4-2-19		Routine.	
	5-2-19		Routine.	
	6-2-19		Routine.	
	7-2-19		Routine.	
	8-2-19		A/A.D.M.S. visits 7/8" Neven Succ Ambulance.	
	9-2-19		Routine.	
	10-2-19		Routine.	
	11-2-19		Routine.	

Army Form C-2118.

WAR DIARY
or
INTELLIGENCE SUMMARY.
(Erase heading not required.)

Instructions regarding War Diaries and Intelligence Summaries are contained in F. S. Regs., Part II. and the Staff Manual respectively. Title pages will be prepared in manuscript.

Place	Date	Hour	Summary of Events and Information	Remarks and references to Appendices
Aircan	12.2.19		A/R.A.M.S visited 2/3rd Wessex F. Ambulance.	
	13.2.19		Routine.	
	14.2.19		Routine.	
	15.2.19		Routine.	
	16.2.19		Routine.	
	17.2.19		Routine.	
	18.2.19		Routine.	
	19.2.19		Routine.	
	20.2.19		Routine.	
	21.2.19		Lt. Col. A.N.B. Pinder, 1 5/2nd W. Lanc. F. Amb. Capt. C.H. Weston, 3/2nd Western F. Amb. Capt. H.D. MacPhayer, M.C., 3/2nd Western F. Amb.	Report for demobilisation
	22.2.19		Routine.	
	23.2.19		Routine.	
	24.2.19		Major M.B. Kane, M.C., D.A.D.M.S proceeds to 51 General Hospital	
	25.2.19		Routine.	
	26.2.19		Routine.	

Army Form C-2118.

WAR DIARY
or
INTELLIGENCE SUMMARY.

(Erase heading not required.)

Instructions regarding War Diaries and Intelligence Summaries are contained in F. S. Regs., Part II. and the Staff Manual respectively. Title pages will be prepared in manuscript.

Place	Date	Hour	Summary of Events and Information	Remarks and references to Appendices
DUISANS	24.2.19		ROUTINE	
	28.2.19		Major Frickard, & Capt Burd Morcusa to report to D.M.S. II Army for duty (for reinforcement).	

28.2.1919

Severd Mutherford
Lieut Colonel
A/A D.M.S. 57th Division

War Diary
of
A.D.M.S., 3ʳᵈ Divisions
from 1ˢᵗ March 1919.
to
31ˢᵗ March 1919.

Army Form C. 2118.

WAR DIARY
or
INTELLIGENCE SUMMARY.
(Erase heading not required.)

Instructions regarding War Diaries and Intelligence Summaries are contained in F. S. Regs., Part II. and the Staff Manual respectively. Title pages will be prepared in manuscript.

Place	Date	Hour	Summary of Events and Information	Remarks and references to Appendices
Dueruno	1.3.19.			
	2.3.19			
	3.3.19			
	4.3.19			
	5.3.19		MAJOR KIDSTON, 2/5 Queen's And. MAJOR FAULKNER, att 8th K. Liver P. Captain HURD, M.O.R.C, U.S.A. left to report to D.M.S. Second Army.	
	6.3.19			
	7.3.19			
	8.3.19			
	9.3.19			
	10.3.19			
	11.3.19			
	12.3.19			
	13.3.19			
	14.3.19			
	15.3.19			
	16.3.19			
	17.3.19			

Army Form C. 2118.

WAR DIARY
or
INTELLIGENCE SUMMARY.
(Erase heading not required.)

Instructions regarding War Diaries and Intelligence Summaries are contained in F. S. Regs., Part II. and the Staff Manual respectively. Title pages will be prepared in manuscript.

Place	Date	Hour	Summary of Events and Information	Remarks and references to Appendices
Duncan	18.3.19		Captain O'REGAN left for England - transferred to Home Establishment.	
	19.3.19		Captain BULLOCH left for England for demobilization.	
	20.3.19		Duncan	
	21.3.19		Orders received for removal to H.Q. of Division at 0005 28th March.	
	22.3.19		Commenced of move of Units of Division from 16 B.O.C., Bu Group and others over the past seven weeks and the A.D.M.S. Office is elsewhere.	
	23.3.19			

Sd/ Hutcheon
Lieut. Colonel
A/D.D.M.S. 52nd Division

57TH DIVISION

C. R. E.

~~FEB 1917 - MAR 1919~~

1915 SEP — 1916 FEB

1917 FEB — 1919 MAR

www.ingramcontent.com/pod-product-compliance
Lightning Source LLC
Chambersburg PA
CBHW081423300426

44108CB00016BA/2288